Pakistan's Freedom
&
Allama Mashriqi

Pakistan's Freedom & Allama Mashriqi

Statements, Letters, Chronology of Khaksar Tehrik (Movement)

Period: Mashriqi's Birth to 1947

Edited & Compiled by:
Nasim Yousaf

Acknowledgements

I extend my heartiest thanks to my mother, relatives, Khaksars, and others, who during my life have contributed to my knowledge on Allama Mashriqi and the Khaksar Tehrik, and have thus helped make this work possible. I am also extremely grateful to those authors and publications whose works I have used in compiling this book.

I would like to extend my deepest gratitude to my children, Mehreen, Zain, and Myra, for helping me in this effort, and my wife for her support.

Declaration

I, Nasim Yousaf, have produced this work to the best of my ability. All events and dates have been collected from credible sources. I have made every attempt possible to list all events in chronological order, however error(s) is possible. In some cases, the exact day and/or month of the event may not available. In case of quotes, any typographical errors have been preserved and may appear in this text. I cannot be held responsible for any error(s) or omission(s) due to any reason.

I am not seeking condemnation of any personality, organization, or political party in this publication. My intent is purely to present the facts. If I have hurt anyone unintentionally, I sincerely extend my apologies.

Updates

It is not possible to include all information related to the period (1846-1947) in this publication. For information on updates to this or any other publications by this author/editor, please visit the following web sites:
http://www.allamamashriqi.info
http://www.allama-mashriqi.8m.com

A Salute

To Allama Mashriqi (Inayatullah Khan) who rendered selfless services and laid his life for the freedom of Pakistan and for the uplift of poor Muslims.

To Allama Mashriqi's brilliant son, Ehsan ullah Khan Aslam, who was injured by the police during the raid at the Khaksar headquarters on March 19, 1940. He died on May 31, 1940 due to fatal injuries. During this time, Mashriqi was in jail and was not allowed to attend his son's funeral.

To the Khaksar martyrs who made history on March 19, 1940 and laid their lives courageously.

To Mashriqi's family that suffered during Mashriqi's struggle to change the destiny of his poor nation. They stood by Mashriqi and faced atrocities of the Government with extreme courage.

To the families of the Khaksars who suffered. They stood behind their men and women who fought for a cause fearlessly.

To the Khaksars who put forth tremendous resistance against the rulers during the struggle for the freedom of their homeland.

Editor's Biography

This publication has been edited and compiled by Mr. Nasim Yousaf, a grandson of Allama Mashriqi. This document is the result of exhaustive study on the Pakistan movement carried out by Mr. Yousaf and his personal knowledge of Allama Mashriqi and the Khaksar Tehrik.

Mr. Yousaf began his career as a Pilot Officer in the Pakistan Air Force. He left the cherished profession and became an exporter and a leader in the business community in Pakistan. The editor is a founding member of the Board of Directors that established The Pakistan Commercial Exporters of Towels Association (PCETA), one of the largest trade associations in Pakistan. He also held other important positions in the PCETA, including Vice Chairman (North Zone), Member of the Central Executive Committee, and Member of the Textile Quota Committee of the PCETA. As part of the Textile Quota Committee, he and other members were responsible for disbursing quota to exporters of PCETA. Mr. Yousaf also represented the business community in front of various levels of the Government of Pakistan, including the ministerial level, to discuss and resolve trade issues. Mr. Yousaf has traveled extensively around the world, which according to him, has been a great source of learning and has opened his vision on global issues.

Since his move to the USA over a decade ago, he has continued to be in his own business, and has simultaneously pursued his passion of writing books and articles, particularly on Allama Mashriqi and the Khaksars' role towards the independence of Pakistan. He has spent many years on research on the Pakistan movement and has continuously devoted a considerable amount of time toward this project.

Mr. Yousaf's other works and books include:
1. *Allama Mashriqi & Dr. Akhtar Hameed Khan: Two Legends of Pakistan*
2. *Import & Export of Apparel & Textiles*
3. Various articles on Allama Mashriqi and the Khaksar Tehrik
His research has also been published on:
http://www.allamamashriqi.info and http://www.allama-mashriqi.8m.com
http://www.akhtar-hameed-khan.8m.com

Preface

I feel greatly thankful to God that I have been able to accomplish this work on Allama Mashriqi and the Khaksar Tehrik (Movement) that Mashriqi founded in 1930.

Allama Mashriqi played a vital role during the freedom movement that resulted in the creation of Pakistan. His movement, the Khaksar Tehrik, is absolutely and completely an unprecedented phenomenon in the sub-continent. This work is a chronology of events highlighting the role of Allama Mashriqi and the Khaksar Tehrik in Pakistan's freedom movement. I took on this task because I felt that the history of Pakistan was incomplete without this information. There are in fact a lot of information sources and references on Mashriqi and the Khaksars that need to be documented for public consumption. The subject is so extensive that a dedicated research academy is needed to cover every event and aspect of Allama Mashriqi and the Khaksar Tehrik. More articles and books on Mashriqi need to be written and a film, documentary, or television serial would also be an excellent source of guidance and learning for everyone. Unfortunately, the Government of Pakistan has made no serious effort in these regards.

This work in conjunction with my book, *Allama Mashriqi and Dr. Akhtar Hameed Khan: Two Legends of Pakistan*, present the study of a man who sacrificed all that he had. A man whose exemplary life is a source of great enlightenment, motivation, and knowledge for everyone. A man whose followers possessed an immense amount of devotion and love for him. This is the study of a man who was probably born before his time.

It has been gratifying to present an extremely important study to the nation. This study covers important statements of Mashriqi, his correspondence with prominent leaders, and momentous and consequential events surrounding the Khaksar Tehrik and that led to independence. This work is like a drop in the ocean, but still I hope that it will serve as a good reference and source of information for historians, authors, researchers, scholars, professors, teachers, students, film and documentary makers, journalists, and anyone else interested in the subject. This will be an eye-

opener for people and will encourage them to more closely study the role of
Mashriqi and the Khaksars' struggle towards independence.

Allama Mashriqi founded the Khaksar Movement with noble causes in mind
including the following:

1. To rebuild the entire nation in every aspect with emphasis on character building
2. To instill peace, solidarity, brotherhood, and extreme discipline amongst the
   followers
3. To instill amongst its followers a sense of providing community service for
   everyone regardless of caste, religion, color, or creed. This was not only to
   provide a clean environment and build the nation, but also to generate a feeling
   of love amongst all
4. To eradicate sectarianism and prejudices from the society
5. To awaken people to convert them into a robust nation by inculcating physical
   fitness, strict discipline, and other qualities of a soldier
6. To adopt simplicity and punctuality and to remove lethargy
7. To bring equality and dignity to the common man and to stop their exploitation
   by the rich and insincere leaders
8. To become role models for the world by practicing the real teachings of Islam
9. Last but not the least, to regain rule of the entire India that once belonged to the
   Muslims.

****

This work is the result of many years of research, and I have used credible sources
that consist of non-Khaksar and Khaksar materials. I have also used my personal
knowledge to provide further information in the sections marked editor's comments
(the sources of this information are my family, Khaksars, others, and personal
knowledge.).

Although a lot of Khaksar material existed, its availability is very limited, for
various reasons. It is very tedious for a researcher to locate this material. This
problem has been pointed out by many. There are many causes for the limited
availability of this material including the following:

1. A lot of material was confiscated by various governments at different times
   during their raids at Khaksar headquarters and other Khaksar places. That
   material is missing
2. Material available with the Pakistan Government and foreign institutions is not
   easily accessible in many cases
3. A lot of material was either lost, mutilated, or damaged over a period of time
4. There is limited availability of material with few public libraries
5. Copies of *Al-Islah* (a true spokesman weekly of the Khaksar Movement
   published prior to partition) are difficult to find

6. Khaksar material is mostly available in Urdu only. The absence of Khaksar material in English causes difficulty for many writers, particularly those with a limited understanding of Urdu and those who are foreign writers
7. Much of the material is not well organized
8. Much of the Khaksar material still remains unpublished.

Keeping all of the above in view, researchers and writers rely on non-Khaksar and even anti-Khaksar materials to carry out their studies. This of course leads to a completely biased study. Thus the Khaksar point of view is not reflected properly and the facts related to the Khaksar Tehrik and movement for the independence of Pakistan end up being distorted. In the absence of original Khaksar material, the study of the Khaksar struggle will always remain incomplete and biased. In consideration of this, the Government of Pakistan is urged to establish an independent research center that should collect and produce Khaksar materials, before it is too late.

These web sites have been dedicated to Allama Mashriqi. Any updates, as and when possible, will be posted on:
http://www.allamamashriqi.info
http://www.allama-mashriqi.8m.com

I hope that readers will find this study useful.
God may bless Pakistan and its people.

Letter to the President of Pakistan

On November 14, 2003, I sent a registered letter (certified mail) to the President of Pakistan, General Pervez Musharraf, via the Ambassador of Pakistan in Washington, D.C. USA. I also sent a similar letter to the Prime Minister, Mir Zafarullah Khan Jamali. In the letter, I made various requests including establishing a research academy in the name of Allama Mashriqi. This letter is reproduced here.

Mohtarram President General Pervez Musharraf Sahib,

Assalam-u-Alaikum

I am delighted to send you the two books that I have authored in the recent past. I am sending these through Mohtarram Ashraf Jehangir Qazi, Ambassador of Pakistan in Washington, D.C.

My first book was published in 2001 in the U.S. and is entitled *Import & Export of Apparel & Textiles*. In Part I of this book, I tried to make a humble effort to apprise Pakistani exporters, particularly those who are new to international trade, on how to export to the USA. In Part II of this book, I made an attempt to assist and encourage importers of apparel and textiles from around the world to import from Pakistan. The second book titled, *Allama Mashriqi & Dr. Akhtar Hameed Khan: Two Legends of Pakistan* was published this year in the U.S.

The purpose of this letter is primarily to draw your attention to the tremendous sacrifices and contributions of two great patriots of Pakistan, Allama Mashriqi and Dr. Akhtar Hameed Khan, towards their countrymen. In my second book, I had promised to the nation that I would send a copy of my work to the President and Prime Minister of Pakistan, so that they would have a chance to read it and take the necessary steps that are very important to the Pakistani nation.

The second book is divided into two parts on Allama Mashriqi and Dr. Akhtar Hameed Khan. This book sheds light on the selfless and exemplary lives that these two giants of our nation led. This book is a fraction of what could be written on them and what needs to be done to acquaint Pakistan with their lives and times. Various aspects of their personalities including distinguished valor and substance are an immense source of inspiration, learning, and guidance for every soul of humanity.

Allama Mashriqi and the Khaksars

The first part of my book discusses Allama Mashriqi's life and the role of the Khaksar Tehrik (Movement) that was founded in 1930 to re-build the nation and to achieve freedom. Mashriqi and the Khaksars mobilized the nation to rise for freedom. During this struggle, Mashriqi and Khaksars' sufferings were unmatched as they valiantly resisted against the rulers who did their best to eliminate the movement altogether.

The role of Allama Mashriqi and the Khaksars in the making of Pakistan has not been made public and in fact many history books have distorted and misquoted their role. The brutal massacre of the Khaksars on March 19, 1940 is a very important part of Pakistan's history, but the facts of this massacre are unknown to the majority of Pakistanis, since they have not been written or discussed in history books. This incident is also excluded whenever there is a discussion or program about Pakistan history on the radio, television, and even in the supplements of the newspapers that are published every year on important days such as March 23 and August 14. There are many other matters relating to Mashriqi and the Khaksar movement that have been ignored in Pakistan history. The nation needs to be apprised of the historical facts that are unknown to a vast majority. These include the following:

1. The massacre of the Khaksars on March 19, 1940 was one of the cruelest killings of innocent people in the history of India. It occurred only three days prior to the beginning of the historic Muslim League Session at Minto Park Lahore (March 22-24, 1940) which passed the Lahore Resolution (Pakistan Resolution).
2. Quaid-e-Azam Mohammad Ali Jinnah made a statement on the massacre of the Khaksars prior to coming to Lahore to attend the historic Muslim League Session held on March 22-24, 1940.
3. A large number of attendees at the historic Muslim League Session at Lahore (March 22-24, 1940) raised slogans in favor of the Khaksars and denounced the actions taken by the Punjab Government including the killing and injuring of innocent Khaksars, arrest of Allama Mashriqi, and ban on the Khaksar movement. The Muslim League had a difficult time controlling the emotions of the people in favor of the Khaksars. History is witness to the reality that this massacre was a turning point in the freedom struggle and the history of Pakistan.
4. The Pakistan Resolution (Lahore Resolution) was passed on the same day (March 24, 1940) when the Muslim League also passed a Khaksar resolution asking for an inquiry into the tragic killing of the Khaksars.

5.   Mashriqi's determination and exemplary courage during his arrest for a long period as well as the resistance of the Khaksars during the ban on the Khaksar Tehrik further attest to the fact that the Khaksars' resistance to the British was the most unparalleled, toughest, and the longest fight in the Indian freedom struggle after the Khilafat movement. Mashriqi and the Khaksars remained steadfast despite the agony they faced and the unmatched atrocities that were inflicted on them.

It is not possible to cover all aspects and matters relating to Allama Mashriqi in depth -- his life, scholarly contributions, vision of our nation, and role in Pakistan history. However, in my book, I have made a modest endeavor to briefly shed light on him and have discussed some issues from Pakistan history that are foreign to the nation.

My Request

I feel extremely good to be presenting this work of mine, that was produced after years of research, in order to bring to your attention the importance of Mashriqi and the Khaksars' roles in the history of our nation. I am earnestly requesting to you to personally look into the matter and issue a directive to the concerned authorities to make Mashriqi and the Khaksars' roles known to the public as they are clearly important from Pakistan history's point of view. I am also requesting that you ask the relevant institutions not to eliminate or distort the facts of Pakistan history because such steps are very dangerous for the growth of any nation. By directing the appropriate authorities to take necessary steps in acquainting the nation about Allama Mashriqi and Khaksars' contributions and sacrifices, you will redress the grievances of the families of Mashriqi and the Khaksars, particularly families of those Khaksars who either laid their lives or suffered in prison for the cause. In the past, myself and members of my family have met heads of the state, federal ministers, etc, in order to apprise them of the injustice that has been done in the history books, but nothing has came out of these meetings. I hope you will take the following steps to address the neglected and unattended important issues pertaining to every Pakistani. Your positive action in this regard will go a long ways in revealing the consequential facts of our history that are still unknown. Of course, if needed, my services to follow through on the following steps shall always be available:

1.   A research academy should be formed to conduct complete research on Mashriqi and his Khaksar Movement. A library exclusively for Khaksar literature should be formed. All Khaksar materials should be collected from the public, government departments, the India Office (U.K.), and historical resources in India. Mashriqi's books and speeches should be translated into English and other languages. An official and unbiased biography on Mashriqi should be published depicting his purpose of establishing the Khaksar Tehrik. His emphasis on equality, non-prejudicial or non-sectarian society, self-sacrifice, and community service, as well as his own exemplary life, including

the fact that he did not seek personal glorification, are just a few points that are beneficial learnings for all of humanity.

2.   Icchara in Lahore (where he laid the foundation of the Khaksar movement in 1930) as well as the Punjab University should be named after Allama Mashriqi. A monument should be erected in Lahore at the site of the massacre of March 19, 1940. March 19 should be declared "Martyrs Day" and special seminars should be held in major cities in remembrance of those Khaksars who laid their lives on that day. Official yearly seminars, on his death and birth anniversaries, should be held on the life and times of Mashriqi.

3.   National media should be directed to broadcast/publish special programs on Mashriqi, particularly on his birth and death anniversaries. A film and television program should be made on Allama Mashriqi's life and the Khaksar Movement. Funds should be allocated for this purpose.

4.   A national holiday should be observed on Mashriqi's birth or death anniversary.

In the end, I would like to add that well over a hundred thousand people attended Mashriqi's funeral on August 29, 1963. For months afterward, mourners kept visiting Mashriqi's family and phone messages from Pakistanis across the world kept pouring in. Thus, he must have done something significant for the nation that so many people came to pay their tributes upon his death.

Dr. Akhtar Hameed Khan

Dr. Akhtar Hameed Khan's services are well known to you, as such I will refrain from reminding you of his contributions. You have already vowed to carry Dr. Khan's mission when you inaugurated a symposium in the March 04, 2000 on his life and times. I thank you for recognizing his services to the nation. Keeping in view his services, I request you to consider the following for what he did for his countrymen:

1.   Orangi Town in Karachi should be named after Dr. Khan. A road leading to Orangi Town should be named after him.

2.   A monument should be erected at Orangi Town. An official biography on Dr. Khan should be published. Official yearly seminars, on his death and birth anniversaries, should be held on the life and times of Dr. Khan.

3.   Dr.Khan's works should be translated into various languages so that they can help alleviate poverty that exists around the world. This will be a service to all of humanity.

Closing

I have enclosed the following books:

1.   *Allama Mashriqi & Dr. Akhtar Hameed Khan: Two Legends of Pakistan*

2.   *Import & Export of Apparel & Textiles - Part I: Export to USA, Part II: Import from Pakistan*

Please acknowledge that you have received these books. In addition, I would certainly appreciate your valuable comments after you have read my book.

Best Regards.
Allah Hafiz.

Nasim Yousaf

P.S. As per my promise in my second book, I will also be sending a copy of this book to the Prime Minister Mir Zafarullah Khan Jamali along with a similar request.

C.C: Ambassador of Pakistan (Washington D.C.)

Introduction

Allama Mashriqi
One of the Founding Fathers of Pakistan

Allama Mashriqi was born in a very well placed and respected family of India. He was born to a Rajput family in Amritsar in 1888 and died in Lahore on August 27, 1963. Mashriqi's father, Khan Ata Mohammad Khan was a very well educated person and a man of means. Khan Ata inherited large property from his father. During the Mughal Empire, Khan Ata Mohammad Khan's predecessors held prominent positions. Khan Ata was a highly regarded and well-connected person with the Muslim luminaries of the time such as Sir Syed Ahmed Khan, Jamal Ud Din Afgahani, Shibli Noamani, and Mirza Ghalib. Mashriqi's father himself was a literary person and a great writer. He owned a bi-weekly, *Vakil,* from Amritsar. This publication was an avenue for discussing political issues and re-awakening the Muslims. The quality of this publication can be judged by the fact that Maulana Shibli Naomani requested Khan Ata Mohammad Khan to let Maulana Abul Kalam Azad work at *Vakil*, so that Maulana Azad could refine his literary knowledge under the guidance of Khan Ata Mohammad Khan. Abul Kalam Azad went on to work as an editor of *Vakil.* Hence, Mashriqi was raised in an environment that was surrounded by highly literate and educated people. Khan Ata Mohammad Khan noticed the genius in his son and he guided him accordingly.

Allama Mashriqi, a born genius, liked reading from his childhood. As an extremely brilliant and confident boy, he was famous amongst his teachers and friends. He completed his Masters degree in Mathematics from the University of the Punjab at the age of 19 and broke all previous records. The Indian press was full of praise for him. As a brilliant student at the Punjab University, Mashriqi went on to Christ's College of the Cambridge University (England) to distinguish himself in Mathematics and emerged as a renowned Mathematician and scholar. He again broke records and completed four Triposes with distinction in various subjects within five years. The British press media, impressed with Mashriqi's educational accomplishments at Cambridge University, paid rich tributes to him. It is believed that his records at Cambridge University are yet to be broken. He completed his education in England in 1912 and returned to India. Upon his return, at the age of 25 he was appointed Vice Principal of Islamia College by Chief Commissioner, Sir George Roos-Keppel (at that time, Chief Commissioner was equivalent to Governor). He was made Principal of the same college in 1917. As a result of his outstanding abilities, he was appointed Under Secretary, Government of India in the Education Department. Sir George Anderson (1876-1943) had held this position prior to Mashriqi's appointment. It is interesting to note that Sir George Anderson was much older to Mashriqi when he had held this position. Mashriqi was directly appointed Vice Principal of Islamia College and Under Secretary, when he was only 25 years and 29 years old, respectively. This speaks to his outstanding caliber, competence, and abilities. Furthermore, he was offered Ambassadorship of Afghanistan at age 32 and title of Sir at age 33, but he declined both. It is believed that he was the youngest Indian to be offered and to hold important positions.

In 1924, at the age of 36, Mashriqi completed his book, *Tazkirah*. This monumental work was highly praised and was nominated for the Nobel Prize. At such an early age, few can achieve the distinction of producing a book that earns worldwide praise. Mashriqi emerged as a great scholar and a prolific writer. Mashriqi's list of achievements does not end there. Soon he emerged as a fine organizer, reformer, leader, an excellent orator, a great philosopher, a thinker, and a visionary. He became one of the most prominent personalities and political leaders of India, with great wisdom and political foresight. He was a truly brave and fervent freedom fighter. Mashriqi was courageous and a true warrior.

In order to lift the masses and bring freedom to India, he resigned from the Government service and laid the foundation of the Khaksar Tehrik in 1930. Allama Mashriqi played a vital role in directing the Muslims towards the independence of India and creation of Pakistan. During the struggle movement, Mashriqi, his family, and a large number of Khaksars heavily suffered and many Khaksars lost their lives. His life story and that of the Khaksar Movement is extremely exhilarating and impressive. It guides and inspires readers, instilling a spirit of patriotism and love for the common man. It also influences leaders to adopt simplicity, provide selfless service to the nation, and lift the masses. This short piece of introduction does not justify the superb and manifold personality of Mashriqi, a great visionary and freedom fighter.

The Khaksar Tehrik

Allama Mashriqi's political thoughts were shaped at home, but he earnestly started thinking about politics while he was a student in England. Mashriqi came to the rescue of the Indians, when other political leadership had failed to deliver and the Indians were almost finished politically, economically, and socially. The only Indians (including Muslims, Hindus, and others) who were influential and strong, were those who were bestowed with large *jagirs*, important positions, and fancy and prestigious titles, such as *Sir*. Obviously, those who were honored were required to serve the British interest. And, the British used this privileged class for their own objectives. This rich and privileged class of Indians was ignorant of the sufferings of the common man. Mashriqi realized that the nation needed awakening and its character re-built. He wanted a nation that had sound character and was well disciplined and mentally and physically fit. He wanted a nation with a sense of community service, tolerance, respect, and mutual love for each other, regardless of religion, color, caste, or creed. He understood that Muslims must have these traits in order to revive the lost glory that they once enjoyed. Mashriqi was the first intellectual Muslim leader, visionary, philosopher and thinker to understand the importance of a soldierly life and community service. Thus, to remedy sufferings of the poor Indians and achieve his goals, the Khaksar Tehrik was born in 1930.

Mashriqi took great pains in delivering his message for the Khaksar Movement. He became a commoner and left the luxuries of life behind. There was nothing on his mind but to revolutionize the lives of the masses. He passed his message through his invigorating and motivational speeches, writings, pamphlets, and personal contact with the common men. By the late 1930's, the Khaksar Tehrik had four million Khaksars and millions of supporters and sympathizers. It had over 3500 centers (Khaksar circle estimates that the numbers of followers and centers were even more) across India and branches in many other countries. In the late 1930's, it had such strong roots in the masses that no other Muslim party was even comparable. Mashriqi was indeed a great organizer of the 20th century. The explosive growth of his movement in a short span of time in a huge country like India is proof of his exceptional abilities and the strength of his message that led people to follow him. The Khaksars were trained to be disciplined, sacrificing, simple, honest, above sectarianism, and helpers in the community. The movement was raised to uplift the masses and welcomed anyone, and this is why non-Muslims also became part of the Khaksar Movement. In the Khaksar Tehrik, the rich and the poor all stood in the same line regardless of their status. Mashriqi, though an extremely powerful leader, made no distinction between himself and any Khaksar. In a formation, he was made to stand like any other Khaksar, in whatever position the leader of the contingent assigned. He was as much accountable as anyone else. Once, he was even punished by the Salar when he marched out of step in a formation while parading. To me, it is this equality and sincerity of uplifting the masses that created dedicated followers for Mashriqi.

Its explosive expansion with millions of dedicated members and supporters in the entire India became a massive threat to British rule. The British feared none except the Khaksars and declared it the most dangerous party in India. They completely understood the objective of the movement, and they knew that such dedicated and disciplined volunteers from all across India could be directed by Mashriqi toward any goal, including the removal of the British from power.

Opponent political parties of the Khaksars, including the Muslim League and the Congress Party also felt threatened. Sir Sikandar Hayat Khan, Premier of the Punjab, felt his political career at risk. To prove his loyalty to the British and to hold on to power in the Punjab, he took action against the Khaksars. A ban was imposed on Khaksar activities (with the support of the British). However, Khaksars refused to accept the ban. They started assembling in Lahore to protest against the restrictions. Opposing the ban, they marched in the streets of Lahore on March 19, 1940. Police opened indiscriminate fire on the innocent Khaksars to get them to stop the demonstration, and a bloody massacre of the Khaksars took place in Lahore. A large number of innocent Khaksars were killed. Mashriqi was arrested and a campaign to arrest the Khaksars was launched. The Khaksar Tehrik headquarters in Lahore, adjacent to Mashriqi's house, were raided. Mashriqi's son, Ehsanullah Khan Aslam, was protesting the police raid when he was hit and injured by one of the tear gas grenades (he later died of injuries). It seems that the police intentionally hit him with the grenade in retaliation for his protests. After these actions, censorship on the media was imposed and the Khaksars were not to be addressed as martyrs. This slaughter was the bloodiest ruthless killing after the Jallianwala Bagh massacre at Amritsar by General Dyer in April 13, 1919. After this tragic incident, the Khaksars came out on the streets, and demonstrations continued on a daily basis for the release of Mashriqi and the Khaksars in jail and for the removal of the ban on the movement. It is also important to note that the merciless and ferocious killing of the Khaksars happened only a few days prior to the historic session of the Muslim League. It is more important to note that the ban on the assembly of people (Section 144) was suspiciously removed right before the Muslim League session, and thus the League was allowed to hold its historic session on March 22-24, 1940. This raised eyebrows of the people and it was sensed that there was a conspiracy against Allama Mashriqi and the Khaksar Movement. The indicators and the Khaksar circle's view that point toward the conspiracy need a separate discussion altogether.

On March 22, 1940, the Muslim League Session commenced at Minto Park in Lahore. It adopted Lahore Resolution (Pakistan Resolution) on March 24 and in the same session the Khaksar resolution was unanimously passed. It is consequential to understand that the Muslim League, prior to massacre of March 19, 1940, had no roots in the masses and that they lost miserably the elections in 1937. The Muslim League's popularity can be gauged from the results of these elections. (In the Khaksars' and nationalists' view, the Muslim League's loss in the 1937 elections prompted the League to demand division of India and therefore hold this session. According to the nationalists, the intention of the Leaguers was not to uplift the masses; rather their aim was to create a separate land and hold full power in their own hands. The indicators then and now prove this theory.)

The people present at the Muslim League Session (March 22-24, 1940) were emotionally charged and grieved because of the Khaksar tragedy. Many a time during the three day session, it was even difficult to control the situation. People were demanding that Sir Sikandar be ousted from the Muslim League, that Mashriqi and the Khaksars be released, and that the ban on the Tehrik be removed. Quaid-e-Azam and others had to speak to the public to solace their feelings. The public looked to Quaid-e-Azam to help them in the time of mourning. Despite the censorship on the public media, newspapers could not avoid writing that the public present was agitated and was raising slogans against Sir Sikandar and in support of the Khaksars. The public was demanding from Jinnah to resolve the Khaksar issue. There is no denying the fact that the public was fully sympathetic to the Khaksars and showed immense support for them. When many Muslims at the session wanted to make speeches in support of the Khaksars, they were prevented from doing so.

The large presence, uproar, and enthusiasm at the Muslim League Session (March 22-24, 1940) was a result of the massacre of the Khaksars on March 19, 1940. Anyone can understand the feelings that prevailed among the Muslims for the Khaksar tragedy. The pro-Muslim League historians have ignored support for the Khaksars during the session and have given full credit of this large presence to the League's popularity. But the facts have been twisted and events are witness to the reality that the large presence at the Muslim League session was due to the Khaksar killings, and the League flourished after the Khaksar massacre of March 19, 1940, the ban on the Khaksar Movement, and Mashriqi's arrest. The truth is that, at the time, the Muslim League was a completely disorganized party. Quaid-e-Azam had many a time admitted that the party needed to be organized. Thus, the massacre of the Khaksars and atrocities against Mashriqi, Khaksars, and their families helped unite the Muslims under the Muslim League. Within seven years of this massacre, the Muslims of the Indian sub-continent had an independent homeland.

****

When the Khaksar resolution was adopted on March 24, Sir Sikandar had observed the public's sympathy with the Khaksars and condemnation against him. Despite this, Sir Sikandar (Muslim Leaguer) continued his actions against the Khaksar Movement. Mashriqi's bank account was seized, his family was brought to the point of starvation, and the chase and arrests of the Khaksars continued. Thousands of Khaksars including Mashriqi and his sons were thrown in jails. Even the supporters and sympathizers of the movement were imprisoned. All were subjected to beatings and other forms of torture and brutalities. Mashriqi himself was a victim of tormenting treatment despite the fact that he was a political prisoner not a criminal prisoner. Mashriqi's sons were also kept in miserable conditions and were mishandled. Mashriqi and the Khaksars were asked to disband the movement or face consequences. But nothing could stop them from maintaining their unwavering stance. They refused to surrender and remained determined, and the movement prevailed. The Government of India failed miserably in their designs to wipe out the Khaksar Movement. This was a clear message to the rulers that their days of power in India were numbered.

Mashriqi, though in jail, enjoyed tremendous faith of his followers and supporters. His followers refused to take any mandate or direction from anyone else except Mashriqi. He was very close to his people; he lived in their hearts. His followers had blind faith in him. In fact the atrocities against Mashriqi and the Khaksars brought the nation together and led them to believe in themselves and that nothing short of independence would be acceptable to them. In the absence of Mashriqi and with the ban on the Khaksar Movement, there was no choice left for the Muslims but to gather under the flag of the Muslim League.

No other movements in the history of the India parallel the resistance put up by the Khaksars after March 19. Mashriqi and the Khaksars continued to suffer. Mashriqi had to fast for 80 days to obtain his and the release of the Khaksars from jail. He was at the brink of death when released. Under tremendous pressure and public outcry, Mashriqi was liberated from Vellore Jail on January 19, 1942, but his movements were restricted to the Madras Presidency. Mashriqi continued his struggle for freedom despite the odds against him. His followers carried Mashriqi's directive forward to every soul they came across. They passed the message to remain steadfast and to believe that nothing short of a free India would be acceptable. Upon arrival of Sir Stafford Cripps on March 23, 1942 in India, Mashriqi sent him a telegram and demanded complete independence of the entire India. Mashriqi also sent a message to leaders, including Quaid-e-Azam Mohammad Ali Jinnah, and offered them of his complete support in this regard.

It is a tragedy that the Muslim League did not avail, on purpose, Mashriqi's offer of cooperation at various points during the struggle for Pakistan. They were in fact intimidated by his strength and did not want him to play a role in politics. They openly denounced Mashriqi's involvement in politics. The British and the Congress were against collaboration between Khaksars and the Muslim League. The Muslim League disregarded public protests and even Mashriqi's offer of cooperation. As a result, the opponents of the Muslims took advantage and a divided Punjab and Bengal and many other areas that should have been part of Pakistan were given to Hindus. If the Muslim League had supported the Khaksars, the map of Pakistan would have been different.

****

Although the Khaksar role has been given a sense of negativity by anti-Khaksar elements and in many cases has been wiped out from the freedom movement of Pakistan, history is witness to the fact that the Khaksar resistance was the longest and boldest fight for independence in the sub-continent. As mentioned earlier, the Muslim League fully capitalized on Khaksar resistance and strengthened its own position, rather than working with the Khaksars. Unfortunately the role of the Khaksars in the creation of Pakistan is denied for vested interests.

The fact of the matter is Khaksars worked for freedom and guided the nation towards it. Mashriqi wanted the entire India to be Pakistan, whereas Muslim Leaguers wanted to divide India as per the Pakistan Resolution. However, Mashriqi's effort towards the creation of Pakistan have been denied by saying that he was anti-Pakistan. Mashriqi was not anti-Pakistan at all. In fact, he had envisioned the *entire* India to be Pakistan. The Muslims had ruled India for a long time; it was not easy to abandon this and let the Hindus rule a major part of the land and the Muslims living there. He firmly believed that India should be returned to the Muslims because it belonged to the Muslims. He further believed that Muslims and Hindus could continue to live together as they had been living. Mashriqi being a visionary was aware that there were far more negatives than this in the partition plan. These negatives are more visible today.

The Muslim League's struggle was based around the Pakistan Resolution, where as Mashriqi's struggle worked toward the liberation of the entire India. The British preferred to divide India rather than to hand it back to the Muslims. Thus this was one of the reasons that the rulers gave preference to and conducted all negotiations with the Muslim League, rather than the Khaksar Tehrik.

It is absolutely wrong to assume that Pakistan was gained through a constitutional fight and that the Muslim League is the sole creator of Pakistan. No freedom can be achieved without resistance and sacrifice of human life. In the process, leaders and supporters of the movement, in almost all cases have to face the atrocities of jail and render many other personal sacrifices. In case of Pakistan's freedom, Mashriqi and the Khaksars had to suffer a great deal, and they paid the real price. Many Khaksars were killed and Mashriqi and the Khaksars rotted in jails. None of the Muslim League leadership made any such sacrifices or put forth any resistance. None of the Muslim League leaders were even jailed. So who paid the price? It was without a doubt, Mashriqi and the Khaksars.

The British, though they avoided the Khaksar Tehrik for negotiations, did understand the significance of the Khaksar Movement and its strength. Khaksars' contributions have been denied by pro Muslim Leaguers and the entire credit for the creation of Pakistan has been given to Muslim League, however the facts of history speak for themselves and cannot be changed or denied no matter what pro-Muslim League historians may say. Liberation can never be won through constitutional fights alone; look at Kashmir and Palestine where so many people are killed and jailed every day.

****

After the creation of Pakistan, the Muslims of India came under complete Hindu Raj, In Pakistan "*gora sahib*" was replaced by "*brown sahib*". The fight for power started in the newly acquired country. Muslim League leadership failed miserably to put the country in the right direction and priorities were never determined. From 1947 to date, the elite have dominated the country's economic, political, and social sectors. Pakistan has been always been ruled by the feudal lords, bureaucrats (civil and military), and the industrial clans. Furthermore, with the creation of Bangladesh, the two-nation theory failed. Hence, the purpose of obtaining Pakistan has never been fulfilled. Masses continue to suffer on many fronts. Even basic rights, such as freedom of speech and a pure justice system, are not available and accountability of the exploiter is superficial. A vast population lives below the poverty line, and Pakistan is regarded as one of the most corrupt nations in the world. The elite continue to exploit the poor. Although Pakistan had technically become autonomous in 1947, the British colonial ruling system continues to prevail. And the common man has drawn very little gain from the creation of Pakistan.

In the Khaksar circle, the Muslim Leaguers' intentions in the creation of Pakistan have always been questioned. This is true because of the facts and the conditions that have prevailed since Pakistan's creation. Providing education to the nation should have been the top priority for the Muslim League, but despite Mashriqi's emphasis, nothing concrete was ever done in this direction. Muslim Leaguers didn't want to share power with the common man. Otherwise, the education sector would not have been ignored and the masses could have been uplifted. This is one of the major reasons why the purpose of obtaining Pakistan—for the uplift of the masses—has never proven true.

So the question arises, was Pakistan acquired for the privileged classes of India (the leadership of the Muslim League), rather than for the masses? Mashriqi and the Khaksars had doubted the intentions of the Muslim Leaguers and that is why when Mashriqi was approached to join the Muslim League Central Working Committee (prior to partition), he asked for the condition that the Muslim League must share power with the non-elite. After the creation of Pakistan, whenever Mashriqi raised his voice and asked the leadership to stop exploitation of the people, he was harassed and crushed, and many a time imprisoned on fabricated and concocted bases. He continued to suffer at the hands of various governments until he died.

****

Unfortunately, the history of Pakistan is incomplete and distorted. If people are kept ignorant of Mashriqi's and the Khaksars' struggle, sufferings, and services, then the history of Pakistan is inadequate. Mashriqi's role has been twisted, misrepresented, and in many cases misquoted. The crux of the movement has been completely ignored. There are various reasons to keep the role of Mashriqi unknown or to deny him credit for his services toward independence. One reason is so that full credit for independence can be retained by the pro-Muslim Leaguers. For the pro-Muslim Leaguers, naming Mashriqi as a great freedom fighter means taking away their credit or at least having to share credit with Khaksar Tehrik in the creation of

Pakistan. Another reason is that because Mashriqi led a simple life, acknowledging this would mean that all those who cherished high profile lifestyles then and now, at the expense of a poor nation, would have to forgo their affluent lifestyles.

Therefore, the easiest way for Mashriqi's opponents was to conceal Mashriqi, distort his image, deny his role in the creation of Pakistan and continue exploitation of the masses for their personal gains. Anyone who raised a voice against misrepresentation of Pakistan history and distortion of the Khaksars' role was given threats of dire consequences. Only Muslim League's point of view was to be projected. If this is not true, then why wasn't Khaksar material collected from Pakistan, U.K., and India and made available for public use. Why wasn't there a research academy formed for collecting Khaksar material? This in itself is proof that many realities of Pakistan history are kept hidden on purpose. This work is witness to the fact that Mashriqi and the Khaksars were a part of the struggle and it is beyond one's comprehension, how a nation can be kept so ill informed of this reality.

****

After the creation of Pakistan, Mashriqi still tried to undo injustices by mobilizing his followers in India and also worked hard for the liberation of Kashmir and to uplift the poor masses in Pakistan. Until his death, Mashriqi continued to guide his nation towards an economic, political, and social resurgence of Pakistan and the freedom of Kashmir. Mashriqi's love for the nation is also evident from the fact that he donated some of his land to the people who cultivated it prior to partition. Throughout his life, Mashriqi used his own money to meet expenses related to his political activities, and Khaksars were never asked for any membership fees. After his death, a trust of his property was left for the public, as per his will.

Allama Mashriqi passed away on August 27, 1963. He must have done something for his nation that well over 100, 000 people came to Lahore to attend his funeral.

These web sites have been dedicated to Mashriqi:
http://www.allamamashriqi.info
http://www.allama-mashriqi.8m.com

Chronology of the Khaksar Tehrik and its Leader, Allama Mashriqi

1846-1938

1846

Khan Ata Mohammad Khan (Mashriqi's father) is born.

1888

1888 August 25

Inayatullah Khan (Allama Mashriqi) is born in Amritsar, India to a Rajput family.

1895

Mashriqi attends an Educational Conference in Rampur with his father. At the conference, Mashriqi's father introduces him to Sir Syed Ahmed Khan.

1897

In the initial years, Mashriqi gets his education at home. Later, he starts school at B.N. Public School in Amritsar, India.

1900

Mashriqi is first in the entire district in middle school examinations.

Mashriqi begins studying at Government High School in Amritsar.

1902

Mashriqi passes the Matric exam with distinction from Government High School and is awarded Certificates of Proficiency in Mathematics, Persian, and Arabic.

Mashriqi begins writing a collection of poetry in Persian under the title *Kharita*. **Editor's Comments:** Mashriqi completed *Kharita* in 1909 and it was published on February 07, 1924.

1904

Mashriqi passes his intermediate examination and stands first in the entire district. He also receives Jubilee Scholarship and Proficiency awards in the subjects of Arabic, Mathematics, and English.

He goes to Church Mission College and wins a Jubilee Scholarship and Proficiency prizes in Mathematics, Arabic, and English.

Mashriqi joins F.C. College (Foreman Christian College) in Lahore for his Bachelor of Arts degree.

1906

Mashriqi obtains a Bachelor degree (B.A.) from F.C. College in Lahore.

1907

Mashriqi passes his M.A. in Mathematics from the University of Punjab and breaks all previous records. The Governor of Punjab congratulates him on his success.

1907 April 14

The Tribune, Lahore writes Inayatullah's (Mashriqi) name on its first page on the top under the heading, "Distinguished Scholars."

The Tribune in Lahore pays rich tributes to Mashriqi on securing First Class in Mathematics. The paper writes, "We offer our hearty congratulations to Mr. Inayatulla of the Foreman Christian College on the brilliant success he has achieved at the last M.A. examination of the Punjab University. It is but the bare truth to say that the success he has achieved is a record one in the history of the University. It is no mean achievement to secure First Class in Mathematics at the M.A. examination and well might our countrymen congratulate themselves at the unique success achieved by Mr. Inayatulla... The brilliant University careers of Dr. Zia ud Din Ahmed... Mr.Inayatulla... unmistakingly indicate that our Mahomedan brethren are second to none in the field of intellectual culture."

1907 October 21

At age 19, Mashriqi joins Christ's College at Cambridge University in England.

1908

Mashriqi places first in a preliminary examination in Mathematics and is declared Foundation Scholar at Cambridge University. He secures a scholarship at Christ's College.

1909

Mashriqi completes *Kharita*, a collection of Persian poetry, which he began writing in 1902.

1909 June 22

Mashriqi obtains a Bachelor of Arts (B.A.) degree. He passes Tripos in Mathematics and wins titles of Wrangler and Bachelor Scholar. He passes Tripos in two years, instead of three years, and stands first in his class.

1911

Mashriqi passes Tripos in Natural Sciences (Physics and Geography) with distinction.

Mashriqi obtains Bachelor of Oriental Languages (B.O.L.) degree. He passes Tripos in Oriental Languages (Arabic and Persian).

1911 June 17

The Times, London writes, "Inayatullah Khan of Christ's College, besides gaining First Class in Oriental Languages obtained Honours in Natural Sciences. He became Wrangler only after two years residence."

The Daily Mirror, London writes, "This year at Cambridge Inayatullah Khan of Amritsar and a student of Christ's College has obtained the unusual distinction of successfully competing for two Triposes at the same time and obtaining a First Class and Honours in them."

The Telegraph, London writes, "Other Tripos lists were issued yesterday. Among the names stands conspicuous the name of Inayatullah Khan whose University career presents a series of remarkable successes."

1911 June 30

Indian Student, London writes, "But it has been given to a few Indian students in England to achieve such academic distinctions as has fallen to the lot of Mr. Inayatullah whose name appears both in the Oriental Languages and the Natural Sciences Tripos this year. Born in 1888 he did his B.A. while yet a boy of 18 in First Class and got his M.A. in Mathematics only one year later taking a First Class for the first time in the history of the Punjab University in 1907. In 1908, he was Foundation Scholar at Cambridge and Wrangler and Bachelor Scholar in 1909. We hope and pray that his exceptional abilities may find adequate opportunities for consecrating themselves to the service of his country and glory of his God."

1912

Mashriqi obtains Bachelor of Engineering (B.E.) degree. He passes Tripos in Mechanical Sciences with distinction.

Mashriqi completes his education at Cambridge University.

Evening News writes, "Two special features gave distinction to the Mechanical Sciences Tripos published today at Cambridge, an Indian scholar, Inayatullah Khan, passing his fourth Tripos…"

The Star, London writes, "It was hitherto considered not possible at Cambridge that a man could take four Triposes in the short period of five years, but it is to the credit of India that Inayatullah Khan of Christ's College has accomplished the feat. In 1909, he was declared a Wrangler, two years later he secured First Class Honours in Oriental Languages Tripos and Natural Sciences Tripos at one and the same time and established a record performance."

The Daily Chronicle, London writes, "The Mechanical Science Tripos result which was published at Cambridge yesterday was notable for the success of Inayatuallah Khan who is believed to be the first man to take honours in four different Tripos. He must be placed in the first rank of Indians who have been educated in this country."

1912 June 12

The Cambridge Daily News lauds Mashriqi's performance at Cambridge University and writes, "A further batch of lists was published this morning. Chief interest was taken in the performance of Inayatullah Khan of Christ's College who has proved himself the best all-round Indian student ever at Cambridge. The best known Indians previously are, perhaps, B.P. Paranjpye and A.T. Rajan, both of whom were bracketed senior Wranglers. A few years ago S.A. Majid came along and besides passing both parts of Law Tripos, obtained honours in Oriental Languages Tripos. All these performances are swept aside by the achievement of Inayatullah Khan of Christ's College who yesterday obtained a First Class in the Mechanical Sciences Tripos…He is believed to be the first man of any nationality to obtain honours in four different Triposes. He established a record at the Punjab University also in Mathematics by gaining First Class for the first time in the history of the University. He has carried off a very large number of awards at Christ's College."

The *Westminster Gazette* writes, "A brilliant Indian Scholar, Inayatullah Khan, who today passed, besides his three other Triposes, another Tripos is one of the most distinguished Indians ever seen up."

1912 June 13

The Yorkshire Post writes, "Inayatullah Khan…has proved himself the best student ever at Cambridge. He is believed to be the first man of any nationality to obtain honours in four different subjects…"

1913

While he is still in England, the Maharaja of Alver offers Mashriqi a State Premiership. He politely declines the offer.

1913 January

Mashriqi returns to India.

1913 April

Sir George Roos-Keppel, the Chief Commissioner (equivalent to Governor) of the NWFP, appoints Mashriqi to Vice-Principal of Islamia College in Peshawar.

1917

Mashriqi is promoted to the rank of Principal of Islamia College, Peshawar (NWFP).

1917 October 17

The British government, through Lord Chelmsford (Governor General in India), appoints Mashriqi to Under Secretary of Education in British India in place of Sir George Anderson.
Editor's Note: A typographical error has been made on page 77 of the book, *Allama Mashriqi & Dr. Akhtar Hameed Khan: Two Legends of Pakistan* by Nasim Yousaf. Sir George Anderson has been written Sir John Anderson.

1918

1918 February 19

Mashriqi, as the Under Secretary, recommends the following Muslims for a vacancy in a government position: Dr. Iqbal (Allama Iqbal), Afzal Hussain (of Cambridge University), Qazi (a Wrangler from Cambridge University), and Mirza Ali Mohammad Khan.

1919

1919 October 15

Mashriqi receives confirmation from the Secretary of Education for his incorporation as member of the Indian Education Service (I.E.S.) and his appointment as headmaster of Government High School in Peshawar.

Editor's Comments: Mashriqi's appointment placed him at a lower rank, from Under Secretary to headmaster of a high school; this was of course a case of victimization. Mashriqi was penalized due to his nationalist thinking and his concern and sympathies for the Indians.

1919 October 21

Mashriqi (I.E.S.) joins as headmaster of Government High School in Peshawar.

1920

Mashriqi is offered Ambassadorship of Afghanistan. He declines the offer.
Editor's Comments: Mashriqi understood the reason for this offer. The British offered him this position, so that they could use his popularity and influence on Muslims to stop people from joining the Khilafat Movement.

Mashriqi begins work on what would become his monumental book, *Tazkirah*.

1920 December

Maulana Mohammad Ali Jauhar invites Mashriqi to become the Head of the Mathematics Department at Jamia Millia Islamia University. Mashriqi does not accept the offer due to his other commitments.
Editor's Comments: Jamia Millia Islamia is an institution, which was originally established at Aligarh in United Provinces in India in 1920. In 1925, it was shifted to Karol Bagh in New Delhi.

1921

Mashriqi is offered Knighthood (Title of Sir), but he declines it.
Editor's Comments: Mashriqi was again offered this position by the British so that they could use him for their own ends.

1922

Mashriqi implements Islamic Studies in schools in NWFP, despite resistance from the British.

1923

Mashriqi is elected Fellow of the Royal Society of Arts-F.R.S.A (London).

Mashriqi is appointed Member of the Board of the University of Delhi in India.

1924

Mashriqi is appointed President of the Mathematical Society.

1924 February 07

Kharita, Mashriqi's collection of poetry in Persian, is published.

1924 March 30

Mashriqi's book, *Tazkirah,* is published.

1924 July

Mashriqi sends a copy of *Tazkirah* to Mustafa Kamal Pasha of Turkey.

1925

Mashriqi's book, *Tazkirah*, is nominated for a Nobel Prize.
Editor's Comments: During these years, many prominent people such as, Sir Abdul Qadir, Sir Fazal Hussain, Barrister Sahibzada Aftab Ahmad Khan (Vice Chancellor of Aligarh Muslim University), and two professors from France, nominated *Tazkirah* for the Nobel Prize.

Mashriqi's father dies.

1925 October 18

Mashriqi writes a letter to Mustafa Kamal Pasha of Turkey.
Editor's Note: For letter, see *Allama Mashriqi & Dr. Akhtar Hameed Khan: Two Legends of Pakistan* (pages 100-01).

1926

1926 April 26

Mashriqi leads a delegation to Cairo, Egypt to attend the upcoming Motamar-i-Khilafat Conference.

1926 May 13

Mashriqi delivers his historic speech, *Khitab-e-Misr*, at the Motamar-i-Khilafat Conference at Egypt.

1926 May 13-22

Mashriqi attends the Motamar-i-Khilafat Conference in Cairo, Egypt.
Editor's Comments: Mashriqi stayed in Egypt for some time and then left for Europe.

Latter Part of 1926

Einstein invites Mashriqi to his house in Europe. Einstein's wife is also present at the meeting.

Mashriqi becomes a Fellow of the Geographical Society-F.G.S. (Paris).

Mashriqi becomes a Fellow of the Asiatic Society of France.

Towards the end of the year, Mashriqi returns to India from his foreign tour, and resumes his duties in Peshawar.

1928

Mashriqi implements vocational and technical education in schools in NWFP.

Mashriqi's mother dies in Aligarh.

1930

Mashriqi resigns from Government service and lays the foundation for the Khaksar Tehrik.
Editor's Note: 24 principles of the Khaksar Tehrik are mentioned in *Allama Mashriqi & Dr. Akhtar Hameed Khan: Two Legends of Pakistan* (pages 111-12).

Mashriqi becomes a member of the International Congress of Orientalists (Leiden).

Mashriqi attends the Palestine World Conference.

1930 August 28

Mashriqi responds to Professor Ghulam Jilani Burq, who sent Mashriqi a letter of appreciation for *Tazkirah*.

1931

1931 August 01

Mashriqi's book, *Ishaa'rat*, is published. It explains the philosophy of the Khaksar Tehrik.

1932

Mashriqi meets Abul Kalam Azad at Dehli. Abul Kalam Azad had said that the Khaksar Tehrik was the only party that could eradicate the problems of Muslims.

1932 October 07

Mashriqi arrives in Peshawar with a group of Khaksars.

1932 November

Alarmed by the Khaksar Tehrik's growing popularity in the NWFP, the Government of NWFP imposes restrictions on the Khaksars' activities.

1934

Al-Islah weekly, a publication of the Khaksar Tehrik, is started from Lahore.

1935

1935 July

Mashriqi plays a vital role during a Muslim-Sikh conflict over Shaheed Gunj mosque in Lahore. Mashriqi's efforts raise his prestige among the Muslims.

1935 July 23

Mashriqi addresses a public gathering in Lahore.

1935 August 01

Mashriqi issues a statement regarding Shaheed Gunj Mosque.

1935 August 30

A meeting is convened in Rawalpindi in connection with the Shaheed Gunj Mosque. Mashriqi addresses the public at the meeting.

1935 October

Mashriqi visits Chakwal.

Raja Mohammad Sarfraz Khan (Member Legislative Assembly) from Chakwal joins the Khaksar Tehrik.

1935 October 27

Mashriqi addresses Khaksars at a Khaksar Camp in Lahore. Mock war exercises are also held at this camp.

1935 November

The Khaksars hold mock war exercises in the cities of Punjab.

1935 November 15

Mashriqi's book, *Qaul-e-Faisal*, is published.

1936

Mashriqi delivers a speech at Shahi Mosque, Lahore.

1936 January 10

Allama Mashriqi addresses the Muslims at Dehli.

1936 April 07

The NWFP Government serves notices to Mian Mohamed Abdur Rashid and Mian Bazarg Shah (two Khaksar leaders) in Peshawar, asking them not to take part in the Khaksar Movement.

1936 April 10-12

A Khaksar Camp is held in Rawalpindi. Two of Mashriqi's sons, Ikramullah Khan Anwar and Ehsanullah Khan Aslam, accompany Mashriqi to the camp.

1936 April 24

A report is made on the activities of the Khaksar Camp in Rawalpindi.

1936 July 23

The Government in Peshawar serves notices to eight people asking them not to take part in the Khaksar Movement.

1936 July 31

Mashriqi addresses Khaksars at Amritsar Khaksar Camp.

1936 August 07

Mashriqi addresses Khaksars at Jhelum.

1936 August 10

Mashriqi addresses Khaksars at a Khaksar Camp in Gujrat.

1936 August 28-30

A Khaksar Camp is held in Murree (near Rawalpindi) under the leadership of Malik Ghulam Rasool. A mock war exercise is also conducted at this camp.

1936 September 25

Mashriqi's book, *Maulvi Ka Ghalat Muzhab*, is published.
Editor's Comments: In this book, Mashriqi criticized Maulvis for wrong interpretation of the teachings of the Holy Quran. Today, many voice that the lack of proper projection of Islam is due to the inadequate elucidation of the Holy book by the Maulvis.

1936 September 27

Mashriqi addresses Khaksars at Lahore Khaksar Camp.

1936 October 02-04

A Khaksar Camp is held in Jhelum. Dr. Nazar Muhammad is the Salar-i-Akbar at this camp. Mashriqi addresses the Khaksars at the camp.

1936 October 09-11

A District Khaksar Camp is held in Rawalpindi. Mashriqi addresses the Khaksars at the camp.

1936 October 16

Al-Islah (Khaksar Tehrik's weekly) publishes Mashriqi's address to the Khaksars at Rawalpindi Khaksar Camp.

1936 November 29

Mashriqi addresses Khaksars at Sialkot Khaksar Camp.

1936 December 14

The Chief Secretary of NWFP writes a letter to Mashriqi barring him from entering the North West Frontier Province. According to the Chief Secretary's letter, the ban is to last until November 29, 1937.

1936 December 28

Mashriqi sends a message to the Khaksars of NWFP. He reminds them that the foundation of the Khaksar Tehrik is based on peace, solidarity, brotherhood, discipline, and obedience. He requests to the NWFP Government that all restrictions be lifted from the Khaksar Movement and the ban on his entry into the province be removed. He states that Muslims should have complete freedom to organize themselves according to the teachings of the Quran and Hadiths.

1937

Mashriqi is elected President of the All World's Faiths Conference, which is to be held at Indore, India on April 18, 1938.

G.M. Syed joins the Khaksar Tehrik.

1937 January 02

The Tribune, Lahore reports that the NWFP Government banned a Khaksar Camp, which was to be held from December 29-31, 1936 in Peshawar.

1937 January 27

Al-Islah publishes the first edition of Mashriqi's *Muqalaat*.

1937 March 14

Mashriqi addresses Khaksars at a Lahore General Camp.

1937 March 25-28

A Khaksar Camp is held in Dehli. Mashriqi addresses the Khaksars at the camp.

1937 August 13-15

Mashriqi addresses Khaksars at a Lyallpur (now Faisalabad, Pakistan) Khaksar Camp.

1937 August 15

August 15 is the deadline that Mashriqi gave to the NWFP Government by which restrictions on the Khaksar Tehrik and on his entry into the province must be removed.
Editor's Comments: Five days after this deadline, the NWFP Government removed all restrictions.

1937 August 20

Nawab Sir Sahibzada Abdul Quyyum Khan lifts restrictions on the Khaksar Tehrik in NWFP and on Mashriqi's entry into the NWFP Province; these restrictions had been in place for five years.

1937 August 20-22

Mashriqi addresses a Khaksar Camp in Lahore.

1937 August 29

After the removal of restrictions on August 20, 1937, Mashriqi visits NWFP.

1937 October

A Khaksar rally is held in Peshawar.

1937 October 15

Mashriqi decrees the Fourteen Points of the Khaksar Tehrik.
Editor's Note: For the 14 Points, see *Allama Mashriqi and Dr. Akhtar Hameed Khan: Two Legends of Pakistan* (pages 112-14).

1937 December 11

Dr. Nazar Mohammad leads a delegation of Khaksars to meet with Sir Sikandar Hayat Khan (the Premier of Punjab). They make the following demands:
1. The Punjab Government needs to set up a system under which khairat, zakat, sadaqat, etc. should be collected for the Bait-al-Maal set up by the Khaksars.
2. The Government should grant the Khaksars permission to set up a radio station at the Khaksar headquarters in order to preach the Quran, Hadith, etc.
3. No restrictions should be placed on Government servants for joining the Khaksar Tehrik.
Sir Sikandar Hayat Khan (Premier of Punjab) refuses to accept the three demands of the Khaksar Tehrik.

1937 December 12

Allama Mashriqi writes a courtesy letter to Sir Sikandar Hayat Khan thanking him for meeting with the Khaksar delegation on December 11, 1937. At the same time, Mashriqi asks the Khaksars to send telegrams, letters, etc. to the Premier asking him to accept the Khaksar demands.

1938

Mashriqi is awarded a Gold Medal by the World Society of Islam.

Nawab Bahadur Yar Jang joins the Khaksar Tehrik.

A picture album of Khaksar activities is published.

1938 January 01

Mashriqi addresses Khaksars at Lyallpur Khaksar Camp.

1938 January 26

Allama Mashriqi sends another letter to Sir Sikandar Hayat Khan (Premier of Punjab). In the letter, Mashriqi seeks Sir Sikandar's support regarding the three demands of the Khaksar Tehrik.

1938 February 25

A Khaksar delegation meets Sir Sikandar Hayat Khan (Premier of the Punjab) in connection with the three demands that were put before him on December 11, 1937.

1938 February 27

Mashriqi addresses Khaksars near Gujrat.

1938 March 04

Nawab Bahadur Yar Jang writes to Sir Sikandar Hayat Khan (Premier of Punjab) to accept the three demands of the Khaksar Tehrik (presented to him on December 11, 1937).

1938 March 05

Allama Mashriqi writes a detailed note to Sir Sikandar Hayat Khan (Premier of Punjab) stressing the importance of the three demands of the Khaksar Tehrik.

1938 March 17

The Premier's office again informs Mashriqi that Sir Sikandar already gave his reply in regards to the Khaksar demands at the meeting with the Khaksar delegation on December 11, 1937.
Editor's Comments: At the meeting on December 11, 1937, Sir Sikandar had refused to accept these demands.

1938 March 28

A Khaksar training camp is held in Rawat near Rawalpindi.

1938 April 01-03

Sir Sikandar Hayat Khan (Premier of Punjab) visits the Khaksar Camp at Chakwal. Sir Sikandar addresses the Khaksars. Dr. Nazar Mohammad (Salar-i-Akbar of the Tehrik) requests Sir Sikandar Hayat to accept the three demands of the Khaksars, which were presented to him on December 11, 1937.

1938 April 08

Al-Islah publishes a letter (dated March 30, 1938) by Sir Sikandar Hayat Khan.

1938 April 13-17

A Khaksar Camp is held in Rawalpindi from April 15-17, and another Khaksar Camp in Bannu takes place from April 13-15.

Mashriqi attends the camp in Rawalpindi along with his sons, Inamullah Khan Anwar and Ehsanullah Khan Aslam. Mashriqi also addresses the Khaksars at the camp. A mock war is conducted during the camp.

Mashriqi then travels to Bannu and addresses the second camp.

1938 April 16

Khaksars parade in the Rawalpindi Cantonment area.

Mashriqi returns to Rawalpindi from Bannu and again addresses the Rawalpindi camp.

Mashriqi leaves Rawalpindi for Indore to preside over the All World's Faiths Conference (to be held on April 18, 1938).

1938 April 18-21

Mashriqi presides over the All World's Faiths Conference in Indore.

1938 April 21

Maharaja (Prince) Deevas invites Mashriqi for a meeting. Mashriqi accepts the invitation.

1938 April 22

Mashriqi leaves Indore for Dehli.

1938 April 23

Mashriqi arrives in Dehli at 8:00 am and conducts a meeting with the Khaksars on the same day.

1938 April 24

Mashriqi returns to Lahore.

1938 May 05

Allama Mashriqi again writes to Sir Sikandar Hayat Khan (Premier of Punjab) about the three demands of the Khaksar Tehrik put up on December 11, 1937.

1938 May 30

Barrister Mian Ahmed Shah and Mian Bashir Ahmed Siddiqui, two Khaksar leaders, meet with Sir Sikandar Hayat Khan in order to discuss the Khaksar demands of December 11, 1937.

1938 June 05

Mashriqi addresses a Khaksar Camp at Ludhiana.

1938 August 28

Mashriqi delivers a speech at the Khaksar Camp in Murree.

1938 November 14

The Punjab Government invites Mashriqi and informs him about the acceptance of the three demands he had placed on December 11, 1937.
Editor's Comments: However, the Punjab Government later backed out of the agreement.

1938 December 26

Mashriqi addresses a Khaksar Camp at Adori, Sind.

1939

January

1939 January 27

Mashriqi's message to women is published in *Al-Islah*, the weekly newspaper of the Khaksar Tehrik.

April

1939 April 07-09

A Khaksar Camp is held in Rawalpindi.

1939 April 25

Dr. Sir Zia ud Din writes a letter to Allama Mashriqi to resolve the Shia-Sunni riots at Lucknow.

May

1939 May 25

Dr. Sir Zia ud Din writes another letter to Allama Mashriqi to resolve the Shia-Sunni riots at Lucknow.

1939 May 28

Shias continue to arrive in Lucknow from Punjab to join the Shias in the clash against Sunnis.

June

1939 June

Khaksar Weekly is started in Calcutta. Its editor is Sultan Zia.
Editor's Comments: *Al-Islah* is the Khaksar Tehrik's own weekly paper and thoroughly reflects the Khaksar Tehrik's point of view.

1939 June 12

Idara-i-Aliya (the Headquarters of the Khaksar Tehrik) makes an announcement asking the leaders of the Sunnis and Shias to stop sending groups of people to Lucknow. Idara-i-Aliya warns the Sunnis and Shias to stop the riots by June 30, 1939 or the Khaksars will intervene in order to ensure peace between the two Muslim Sects.

Editor's Comments: These groups were arriving to join their respective sides in Lucknow. However, these support groups were further deteriorating the situation. Thus, Idara-i-Aliya asked them to stop the riots and gave them a deadline of June 30, 1939. This deadline was later extended to July 21, 1939.

1939 June 25

Mashriqi addresses Central Camp at Abbotabad.

1939 June 27

Haq (Lucknow) newspaper publishes the appeal of a local Khaksar leader to end the Shia-Sunni riots.

July

1939 July 02

Khaksars hold mock wars in various cities. Thousands of men and women witness these events. Allama Mashriqi travels extensively to many Khaksar Camps to address the Khaksars and witness their activities.

Khaksars hold a mock war at Minto Park, Lahore. The mock war is held under the command of Salar-i-Azam Ahmed Rafi. Allama Mashriqi addresses a big gathering at Minto Park, Lahore and gives "hope and unity" to the people and the Khaksars. *The Tribune* would write on July 03, 1939, "He [Allama Mashriqi] said that he was preaching unity between the two…communities of India even at the risk of being abused and misrepresented by men of his own community. He believed that the salvation of India lay neither through the 'paper resolutions of the Congress nor through the arm-chair politicians of the Turkish caps of the Muslim League but through unity and spirit of selfless service of one another.'" Mashriqi also stated, "Your duty is to render selfless service and thus move the hearts of your opponents and critics, not by oppression of any kind." *The Tribune* would further write, "Unity, he [Mashriqi] said, could not be achieved by distribution of seats or by constitution. Real unity would be achieved when the true spirit of the two cultures as preached by the holy Quran and the holy Gita was grasped, understood and practiced by the followers of the two faiths."

Mashriqi addresses Khaksars near Gujranwala.

Haji Amir ud Din Sehra, a prominent Muslim Leaguer, announces his decision to join the Khaksar Tehrik.

1939 July 03

Mashriqi again appeals to the leaders of the Sunnis and Shias to stop rioting.

1939 July 07

Al-Islah publishes a letter from the high command of the Shias stating their desire for a truce.

1939 July 16

Mashriqi addresses the Khaksars at Quetta.

1939 July 22-24

A Khaksar Camp is held at Jehlum under the leadership of Muhammad Sarfraz Khan, Member Legislative Assembly (M.L.A.). Dr. Nazar Muhammad from Jehlum is also present.

1939 July 29

Khaksars hold parades in Amritsar. Khaksar leader Mir Manzoor Wali addresses the Khaksars and explains the need for discipline among Muslim youths.

August

1939 August

A Khaksar Camp is held in Delhi.

1939 August 05

Khaksars attempt to stop people in Lahore from proceeding to Lucknow to take part in the Shia-Sunni conflict.

1939 August 07

Mashriqi sends a telegram to Pandit Govind Ballabh Pant (the Premier of U.P.) asking him to end the Shia-Sunni riots in Lucknow. Mashriqi also offers the services of the Khaksars in this regard.

1939 August 08

Mashriqi meets with Sir Sikandar Hayat Khan (the Premier of Punjab) in the presence of Nawab Ahmed Yar Khan Daultana and Mir Maqbool Mehmood. The meeting lasts two and a half hours. Mashriqi asks about the acceptance of the Khaksars' three demands. Mashriqi also discusses the Shia-Sunni riots in Lucknow.

1939 August 09

Mashriqi sends another telegram to the Government of U.P. in regards to the Shia-Sunni riots.

1939 August 10

Mashriqi sends another telegram to Pandit Govind Ballabh Pant (the Premier of U.P.) offering the services of 3,000 Khaksars to end the Shia-Sunni riots.

1939 August 11

Mashriqi sends a telegram to a Khaksar leader in Lucknow. In the telegram, Mashriqi informs the Khaksar to meet with the Premier of U.P. and seek a reply in regards to Mashriqi's offer of 3,000 Khaksars (to settle the Shia-Sunni riots).

Mashriqi receives a telegram from a Khaksar leader in Lucknow, who states that he met with the Premier of U.P. for about one hour. The Khaksar further informs Mashriqi that the Premier of U.P. does not agree that the Khaksars should intervene in the Shia-Sunni riots.

Mashriqi announces his decision to go to Lucknow (U.P.) to end the Shia-Sunni riots.

1939 August 12

At its meeting, the Executive Committee of the U.P. Muslim League decides not to interfere in the Shia-Sunni clash.

1939 August 14

Mashriqi sends another telegram to the Government of U.P. in regards to the Shia-Sunni riots.

The Government of U.P. writes to Mashriqi. The government acknowledges receipt of Mashriqi's telegrams of August 07, 09, and 14, 1939, in regards to the Shia-Sunni riots.

1939 August 16

Mashriqi sends a reply to the Government of U.P. in regards to the Shia-Sunni riots.

1939 August 19

Mashriqi sends another telegram to the Premier of U.P and informs him about his arrival in U.P on August 25, 1939.

1939 August 25

Mashriqi arrives in Lucknow (U.P.) to settle the Shia-Sunni dispute and put an end to the riots. A rigorous effort to ensure settlement between Shias and Sunnis is launched.

1939 August 27

The Hindustan Times, Delhi publishes news of an interview with Allama Mashriqi regarding the aim of the Khaksar Tehrik. The newspaper writes, "…Interviewed by the *United Press* Allama Mashriqi, who is here [in Lucknow] with a view 'to settling the *Madhe Sahaba-Tabarra* agitation,' claimed that his was not a communal movement. He said that the Khaksar movement contained a receipe for all ills to which India was subject nowadays."

Khaksars hold discussions with Ministers of the Government of U.P.

1939 August 28

As a result of Mashriqi and the Khaksars' efforts, the Shias and Sunnis agree to stop the agitation in Lucknow. Shias stop recitation of *Tabbarra*.
Editor's Comments: A steady flow of Khaksars continued to arrive in Lucknow in the following days. Many Khaksars were unaware of the fact that the Shia-Sunni riots had been resolved by Mashriqi, and they continued to arrive in Lucknow.

After the Shia-Sunni settlement Mashriqi addresses the public in Lucknow. The public is extremely happy at Mashriqi's achievement.

Khaksars hold a rally (lasting three days) in Karachi and present a Guard of Honor to the Premier Khan Bahadur Allahbuksh at the Secretariat.

1939 August 30

Four Khaksars are arrested in Lucknow.

The District Magistrate in Lucknow prohibits the carrying of belchas (spades) by Khaksars for two months.

1939 August 31

Section 144 remains in place in the city of Lucknow.

The Khaksar situation is discussed at length at a Cabinet meeting of Ministers in Lucknow. After deliberating late into the night, the Cabinet decides to allow the District Magistrate a free hand to deal with the Khaksars.

Khaksar batches parade in a procession in Amritsar before leaving for Lucknow.

September

1939 September 01

Allama Mashriqi, who was in Lucknow to resolve the Shia-Sunni conflict, is arrested in the early hours (4:05 A.M.) of the morning.
Editor's Comments: The Government of U.P. resented Mashriqi and the Khaksars' involvement in the Shia-Sunni issue and frowned at credit given to him for settling the issue. Mashriqi's selfless labor was highly appreciated by Muslims in this regard.

Police continue their arrests of the Khaksars in Lucknow. Approximately 30 Khaksars are arrested on this day.

An adjournment motion, moved by Khan Bahadur Masood-uz-Zaman in the U.P. Council to discuss the arrest of Allama Mashriqi, is disallowed.

Further restrictions are imposed on the Khaksars by the Government of U.P. According to *The Hindustan Times*, Delhi of September 02, 1939, the District Magistrate in Lucknow "orders that no Khaksars shall, for a period of two months, enter into the city and the district of Lucknow and for a period of two months no Khaksars will join in the activities of Khaksars in the city, nor will they go out in the area in Khaksar uniforms or wear distinctive badges or banners associated with Khaksars and their organization."

A strike is observed in Lucknow in protest of Mashriqi's arrest and the Government's restrictions on Khaksar activities in Lucknow.

1939 September 02

As a result of protest from the public and the Khaksars, Mashriqi is released (in the evening) from jail in Lucknow.
Editor's Comments: It was reported that Mashriqi was released from jail upon the agreement that he would not enter U.P. for one year, would not permit Khaksars from outside the U.P. to work in the U.P., and would direct U.P. Khaksars not to interfere in the Shia-Sunni riots.
    However, Mashriqi never gave or agreed to any such statement and his signature was forged. In order to prove that no such undertaking was given, Mashriqi returned to Lucknow on September 13, 1939.

Mashriqi leaves Lucknow along with a large number of Khaksars.
Editor's Comments: Well over 10,000 people had gathered at the Lucknow railway station to bid farewell to Mashriqi and the Khaksars and appreciate their efforts for bringing settlement between Shias and the Sunnis.

Khaksars leave Lucknow after the Shia-Sunni matter is brought under control. The Government of U.P. agrees to pay their fares so they can return to their respective homes.

1939 September 03

Mashriqi, along with a large number of Khaksars, arrives in Delhi.

1939 September 07

Mashriqi arrives in Lahore and addresses a large gathering. He vehemently denies signing any undertaking (stating that he would not return to Lucknow for one year) to obtain his release from jail.

The Government of U.P. bans the Khaksars from entering U.P. The Khaksars living in U.P. are also forbidden from carrying spades and marching in formation.

1939 September 08

The District Magistrate issues an order under Section 144 forbidding Khaksars from carrying spades and marching in formation in Cawnpore.
Editor's Comments: The Government of U.P. took preventive measures as they feared reaction from the Khaksars due to false allegations against Mashriqi.

1939 September 09

Khaksars demonstrate in Bareilly (U.P.), protesting that Allama Mashriqi had been arrested deceitfully on September 01, 1939. They also announce that Mashriqi had not issued any undertaking stating that he would not enter U.P. for one year. They state that the Government of U.P. forged his signature.
Editor's Comments: Khaksars highly resented the Government of U.P.'s conniving act that Mashriqi signed the undertaking for his release. Khaksars knew Mashriqi was a man of integrity and would never have taken such an action regardless of any pressure or circumstance. Thus, they protested.

The District Magistrate in Bareilly (U.P.) announces that no Khaksar in uniform with a spade could parade in the city for two months.

1939 September 10

Revenue Minister replies to a local Congressman via telegram regarding the basis on which Mashriqi was released from jail in Lucknow on September 02, 1939.
Editor's Comments: In his reply, the Revenue Minister states that Allama Mashriqi was released upon giving an undertaking not to visit the U.P. for one year, not to depute or permit Khaksars from outside the U.P. to work in the province, and to direct U.P. Khaksars not to interfere in the Shia-Sunni dispute.

This statement was false as Mashriqi's signature was forged on the undertaking. Mashriqi vehemently denied making any apology to the Government. In order to prove that no such undertaking was given, Mashriqi returned to Lucknow on September 13, 1939.

The Statesman, Calcutta reports that the Government of U.P. is annoyed over Allama Mashriqi's press statement refuting the Government's claim that Mashriqi had signed an undertaking to obtain his release.

1939 September 13

Allama Mashriqi and six others, including Raja Mohammad Sarfaraz Khan (Member Legislative Assembly, Punjab), are arrested in Maliahabad while on their way to Lucknow. Allama Mashriqi is returning to Lucknow to prove that he did not give any kind of undertaking stating that he would not enter U.P.
Editor's Comments: The news of Mashriqi's arrest spread like a wild fire and Khaksars from all over the country were shocked and angered at the Government of U.P. Thousands of Khaksars from various parts from the country, from Calcutta to Peshawar, rushed to Lucknow for his release. The public and the Khaksars heavily resented Mashriqi's arrest.

1939 September 14

A strike is observed in Lucknow in protest of the arrests of Mashriqi and the Khaksars.

1939 September 15

The people of Lucknow remain disturbed and show their anger at Juma gatherings in response to Mashriqi's arrest.

1939 September 16

Allama Mashriqi and six others (arrested on September 13, 1939) are tried by the First Class Magistrate in Lucknow. Allama Mashriqi is sentenced to one month of simple imprisonment and a fine of Rs. 50. Five of the others are fined Rs. 10 each and the sixth is let off. The public and the Khaksars resent the court's decision.

Maulana Zafar Ali Khan, the editor of *Zamindar* newspaper, pays tributes to the Khaksar Tehrik in *Zamindar*.

1939 September 17

Khaksars demonstrate in Lucknow against Mashriqi's arrest and the Government's attitude toward the Khaksars. Police arrive at the scene and arrest eight Khaksars. The police also injure a Khaksar and some onlookers.

1939 September 18

The Bihar Assembly discusses the Khaksar Movement.

25 Khaksars are arrested in Aligarh. The Khaksars were on their way to Lucknow to join protests for Mashriqi's arrest.

1939 September 19

Questions are raised in the Bihar Assembly about the Khaksar Movement's political objectives.

Khaksars continue to demonstrate in Lucknow against Mashriqi's arrest and the Government's attitude toward the Khaksars. 24 Khaksars are arrested.

A large number of people in Aminabad (Lucknow) condemn police for arresting Khaksars.

Six Khaksars from Aligarh are convicted in Lucknow for wearing the Khaksar uniform, parading in formation, and carrying spades. They are fined and sentenced to rigorous imprisonment.

In a statement to the press, Dr. Sir Zia ud Din expresses his regret over Allama Mashriqi's arrest.

1939 September 20

Khaksar activities are questioned in the Bihar Assembly. Members of the Assembly are informed that the Khaksar Tehrik's activities are being watched.

Khaksars continue to arrive in Lucknow for Mashriqi's release and to join in ongoing demonstrations.

A batch of Khaksars leave Campbellpur for Lucknow in connection with Mashriqi's arrest.

16 Khaksars from Delhi (on their way to Lucknow) are arrested in Aligarh upon arrival. Other batches from Punjab continue to arrive in Aligarh on their way to Lucknow to join ongoing protests for Mashriqi

Thousands of Muslims in Aminabad (Lucknow) condemn police for arresting Khaksars. Slogans against Government of U.P are raised.

1939 September 21

The Statesman, Calcutta reports that the Government of U.P. has issued instructions to authorities to stop the entry of Khaksars (who are collecting at Jagadhari) into

U.P. The newspaper further reports that the Government will use special camps for imprisoning arrested Khaksars.
Editor's Comments: A large number of Khaksars, who had arrived from various parts of India in connection with Mashriqi's arrest, were thrown in jail. This was causing difficulties for the Government of U.P., including shortage of space and staff in jail.

Khaksar arrests continue in U.P. Many Khaksar leaders are arrested. Included in the arrests are Barrister Wahid ud Din Hyder, Barrister Mian Ahmed Shah, Advocate Habib ullah Khan, Hakim Mohammad Akram Khan, Nawazzada Arbab Sher Akbar Khan. They are arrested under Section 107 Cr.P.C. and each one is asked to provide two sureties of Rupees 1,500 and a personal bond of Rupees 2,000.

The public in Lucknow is angered at the arrest of the Khaksars. Slogans against Government of U.P. are raised.

Khaksars offer court arrest. 27 Khaksars are taken into custody and a large crowd gathers to watch the arrests. Police injure spectators and sympathizers while dispersing the crowd.
Editor's Comments: The Khaksars would have taken any step to ensure Mashriqi's release. Their demonstrations and offers of court arrest were part of their efforts toward this cause. The police did not even spare Khaksar sympathizers and spectators.

In a Press Note, the U.P. Government denies allegations that it is trying to crush the Khaksar Tehrik.
Editor's Comments: The Government was highly troubled by the ongoing Khaksar demonstrations and public support, therefore, the Government felt compelled to issue a Press Note stating that it had no intentions of crushing the Khaksar Movement.

1939 September 23

24 Khaksars are arrested on charges of parading and wearing Khaksar Movement badges.

Five Khaksars are arrested in Ghaziabad, U.P. under Section 144 and sent to lock-up at Meerut.

1939 September 24

24 Khaksars are arrested in Aminabad (Lucknow). Two are arrested at the railway station on their way from Bareilly.

The Women's Sub-Committee of the All-India Muslim League passes a resolution declaring their sympathies with the Khaksar Movement and congratulating the

Khaksars on their firm stance against the curtailment of civil rights by the U.P. Government.

The Lucknow City Muslim League Council passes a resolution condemning the Government of U.P. for suppressing civil liberty and for its anti-Muslim attitude. The Government fears that the Muslim League may join hands with the Khaksar Tehrik. Armed police are placed in Aminabad Park, Lucknow and the U.P. Government continues its strict watch of Khaksar activities.

The Government of U.P. distributes thousands of pamphlets to people throughout the province, in an attempt to clarify its actions against the Khaksars.
Editor's Comments: The Government of U.P. was highly perturbed and nervous at the public outcry in favor of Mashriqi and the Khaksars. Thus the Government of U.P. distributed pamphlets explaining their position and to pacify the feelings against the Government's action in regards to the Khaksars and Allama Mashriqi.

1939 September 25

Police attempt to prevent a batch of Khaksars from proceeding towards Ghaziabad, U.P. This results in a clash and upon reaching Ghaziabad, 75 Khaksars are arrested.

Police attempt to stop Khaksars at Charbagh Railway Station, Lucknow from entering the city. The Khaksars ignore the police and proceed to a local Mosque. Police reinforcements arrive, surround the mosque, and arrest the Khaksars.

Six Khaksars are arrested in Lucknow.

1939 September 26

The Tribune quotes a report by *Al-Islah* regarding the mistreatment of Khaksars in jail.

The Hindustan Times, Delhi reports that the Government in Delhi is very concerned about the Khaksar situation.

There is a clash near Delhi between Khaksars (who are heading to Meerut to protest Allama Mashriqi's arrest) and the police. The Acting District Magistrate, the Superintendent of Police, and other police officers arrive on the scene. Many Khaksars are arrested and schools and shops are closed. A large crowd gathers to witness the arrests of the Khaksars.

Khaksars continue to demonstrate (in protest of Mashriqi's arrest and the U.P. Government's attitude towards Muslims) in various places in U.P. In Lucknow, many people gather to watch the demonstrations. Khaksars are arrested daily.

A large police force guards the Hindon River Bridge to prevent a batch of Delhi Khaksars from reaching Ghaziabad (Lucknow). A permanent police force is ordered to guard the bridge.

In Ghaziabad, cases are registered against 75 Khaksars (arrested following a clash with police on September 25, 1939).

17 Khaksars (arrested on September 17, 1939) are tried in Agra and sentenced to one month of simple imprisonment each.

Five Khaksars are arrested in Meerut and moved to Meerut Jail.

1939 September 27

The Statesman publishes news about the arrest of the Khaksars at Ghaziabad.

12 Khaksars from Bihar are arrested at Benares Cantonment Railway Station under Section 144.

The Hindustan Times, Delhi reports "…earlier in the week the City Muslim League passed a resolution holding the Ahrars entirely responsible for the present state of affairs and deploring the [U.P.] Government's 'trampling upon Muslim civic rights.'"

1939 September 28

Mr. Rafi Ahmed Kidwai (the acting Premier of U.P.) makes advances for a settlement with the Khaksars through Mr. Mubashar Hussain Kidwai, Secretary of the U.P. Muslim League. Several personalities including Mr. Mubashar Hussain Kidwai visit Mashriqi in jail. They insist on Mashriqi seeing Quaid-e-Azam and leaving him to settle the matter with the U.P. Government.
Editor's Comments: As a result of the Khaksar and public support for the Khaksars, the Government of U.P. felt compelled to reach a compromise with the Khaksars.

Amidst allegations that the U.P. Government is trying to crush the Khaksar Tehrik, Rafi Ahmed Kidwai (the Acting Premier of U.P.) issues a statement attempting to explain the U.P. Government's position.

The Government of NWFP issues a communique regarding allegations that the U.P. Government is trying to crush the Khaksar Tehrik.

1939 September 29

Police clash with Khaksars at Aminabad. Some Khaksars are injured, and 18 Khaksars are arrested.

Khaksars from Calcutta arrive at Lucknow railway station to join other Khaksars who had gathered in connection with Allama Mashriqi's arrest. Police ask the Khaksars to surrender, but the Khaksars refuse. Police clash with the Khaksars and reinforcements arrive. Nine Khaksars are arrested.

1939 September 30

Acting Premier of U.P. issues another statement attempting to clarify the Government's position regarding the Khaksar Tehrik.

October

1939 October 01

15 Khaksars are arrested in Lucknow.

Ten Khaksars are arrested near Charbagh Railway Station.

Nine Khaksars are arrested in Aminabad.

1939 October 03

Five Khaksars are injured by the police at Charbagh Railway Station in Lucknow. Special police is posted at all entrances to the Assembly Chamber in Lucknow to prevent Khaksar demonstrations.

Seven Khaksars are arrested in Lucknow.

Police lathi charge Khaksars outside a mosque in Aligarh. 20 Khaksars are arrested. Police patrols the entire city.

1939 October 04

Mashriqi receives a letter in Lucknow jail from Quaid-e-Azam from Delhi. The letter asks that Mashriqi give authority to Jinnah to discuss the question of the Khaksar Movement with the Viceroy. The messenger who brought the letter demands immediate response, however Mashriqi provides no such response. **Editor's Comments:** According to the Khaksar circle, the Muslim League was interfering in the Khaksar-U.P. conflict without any request from Mashriqi. The Muslim League was getting involved so that they could use the strength of the Khaksars for their own political ends. Muslim League leadership wanted to show to the Viceroy that Khaksars were at the back of the League.

Mashriqi writes the following letter to the Viceroy of India:
"My imprisonment and that of hundreds of prominent Khaksars by the United Provinces Government and their intention to crush the Khaksar Movement need not detain me further from announcing our attitude towards the war. I consider

bargaining even with an enemy in trouble mean and unmanly. Moslem character forbids it. Islam prohibited double dealing. England is now engaged in struggle involving life and death and most certainly India's future also...We must prove to the British again that we Musalmans are the actual defenders of India and therefore, we, above all, have natural, also inheritary, right to control it. BLOOD AND RULE HAVE ALWAYS GONE TOGETHER IN ALL HISTORY.

I doubt if the Indian National Congress can supply a single soldier for the defence of India anywhere. Any posing, therefore, by a party that cannot deliver goods is ridiculous and preposterous. Only Khaksars all over India, who have rendered selfless and practical social service irrespective of caste or creed for past nine years, can claim playing game of blood at this moment. Or again the Punjab Premier can give real aid for defence of country. I have thought over the problem and have closely examined all real, false and conditional offers. I hereby declare that within three months of this announcement I shall be able to place at the disposal of Your Excellency 30,000 well drilled and best-disciplined Khaksar soldiers after minimum military training for internal military defence of India, 10,000 for police purposes for maintaining internal peace and another 10,000 of the very best quality for help of Turkey, our ally, if need be for a fight on European soil. Government has only to test us in order to prove Khaksar's fidelity to Motherland to the last drop of his blood. I request widest publicity of this declaration as I am in prison."

Editor's Comments: World War II started on September 01, 1939. Mashriqi was loyal to the land, thus he made the offer of 50,000 Khaksars for the defense of India. Sir Sikandar did not like Mashriqi's offer of 50,000 Khaksars to the Viceroy. He knew that if he couldn't make a similar offer, Mashriqi would appear stronger than himself in the eyes of Viceroy.

Two Khaksars are arrested in Lucknow.

In Mordabad, a resolution demanding the removal of the ban by U.P. Government on the Khaksars is passed at a crowded meeting of Muslims.

Nehru asks Rafi Ahmad Kidwai to send full account of Khaksar-U.P. Government dissension to Quaid-e-Azam.

1939 October 05

Rafi Ahmed Kidwai, the Acting Premier of U.P., meets Khaksar leaders from Punjab in order to discuss a settlement between the Khaksars and the Government of U.P. The Minister for Law and Order and the Chief Secretary are also present at the meeting. The Government of U.P. demands the following:
1.   All Khaksars from outside the province must leave U.P.
2.   Local Khaksars must not indulge in Khaksar activities.
3.   Allama Mashriqi should withdraw his statement that the Government forged his undertaking.
The Khaksar leaders state that they will need to consult Allama Mashriqi in jail before they can carry out the Government's instructions.

In Benares, 12 Khaksars are sentenced to six months of imprisonment and fined Rs. 50 each for defying the ban on Khaksar entry into U.P.

The U.P. Government issues a Press Note in an attempt to clarify their actions in regards to the Khaksars.

1939 October 06

Quaid-e-Azam sends another letter to Mashriqi in Lucknow jail.
Editor's Comments: Quaid-e-Azam had already sent a letter to Mashriqi on October 04, 1939. Mashriqi did not respond to either of these two letters. According to the Khaksar circle, Jinnah was insisting on getting involved in the Khaksar-U.P. conflict to achieve political benefits for the Muslim League.

Sir Raza Ali informs the Associated Press that he is proceeding to Lucknow to meet Allama Mashriqi in jail. He also issues a notice of a resolution for the U.P. Provincial Muslim League Council (which is to meet on October 08, 1939). The resolution condemns the Government of U.P. and states that the Government's actions toward the Khaksars are against the basic principle of civil liberties. It particularly mentions the following:
1. The Government's ban on the entry of Khaksars into certain places in U.P.
2. The restrictions imposed on the Khaksar Movement
3. Resorting to the use of Section 144
4. Obtaining undertakings from the arrested Khaksars.
The resolution further states that the actions of the Government of U.P. are no different than those of the previous Governments during the civil disobedience movement.

A Khaksar influx from Punjab into Ghaziabad, U.P. results in a standoff between Khaksars and the police. The market in Ghaziabad is closed, as the situation remains tense.

The local Congress Committee in Ghaziabad holds a special sitting in light of the Khaksar situation. The President of the Congress Committee informs the Premier of U.P. about the situation in the city.

1939 October 07

Quaid-e-Azam has a telephone conversation with Rafi Ahmed Kidwai, Acting Premier of U.P., regarding the Khaksar issue.

The U.P. Premier sends Mashriqi his proposals regarding the U.P. Government-Khaksar conflict.

There is military and police presence in Ghaziabad to guard Khaksar activities. Tension prevails in the city.

A Khaksar-police clash is averted in Lucknow after Khaksars are allowed to enter Ghaziabad.

20 Khaksars are arrested in Lucknow.

The number of Khaksars in Dehra Dun continues to increase.

In Aligarh, Police lathi charge on Khaksars from Delhi.

1939 October 08

Quaid-e-Azam offers his services to the Government of U.P. to resolve the differences between the Government and the Khaksars.

Quaid-e-Azam discusses the U.P. Government's attitude toward the Khaksars with Rafi Ahmed Kidwai, the Acting Premier of U.P. Jinnah asks Rafi Ahmed Kidwai to release Allama Mashriqi on parole so that Mashriqi can meet with Jinnah.

Quaid-e-Azam speaks over the phone with Moti Lal Nehru and Nawab Ismail Khan, President of the U.P. Provincial Muslim League, regarding the Khaksar issue.

Nehru telegraphically requests the Premier of U.P. to forward to Quaid-e-Azam the Government's papers in regards to the Khaksar Tehrik.

Dr. Zia ud Din visits Mashriqi after seeing the Premier. He insists that Mashriqi should see Quaid-e-Azam.

Nawab Ismail Khan insists on interviewing Mashriqi (in Lucknow jail) to discuss the Khaksar-U.P. Government settlement. Nawab Ismail Khan along with Begum Habibullah and Mr. Kidwai meet Mashriqi.
Editor's Comments: According to the Khaksar circle, Muslim Leaguers' continued interest in the Khaksar-Government of U.P issue was for vested motives. Mr. Mubashar Hussain Kidwai, Secretary of the U.P. Muslim League, himself had admitted to Mashriqi in Lucknow jail that Khaksars' conflict with the U.P. Government had put new life into the Muslim League in U.P. Owing to the insistence of the Muslim Leaguers and Jinnah, Mashriqi did meet with Jinnah later on October 15, 1939.

Allama Mashriqi does not agree to be released on parole or to conduct a phone conversation with Quaid-e-Azam. Mashriqi decides to wait until his release (which is set for October 15, 1939), after which he is willing to meet with Quaid-e-Azam.

The Muslim League Council Meeting

The Muslim League Council meets and discusses the Khaksar issue. The Muslim League protests the U.P. Government's treatment of the Khaksars and demands that the Government withdraw the ban on Khaksars entering U.P. A committee is also appointed to negotiate with the Government. The Council decides to wait until October 22, 1939 for the outcome of the negotiations with the Government.

At its meeting, the U.P. Muslim League Council discusses the Khaksar Tehrik. *The Tribune*, Lahore of October 10, 1939 would report, "Discussion appears to have taken place at…[the] meeting of the U.P. Muslim League Council over the question of attitude to be adopted by the Muslim League towards the Khaksar movement. It was emphasised that in so far as the Khaksar movement had proved a source of strength to the Muslim community it was the duty of the Muslim League to stand by them and prevent their effacement…Prominent leaders among those who spoke were Sir Raza Ali (who was the sponsor of the resolution), Ch. Khaluquz Zaman, Mr. Z.A. Lari and other prominent Muslim U.P. legislators."

Bulandshahr

A large number of Khaksars are stationed near Bulandshahr. The military and an armed police force are in place to stop additional influx of Khaksars (from different cities of India) and to control their ongoing activities. A special train with a cavalry unit has also just arrived to further these efforts.

Armed police and military remain on alert in Bulandshahr. A number of Khaksars are arrested 9 miles from Bulandshahr and taken to the district jail in Bulandshahr. As the Khaksars enter the jail, police opens fire. Five Khaksars are brutally killed and 20 injured.
Editor's Comments: There was no justification to open fire and ruthlessly kill the Khaksars under arrest. The Khaksars were completely peaceful, and this firing demonstrates the arrogance of the authorities against the Khaksars.

Delhi authorities remain vigilant following the Bulandshahr incident and search cars for Khaksars. The Deputy Commissioner, Senior Superintendent of Police, and many other Delhi officials are present at the boundary of Delhi and U.P.

The Commissioner of Meerut Division arrives in Bulandshahr to hold an inquiry about the killing of the Khaksars. The Government appoints Justice Hunter of the Allahabad High Court to hold an inquiry.

Sir Harry Graham Haig (the Governor of U.P.) sends a secret official inquiry report to Lord Linlithgow. According to the report, the Khaksars at Bulandshahr had agreed to surrender their belchas in the jail. The police officers, nevertheless, open fired. This report proves that the Khaksars did not attack first.

In Other Areas

The Statesman, Calcutta reports that the curfew order in Meerut is now in place from 6:30 pm to 6:30 am.
Editor's Comments: Curfew was imposed in anticipation of public outcry due to killing of the Khaksars at Bulandshahr jail.

The Statesman reports that the Khaksar presence in the Meerut Division has been the subject of discussion by the U.P. Government.

A batch of Khaksars arrives from Calcutta in Lucknow. Police try to stop them at the railway station, but they manage to reach Aminadaula Park in Lucknow. A scuffle takes place here and the police injure five Khaksars. All 31 Khaksars who came from Calcutta are arrested.

Two Khaksars are arrested in Ammabad.

25 Khaksars pass through Ghaziabad on their way to Aligarh.

A batch of 125 Khaksars from Delhi arrives in Aligarh. Local authorities encircle these Khaksars. Another batch of Khaksars arriving in Aligarh manages to evade police.

20 Khaksars from Delhi are arrested in Aligarh. (Police had resorted to lathi charge against these Khaksars on October 07, 1939.)

1939 October 09

Sir Raza Ali leaves Lucknow. Sir Raza Ali had come to Lucknow to interview Mashriqi in jail, but was unable to do so because the Government attached unacceptable restrictions in regards to him meeting Mashriqi. Sir Raza Ali criticized the Government of U.P. for imposing these restrictions.

The Tribune, Lahore reports that Sir Raza Ali further states that in 1922, the Government had allowed him to see Moti Lal Nehru without any such conditions.

The Tribune reports that the Government of U.P. has sent its documents regarding the Khaksar Tehrik to Quaid-e-Azam.

Nawab Ismail Khan also meets with the Viceroy and discusses the Khaksar issue.

Nawab Ismail Khan meets Quaid-e-Azam and explains various developments regarding the Khaksar Tehrik issue with the Government of U.P.

The Tribune, Lahore reports that the Government of the U.P. has appointed Justice Hunter of the Allahabad High Court to conduct an inquiry into the killing of the Khaksars in Bulandshahr on October 08, 1939.

The bodies of the five Khaksars that had been killed at Bulandshahr by the police firing on October 08, 1939 are brought to Lahore to their families (two of these bodies are en route to Peshawar). City and police officials remain present at the time of delivery. The Khaksars plan to hold a procession through the streets of Lahore with the bodies of the deceased, but they are prevented from doing so by the Government officials.

130 Khaksars are arrested at Aligarh.

Sikandar Hayat Khan states that the Khaksars cannot be made part of the Territorial Army in Punjab.

Editor's Comments: Sir Sikandar did not like Mashriqi's offer of 50,000 Khaksars to the Viceroy. He felt that this undermined his position in the eyes of the Viceroy of India. Sir Sikandar felt compelled to come up with an equivalent or even higher number of trained and disciplined people like the Khaksars for the defense of India.

Sir Sikandar had observed the strength of the Khaksars during Government of U.P-Khaksar issue. Khaksars were able to pressure the Government of U.P. not to cause split between Shias and Sunnis. Sir Sikandar had also witnessed the dedication of the Khaksars towards Mashriqi, when thousands of Khaksar came to Lucknow, at their own expense, in protest of Mashriqi's arrest.

Sir Sikandar was alarmed by the strength of Mashriqi and the Khaksars. In the coming days he would declare them to be a communal organization (even though this was not the case) and in the coming months, a ban would be placed on the Khaksar Movement. Sir Sikandar would declare them communal so that he could justify the ban.

1939 October 10

Dr. Sir Zia uddin meets Dr. Kailash Nath Katju (U.P. Government Minister) and discusses with him the Khaksar situation. *The Tribune*, Lahore would write on October 12, 1939, "…difficulty is being experienced in drafting an announcement which would show that neither the Government had yielded nor the Khaksars have done so."

Khan Bahadur Moulvi Obaidur Rahman Khan, Member Legislative Assembly (M.L.A), visits injured Khaksars in Aligarh jail.

Khaksars continue to arrive in Bulandshahr. The police remain on high alert.

Of the five bodies (killed by the police firing in Bulandshahr on October 08, 1939) two are brought to Peshawar. The funeral procession for one of the Khaksars takes place in Peshawar while the other is delivered to D.I. Khan for burial.

Muslims observe a complete strike in Peshawar out of respect for the Khaksars who were killed on October 08, 1939 at Bulandshahr.

Khaksars from Delhi arrive in Agra and march through the bazaar. Police try to stop the parading Khaksars and call in more constables armed with lathis and other weapons. The entire market is closed and large crowds witness the Khaksars marching. Khaksars offer prayers and deliver speeches in front of the crowd. The Khaksars spend the night at a mosque. Tension between the police and the Khaksars remains high. Police block all roads leading to the mosque and prevent the crowds from approaching the mosque.

Editor's Comments: 27 Khaksars were arrested the following morning (October 11, 1939) when they emerged from the mosque.

Approximately 100 Khaksars arrive in Aligarh and establish a camp on the outskirts of the city.

The District Magistrate of Meerut visits Ghaziabad to inquire about the activities of the Khaksars.

One Khaksar is arrested at Sikandarabad.

Ten Khaksars are arrested in Aminabad.

1939 October 11

Quaid-e-Azam writes a letter to Mashriqi from New Delhi:

Dear Allama Mashriqi,

This is just to inform you that at my request the acting Prime Minister of U.P. sent me all the papers relating to the conflict between the Government and the Khaksars from the Government point of view with his covering letter dated the 5th of October.

Thereafter at my suggestion he agreed to release you without imposing any condition so that you may come to Delhi and meet me, and if there was any hitch in your agreeing to this suggestion you should be enabled to speak to me on the phone from Lucknow jail.

Hon'ble Mr. Rafi Ahmad Kidwai informed me that you were not willing to do either. I, therefore, apprehending some misunderstanding, got in touch with Nawab Ismail Khan, who was in Lucknow, on phone to communicate to you personally my suggestion. He had an interview with you on the 8th [October, 1939] at the Lucknow jail and on his arrival at Delhi on the 9th [October, 1939] he informed me that you told him that you would only come after your present term of imprisonment expires about the 15th of October [1939].

Since then Dr. Sir Ziauddin Ahmad met me today and explained to me the situation further. You know that I am anxious to do all I can to help the Khaksars in the matter, and I once more request you to come to Delhi without delay. I would have come to Lucknow but just at this moment it is not possible for me to do so and Dr Sir Ziauddin will explain to you why at this critical moment I can't leave Delhi.

I do hope that you will in these circumstances come to Delhi, so that we could handle the matter at once as any delay may complicate the situation.

I shall be obliged if you will send me an immediate reply.

Yours sincerely,

Sd. M.A. Jinnah

Dr. Sir Zia ud Din meets Quaid-e-Azam to discuss the Khaksar-Government of U.P. issue.

Khaksars organize a camp in Anjuman Park (Amritsar). Parades are held, and Manzur Ali and Sheikh Muhammad Umar deliver speeches criticizing the Government of U.P.'s actions against the Khaksars.

In Agra, 27 Khaksars (who had arrived in Agra from Delhi on October 10, 1939) are arrested when they emerge from a mosque.

1939 October 12

Three lorry loads of Khaksars arrive in Amritsar from the North West Frontier Province (NWFP) in order to proceed to Lucknow to join their fellow Khaksars.

37 Khaksars are arrested in Lucknow under Section 144.

Two volunteers wearing Khaksar badges are also taken into custody in Lucknow.

1939 October 13

In the U.P. Council, an adjournment motion is denied to Sheikh Masood to discuss the police firing in Bulandshahr that killed five Khaksars. The Minister of Justice, Dr. K.N. Katju, informs the Council that an open judicial inquiry would be held shortly to discuss the incident.

The Hindustan Times, Delhi reports that Sir Raza Ali spoke about the Khaksar Movement in front of a large gathering at Juma Mosque in Budaun. The newspaper further reports that Sir Raza Ali is to meet with Jinnah and other leaders in Delhi in order to bring about a settlement between the Government of U.P. and Khaksars.

Another batch of Khaksars arrives in Anjuman Park (Amritsar) from the North West Frontier Province (NWFP) en route to Lucknow.

Over a dozen Khaksars are arrested in Lucknow.

More Khaksars arrive in Bulandshahr.

1939 October 14

In Lucknow, there is a clash between Khaksars from Peshawar and the police, after police prevent the Khaksars from marching in the streets. Police injure 15 Khaksars, and three of the Khaksars remain in serious condition in the hospital.

Allama Mashriqi is released from Lucknow jail after completing his jail sentence (he had been arrested on September 13, 1939). After his release, he leaves for Delhi (accompanied by Dr. Sir Zia ud Din) to meet Jinnah in order to discuss the Khaksar situation.

Mashriqi writes the following letter to Quaid-e-Azam from the waiting room of Delhi Railway Station:

My dear Jinnah,

Your letter sent through Dr. Sir Ziauddin Ahmad asking me to have a talk with you concerning the struggle between Idara-i-Aliyyah and the U.P. Govt.

The U.P. Government have given me in writing that they desire peace. It was on account of this undertaking that I came over to have a friendly talk with you, but in view of the most shameful demonstration of force and heartless cruelty displayed by the U.P. Government to-day at 9 a.m. at the very moment when I was released from jail and more especially when they gave me an undertaking of desire of peace, I find that it will be impossible for me to begin any talk of peace with you until U.P. Govt. stop at once all exhibition of force, e.g., lathi charge and firing. One Khaksar is reported to have been so very seriously injured that he must have died by now.

Till negotiations go on Government should stop all force. I shall then arrange to have the matter discussed with you.

Please let me know the intentions of the Govt. through Sir Ziauddin Ahmad. I shall remain in Delhi tomorrow Sunday and if necessary Monday also.

I appreciate the trouble you are taking in the matter.

Yours Sincerely,
Inayatullah Khan

Barrister Mian Ahmed Shah is released from Lucknow jail.

Another batch of Khaksars arrives in Bulandshahr and marches through the streets.

Over 10,000 Muslims gather at Jamia Masjid in Aligarh and pass a resolution condemning the actions of the U.P. Government against the Khaksars and demand the release of the Khaksars.

1939 October 15

Quaid-e-Azam writes the following letter to Mashriqi from New Delhi:

Dear Inayatullah Khan,

I am in receipt of your letter. I am afraid you have not understood my position in this matter and I did not think that I shall have to carry on any correspondence with you. I do not represent the U.P. Government and I am sorry to find that you are treating me as if I were the agent of the U.P. Government.

I was moved entirely in the interest of Muslim India as many letters and telegrams were sent to me and also several influential Musalmans [Muslims] saw me and urged me to do something with regard to the unfortunate conflict that was created between the U.P. Government and the Khaksars and hence I wanted to know all the facts correctly.

In the course of my conversations with Pandit Jawaharlal he offered to ask the U.P. Government to send me all the facts from the point of view of the Government. When I received the papers from Mr. Kidwai, the acting Prime

Minister of U.P., it naturally struck me that I should know first hand from you the version of the Khaksars and hence my suggestion to Mr. Kidwai that you should be released without any condition being imposed upon you to come and meet me so that I may know exactly all the facts and then see what I can do in the matter in the interest of the Musalmans.

I regret deeply the loss of life and serious injuries to the Khaksars that have been caused.

I am sorry you are imposing conditions upon me before you can come and talk to me as if I was acting on behalf of the U.P. Government. I am not asking you to 'begin any talk of peace with me' but U.P. Government in the best interests of Musalmans.

I don't know what undertaking the U.P. Government has given to you. There are no negotiations going on between the U.P. Government and myself except that at my suggestion you were released for the purpose indicated above…
Yours sincerely,
M.A. Jinnah

In Delhi, Mashriqi and Jinnah meet at the house of Nawabzada Liaquat Ali Khan. Dr. Zia ud Din Ahmed also meets with Jinnah to discuss the Khaksar issue.
Editor's Comments: During the meeting, Jinnah convinced Mashriqi that he could bring a settlement in the Khaksar-U.P. issue. Mashriqi agreed, and in the coming days, he sent telegrams to Jinnah to bring about a settlement. He also gave full power to Dr. Sir Zia ud Din and Barrister Mian Ahmed Shah to resolve this issue.

Six Khaksars are arrested upon their arrival at Lucknow railway station.

13 Khaksars are arrested in Lucknow.

43 Khaksars from the North West Frontier Province (NWFP) leave Amritsar for Bulandshahr in U.P.

Khaksars demonstrate in Aligarh. Military and police force remain present to watch Khaksar activities.

1939 October 16

Quaid-e-Azam visits Mashriqi in the evening at the Khaksar Camp at Karol Bagh in Delhi. Nawabzada Liaquat Ali Khan accompanies him. Dr. Sir Zia ud Din Ahmed, Sir Abdur Rahim (President of the Legislative Assembly), and Sir Abdullah Haroon also visit Mashriqi.
Editor's Comments: Upon arrival, these men were given a Guard of Honor by the Khaksars. This was Quaid-e-Azam's third interview with Mashriqi since October 15, 1939. A historic photo was taken at this occasion when Quaid-e-Azam visited Mashriqi at the Khaksar Camp at Karol Bagh. The people in the photograph were Mashriqi, Quaid-e-Azam, Liaquat Ali Khan, Barrister Ahmed Shah, and Dr. Sir Zia ud Din. (See first photo in the section, "Some Prominent Personalities & the Khaksar Movement," near the end of this book.)

The Tribune, Lahore reports, "It is considered here that Mr. Jinnah has represented their [Khaksars] point of view to the Viceroy and some of the other supporters of the Khaksar movement are urging the Viceroy to intervene in this matter."

Quaid-e-Azam also meets with Sir Raza Ali to discuss the Khaksar situation.

Mashriqi leaves Delhi for Lahore.

The official inquiry into the Bulandshahr firing commences. D.C. Hunter, who was appointed by the Government, conducts the inquiry. The District Magistrate is examined.

1939 October 17

Mashriqi sends four telegrams to Quaid-e-Azam between October 17 and October 24 to bring about a settlement in the Khaksar-U.P. issue.

A batch of Khaksars arrives in Lucknow. They march in uniform near the railway station.

Three Khaksars are arrested in Aminabad in Lucknow.

The Statesman, Calcutta reports that the Government of U.P.'s side of the story (regarding their clash with the Khaksars) is in Jinnah's possession.

1939 October 18

According to *The Hindustan Times*, Delhi, Mashriqi appoints Khaksar Dr. Sir Zia ud Din Ahmed and Khaksar Mian Ahmed Shah (Bar at Law) to conduct negotiations with the Government of U.P. Allama Mashriqi expresses his determination to carry on their campaign in the U.P. until the Government of U.P. accepts all demands.

Dr. Kailash Nath Katju, Minister for Justice (U.P.), meets Quaid-e-Azam in connection with the Khaksar issue. Quaid-e-Azam presents the Khaksar demands to him. Dr. Katju promises to discuss the proposal with his colleagues and inform Quaid-e-Azam about their decision by October 25, 1939.

58 Khaksars arrive in Agra. They hold a procession and salute the Khaksar flag.

The Government of U.P. calls in the military to aid local authorities in suppressing Khaksar activities in Lucknow. Military, along with the police, patrol the city. The army and police maintain close watch at railway and bus stations to check arriving Khaksars.

Two Khaksars are arrested in Lucknow.

A batch of Khaksars arrives in Ghaziabad from Delhi and marches through the town.

1939 October 19

The Tribune, Lahore reports that the Government of U.P. will issue a statement on the Khaksar agitation.

Mashriqi sends a telegram to Quaid-e-Azam regarding the ongoing negotiations with the Government of U.P.

Quaid-e-Azam replies to Mashriqi's telegram regarding the ongoing negotiations with the U.P. Government: "Discussed matter fully with Dr. Katju he informed me that he will let me know from Lucknow on his return the Government answer to your proposals."

Khaksars demonstrate in Ghaziabad. A crowd witnesses and follows the Khaksar demonstrations.

1939 October 20

D.C. Hunter, President of the official inquiry committee into the Bulandshahr firing on October 08, 1939, visits the scene of the firing. He also asks the District Magistrate and the Superintendent of Police to provide information about the occurrence. No Khaksars are requested to explain their point of view.

The Tribune, Lahore reports that Dr. Kailas Nath Katju, Minister for Justice (U.P.), is to meet with prominent Muslim Leaguers to reach a settlement between the Khaksars and the Government of U.P.

1939 October 21

The official inquiry into the Bulandshahr firing is resumed. D.C. Hunter records the statements of four witnesses. Among those testifying is Sergeant Beacon, who escorted the Khaksars to Bulandshahr Jail on the day of the firing.

Since Quaid-e-Azam is still considering the Khaksar issue, the Muslim League decides not to launch a civil disobedience movement in support of the Khaksars. **Editor's Comments:** The movement, which was set to begin on October 22, 1939, had been agreed upon at an earlier meeting of the Muslim League Council in the event that no settlement was reached between the Khaksars and the U.P. Government by October 20, 1939.

Military and police again guard the Lucknow railway station in order to prevent Khaksars (from various parts of the country) from entering the city. 16 Khaksars in uniform are arrested upon arrival at Lucknow railway station.

Four more Khaksars are arrested in the evening in Lucknow.

Sardar Auregzeb Khan (Opposition leader in the Frontier Assembly) and Khan Bahadur Saadullah Khan (Former Education Minister and Member of the Working Committee of the Muslim League) visit a Khaksar Camp in Delhi.

1939 October 22

Military and police remain stationed at Lucknow railway station to arrest arriving Khaksars.

21 Khaksars are arrested in Lucknow. 18 of these Khaksars are from Cawnpore and are arrested at the railway station while three are arrested in Aminabad Park.

1939 October 23

24 policemen record their evidence at the court of D.C. Hunter in connection with the firing on the Khaksars at Bulandshahr jail.

Khaksars continue to leave Bulandshahr.

1939 October 24

Three Khaksars are arrested in Lucknow.

1939 October 25

Mashriqi arrives in Delhi from Lahore to attend a Khaksar Camp.

Mashriqi writes the following letter to Quaid-e-Azam from the Khaksar Camp at Karol Bagh, Delhi:
My dear Mr. Jinnah,
        I have just come over from Lahore. Twelve precious days have been wasted and I understand from [Barrister] M. Ahmad Shah that nothing particular has come about except what Government already agreed to on October, 8. I am sure I would have moved mountains in these twelve days. It is a shame if Government has ignored your presence in the peace discussions.
        I want a quick and final reply now. If Government declines to accept the terms in toto and most especially the compensation that we demand per Khaksar as well as a guarantee for the protection of Muslim rights, I fear I shall have to do something very drastic in order to bring the present Ministry down to reason and I am sure that I shall succeed. You know we are pledged to bring the Ministry down if they do not accede to our demands, and you will see in the next few days that we shall have that done at all costs provided they do not resign of their own accord. Of course, I shall be ready to listen if you can make the Ministry see the seriousness of the situation.
Yours Sincerely,

Inayatullah
P.S. I have already sent you three telegrams in this connection.

Dr. Katju replies to Jinnah with a proposal on behalf of the Government of U.P. The proposal states the degree to which the Government is willing to meet the Khaksars' demands (which Jinnah had presented to Dr. Katju on October 18, 1939).

Three more Khaksars are arrested in Lucknow.

In Bulandshahr, the inquiry into the police firing at Bulandshahr continues. The District Magistrate, the Deputy Collector, and a Police Inspector are examined in court.

Khaksars continue their daily marches in Ghaziabad. Local Muslims in Ghaziabad also join the Khaksar Tehrik.

1939 October 26

Quaid-e-Azam issues a press statement regarding the conflict between the U.P. Government and the Khaksars:
"Dr. Katju saw me in Delhi on October 18 [1939] on behalf of the United Provinces Government in connexion with the situation created with regard to the Khaksars and I placed before him the proposals of the Khaksars. After a full discussion he told me that he would go back to Lucknow and confer with his colleagues and let me know finally on or before October 25 how far the United Provinces Government is prepared to meet the demands formulated by the Khaksars.
I received from him last night the proposals on behalf of the Government showing how far it is prepared to meet the Khaksars' demands. I have forwarded the Government's proposals in answer to the Khaksars' demands to Allama Mashraqi (their leader) to-day for him to consider and deal with them in such manner as he may be advised." *The Statesman*, Calcutta, October 28, 1939

Quaid-e-Azam writes a letter from New Delhi to Mashriqi (in response to Mashriqi's letter dated October 25, 1939).
Editor's Comments: For Quaid-e-Azam's letter, see *Al-Mashriqi: The Disowned Genius* by Syed Shabbir Hussain (pages 117-119).

More witnesses are examined as the inquiry into the police firing at Bulandshahr continues.

The Working Committee of the U.P. Muslim League passes a resolution condemning the police firing on the Khaksars at Bulandshahr. The Committee also decides not to take any action in regards to the Khaksar issue until they receive final word from Jinnah. The Committee meeting is presided over by Ch. Khaliquzzaman.

Mashriqi issues a statement saying that the proposals sent by the Government of U.P. through Jinnah are unacceptable. He further states that they are not even better than the ones the U.P. Premier had sent to him on October 07, 1939 (while he was in jail).

1939 October 27

Shaukat Ali moves an adjournment motion in the U.P. Assembly to discuss the police firing on the Khaksars in Bulandshahr. The motion is discussed in the Assembly and the Nawab of Chhatari and others speak in favor of the Khaksars. **Editor's Comments:** Syed Mohammad Ahsan (Member Legislative Assembly) denounced the U.P. Government's actions against the Khaksars. The exact date of this statement is not known.

Khaksars demonstrate in Cawnpore. The military is called in to handle the situation.

A Khaksar Camp is established in Saharanpur. The number of Khaksars continues to increase, and police in Dehra Dun remain on high alert and are ready to leave for Saharanpur.

Rafi Ahmed Kidwai (the Minister of Jails) sends Chaman Lal to persuade Barrister Mian Ahmed Shah to meet him (Kidwai) for a truce. Mian Ahmed Shah accepts the offer and would leave for Lucknow on October 28, 1939.

1939 October 28

Barrister Mian Ahmed Shah, a prominent Khaksar leader, arrives in Lucknow.

Khaksars parade in Aminabad (Lucknow). Five Khaksars are arrested.

Khaksars being taken by the police from Lucknow to Saharanpur delay a train because they state that they have not been given any food.

1939 October 29

Barrister Mian Ahmed Shah, a lieutenant of Mashriqi, meets with R.A. Kidwai, the Minister of Jails, regarding the Khaksar conflict with the Government of U.P.

1939 October 30

Barrister Mian Ahmed Shah informs Mashriqi that Rafi Ahmed Kidwai was never sincere about settling the issue with the Khaksars.

The Khaksar issue is a main topic of discussion during the U.P. Assembly meeting. When asked about the aims of the Khaksar Movement, Hafiz Mohammad Ibrahim, Minister for Communications (U.P.), replies "that the Government had no authoritative information on the point but the Khaksar leader had stated in the course of a press statement that their aims were to bring about peace and brotherhood among different communities in India by doing social service." *The Tribune*, Lahore October 31, 1939

Dr. Kailash Nath Katju makes a statement to the press: "As requested, Mr Jinnah was supplied with the copies of various press *communiques* issued by the U.P. Government from time to time relating to the Khaksar situation...I met Mr. Jinnah who put before me the various demands made by the Khaksars..." *The Tribune*, Lahore October 31, 1939

1939 October 31

The ban on the Khaksars in Lucknow expires.

Punjab Assembly discusses the Khaksar Movement.

The Tribune, Lahore reports that "Mr. Rafi Ahmed Kidwai, Minister for Revenue [U.P.]...suggested [in reply to a question regarding the Khaksars at the U.P. Assembly on October 30, 1939] that the Muslim League had lost their influence in the U.P. and were, therefore, trying to regain it through the Khaksar organisation."

Hundreds of Khaksars in uniform hold a demonstration in Lucknow under the command of a female leader.

Another group of Khaksars holds a demonstration in Lucknow in the evening. Police keep a close watch over the procession.

Khaksars parade in Aminabad (near Lucknow).

November

1939 November 01

The Hindustan Times, Delhi, reports that Allama Mashriqi issued instructions to suspend Khaksar activities for ten days to allow the new U.P. Government (the Congress Ministry resigned) to remove "the causes of friction between the Khaksars and the authorities." The newspaper also reports that Dr. Sir Zia ud Din, who has been appointed Khaksar organizer for the U.P., has taken it upon himself to spread the movement amongst students of Aligarh.
Editor's Comments: Studying the clash between the Government of U.P and the Khaksars, it is evident that there was no reason for the Government of U.P to convert this into a large issue, when Mashriqi's sole purpose was to bring peace between the Muslim sects (Shia-Sunni). In fact Mashriqi's offer to bring a settlement should have been encouraged and welcomed. But the Government of U.P's actions against the Khaksars recounts the intention of the Government of U.P.

The Hindustan Times, Delhi publishes Mashriqi's account explaining negotiations in the Khaksar-U.P. issue.

Maulvi Fazlul Haq (Premier of Bengal) visits a Khaksar Camp in Delhi. He is extremely impressed with the Khaksars. He addresses the Khaksars and appreciates their role in changing the fate of the Muslims. Mashriqi thanks him for his comments.

1939 November 04

In a telegram to the headquarters of the Khaksar Tehrik, Barrister Mian Ahmed Shah states that an agreement has been reached between the new U.P. Government and the Khaksars.

The new Government of U.P. decides to release all imprisoned Khaksars, whether convicted or otherwise in jail.

1939 November 05

A settlement is reached between the Khaksars and the Government of U.P. Authorities issue orders to remove restrictions on and release all imprisoned Khaksars from Camp Jail Lucknow. 72 Khaksars are released from Camp Jail in Lucknow.

The U.P. Government pays the railway fares for the Khaksars from Punjab, North West Frontier Province (NWFP), and other provinces, and the Khaksars depart Lucknow for their respective destinations.
Editor's Comments: Finally the Government of U.P. gave in to Khaksars' demands and came to an agreement with them, including release of the Khaksars and payment of fare for the return of the Khaksars to their homes. The Khaksars came out victorious as a result of their strength.

Shan Muhammad wrote in his book, "The new government of the United Provinces…started negotiations with the Khaksars and reached an agreement on November 4 [1939]… The Khaksar volunteers, when back home, received a rousing ovation and their campaign in the United Provinces was hailed as a great episode, enhancing the prestige of the organisation…the Khaksars emerged from this campaign as champions of the Muslim cause against the alleged pro-Hindu policy of the Congress ministry of the United Provinces." (Muhammad 1973, 43)

The exact number of Khaksars who came to Lucknow and total number of arrests are not known. According to the Khaksar circle, the number of Khaksars who came to U.P. from various parts of India is in thousands.

Section 144 Cr.P.C against the Khaksars is canceled in Bulandshahr.

1939 November 06

After the settlement with the Government of U.P., 400 Khaksars are released from Meerut Jail. (They had been imprisoned while in Lucknow to resolve the Shia-Sunni issue.) The Government pays for their food and travel expenses for their return home.

Following the settlement between the Khaksars and the Government, over 600 Khaksars leave Meerut district for Delhi en route to their respective homes.

Khaksars from other provinces continue to leave Lucknow.

By this date, most of the Khaksars from Punjab and NWFP have left Lucknow, while those from other places are still leaving.
Editor's Comments: Upon return to their homes, Khaksars were given rousing welcomes by the public everywhere. They were considered champions for winning the Muslim cause.

1939 November 07

The Tribune, Lahore writes, that D.C. Hunter has submitted his report of the inquiry into the police firing in Bulandshahr (on October 08, 1939).
Editor's Comments: D.C. Hunter's report held the police responsible for opening fire and recommended compensation for the Khaksar victims. The report was never published.

The Tribune, Lahore reports that 550 more Khaksars are to be released shortly.

1939 November 12

The Hindustan Times, Delhi reports that Allama Mashriqi sent telegrams to Dr. Khan Sahib.

1939 November 27

The Statesman, Calcutta reports that, to further strengthen the Khaksar Movement, Khaksars in Bihar continue to hold daily parades. At the parades, they explain the objectives of the Khaksar Movement to crowds who gather. The newspaper further reports, "Much interest has been caused among the people here by the report that four Khaksar leaders will visit our province in the next month..."

December

1939 December 04

Sir Sikandar Hyat Khan, Premier of Punjab, replies to questions about the Khaksar Tehrik during the Punjab Assembly session. The Premier declares the Khaksar Tehrik to be communal.
Editor's Comments: In order to undermine the Khaksars, Sir Sikandar began to lay the groundwork for justification for a ban on the Khaksar Movement that would be imposed in the coming months. Mashriqi had always stated that the Tehrik was non-communal and did not discriminate against caste, color, religion, or creed. In fact, many members of the Tehrik were non-Muslims. However, Sir Sikandar still declared the Khaksar Tehrik to be communal, so as to prompt non-Muslims, such as Hindus and Sikhs, to raise their voices in favor of restrictions on the Khaksar Tehrik.

1939 December 05

Sir Sikandar and Mir Maqbool Mahmud, Parliamentary Secretary, reply to questions about the Khaksar Tehrik in the Punjab Assembly session.

The Khaksar Tehrik is again the main subject of discussion in the Punjab Assembly.

1939 December 07

Sir Shah Suleiman writes a letter to Allama Mashriqi.

1939 December 21

The Hindustan Times, Delhi reports that Sir Sikandar Hayat Khan left Lahore suddenly on December 19, 1939 for a secret mission. According to the newspaper, it is believed that he went to meet Quaid-e-Azam in Bombay.

1939 December 24

Sir Sikandar Hayat Khan meets with Jinnah in Bombay for three hours.
Editor's Comments: The Khaksar Movement had become the most powerful Muslim party in the entire India by that time. This was proven during the Shia-Sunni riots. This had become a matter of concern for the Government and many Muslim Leaguers.
 It was believed in the Khaksar circle that discussion about the Khaksars had occurred at Sir Sikandar and Jinnah's meeting, although no such discussion was made public. This meeting had great significance for the Khaksars, as the Khaksar Movement came under restrictions within weeks after. On February 22, 1940, Mohammadi Press in Lahore, which printed the Khaksar weekly *Al-Islah*, was raided. On February 28, 1940, the Government imposed a ban on the Khaksar Tehrik.

1940

January

1940 January 04

Mashriqi writes a letter to Sir Shah Suleiman reiterating that he has made an offer of 50,000 Khaksars to the Viceroy for the defense of India.
Editor's Note: For full letter, see *Al-Mashriqi: The Disowned Genius* by Syed Shabbir Hussain (page 125).

1940 January 12

Mir Maqbool Mahmud replies to questions in the Punjab Assembly session regarding the Khaksar Tehrik. He states that the Khaksar leader's demand for certain broadcasting privileges has been forwarded to the Government of India. However, he refuses to give any details of the Khaksar leader's proposal or the remarks made by the Government.
Editor's Comments: It was understood in the Khaksar circle that members of the Punjab Assembly were encouraged by Sir Sikandar Hayat Khan (Premier of the Punjab) to raise questions about the activities of the Khaksar Movement, so that a ban on the Khaksar Movement could be justified.

1940 January 28

Khaksars parade daily through the bazaar in Muttra. More Khaksars continue to be enrolled in large numbers in Muttra.

February

1940 February 03-06

The Working Committee of the All India Muslim League meets at New Delhi under the Presidentship of M.A. Jinnah. Sir Sikandar is also present at the meeting. They pass a number of resolutions, including the following:
RESOLUTION NO. 10
  'Resolved that the consideration of the Report of the National Guards Committee be postponed till the next meeting of the Working Committee.'
  In this connection some members raised the question of the Khaksars and wanted that some definite statement in this connection should be issued on behalf of the Committee as there was a great misunderstanding regarding the activities of the Khaksars. It was mentioned in the course of the discussion that on account of the attitude of the Muslim League not being definitely clear the Muslim League work was suffering in some parts of the country as the Khaksars are doing some propaganda which was not in the interest of the League. The Committee decided not to take any action or make any statement at present.
Editor's Comments: The Khaksars were not indulging in any propaganda at all, in fact, as per their charter, they were bringing unity among the people. Anti-Khaksar

elements in the Muslim League raised unnecessary alarm (as a result of certain motives). The Khaksars viewed the resolution as a clear sign that the strength of their movement was a source of worry for many of the Muslim Leaguers and that the Muslim Leaguers were considering various options on how to deal with it. Within a few days of this resolution, Sir Sikandar, a Muslim Leaguer, imposed restrictions on the Khaksar Tehrik.

1940 February 19

A three-day Khaksar Camp concludes in Amritsar. A large number of men and women witness the activities at the camp.
Editor's Comments: All Khaksar camps and their marches drew keen interest from the public. They had become a source of uprising.

1940 February 20

The Punjab Government orders the confiscation of *Kiya Ainda Mayar-I-Hukumat Aksariat Ya Khoon Ho Ga,* a pamphlet/article of the Khaksar Movement. The Government also demands security from Mohammadi Press, which prints *Al-Islah.*

1940 February 21

Mashriqi sends a telegram to the Viceroy of India regarding the confiscation of the Khaksar pamphlet *Kiya Ainda Mayar-I-Hukumat Aksariat Ya Khoon Ho Ga.* He also sends a copy of the telegram to the Governor of Punjab.

1940 February 22

Mohammadi Press in Lahore, which prints the Khaksar weekly *Al-Islah,* is raided.

Police raid different locations in Lahore where Khaksar literature is sold.

The editor and assistant editor of *Al-Islah* meet with Sir Sikandar Hayat Khan to discuss the confiscation of Khaksar materials at Mohammadi Press. However, Sir Sikandar fails to help the Khaksars in this regard.

1940 February 27

Mashriqi arrives in Delhi from Lahore to meet with the Viceroy of India. Mashriqi wants the Viceroy to intervene in the unjust behavior of the Punjab Government against the Khaksars.

Mashriqi meets with Quaid-e-Azam, Dr. Sir Zia ud Din, Sir Suleiman, Sir Zafarullah Khan, and others in Delhi to discuss the Punjab Government's attitude toward the Khaksars.

Editors Comments: Mashriqi's purpose was to ask them to use their influence over Sir Sikandar Hayat Khan who was attempting to crush the Movement which was mobilizing the masses and directing them towards a cause.

The editor and assistant editor of *Al-Islah* again meet Sir Sikandar Hayat Khan to persuade him to stop his actions against the Khaksars. Sir Sikandar again refuses to budge from his stance.

1940 February 28

The Government of Punjab imposes restrictions on the Khaksar Tehrik. The orders are issued under Rules 54 and 58 of the Defence of India Rules.

The Punjab Government reiterates that government servants are not allowed to join the Khaksar Tehrik.

The Khaksars hold their usual evening parades in various parts of Lahore.

1940 February 29

Sir Suleiman confirms Mashriqi's appointment with the Viceroy of India. However, the Viceroy of India declines to help the Khaksars and cancels the meeting at the last minute.

March

1940 March 03

Mashriqi sends the following telegram to Fazlul Haq, seeking his intervention to resolve the Khaksar issue with Sir Sikandar Hayat Khan (Punjab Premier): "Pb. [Punjab] Premier bent on crushing Khaksar Movement. Terrible clash inevitable. Intervene effectively."

1940 March 05

Allama Mashriqi issues the following statement regarding the Punjab Government's ban of February 28, 1940:
"I do not see legally anything in the wording of the prohibitory orders of the Punjab Government, dated the 28th February [1940], which can directly or indirectly apply to the Khaksar Movement. I do not expect that the intention of the Government is to put ban on a movement whose action for the past nine and a half years is that it has not taken part in communal disturbances, in fact any disturbance, whose accepted and declared practical principal is social service irrespective of caste or creed and in whose literature and actual deeds respect for religious leaders of all communities, their traditions and culture is included as a declared principle...
Khaksar Movement was founded in October, 1930...the Khaksar Movement, during the first eight and a half years of its existence, when no

organization among the sister communities exhibited its semi-military power and when they could be easily cowed down, did not show any communal prejudice, nor during this year any opportunity arose which could give the Movement a communal tinge. The reason is that people of all communities, irrespective of caste or creed, have remained as members in the Movement and are now joining in large number.

That the Movement is strictly non-communal and non-political is evidenced by actual deeds of the past nine and a half years and no order or law of Government can put a wrong interpretation on this evidence. If the Government has any apprehensions about the keeping of tranquility, it should bring those organizations under the grip of law about which apprehension for breach of peace exists on the ground that their future line of action is not known. No such apprehension can possibly exist in the case of the Khaksar Movement, which is under strong discipline and in which orders emanate from one centre of Authority.

In the explanatory remarks on Government orders, issued by the Director of Information Bureau, it is clearly stated that 'the order will not interfere with the activities of bodies engaged in purely social service.' Prayer and social service form an indispensible part of the Khaksar Movement from the very beginning and for this reason alone the Khaksar Movement cannot come under those orders.

In spite of all this I am waiting for an explanation from the Punjab Government after this public statement. In case the Punjab Government do not issue any particular statement in regard to this matter by the 16th March, 1940, Khaksars are hereby ordered to continue their unlimited social service in accordance with the set programme and congregate for the night prayers as usual.

Khaksars who have arrived and are arriving in large numbers in Lahore from distant places in a mood of uneasiness as well as those Khaksars who belong to Lahore are hereby ordered to continue their programme of social service and night prayers outside the Mochi Gate and inside their local mosques. Further orders in connection with the Khaksars of the Punjab will be shortly published in *Al-Islah*."

1940 March 06

The Khaksars present a Guard of Honor to Quaid-e-Azam upon his arrival in Aligarh.

1940 March 07

The Hindustan Times, Delhi publishes Allama Mashriqi's statement, which was issued on March 05, 1940.
Editor's Note: For Mashriqi's statement, refer to date March 05, 1940 in this publication).

Dr. Sir Zia ud din Ahmed, Sir Zafarullah Khan, the Nawab of Kunjpura, and many other Muslim personalities meet with Sir Sikandar Hayat Khan to protest the restrictions on the Khaksar Movement. However, Sir Sikandar Hayat Khan refuses to yield to their pressure.

1940 March 08

The Khaksars welcome Quaid-e-Azam upon his arrival in Bareilly from Aligarh and present him with a Guard of Honor.

1940 March 09

Khaksars continue to increase their numbers in Cawnpore and plan to demonstrate in Punjab against the Government's ban on their activities.

1940 March 12

Mashriqi issues a statement:
"We have been doing social service openly and collectively for the last ten years and no Government has taken exception to this. We now consider it our right and are prepared to give a physical fight, without transgressing any law, to any power which would want to snatch this right of ours…It is ridiculous that a jamaat [party] which has offered services of 50,000 of its members for the defence of India should be proceeded against under the Defence of India Rules. I am filing a case in the court of law and would try to obtain a stay order till its final disposal."

1940 March 14

Mr. Jinnah meets with the Viceroy.
Editor's Comments: The restrictions on the Khaksars were a vital issue at the time, and Jinnah's meeting with the Viceroy was considered very important. It was believed that the Khaksar issue was discussed, however no details were revealed, and this raised eyebrows in the Khaksar circle.

1940 March 15

Al-Islah condemns the Government's orders imposing restrictions on the Khaksar Tehrik.

Khaksars from the North West Frontier Province demonstrate in Lahore. Six Khaksars are arrested near the Assembly Chamber.

1940 March 17

5,000 Khaksars from the North West Frontier Province arrive in Lahore.

1940 March 18

Mohammad Sharif (Salar-i-Awwal of the Khaksar Tehrik in Lahore) leaves for Delhi to seek Mashriqi's guidance regarding the future actions of the Khaksars in Lahore. In Mohammad Sharif's absence, Khushal Khan Jadoon takes over as the Salar-i-Awwal of the Khaksars in Lahore.

1940 March 19

The Khaksar Massacre

313 Khaksars hold a peaceful demonstration in protest against the ban and march toward the Badshahi Mosque in Lahore to offer prayers. Police fires indiscriminately on the Khaksars. The police is headed by Gainsford (Senior Superintendent of Police, Lahore), Beaty (Deputy Superintendent of Police), and Frederick Chalmers Bourne (District Magistrate). Many Khaksars are brutally killed, while others are injured and admitted to Mayo Hospital. This massacre opens a new chapter in the history of the Pakistan movement.
Editor's Comments: According to an official report, 32 people died on that fateful day (*The Tribune* April 16, 1940). However, "According to eye witnesses the dead were more than 200" (Gauba 1974, 204).

To avoid public outcry, police quickly move the dead bodies of the Khaksars killed in Lahore.

The Aftermath

After the firing, police round up Khaksars in Lahore.

The Inspector General of Police (I.G.) and the Deputy Inspector General of Police (D.I.G.) as well as many other officers arrive at the scene of the firing in Lahore.

The military forces are called in support of the police in Lahore.

Police pickets are stationed throughout Lahore. All Police stations remain on high alert.

Shopping centers in Lahore are closed as a result of the police firing.

Sir Sikandar Hayat Khan visits the injured police officers, including Gainsford and Beaty, as well as the injured Khaksars at Mayo Hospital in Lahore. He praises the police officers.

Special police is posted at the Sir Sikandar Hayat Khan's (Premier of Punjab) house in Lahore.

The Government's Actions Following the Massacre

The Punjab Government issues warrants of arrest for Allama Mashriqi (who is in New Delhi on this day) and his Lieutenants.

Following the police-firing in Lahore, the Government of Punjab issues a Gazette Extraordinary banning the Khaksar Tehrik and stating that the Government is to take possession of the Khaksar headquarters in Ichhra, near Lahore. The District

Magistrate also issues an order prohibiting for two months the gathering of five or more persons in any street or public place within Lahore. He also warns the public not to organize or join any such gathering.

In a Gazette Extraordinary, the Government imposes censorship on newspapers. The Government of Punjab appoints a Censor Officer and directs editors, publishers, and printers of the news media not to print anything regarding the firing incident on March 19, 1940 in Lahore, unless it has been censored by the Censor Officer. No such item is to be published without the approval of the Special Press Advisor.

**

The Joint Secretary of the Punjab Government issues an order stating:
        Whereas in the opinion of the Punjab Government it is expedient for the enforcement of the Defence of India Rules that all matters relating to the unlawful association, commonly known as the Khaksars, shall, before publication, be submitted for scrutiny to the Special Press Advisor, Lahore;
        Now, therefore, in exercise of the powers conferred by sub-rule (I) of rule 41 of the Defence of India Rules, the Governor of the Punjab is pleased to direct by this order issued generally to all printers, publishers and editors in the districts of Lahore and Amritsar that any matter relating to the aforesaid Khaksars Association shall before publication be submitted to the said Special Press Adviser, Lahore, at his office in the Punjab Civil Secretariat, Lahore, and shall not be published until he has given his approval.

**

The Punjab Government issues a notification in regards to the Khaksar Tehrik:
        Whereas in the opinion of the Governor of the Punjab the association known as the Anjuman-i-Khaksaran interferes with the maintenance of law and order and constitutes a danger to the public peace;
        Now therefore in exercise of the powers conferred by section 16 of the Indian Criminal Law Amendment Act, 1908, the Governor of the Punjab is pleased to declare the said association to be unlawful.

**

Another notification by the Punjab Government says:
        Whereas by a notification this day issued by the association known as the Anjuman-i-Khaksaran has been declared to be an unlawful association:
        And whereas in the opinion of the Governor of the Punjab the premises known as Idara-i-Aliya, in the village of Ichhra, near Lahore, are used for the purposes of the said Anjuman-i-Khaksaran:
        Now, therefore, the Governor of the Punjab is pleased hereby to notify the said premises for the purposes of section 17-A of the Indian Criminal Law Amendment Act, 1908.

**

The District Magistrate, F.C. Bourne, imposes a curfew in Lahore:
Whereas the members of an organization known as Khaksars have gathered in Lahore to defy Government orders contained in Punjab Government Notifications No. 2417-B.D.S.B., and No. 2415-B.D.S.B., dated the 28th of February 1940, banning the taking of armed processions, the parading in military formation etc;
Whereas, in pursuance of their concerted plan, the members of the aforesaid organization have to-day committed a serious riot armed with deadly weapons, killing policemen on duty and seriously wounding others;
Whereas, by such act of the members of the aforesaid organization, the city of Lahore is in a great disturbed state;
And whereas the remaining of people outdoors before and after certain hours is considered very dangerous to public tranquility;
Therefore, I, Frederick Chalmers Bourne, I.C.S., District Magistrate of Lahore, in exercise of the powers conferred on me under Section 144, Cr.P.C., hereby direct that until further notice no person within the limits of the walled city of Lahore shall remain outdoors between the hours of 7 p.m. and 6 a.m. with effect from to-day, the 19th day of March 1940.
Given under my hand and seal of this Court this 19th day of March 1940.

**

The District Magistrate issues an order under Section 144:-
(1) Whereas it has been made to appear to me, Frederick Chalmers Bourne, I.C.S., District Magistrate of Lahore, that owing to a serious disturbance having occurred in Lahore City in consequence of the Defiance of Government orders contained in Punjab Government Notifications No. 2417-B.D.S.B., and No. 2415-B.D.S.B., dated the 28th of February 1940, banning the taking of armed processions, the parading in military formation, etc;
Whereas the members of the aforesaid organization have to-day committed a serious riot armed with deadly weapons;
And whereas, by such acts of the members of the aforesaid organization, there is a likelihood of a disturbance of the public tranquillity, and immediate prevention and speedy remedy is necessary;
Now, therefore, in exercise of the powers conferred on me by section 144, Criminal Procedure Code, I, Frederick Chalmers Bourne, I.C.S., District Magistrate, Lahore, do hereby forbid all persons to carry in the streets and public places within the limits of the Lahore Municipality any firearm, knife, sword, kirpan, belcha, lathi, or any other article capable of being used as an arm, for a period of two months.
Given under my hand and Seal of Court this 19th day of March 1940.
(2) Whereas it has been made to appear to me, Frederick Chalmers Bourne, I.C.S., District Magistrate of Lahore, that owing to a serious disturbance having occurred in Lahore City in consequence of the defiance of Government orders

contained in Punjab Government Notifications No. 2417-B.D.S.B., and No. 2415-B.D.S.B., dated the 28th of February 1940, banning the taking of armed processions, the parading in military formation etc.

Whereas the members of the aforesaid organization have to-day committed a serious riot armed with deadly weapons.

And whereas, by such acts of the members of the aforesaid organization, there is a likelihood of a disturbance of the public tranquility, an immediate prevention and speedy remedy is necessary;

Now, therefore, in exercise of the powers conferred on me by section 144, Criminal Procedure Code, I, Frederick Chalmers Bourne, I.C.S., District Magistrate of Lahore, do hereby prohibit for a period of two months, any gathering or assembly of five or more persons in any street, lane, or public place of any kind whatsoever within the limits of the Lahore Municipality, and strictly warn all members of the public not to organize, join or take part in any such gathering or assembly.

Given under my hand and the Seal of Court this day, the 19th March 1940.

**

The Director of Information Bureau, Punjab Government, issues a press communique:

Some 150 or 200 Khaksars mainly from the North-West Frontier Province collected in Lahore City this morning with the object of holding a procession in military formation in defiance of recent Government orders under the Defence of India Rules. The District Magistrate and the Senior Superintendent of Police on getting the information immediately proceeded to the spot and warned them that such processions were forbidden and attempted to dissuade them from their intention. They refused, however, to abandon their procession and when they found their way barred by a posse of police they attacked them with their spades and inflicted a number of injuries. They were subsequently held up by a larger body of police whom they also attacked and the police were forced to fire. The exact number of casualties is not yet known but some Khaksars are reported to have been killed. The Senior Superintendent of Police and the Deputy Superintendent of Police received serious injuries from spades and have been admitted to hospital and their condition is causing anxiety. The District Magistrate was also injured. One constable has been killed and five or six others injured. Police and military reinforcement have arrived and are patrolling the city.

**

Sir Sikandar Hayat Khan holds a conference at the Secretariat (in Lahore) with the Chief Secretary, the Joint Chief Secretary, the Commissioner, the District Magistrate, and other officials.

Sir Henry Duffield Craik, the Governor of Punjab, sends a telegram to Lord Linlithgow (Viceroy of India) about the Khaksar incident in Lahore.

The Chief Commissioner of Delhi and the Home Member of the Government of India meet to discuss ways to control the Khaksar Tehrik and ensure that the Khaksars do not demonstrate in Delhi against the Punjab Government.

The Deputy Commissioner holds a conference with police officers in Amritsar District Court. Steps are taken to stop any further demonstrations by Khaksars or in support of the Khaksars. Police forces are strengthened throughout the city.

The Raid at the Khaksar Headquarters

Police, accompanied by F.C. Bourne, raid the Khaksar Tehrik's headquarters at Ichhra. Police also enter Mashriqi's house, which is adjacent to the headquarters, despite the purdah-observing women occupants inside. Police use tear gas grenades to arrest the Khaksars. According to *The Tribune* of March 21, 1940, "This was the first occasion when tear gas was used in the Punjab on a number of people in the open." The police confiscate literature of the Tehrik, Khaksar uniforms, and spades and they seal and lock the Khaksar Tehrik's headquarters.

During the raid at the Khaksar headquarters, police arrest a number of Khaksars. Police also continue to search other Khaksar houses and round up Khaksars in Lahore.

During the raid at the Khaksar headquarters in Lahore (adjacent to Mashriqi's residence), Mashriqi's sons, Akram and Anwar, are arrested. Police injures Mashriqi's other son, Ehsanullah Khan Aslam, by hitting him with a tear gas grenade.
Editor's Comments: Ehsanullah Khan Aslam later died (on May 31, 1940) as a result of the injury from the tear gas grenade.

Mashriqi's Arrest

Allama Mashriqi is arrested in Karol Bagh, New Delhi around 11:30 pm under section 46 of the Defence of India Act. The Secretary to the Home Department of the Government of India had signed the order for his arrest. The police officer declines to give a copy of the arrest order to Mashriqi's lieutenant. Khaksars salute Mashriqi as he drives off with police officials.

At the time of arrest, Allama Mashriqi tells the Press correspondents that he has no details of the incident at Lahore on this day, other than what he had read in a Delhi evening newspaper, *Tej*. He adds, that he had not issued any orders to start demonstrating, and he was surprised that the Khaksars went ahead without any such orders from him.
Editor's Comments: Prior to his arrest, Mashriqi was in Delhi for some time. During his stay in Delhi, he met with Quaid-e-Azam, Sir Shah Sulaiman, Sir Zia ud Din, and Nawab Bahadur Yar Jang to seek their support to remove the restrictions on Khaksar activities.

The Muslim League Session

Despite the Khaksar massacre of March 19, 1940 in Lahore, the All-India Muslim League decides not to cancel their upcoming session at Minto Park, Lahore. **Editor's Comments:** In spite of the great tragedy of March 19, 1940 when a large number of innocent Khaksars were killed and the ban on public assemblies was in place, the Muslim League decided not to postpone their session (where Pakistan Resolution was passed) in Lahore. This raised eyebrows among the public. In the Khaksar circle, it was viewed that the Muslim League wanted to use the massacre for political ends. The Khaksars sensed a conspiracy against their movement. If one studies the history, prior to and after March 19, 1940 massacre, this leads one to believe that there was in fact a conspiracy against the Khaksar Movement.

*****

News of the massacre spreads throughout India. Muslims feel hurt and show great resentment towards the actions of the Government.

Partial List of the 313 Khaksars (full record was taken by the police during the raid at the Khaksar headquarter) that were part of the Contingent on March 19, 1940:

Abdul Aziz
Abdul Ghafoor
Abdul Ghani
Abdul Ghanni
Abdul Hameed
Abdul Hayee
Abdul Kareem
Abdul Kareem Urffi Janbaz
Abdul Karim
Abdul Khaliq
Abdul Latif
Abdul Majeed
Abdul Majeed Shah
Abdul Qayyum
Abdul Rehman
Abdul Shakoor
Abdul Sharif
Abdul Wahid
Abdullah
Abdullah Khan Janbaz
Ahmed Khan
Ali Akbar
Ali Muhammad
Ali Shan
Allah Buksh
Allah Bussaia

Allah Ditta
Allah Ditta Khan Janbaz
Allah Rakhha
Altaf Hussain
Amir Ahmed
Amir Din
Ashiq Hussain
Atta Muhammad
Aurangzeb
Ayub Khan
Bagh Ali Janbaz
Barkat Ali
Bashir Ahmed
Bashir Ahmed
Ch. Sher Muhammad
Dost Muhammad
Faiz Muhammad
Faqir Hussain
Faqir Muhammad
Farman Shah Janbaz
Fateh Muhammad
Fazal Din
Fazal Kareem
Fazal Karim
Fazal Karim Sani
Feroze Din
Fida Hussain
Gary Michael
Ghulab Khan
Ghulam Ali
Ghulam Farid
Ghulam Haider
Ghulam Hussain
Ghulam Mohammad Ajab Khan
Ghulam Muhammad
Ghulam Muhammad Janbaz
Ghulam Murtaza
Ghulam Nabbi
Ghulam Qadir
Ghulam Rabbani
Ghulam Rasool
Ghulam Sabir
Ghulam Sarwar
Ghulam Shabbir
Ghulam Yaseen Janbaz
Gul Muhammad
Habib ur Rehman

Hafeez Ullah
Haji Muhammad
Hassan Din
Hdayatullah Salar Wazirabad city
Hukkam Dad
Islam ud Din
Jaffar Hussain
Kala Khan
Karam Elahi
Karim Dad
Karim Dad
Kazi Ali Asghar
Kazi Syed Rasool
Khan Badshah
Khan Muhammad
Khan Sikandar
Khuda Buksh
Khursheed Ahmed
Khursheed Alam
Lal Khan
Malik Allah Baksh
Mansoor Zaigham M.A.
Maula Buksh
Mehboob Alam
Mehboob Shah
Mehmood
Mian Khan
Mir Inayatullah
Mir shah
Mir Wali
Miran Buksh
Mirza Abdul Hakeem
Mistri Abdil Aziz
Mistri Muhammad Din
Mohammad Shaffi
Mubbarak Shah
Mubbarak Shah
Muhammad Abdullah Khan
Muhammad Afzal Khan
Muhammad Ajaib
Muhammad Akbar
Muhammad Akhtar Janbaz
Muhammad Akram
Muhammad Alam Janbaz
Muhammad Ali
Muhammad Ashraf
Muhammad Aslam

Muhammad Aziz Khan
Muhammad Bashir
Muhammad Dawood
Muhammad Din
Muhammad Ghulshan
Muhammad Hussain
Muhammad Hussain Janbaz
Muhammad Ibraheem
Muhammad Iqbal
Muhammad Ismail
Muhammad Ismail Khan
Muhammad Jan Janbaz
Muhammad Khan
Muhammad Muzaffar
Muhammad Nawaz
Muhammad Nazeef Khan
Muhammad Noor
Muhammad Rafiq
Muhammad Rahim
Muhammad Ramazan
Muhammad Ramzan
Muhammad Rauf
Muhammad Sadiq
Muhammad Sadiq Sani
Muhammad Saeed
Muhammad Sarwar
Muhammad Shaffi
Muhammad Shafi
Muhammad Shakir Khan
Muhammad Sharif
Muhammad Younus
Muhammad Yousaf
Muhammad Zaman
Mukhdoom Buksh
Mukhhan Khan
Mumtaz Ahmed
Munshi Mukhtar Ahmed
Nabbi Buksh
Nadir Ali
Naimat Ali
Nawab Din
Nazam Ali
Nazeer Ahmed
Nazeer Hussain
Nizam Din
Noor Ahmed
Noor Din

Noor Hassan
Noor ud Din
Pir Buksh
Qadir Buksh
Qaim Din
Raheem Dad
Rahim Buksh
Ramazan Baig
Rehmat ullah
Roshan Din
Sabzoo Khan Janbaz
Sadeeq Muhammad
Sadeer Saddar
Sardar Ahmed
Sardar Khan
Sardar Muhammad
Shaikh Inayat Hussain
Shaikh Mushtaq Ahmed
Shaukat Ali
Sheikh Ghulam Muhammad Janbaz
SiraJ Din
Sufi Ahsanullah
Sultan Ahmed
Sultan Mehmood
Tah Muhhamad
Taj
Taj ud Din
Ummat Rasool
Walayat Hussain Janbaz
Yaqoob Khan
Yousaf Ali
Zahoor Ahmed
Zardad Khaksar

Names of the Commanders of the contingent (313 Khaksar March 19, 1940):
Farman Shah
Vilayat Hussain
Subzoo Khan
Mirza Zahoor Ahmed

(Source for names: *Al-Islah*)
Editor's Comments: The exact number of Khaksars killed and injured was never published by the Government.

1940 March 20

The Aftermath of the Massacre

The Tribune, Lahore publishes a front-page headline "Serious Clash Between Khaksars And Police."

The police maintain a strict watch on Khaksar activities. Police officers and district authorities hold a conference to discuss the Khaksar situation.

The number of arrests in connection with the March 19th incident also rises.

Remands are taken for all Khaksars who were put under arrest.

Malik Khizar Hayat Khan (Minister for Public Works), Mian Abdul Haye (Minister for Education), Col Bharucha (Inspector General of Hospitals), and Sardar Ujjal Singh (Parliamentary Secretary [Home]) go to Mayo Hospital to visit the Khaksars who had been injured by the police firing on March 19, 1940.

Three more Khaksars die at Mayo Hospital due to injuries sustained from the police firing on March 19, 1940. Meanwhile, police officers admitted to the hospital are recovering.

The Khaksars who were killed by police firing on March 19, 1940 are buried at a funeral arranged by the police. Photos are also taken of the dead Khaksars. Most of the Khaksars were from the North West Frontier Province. The City Magistrate is also present at the burial of the Khaksars who were killed on March 19, 1940. **Editor's Comments:** Funeral processions of Khaksar martyrs were not allowed. The police rushed their burial to avoid public protests and reaction.

The Government's Actions

The Government of India writes to the Provincial Governments urging them to declare the Khaksar Tehrik an unlawful organization.

A Punjab Gazette Extraordinary publishes the following notification:
        Whereas by a notification issued on the 19th day of March, 1940, the association known as the Anjuman-i-Khaksaran was declared by the Punjab Government to be an unlawful association:
        And whereas in the opinion of the Governor of the Punjab the four places in Rawalpindi described below are used for the purposes of the said Anjuman-i-Khaksaran:
        Now, therefore, the Governor of the Punjab is pleased hereby to notify the said four places for the purposes of section 17-A of the Indian Criminal Law Amendment Act, 1908.
1.   Shop of Muhammad Ramzan, seller of Ghee, in Chhachhi Road
2.   Shop of Doctor Mahmud in Chauk Shah Nazar

3.   House of Master Sher Zaman in Mohalla Imambara
4.   House of Abul Jabbar in Mohalla Pir Harra

The District Magistrate in Lahore modifies his order of March 19, 1940 that banned the gathering of five or more people in a public place. He states that the order shall not apply to gatherings related to the conference of the All-India Muslim League which is opening in Lahore or to any procession licensed under the Police Act.

The District Magistrate states: "In my order of the 19th of March, 1940 passed under section 144 of the Criminal Procedure Code, prohibiting any gathering or assembly of five or more persons in any street, etc. within the limits of the Lahore Municipality, the following proviso shall be added:- 'Provided that this order shall not apply to gatherings or assemblies formed in pursuance of the legitimate objects of the Conference of the All-India Muslim League now opening at Lahore, or to any procession duly licensed under the Police Act.' (2) In my order of the 19th of March 1940 passed under Section 144 of the Criminal Procedure Code, forbidding the carrying of firearms, etc. in the streets and public places within the limits of the Lahore Municipality, the word 'Kirpan' should be deleted." *The Tribune*, Lahore March 21, 1940

The modification to Section 144 by the District Magistrate is seen with great suspicion among the masses.
Editor's Comments: Sir Sikandar Hayat Khan's (Premier of Punjab and Muslim Leaguer) government amended the order so that the Muslim League session at Minto Park could be held. Public suspicion of conspiracy against the Khaksar Movement intensified.

Sir Henry Duffield Craik, the Governor of Punjab, sends a telegram to Lord Linlithgow (Viceroy of India) about the Khaksar incident on March 19, 1940. He also sends a secret letter to Lord Linlithgow about the banning of the Khaksar Tehrik.

The Chief Secretary of Punjab sends a confidential letter to the Deputy Commissioners in Punjab instructing them to prosecute all Khaksars who do not quit the Tehrik. He also instructs them to prosecute any individual helping the Khaksars.

The Deputy Inspector General of Police (CID) of Punjab writes a confidential letter to all Superintendents of Police (SPs) of Punjab asking them to "deal with them [the Khaksars] effectively if they actually do resist." (Muhammad 1973, 63).

K.L.Gauba, Member of the Punjab Assembly, moves an adjournment motion in the Punjab Assembly to discuss the firing on the innocent Khaksars. The motion is to be taken up on March 26, 1940.

The Chief Commissioner, Delhi declares the Khaksar Tehrik unlawful. A notice issued by the Chief Commissioner states:

In exercise of the powers conferred by Section 16 of the Indian Criminal Law Amendment Act, the Chief Commissioner of Dehli, being of opinion that the Association commonly known as the Anjuman-i-Khaksaran interferes with the maintenance of law and order and constitutes danger to the public peace, hereby declares the said Anjuman-i-Khaksaran to be an unlawful association.

In exercise of the powers conferred by section 17-A, of the same Act the Chief Commissioner of Dehli is pleased to notify No.16/267 Faiz Road, Karol Bagh, Dehli, as a place which is in his opinion used for the purposes of an unlawful association, namely, for the purposes of the Anjuman-i-Khaksaran.

Al-Islah

The Government demands security from *Al-Islah* weekly, which recently moved from Lahore to Delhi as a result of the restrictions placed upon it in Lahore. The Government's demand for security is addressed to Mr. Fazal Kashmiri, the editor, printer, and publisher of the newspaper, *Al-Islah*.

The Hindustan Times, Delhi would report on March 22, 1940 that a security of Rs. 3,000 has been demanded from the editor, publisher, and printer of the Khaksar newspaper, *Al-Islah*. The keeper of the Adbe-Jadid press where *Al-Islah* is printed is asked to deposit Rs. 2,000.

Quaid-e-Azam

In Delhi, Jinnah issues a statement to the Press and appeals to the citizens to maintain peace. "I…appeal to the citizens of Lahore particularly to maintain peace and order and to prove to the world that we are capable of adjusting controversial matters justly and fairly. At this critical moment the prestige and honor of the All-India Muslim League is in the hands of the Musalmans of the Punjab. I feel confident that they will fully respond to my appeal and will conduct the deliberations of the session of the League in a manner which will do credit to Islam." *The Hindustan Times*, Delhi March 21, 1940

Quaid-e-Azam issues another statement to the Press regarding the police firing on March 19, 1940: "I am deeply grieved to hear the tragic account of the incident in Lahore last evening regarding the clash between the police and the Khaksars, resulting in terrible loss of life and injury on both the sides. I hope the Khaksars will carry out the instructions issued by their leader, Mr. Innayatullah Mashraqi, published in the newspapers of this morning. As one who has always been so kindly treated by the Khaksars, I appeal to them most earnestly to keep the peace and not precipitate matters by defying law and order. It is difficult to say anything till I am in possession of full facts of the situation." Jinnah also states that the upcoming Muslim League Session would still be held in Lahore as planned. *The Hindustan Times*, Delhi March 21, 1940, *The Statesman*, Calcutta, March 21, 1940 (Ahmad, 481)

Quaid-e-Azam leaves Delhi for Lahore by train.

At every railway stop, Jinnah encounters people protesting against the behavior of the Government in regards to the Khaksars and demanding settlement of the Khaksar issue.

Other Parts of India

Police raid and search four centers of the Khaksar Tehrik in Rawalpindi. Khaksar materials, documents, and literature are seized. The houses of prominent Janbazs and Salars are also searched.

William (District Magistrate) and Scott (Superintendent of Police) are present at the Rawalpindi raids.

Armed police also raid the Khaksar Tehrik's office in Delhi. No one is present at the house. Police conduct a thorough search and confiscate all Khaksar materials. The Khaksar flag and signboard are also removed. Armed policemen are posted to guard the headquarters.

In Ambala, Khaksar houses are searched and Khaksar literature is seized. About 15 Khaksars are arrested in Ambala City and Cantonment.

Police arrest Khaksars and seize Khaksar materials in Lyallpur (now Faisalabad). They also raid the house of Mohammed Afzal, Salar-i-Azam of the Lyallpur District of the Khaksar Tehrik.

Armed police raid the Khaksar office in Multan. Khaksar literature and belongings are confiscated.

Three more Khaksars are arrested in Ferozepur. One of them would be produced before the Additional District Magistrate and remanded to police custody until March 29, 1940.

Police in Amritsar take precautionary measures to prohibit Khaksar demonstrations. A large contingent of Amritsar Police along with other officials, armed with rifles, station themselves at a Railway over-bridge to arrest any incoming Khaksars. The contingent includes A.A. Macdonald (I.C.S Deputy Commissioner), J.A. Scott (Superintendent of Police), Sardar Narinder Singh (City Magistrate), Khan Sahib Mirza Ata Ullah, S.C Terry (D.S.P.), and Chaudhry Sunder Das Midha (A.F.D.M.). Lorries are searched for Khaksars and a large number of people gather to witness the activities of the police against the Khaksars.

1940 March 21

The Aftermath of the Massacre

The Hindustan Times, Delhi reports details of the police raid on the Khaksar Tehrik headquarters in Ichhra on March 19, 1940. According to the newspaper, police raided the Khaksar Tehrik headquarters and arrested Khaksars using tear gas. This was the first time that tear gas had been used on people in the open in Punjab.

Two more Khaksars, who had been injured due to the police firing on March 19, 1940, die at Mayo Hospital.

The Tribune, Lahore publishes a photo of Sir Sikandar Hayat Khan, Premier of Punjab, visiting Khaksars at Mayo Hospital. There is also a photo of a dead body being removed from Mayo hospital and photos from the site of the massacre of the Khaksars in Lahore on March 19, 1940.

At a meeting called by Maulana Daood Ghaznavi and presided over by Maulana Habib ur Rahman Ludhianavi, the Ahrar party decides to arrange medical relief for Khaksars injured on March 19, 1940 and legal help for those who were arrested.

The public remains highly distressed as a result of the massacre on March 19, 1940. Mayo Hospital continues to receive innumerable phone calls from the general public inquiring about the injured Khaksars. The hospital authorities find it impossible to answer all the inquiries and request the general public not to make these calls as it hampers their work.

The Tribune, Lahore publishes the details of Mashriqi's arrest.

The Muslim League Session and Jinnah's Arrival in Lahore

In the wake of the police firing on March 19, 1940, approximately 50,000 people gather when Jinnah arrives in Lahore for the Muslim League Session. A state of hysteria prevails among the masses. The unnerved public is looking to Jinnah to resolve the current issue.

Upon arrival at his host's residence in Lahore, Jinnah makes a statement to the Press, "The unfortunate tragic events that have taken place during the last three days resulting in loss of life and injury must not lead you to lose your balance. You must deal with the situation calmly and dispassionately and I feel confident that you shall find a solution of the situation." *The Tribune*, Lahore March 22, 1940 and *The Hindustan Times*, Delhi March 22, 1940

Editor's Comments: Quaid-e-Azam witnessed the concern of the people everywhere—en route to and upon arrival in Lahore. Keeping in view the public's restlessness and sympathy with the Khaksars, he feared that there could be an outbreak. He also realized that the Muslim League session could be in jeopardy and could turn into a chaotic situation, if at that critical moment, people's heightened emotions due to Khaksar massacre were not solaced. Sensing the feelings of the public, Quaid-e-Azam pacified them and requested that they remain calm. At the same time, he gave them hope for a solution.

Quaid-e-Azam, accompanied by Sir Raza Ali and Mian Abdul Haye (Education Minister), visits the injured policemen and Khaksars in the hospital in Lahore. He first visits the police officers D. Gainsford (Senior Superintendent of Police) and Beaty (Deputy Superintendent of Police). He then also makes a short visit to the injured Khaksars who ask Quaid-e-Azam to see their injuries.
Editor's Comments: Muslims did not appreciate that Quaid-e-Azam first visited and sympathized with the police officers who were responsible for the mass killing of the Khaksars.

Sir Sikandar Hayat Khan (Premier of Punjab) meets with Jinnah at Mamdot Villa, Lahore and apprises him of the situation regarding the police firing on the Khaksars on March 19, 1940.
Editor's Comments: Sir Sikandar briefed Quaid-e-Azam on the extreme resentment that prevailed amongst the Muslims toward Sir Sikandar's actions against the Khaksars and talked over the strategy to control the situation.

In the afternoon, Quaid-e-Azam makes a speech at Minto Park, Lahore in front of 10,000 Muslims. While unfurling the Muslim League flag, he states that he wants to tell the people what is uppermost in his mind as he has just returned from Mayo Hospital. Upon hearing of his visit to the injured Khaksars, the crowd shows its appreciation by shouting "Quaid-e-Azam Jinnah Zindabad."

Jinnah performs the flag hoisting ceremony at the Muslim League pandal. In light of the Khaksar tragedy, people's emotions are at their peak. Quaid-e-Azam calms the emotions of the general public and makes the following statement:
"You have today given me the privelege... of unfurling the flag of the All-India Muslim League... Before I say anything more, I want to tell you what is uppermost in my mind as I have just returned from the Mayo Hospital. I'm sure that we all deeply grieve the unfortunate tragedy which has resulted in a large number of lives being lost and injured. I think every man and every woman must sympathise with the families and the dependents of those who have died and those who have been injured. The session of the All-India Muslim League is going to open on the eve of this most unfortunate situation that has been created in Lahore.
Let me put to you what is the acid test of a great nation and of a great people. The answer is the greater the difficulties, the more we should keep ourselves calm and cool.
The Muslim League, I am sure will not fail to rise to the occasion, irrespective of the parties concerned, to handle this question in a manner which is just and fair. You must, therefore, rely that this is the one and the only organization of the Muslims of India. We must, therefore, stand as one man with one voice under this flag which you have honoured by asking me to unfurl. I have no doubt. I have full confidence in my people, and we shall face any and every difficulty in a manner which will be worthy of this great Muslim nation. I, therefore, earnestly appeal to

you—let us not have any kind of doubt or suspicion with regard to the decisions of the Muslim League and let us take a right decis'n and stand by it" *The Hindustan Times*, Delhi March 22, 1940

Editor's Comments: At the ceremony, people's sympathy with the Khaksars was worth witnessing. They rose slogans in support of the Khaksars such as, "Allama Mashriqi Zindabad," "Khaksar-e-Azam Zindabad," and "Khaksar Shuhdha Zindabad." Once again, Jinnah consoled people and gave them hope when he stated, "The Muslim League, I am sure will not fail to rise to the occasion..." *The Hindustan Times*, Delhi March 22, 1940

At a Muslim League Council meeting in the evening, Z.H. Lahri (M.L.A. Deputy Leader of the Muslim League in the U.P.Assembly) wants to move a resolution regarding the tragic killing of the Khaksars at Lahore on March 19, 1940. Jinnah disallows this on the technical ground that a resolution can only be moved with 15 days prior notice. However, Z.H. Lahri responds that it would have been impossible to provide 15 days notice when the incident took place only three days ago. Thus, it is finally agreed that the resolution will be moved in the meeting of the Subjects Committee. *The Tribune* would report on March 23, 1940 that "The Press was excluded from the meeting of the Council of the Muslim League...this was done...for the first time because previously the Press was always allowed to watch the proceedings of the Council."

The Government's Actions

The District Magistrate withdraws the curfew that had been imposed in Lahore on March 19, 1940.

The Hindustan Times, Delhi reports that all the funds of the Khaksar Tehrik are to be confiscated.

The Government asks the Imperial Bank of India to stop payments from the funds of Allama Mashriqi.

The Punjab Government issues a communique announcing the appointment of an inquiry committee to investigate the police firing on March 19, 1940. The inquiry is to be conducted by two High Court Judges.

The Viceroy sends a telegram to the Secretary of State of India stating: "This [the arrest of Allama Mashriqi] was considered necessary in view particularly of orders contained in official organ of Khaksars to effect that quota from other provinces should march on Lahore. He [Allama Mashriqi] was arrested on the night of 19th in Delhi. Also decided the Chief Commissioner, Delhi should follow example of Punjab and by notification under Criminal Law (Amendment) Act declare Khaksars organisation to be unlawful association."

The Chief Secretary of the Government of U.P. sends a telegram to the Secretary of the Government of India (Home Department) regarding the ban on the Khaksar Tehrik.

The Government of NWFP writes a telegram to the Secretary, Home Department, stating that it does not recommend declaring the Khaksar Tehrik to be an unlawful organization in NWFP.

Continued Demonstrations and Arrests

The Tribune, Lahore reports that 217 Khaksars are arrested. This includes 60 to 70 Khaksars arrested last night from the Headquarters of the Khaksar Tehrik at Ichhra, Lahore.

Khaksar Abdul Haye from Peshawar is arrested in Lahore.

Khaksars hold a demonstration at Anarkali, Lahore. Police, including J.T.M. Benett (Inspector General of Police), F.C. Bourne (District Magistrate), Sardar Abdul Samad (City Magistrate) and other officials, are present. A large crowd gathers to witness the scene. The tear gas squad arrives on the scene and launches a tear gas grenade at the Khaksars. The Khaksars fall to the ground due to the heavy smoke from the tear gas. The police then arrest the Khaksars. Shops are closed in Anarkali as a result of the Khaksars arrests.

15 Khaksars (who were heading from Delhi to Lahore) are arrested near the Ambala railway crossing.

In Amritsar, Mohammad Hussain Bhatti (a Khaksar leader) and other Khaksars are arrested.

At an extraordinary meeting of the M.A.O. College (Amritsar) Union, the students request the Principal of the College, Dr. M.D. Taseer, to close the College as a mark of sympathy for those who were injured or killed on March 19, 1940. Dr. M.D. Taseer addresses the students of the College and expresses profound sorrow at the tragic incident in Lahore on March 19, 1940. The College remains closed for the rest of the day.

Khaksars are arrested in Okara, Montgomery, and Pakpattan.

A Khaksar is arrested near Ramgali.

Five Khaksars (arrested in Lahore on March 20, 1940) are brought in court. Their bail application is denied.

The house of Noor Mohammad Kabali, a Khaksar organizer in Multan, is searched and Khaksar materials are seized.

1940 March 22

A meeting of prominent citizens of Lahore is held. They decide to set up a public inquiry into the police firing on March 19, 1940.

The public supports and helps the Khaksars enthusiastically. Women volunteers look after the injured Khaksars in Mayo Hospital.

The Tribune, Lahore publishes two photos. The first picture shows smoke on the street after police used tear gas against the Khaksars in Anarkali, Lahore. The second picture shows policemen putting on gas masks prior to using the tear gas.

Khaksar batches continue to leave Lucknow for Lahore.

The Government's Actions

The U.P. Government continues to watch the activities of the Khaksars.

Sir Henry Duffield Craik, the Governor of Punjab, visits injured Khaksars and police officers at Mayo Hospital.

The Tribune, Lahore publishes Home Member Sir R. Maxwell's statement in the Central Assembly about the arrest of Allama Mashriqi and the restrictions on the Khaksar Tehrik.

The Hindustan Times, Delhi reports that Sir R.Maxwell, Home Member, replied to a short notice question raised by Sir Zia ud Din Ahmed, that "The Government of India have detained Allama Inayatullah Khan Mashriqui under the Defence of India Rules with a view to preventing him from acting in a manner prejudicial to the efficient prosecution of the war, to the defence of British India and to public order."

The Tribune, Lahore reports that Williams, District Magistrate, informed the Associated Press that the police have taken all precautionary measures and are fully prepared to meet any kind of emergency caused by the Khaksars.

The Muslim League Session

The 27th Session of the All-India Muslim League commences in Lahore. People congregate in anticipation and want to see the Khaksar issue resolved. Restlessness prevails and many tears are shed. Slogans in support of the Khaksars and against Sir Sikandar are raised. People's support for the Khaksars is praise worthy.

The All-India Muslim League Session (to pass the Pakistan Resolution) commences at Minto Park, Lahore at 2:45 pm. There is a demonstration against Sir Sikandar Hayat Khan (Premier of Punjab) at the session. *The Tribune* would write on March 23, 1940:

"Shouts of 'Sikander Hyat Murdabad' were raised by...the audience in the 'pandal' when the name of the Punjab Premier was mentioned by the Chairman of the Reception Committee...The demonstration created a sensation in the 'pandal.'

Immediately after Mr. Jinnah finished his speech a Muslim woman got up on the platform and referred to the happenings at Lahore [the massacre on March 19, 1940].

A crowd held demonstrations against the Punjab Ministers as they left the 'pandal' in their cars."

The Subjects Committee of the All-India Muslim League meets at night behind closed doors. The Press is once again excluded from this meeting.

Continued Arrests

The Tribune, Lahore reports that Abdulla Khokhar and Abdul Razak (two Khaksars) were arrested in Jullundur; their bail was rejected by the District Magistrate, and their remands were taken.

In Lyallpur (now Faisalabad), police search the houses of leading Khaksars including Mohammad Afzal (Salar-i-Azam, Lyallpur). Khaksar literature and materials are seized.

1940 March 23

The Muslim League Session

At Minto Park, Lahore, the second open sitting of the All-India Muslim League begins at 3:30 pm, an hour later than the time announced. Another demonstration against Sir Sikandar Hayat Khan (Premier of Punjab) is held at the session. A big crowd surrounds the pandal. Great excitement prevails; the crowd is restless and demands that a resolution on the Khaksars be taken up immediately.

People shout "Sikandar Hayat Muradabad" and "Turn out Sikandar Hayat from the League." National Guards and volunteers are rushed in to control the situation. News of this demonstration would be reported in *The Tribune*, Lahore of March 24, 1940. The newspaper would also report:

"Mr. Jinnah on coming out of the *pandal*, acceded to the demand of the crowd to speak to them...He addressed the crowd and appealed to them to have patience and remain quiet and orderly.

Referring to the demand of the crowd [that a resolution on the Khaksars be taken up immediately], Mr. Jinnah said that the matter would be thoroughly examined by the Subjects Committee and they would not be influenced by anybody. The issue, he said, would be taken up tonight by the Subjects Committee and they would rise only after coming to some final decision."

Editor's Comments: Restlessness in favor of the Khaksars continued amongst the people. Slogans in favor of Khaksars and against Sir Sikandar were raised continuously. People were uneasy and wanted to hear of the Muslim League's action against Sir Sikandar. Jinnah had to appeal to the jittery and angered crowd to remain patient. He again gave hope to the crowd.

The Subjects Committee meets once again and discusses the Khaksar resolution. Sir Sikandar Hayat Khan is present at the meeting and makes a statement to explain his position.

Many Muslim Leaguers severely criticize and blame Sir Sikandar for the tragedy that occurred on March 19, 1940. Demonstrations are also held during the Subjects Committee meeting.

The Subjects Committee passes a resolution on the Khaksar issue.

Meetings, Demonstrations, and Arrests

A public meeting is being organized by the Khaksars at Kohat (NWFP).

The Governor of the North West Frontier Province, Sir George Cunningham, meets with Abdullah Jan, a Khaksar leader.

Khaksars parade the streets of Peshawar in protest of the March 19th incident. After parading, they enter Jumma mosque to offer prayers. 15 Khaksars are arrested by the police when they emerge from the mosque.

15 Khaksars are arrested in Rawalpindi.

On Grand Trunk Road (G.T. Road) near Gujrat, police search lorries for Khaksars going towards Lahore to participate in ongoing demonstrations there. No Khaksar is allowed to proceed to Lahore.

Police try to prevent any demonstrations in favor of the Khaksars. In their attempts to quell demonstrations, they continue to arrest members of the general public who they suspect may be Khaksars.

The Tribune, Lahore reports that the Government of U.P. is maintaining a close watch on the activities of the Khaksars in Punjab.

1940 March 24

The Tribune, Lahore publishes a partial Khaksar casualty list. The list consists of 44 names of those injured or killed as a result of the police firing on March 19, 1940.

Prior to this date, the Government had failed to publish a complete list of Khaksars that were wounded or killed on March 19. Under public pressure, the Information Bureau of the Punjab Government announces that they will do their utmost in tracing the missing Khaksars. They announce that a list of wounded Khaksars and an incomplete list of the Khaksars killed on March 19 have already been published.

They also state that efforts are being made to prepare a complete list of those Khaksars that had been killed on March 19, 1940.

Public Outcry for Khaksar Tragedy

The public continues to be highly restless and is demanding that the Kkaksar issue be addressed.

The Muslim League holds an open session in the morning. Nawabzada Liaquat Ali Khan informs the people (amidst cheers) that the Khaksar issue will be taken up at the night session of the Muslim League.
Editor's Comments: Knowing that the people were extremely supportive of Allama Mashriqi and the Khaksars, Liaquat Ali informed a rowdy and uneasy crowd that the Khaksar issue would be dealt with.

Khaksars demonstrate in Lahore and a large crowd gathers to watch. Shops in the area are closed and traffic is suspended. Police arrive on the scene and call in a tear gas squad. Prominent Muslims including K.L.Gauba (Member Punjab Legislative Assembly) and Mian Amir ud Din assure the Khaksars that the Khaksar massacre is on everyone's mind and cannot be avoided as a topic of discussion in the Muslim League Session. Upon hearing this assurance, the Khaksars agree to stop the demonstration. The Khaksars then proceed to the Muslim League Session with the Muslim leaders.

Khaksars hold a demonstration in Anarkali, where a large crowd gathers.

Another Khaksar demonstration takes place in Lahore.

Nawab Bahadur Yar Jang, a leader of the Khaksars in Hyderabad (Deccan), meets with the Naib Salar-i-Azam of the Khaksar Tehrik, Punjab in jail in Lahore. Nawab Yar Jang requests the Naib Salar of Punjab to authorize him to stop the ongoing demonstrations by the Khaksars. Nawab Yar Jang assures the Naib Salar that the question of the removal of the ban on the Khaksar Tehrik has been taken up by the Muslim League. Upon this assurance, the Naib Salar authorizes Nawab Bahadur Yar Jang to instruct the Khaksars in Lahore to suspend their demonstrations.

Khaksars arrive from other cities to join the ongoing demonstrations in Lahore. At a demonstration at Golden Mosque in Dabbi Bazaar, the Khaksars address the large crowd that has gathered. The City Magistrate asks the Khaksars to surrender, but the Khaksars refuse. At this point, Nawab Bahadur Yar Jang arrives and informs the Khaksars that negotiations for a compromise regarding the Khaksar issue are in progress between Mr. Jinnah and the Government. He also informs them that the imprisoned Naib Salar-i-Azam of the Khaksar Tehrik, Punjab has authorized him to stop the demonstrations. He thus appeals to the Khaksars to surrender their belchas and uniforms, and suspend their *satyagraha*. The Khaksars accede to Nawab Jang's appeal.

Editor's Comments: The fact that the Khaksars turned down the request of the City Magistrate but accepted the orders of imprisoned Naib Salar-i-Azam, speaks of the discipline and obedience of the Khaksars toward their superiors.

Eight Khaksars are arrested at Jullundur.

In front of a crowd of 10,000, Maulana Habib ur Rehman (President, All-India Majlas-i-Ahrar-i-Hind) announces the appointment of an independent inquiry committee by the Ahrars to investigate the police firing on March 19, 1940. According to the Maulana, the purpose of the independent inquiry committee is to ascertain the real facts and causes of the March 19th incident, particularly since Allama Mashriqi had stated that he did not direct the Khaksars to launch the civil resistance movement. The inquiry committee is to consist of Mian Abdul Aziz (M.L.A. Chairman), K.L.Gauba (M.L.A.), Maulana Daud Ghaznavi, and Maulana Syed Habib. Maulana Habib ul Rehman also offers to include any Government member or members from any other party into the committee. He states that the Ahrars will extend every possible assistance to the Khaksars, including raising funds, to help them in the matter of their defense. Closing, the Maulana sympathizes with the relatives of Khaksars that were killed on March 19, 1940.

Maulana Shahid Fakhri (President of the City Congress Committee, Allahabad and U.P.) says in a statement: "The statement that Mr. Jinnah issued to the Press, after the firing in Lahore [on March 19, 1940], and in which Mr. Jinnah advised the Khaksars to maintain peace but did not utter a word against the action taken by the Punjab Government was surprising. It appears that the personalities of Mr. Jinnah and Sir Sikandar Hayat Khan have been considered above human criticism." *The Hindustan Times*, Delhi Mar 27, 1940
Editor's Comments: People resented the fact that Quaid-e-Azam was using diplomatic language and was not openly criticizing the Punjab Government.

Before the Night Session of the Muslim League

Sir Sikandar Hayat Khan throws a party. Quaid-e-Azam is the guest of honor at the party. The party is also attended by the Sir Henry Duffield Craik (Governor of Punjab), Sir Douglas Young (Chief Justice of the Lahore High Court), other Judges of the High Court, Fazal ul Haq (Premier of Bengal), heads of various government departments, prominent citizens, ministers, and leading Muslim Leaguers.
Editor's Comments: The presence of Sir Henry Duffield Craik (Governor of Punjab) at Sikandar's party for Jinnah was viewed with suspicion in the Khaksar circle. It was evident that the British were supporting Jinnah for their own ends.

Sir Sikandar Hayat Khan and his Muslim Ministers do not attend the night session of the Muslim League.
Editor's Comments: In view of the public resentment and slogans against Sir Sikandar and the Punjab Government, Sir Sikandar did not go to the Muslim League session.

The Night Session of the Muslim League

The All-India Muslim League commences its deliberations at its fourth and final sitting at Minto Park, Lahore, which begins at 9:00 pm, an hour later than the time announced. Demonstrations continue at this final sitting. There is a large crowd present and upon Jinnah's arrival at the session, there are shouts of "Khaksar Zindabad." *The Tribune*, Lahore would report on March 25, 1940, "Immediately after Mr. Jinnah came and occupied the chair continuous shouts of 'Khaksars Zindabad' and 'Turn out Sir Sikander from the League' were raised..." The shouts continue throughout the session.

People are anxious and want to know first what has been decided about the Khaksar issue. Owing to the sensitivity of the issue, Nawabzada Liaquat Ali Khan has no choice but to address the crowd once again. He begs the audience to remain calm and assures them that the session will not end without the resolution regarding the Khaksars being placed before the House.

The Pakistan Resolution (Lahore Resolution) is passed at this Session.

The Khaksar Resolution

Soon after the Pakistan Resolution (Lahore Resolution), Quaid-e-Azam moves the Khaksar Resolution and it is passed unanimously. It states:
> This Session of the All India Muslim League places on record its deep sense of sorrow at the unfortunate and tragic occurrence on the 19th March, 1940, owing to a clash between the Khaksars and the Police resulting in the loss of a large number of lives and injuries to many more and sincerely sympathizes with those who have suffered and with their families and dependents.
> This Session calls upon the Government to forthwith appoint an independent and impartial committee of inquiry, the personnel of which would command perfect confidence of the people with instructions to them to make full and complete investigation and inquiry in the whole affairs and make their report as soon as possible.
> This Session authorizes the Working Committee to take such actions in the matter as they may consider proper immediately after the publication of the report of the Committee.
> This Session urges upon the various governments that the order declaring the Khaksar organisation unlawful should be removed as soon as possible.

Editor's Comments:
The resolution on the Khaksars had no results:
1. The inquiry committee was appointed by the Government itself and did not include anyone from the public
2. The report of the inquiry committee was never made public
3. The ban on the movement was removed due to Mashriqi and the Khaksars' resistance and long struggle.

At the close of the session, Quaid-e-Azam is very happy that he handled the critical situation and was able to pacify the public outcry.

Press Reports of the Last Session of the Muslim League

The Tribune, Lahore would write on March 25, 1940, "In view of the expected discussion on the resolution on the Lahore situation [massacre of the Khaksars on March 19, 1940], there was tremendous rush of visitors. Big crowds stood at the gate and even the Pathan volunteers had a 'miserable' time in keeping back the surging tide of crowd." Begum Mohammad Ali (widow of late Maulana Mohammad Ali) appeals to the Muslims to have patience and remain calm during this difficult time. She also emphasizes the need for unity in the ranks of the Muslims. Later, amidst loud cheers, Jinnah moves a resolution from the chair on the Khaksars, stating that it (the resolution) was the result of deliberations in the Subjects Committee from 9:00 pm to 2:00 am (9:00 pm on the night of March 23 until 2:00 am on March 24).

Editor's Comments: The public's support for Allama Mashriqi was evident from their behavior and anxiety. At every session, they had to be pacified. When Quaid-e-Azam moved the Khaksar Resolution, thunderous and resounding cheers were heard.

The Hindustan Times, Delhi of March 25, 1940 would further report:

"Moving the resolution, Mr. Jinnah assured the gathering that whether it be the Punjab Government, the Government of India, the Punjab Ministry or the Punjab Premier they would not rest until they had got justice. Mr. Jinnah requested every Muslim in the Punjab and particularly Khaksars in the Punjab and elswhere in India to put their heads together and see that at the time of inquiry they placed their material before the investigating authority.

Mr. Jinnah said: 'The [Khaksar] resolution is the result of discussion in the subjects committee from 9 to 2' o'clock in the morning. The Subjects Committee adopted this resolution in the form in which it is now placed before you. They have passed it unanimously, and now it is for you to deal with it. The resolution represents their considered opinion and they want me to convey to you that this resolution should be put from the chair.'

Mr. Jinnah added: 'There are many reasons for this course to be adopted. The first reason is that it will not be desirable to have people coming and making speech after speech. It is very difficult to restrain passions and some may say something which might be considered harmful to our interests. Another reason is that, the matter is *sub judice*.'

…Explaining the resolution, Mr. Jinnah said: 'It asks for a full and complete investigation and inquiry, and it will not be in the fitness of things that, on the one hand, we ask for an inquiry, and on the other, we pronounce our judgement.'"

Editor's Comments: There was a lot of demand from the attendees to make speeches about the Khaksar tragedy and demand action against Sir Sikandar Hayat Khan. However, Jinnah, sensing the emotions of the people, did not allow them to speak up. He wanted to avoid embarrassment to Sir Sikandar, whose support to the

Muslim League was essential at this critical moment, and he did not want to give too much prominence to the Khaksar issue.

Editor's Comments:

Public Outcry Throughout the Three-day Session

Since the day of the massacre on March 19, 1940 and the arrest of Allama Mashriqi, everyone including Jinnah witnessed the increasing support of the public in favor of Mashriqi and the Khaksars. The public outcry was well observed throughout the Muslim League session and wailing and crying by the Khaksars and the general masses was worth seeing. The large attendance at the Muslim League Session, due to the grave tragedy of March 19, showed that the Muslims wanted to see a resolution in respect to the Khaksar Tehrik. People remained restless throughout the session, which lasted from March 22 until March 24, 1940. The public shouted slogans in support of Mashriqi and the Khaksars and vehemently denounced the Punjab Government and raised anti-Sir Sikandar slogans. At every session slogans in favor of Khaksars such as, "Khaksars Zindabad," "Allama Mashriqi Zindabad," and "Khaksar-e-Azam Zindabad," were raised. Hooting and shouting against Sir Sikandar Hayat Khan continued everyday and people shouted slogans such as, "Sikandar Murdabad," "Punjab Government Murdabad," "Down with Sikandar," "Shame Shame," and "Sikandar Ko League Se Nikal Do (expel Sikandar from the Muslim League)." Whenever Sir Sikandar's name was mentioned by any speaker, the public yelled "Sit Down" and "Do Not Mention Sikandar."

The public and the Khaksars wanted the Muslim League to take actions against Sir Sikandar in order to redress their grievances. The crowd's demands included the following:
1. To hold Sir Sikandar responsible for the massacre of the innocent Khaksars in Lahore on March 19, 1940
2. To openly condemn Sir Sikandar and take serious action against him, including expelling him from the Muslim League
3. To provide compensation to the families of the Khaksar martyrs
4. To release Allama Mashriqi and other Khaksars from jail
5. To remove the ban on the Khaksar Tehrik.

At the Last Session

"When the open session met at 8.50 p.m. on Sunday [24 March], the atmosphere in the *pandal* was surcharged with excitement in expectation of the Khaksar resolution being taken up. From the very start the proceedings were interrupted with shouts of 'Khaksars Zindabad' and 'Sikandar Ko League Se Nikal Do (expel Sikandar from the [Muslim] League).'" "An atmosphere of subdued excitement created by the prospect of the resolution on the Khaksar question" prevailed. (*The Hindustan Times*, Delhi March 25, 1940). A huge crowd was present to hear the outcome of the proceedings on the Khaksar issue. Nawabzada Liaqat Ali Khan again had to assure the restless congregation that the Khaksar resolution was forthcoming and the session would not end without it. He had to make requests to the people "to be peaceful and calm." (*The Hindustan Times*, Delhi March 25, 1940). The crowd was highly impatient and such assurance was needed to keep the people's emotions from getting out of hand. Finally, keeping in view the sympathies of the Muslim public, the Muslim League did pass the Khaksar resolution. The Pakistan Resolution was passed first and the Resolution on the Khaksars was passed third.

Great jubilation was seen when Jinnah rose amidst cheers and proposed the Khaksar resolution that was unanimously passed to the Central Committee of the Muslim League. Jinnah handled the situation very smartly and tactfully and was able to pacify the people by passing the resolution. People breathed sighs of relief at the passing of the Khaksar resolution hoping that a fair and independent inquiry would be conducted and action would be taken against Sir Sikandar. The general public tied their hopes to the Muslim League, and it was understood that the League would ensure the release of Mashriqi and the Khaksars as well as the removal of the ban on the Khaksar Movement. The intense emotions that were witnessed throughout the three-day session provide substantial evidence that if this resolution had not been passed, the standing of the Muslim League among the general Muslims would have been in jeopardy, and it was likely that the Muslim League would have broken apart.

Time wore on, but the Muslim League did nothing concrete. To everyone's disappointment, Mashriqi remained in jail and the chase and imprisonment of the Khaksars continued. The Khaksars came to the understanding that the Muslim Leaguers did not want Mashriqi to be released, so that the Muslim League would become the sole representative of the Muslims.

Closing Words

This massacre was the most brutal massacre of innocent people since the Jallianwallah Bagh (Amritsar, India) massacre by General Dyer on April 13, 1919. It is highly deplorable that this important event, a turning point in the history of Pakistan, has been completely ignored and that the Khaksars' role in the resistance movement afterwards has been completely disregarded. This has been done on purpose for many reasons. History is witness to the fact that the Khaksar massacre brought the Muslims of India together under the flag of the Muslim League and led to the creation of Pakistan. Furthermore, the Khaksars' resistance to the imperialists in the Indian freedom struggle was the longest, toughest, and most unparalleled fight since the Khilafat Movement. Freedom is not achieved without personal sacrifice, martyrs, and resistance; and the Khaksars provided all of these for the freedom of Indo-Pakistan. Pakistan's history is incomplete since this massacre and the services of Mashriqi and the Khaksars following this incident have been ignored.

1940 March 25

Headlines in *The Tribune* read "Sorrow Expressed at Lahore Tragic Happenings," "Govt. asked to hold Impartial Enquiry," "'My life is shortened by 10 years', says Mr. Jinnah," and "Resolution Passed at Muslim League session."

Quaid-e-Azam sums up his impression of the Muslim League Session and acknowledges that the Khaksar tragedy brought all Muslims together. He states: "The first thing that has emerged from the session of the All-India Muslim League is that in the face of the unfortunate occurrence on March 19 resulting in the loss of a large number of Muslims, which shook the Muslims of India and, particularly of the Punjab and Lahore, the Subjects Committee, after many hours of deliberations, came to a unanimous decision and a still more remarkable fact is that the entire body of delegates in the open session and the vast public accepted the [Khaksar] resolution moved by the chair also unanimously. This has shown beyond doubt that the Muslims are capable of standing and going through an ordeal and trial worthy of any great political organization. In my opinion, therefore, this session was far more successful than it would have been otherwise...." *The Hindustan Times*, Delhi March 26, 1940 and *The Tribune*, Lahore March 26, 1940

The Star of India, Calcutta reports that a security of Rs. 2,000 has been demanded from Din Duniya Press that publishes *Al-Islah* (organ of Khaksars).

Khaksars hold a demonstration in Rawalpindi. Seven Khaksars are arrested by the police in the presence of the District Magistrate and the Superintendent of Police. A large crowd gathers at the scene.

Police arrest 12 Khaksars at Lahore Railway station.

Mohammad Afzal, Salar-i-Azam of the Lyallpur district, is arrested in Lyallpur (now Faisalabad).

Police raid various locations in Lyallpur and seize Khaksar materials, including literature, tents, uniforms, and spades.

The Hindustan Times, Delhi reports that Khaksar drills at night have become a feature of the city's life.

The Statesman, Calcutta, publishes a photo showing police using tear gas at Anarkali Bazar, Lahore to arrest Khaksars (who refused to stop their demonstration). Smoke from the tear gas can be seen throughout the photo.

1940 March 26

In the News

The Civil & Military Gazette (Lahore) writes "The three-day session commenced under the heavy shadow of the Khaksar disturbance, but the use of hard words with reference to it was carefully avoided throughout the proceedings in distinct contrast to the League's methods of approach to other problems...The wording of the resolution was cautious, attempting to avoid embarrassment to the Punjab Government and at the same time satisfying all sections of opinion...Thus the League has taken on a position which in substance confirms the attitude taken by the Punjab Government...As regards the part [of Khaksar resolution] which urges the removal of the ban declaring the Khaksar organisation an unlawful body, the words 'as soon as possible' in the [Khaksar] resolution are significant and place the onus on the Khaksars themselves."

The Civil & Military Gazette (Lahore) writes in its editorial "As for the resolution touching on the Khaksar incident in Lahore, its only admirable feature was the diplomatic manoeuvre of its presentation...By the stratagem of putting the resolution from the chair and by couching the resolution in language as unexceptionable as it was colourless, Mr. Jinnah cleverly avoided a debate which would most certainly have been acrimonious and might easily have resulted in schism not easily healed. The by no means silent section which condemned Sir Sikandar Hyat Khan and his government for the ban which precipitated the clash between police and Khaksars in Lahore might have adopted methods which would have forced the Punjab Premier to withdraw altogether from his association with the League. Fortunately for Mr. Jinnah and the League (so far as the Punjab is concerned) this was avoided."

The Punjab Assembly

In front of a packed visitor's gallery at the Punjab Assembly, K.L. Gauba (M.L.A. in the Punjab Assembly) moves an adjournment motion at 4:30 pm regarding the March 19th incident. Miss Fatima Jinnah, Nawab Bahadur Yar Jang, Nawab Mohammad Ismail Khan, Raja and Rani of Mandi, Nawabzada and Begum Liaquat Ali Khan, and other Muslim League leaders are among those present at the proceedings. Mr. Gauba states that the Government should issue a list of all those who were injured or killed on March 19, 1940. He also narrates the story of the incident, saying that he saw pools of the Khaksars' blood on the streets. Mr. Gauba states that according to his information, 100 Khaksars lost their lives. He further adds, "The act of shooting was no less than cold-blooded murder." *The Tribune*, Lahore March 27, 1940. Supporting K.L. Gauba, Dr. Gopichand Bharghava (Leader of the Opposition) states that the firing was not just to disperse the Khaksars and was done in a vindictive spirit. K.L. Gauba asks the Premier to provide a full explanation of the incident.

Sir Sikandar Hayat Khan (Premier of Punjab), while replying to the adjournment motion in the Punjab Assembly, attempts to justify the police firing on March 19, 1940. He also sympathizes with the British Police officers (and their families) who were injured during the clash. *The Tribune*, Lahore of March 27, 1940 would write, "The Premier paid a handsome tribute to the sense of duty and gallantry displayed by Mr. Gainsford and Mr. Beaty."

At the Punjab Assembly, the mover is never given a chance to reply to Sir Sikandar's statements. Mian Abdul Aziz and D. Chaman Lal protest, "We have never heard of the movers not being given the right to reply." As time runs out, a vote is called, and K.L. Gauba's adjournment motion is defeated. *The Tribune*, Lahore March 27, 1940

Other Events

Nawab Bahadur Yar Jang (Hakim-i-Aalah of the Khaksar Tehrik) calls a meeting of the Khaksars to be held in Meerut on March 28, 1940 to choose a successor to Allama Mashriqi (who is in jail). Nawab Jang states that he is conducting negotiations with the Punjab Government in order to remove the ban on the Khaksar Tehrik. He appeals to the Khaksars not to send volunteers to Punjab until a successor to Allama Mashriqi has been chosen.

Jinnah, Jinnah's sister (Fatima Jinnah), Liaquat Ali Khan, and Begum Liaquat Ali Khan leave Lahore for Delhi in the evening. Nawab Bahadur Yar Jang also leaves on the same train.

17 Khaksars leave Peshawar for Lahore.

Arrests

The police force in Rawalpindi is strengthened. Police guard various places, including Juma mosque in Rawalpindi, to prevent Khaksar demonstrations.

Police in Rawalpindi raid the houses of prominent Khaksars. Khaksar materials, including literature, uniforms, and spades, are seized.

Khaksar Salars, Akhtar Hussain and Suramdani, are arrested in Rawalpindi.

Police search the Sheikupura district for Khaksars. 20 Khaksars are arrested.

Police are posted at various locations in Sheikhupura to prevent Khaksars from proceeding to Lahore to join ongoing demonstrations.

Seven Khaksars are produced before the Additional District Magistrate in Multan. Their bail requests are rejected.

1940 March 27

The Tribune, Lahore reports that "there is a likelihood of talks between the Viceroy and the Governors of those provinces in which the Khaksar organisation has made considerable headway..."

Quaid-e-Azam arrives in Delhi from Lahore.
Editor's Comments: Khaksars and public supporters of Khaksars were hoping that Quaid-e-Azam would not leave Lahore until he had settled the issue with Sir Sikandar, but his departure from Lahore brought disappointment.
Dr. Gopichand Bhargava (Leader of the Punjab Assembly Congress Party) and Mian Iftikhar ud Din (President, Punjab Provincial Congress Committee) visit wounded Khaksars in Mayo Hospital in Lahore.

A large number of police are posted at Lahore Railway Station to arrest Khaksars arriving in Lahore. The officials include F.C. Bourne (Deputy Commissioner), Deputy Inspector General of Police, S. Abdul Samad Khan (City Magistrate), and F.H. de'Hume (Principal of Police Training School). The tear gas squad is also present.

26 Khaksars arriving from U.P. are arrested in two batches at Lahore Railway Station. A large crowd gathers and witnesses the arrest of the Khaksars.

A batch of Khaksars is arrested in the morning while marching at Raja Bazaar, Rawalpindi.

Khaksars from the North West Frontier Province demonstrate in Rawalpindi. Nine Khaksars are arrested.

1940 March 28

Inquiry Committee

The Governor of Punjab decides to appoint a committee to conduct an inquiry into the police firing on March 19, 1940. The Committee is to consist of Sir Douglas Young (Chief Justice of the Lahore High Court) and Chaudhry Niamat Ullah (Judge of the Allahabad High Court). D.A.Bryan, I.C.S., is to be the Secretary to the Committee.

The inquiry proceedings are to begin on April 08, 1940 at the Lahore High Court. The Committee will conduct its proceedings in public, however any part of the proceedings may be conducted in private at the discretion of the President. Those who desire to appear as witnesses should apply in writing, however, it is the decision of the Committee to decide what evidence it will hear.

The Committee will ascertain the following facts:
1. How and with what object in spite of the orders contained in Punjab Government notifications Nos. 2415- B. DSB and 2417-B. DSB, dated the 28th February, 1940, a number of Khaksars came to collect in Lahore City on the morning of Tuesday, the 19th March, 1940, and began to march through the City.
2. How the Deputy Commissioner, the Senior Superintendent of Police, the Deputy Superintendent of Police and other Police Officers came to receive injuries and two constables were killed.
3. How the Police came to fire upon the Khaksars and kill and wound a number of them.

The Committee will also report:
    i. Whether the Police were justified in opening fire; and
    ii. Whether the firing was uncontrolled or in excess of the necessities of the situation.

Attempts to Replace Mashriqi

Nawab Bahadur Yar Jang calls a meeting of the Khaksars in Meerut.

Nawab Ismail Khan (M.L.A., President of the U.P. Provincial Muslim League) holds a meeting of the Khaksars at his house in Meerut. The meeting is convened by Nawab Bahadur Yar Jang to choose a successor to Allama Mashriqi. Efforts are made to replace Mashriqi with Nawab Bahadur Yar Jang as the leader of the Khaksar Tehrik. This move to replace Mashriqi is seen as a conspiracy and is highly resented by the Khaksars. The Khaksars refuse to accept anyone other than Allama Mashriqi as their leader. However, they do authorize Nawab Jang to act as an emissary and conduct negotiations with the Punjab Government for the release of Allama Mashriqi and the Khaksars and the removal of the ban on the Khaksar Tehrik. Disappointed at not being appointed the new leader of the Khaksar Tehrik, Nawab Bahadur Yar Jang would leave for Delhi the following morning (March 29, 1940) in order to consult Jinnah.

Editor's Comments: In the Khaksar circle, this was a clear act of conspiracy attempting to hijack the Khaksar Tehrik and bring it under the flag of the Muslim League. This would strengthen the Muslim League's position not only in Punjab but in the entire India, since the Khaksar Tehrik was considered the most well-organized movement in the entire India by this time.

Continued Demonstrations and Arrests

The Chief Secretary of Punjab writes another confidential letter (No. 2096 -2124 CDSB) to all Deputy Commissioners of Punjab instructing them to deal with Khaksar leaders and Janbazs severely, even if they had "ceased to wear the outward emblems of the Khaksar Movement." (Muhammad 1973, 65).

Khaksars continue to do everything in their power to join their fellow Khaksars for the ongoing demonstrations in Lahore. To avoid police arrest on their way to Lahore, Khaksars cross the Indus River above Attock by ferryboat.

The police in Lahore remain on alert and carefully watch all incoming trains for Khaksars. Five more Khaksars arriving from U.P. are arrested at Lahore Railway Station.

Five Khaksars are arrested in Lahore and remanded to police custody.

Khaksars pass through Delhi en route to Punjab.

The group of 26 Khaksars who were arrested at Lahore Railway Station on March 27, 1940 are brought before Lahore Magistrate Mehta Ram Rattan and are remanded to judicial lock-up for 15 days.

The police visit Khaksar houses in a village near Amritsar and force them to either renounce their relationship with the Khaksar Tehrik and surrender their spades and uniforms or face arrest.

In Other News

The Hindustan Times, Delhi reports that out of the 70 Khaksars who were admitted to Mayo Hospital in Lahore as a result of the police firing on March 19, 1940, 11 have died and 33 are still under treatment. According to the newspaper, the others have been discharged.

Begum Shah Nawaz (M.L.A. and Parliamentary Secretary, Punjab Government), accompanied by Begum and Mian Bashir Ahmed (Joint Secretary Muslim League), visit the wounded Khaksars at Mayo Hospital.

The Hindustan Times, Delhi reports that Allama Mashriqi has been transferred from a jail in Delhi to a jail in South India.

1940 March 29

The Tribune, Lahore reports that "the total number of Khaksars arrested so far in Lahore or elsewhere in the province is about 400."
Editor's Comments: The number of Khaksar arrests continued to increase in the coming days.

The Tribune publishes the report of a correspondent stating, "The statements made by some of the Khaksars who have been arrested are understood to point to one of the most daring political conspiracies of recent years in India."
Editor's Comments: It was firmly believed in the Khaksar circle that the arrest of Allama Mashriqi and action against the Khaksar Movement was a result of the intrigue by anti-Khaksar elements to finish the Khaksar Movement.
　　　　Four million Khaksars with centers all across India and in some other countries had become a massive threat to anti-Khaksar elements and the very existence of the rulers. The Britishers were worried of the Khaksars' strength in India especially in light of World War II. The Congress Party feared Muslim domination over Hindus, and the Muslim League feared its own bleak future. The Muslim Leaguers did not want the Khaksar Movement to be involved in politics and wanted its separate identity to be eliminated and brought under the flag of the Muslim League.

Two Khaksars are arrested at Lahore Railway Station.

Two Khaksars from Sind are arrested upon arrival in Lahore.

The Governor of NWFP orders the confiscation of all copies of the Khaksar Tehrik pamphlet entitled *Khitab*.

Nawab Bahadur Yar Jang leaves Meerut for Delhi to consult Quaid-e-Azam.

1940 March 30

The Tribune, Lahore writes an editorial about the Inquiry Committee (to investigate the incident on March 19) appointed by the Governor of Punjab.

Batches of Khaksars continue to leave the North West Frontier Province for Punjab.

1940 March 31

The Tribune, Lahore publishes a constitutionalist's analysis in regards to the Government appointed Inquiry Committee to investigate the March 19th incident. The constitutionalist questions whether the Government can properly "invite a Committee appointed by itself to examine and pronounce a verdict on its [own] administrative policies on any subject."

Nawab Bahadur Yar Jang states that no successor to Allama Mashriqi was chosen at the Khaksar Conference in Meerut on March 28, 1940. He also states that Jinnah is negotiating with the Punjab Government on behalf of the Khaksars and that efforts are being made to obtain Mashriqi's release.

Nine Khaksars from Peshawar are arrested in Rawalpindi.

April

1940 April 01

Khaksars demonstrate in Rawalpindi. 8 Khaksars are arrested.

1940 April 02

The Tribune, Lahore reports that the proposal to appoint Nawab Bahadur Yar Jang as leader of the Khaksar Tehrik (in place of Allama Mashriqi) was vehemently opposed by the majority of those who gathered in Meerut to decide the future of the movement.

1940 April 03

Nawab Bahadur Yar Jang meets Sir Sikandar Hayat Khan.

Mian Abdul Aziz, Bar at Law, writes a letter to Sir Douglas Young (Chief Justice of the Lahore High Court and Head of the Government Inquiry Committee into the March 19th incident), Sir Sikandar Hayat Khan (Punjab Premier), and the Chief Secretary to the Punjab Government. He informs them that the public has appointed a committee with Chairman Mian Abdul Aziz Sahib (M.L.A. Punjab, Bar-at-Law) and other members, K.L. Gauba (M.L.A. Punjab, Bar-at-Law), Maulana Syed

Mohammad Daud Ghaznavi (Amir Jamit Ahli-Hadis, Lahore), and S.M. Habib
(Editor, the daily 'Siyasat' and 'Manshur,' Lahore). The objectives are as follows:
"

1. That the Government should notify, very clearly, that no person will be
   victimised, prosecuted and harassed by the police or any official agency by
   reason of any evidence or disclosure made to the Committee...
2. That the Government should clearly state that no officer connected with the
   incident will be in charge of the investigation. The officers concerned with the
   incident should also be transferred.
3. Adequate opportunity is given for the cross-examination of the witnesses
   appearing before the Committee, and adequate access is permitted to jails and
   the places of detention of the Khaksars, I am desired by the members of the
   Committee to enquire what facilities would the Committee and the Government
   grant in this connection.
4. The terms of enquiry of the Committee appear to be too narrow for a proper
   investigation of the real causes that led to the unfortunate tragedy of 19th March
   and my Committee are prepared to make suggestions in this sense provided the
   Government agree to review the terms." *The Tribune*, Lahore April 05, 1940

Editor's Comments: The public was suspicious of the Inquiry Committee set up by
the Punjab Government as its results could be biased.

1940 April 04

Military troops are called into Lahore to prevent any Khaksar demonstrations.
Editor's Comments: Sir Sikandar Hayat was doing everything in his capacity to
finish the Khaksar Movement.

A Khaksar, Abdulla Shah Zayain, is arrested in Lahore.

1940 April 05

Nawab Bahadur Yar Jang is expected to meet with Quaid-e-Azam in Delhi before
returning to Lahore to see Sir Sikandar Hayat Khan.

Police arrest one Khaksar in Lahore.

A Lahore Magistrate sentences eight Khaksars (arrested in Lahore on March 21,
1940) to three and a half years of imprisonment each. Six more Khaksars are
sentenced to six months of imprisonment each.
Editor's Comments: Long term imprisonment was given to innocent Khaksars.

Police keep a night-long vigil in Lahore to prevent any activities by the Khaksars.
Extensive precautionary measures remain in place, and military troops are called in
to curb any Khaksar activity.

1940 April 07

Police remain vigilant in Lahore and continue to watch Khaksar activities.

1940 April 09

Twelve Khaksars (ten from U.P. and two from Quetta), who were arrested at Lahore Railway Station on March 25, 1940, are sentenced to six months imprisonment each by the Lahore court.

The Statesman, Calcutta reports that "an important meeting of Khaksar leaders from various provinces is being held at Aligarh to consider the future of the movement in the light of the negotiations which took place between a Khaksar leader and the Punjab Government."

1940 April 10

Jinnah returns to Bombay from Delhi.

The Tribune, Lahore, reports that the Khaksars do not feel "optimistic about the immediate withdrawal of the ban on the Khaksars by the Punjab Government."
Editor's Comments: Khaksars were nervous at the lukewarm efforts of the Muslim Leaguers to obtain the release of Mashriqi and the Khaksars as well as the removal of the ban on the Khaksar Movement.

The Inquiry Committee

The Tribune, Lahore reports that the Government Inquiry Committee will begin to record evidence on April 11, 1940. The newspaper also reports that admission into the Courtroom in the High Court will be restricted to those having passes.

Preliminaries regarding the Khaksar-police clash are held by the Inquiry Committee at Lahore High Court. Sir Douglas Young, Chief Justice of the Lahore High Court, conducts the meeting in front of a courtroom packed with members of the Bar.

During the preliminaries at the High Court, K.L. Gauba (Member Punjab Legislative Assembly) informs Sir Douglas Young that a non-official committee had also been appointed to conduct an inquiry into the Khaksar-Police clash. Mr. Gauba states that the non-official committee is willing to cooperate with the Government appointed committee provided that certain conditions are met. One condition is that the Government must not harass or intimidate witnesses. K.L. Gauba states that the communique issued by the Government to this effect is insufficient, but Sir Douglas Young replies that this is the only assurance that the Government can give.
Editor's Comments: The public made an effort to be a part of the Inquiry Committee as they suspected unfair results. The Governments did not accept this offer.

During the preliminaries at the High Court, Syed Mohsin Shah of the Anjuman-i-Islamia states that the Anjuman is willing to provide all possible assistance to the Khaksars in regards to this inquiry and that the Anjuman-i-Islamia has passed a resolution to this effect.

At the preliminaries at the High Court, Dr. Khalifa Shujah ud Din, Mian Abdul Aziz, and Malik Barkat Ali's names are suggested to Sir Douglas Young to represent the Khaksars in the High Court for the Government Inquiry Committee's proceedings.

The Director Information Bureau Punjab issues a communique:
In order that Khaksars may not be deterred from coming forward to give evidence before the Committee that is enquiring into the events of the 19th March by fear of prosecution under Section 17 of the Criminal Law Amendment Act (XIV) of 1908, the Punjab Government guarantee that no person, who is assisting at the enquiry or giving evidence before the Committee, or instructing counsel will be arrested merely because he is a member of the Khaksar Association, provided that he does not wear the Khaksar uniform or carry a belcha or take part in any procession or demonstration.
Editor's Comments: Khaksars and other witnesses were harassed despite this order. As such, this order did not work.

1940 April 11

The police arrest 12 Khaksars in Gurgaon.

The Inquiry Committee

In the morning, members of the Government Inquiry Committee, including Sir Douglas Young, Ch. Niamat ullah, and D.A. Bryan, visit the scene of the police firing on the Khaksars on March 19, 1940. The Advocate General (representing the Punjab Government) and Dr. Khalifa Shuja ud Din (representing the Khaksars) are also present at the scene.

After the visit to the scene of the police firing (on March 19, 1940), the inquiry into the Khaksar-Police clash commences at the Lahore High Court. Entry into the courtroom is highly restricted and police surround the courtroom. The Punjab Government is represented by Mohammad Saleem (Advocate General) and Mohammad Muneer. Dr. Khalifa Shuja ud Din (Bar-at-Law), Mian Abdul Aziz (Bar-at-Law), M.M. Aslam, and others represent the Khaksars. Mohammad Saleem gives a graphic account of the Khaksar-Police clash on March 19, 1940. In the course of his statement, the Advocate General informs the court that Beaty (Deputy Superintendent of Police) ordered the police to fire.

1940 April 15

Sir Sikandar Hayat Khan responds to questions in the Punjab Assembly. He refuses to comment on the negotiations regarding the Khaksar issue. Lala Duni Chand asks, "The practice of the Government has been to catch all poppies. Why has not Nawab Yar Jung been caught. Is it because he is a tall poppy? [laughter]" To this, Sir Sikandar replies, "No, Nawab Yar Jung is a member of the Khaksar movement but he came to the Punjab as a member of the Muslim League." *The Tribune*, Lahore April 16, 1940, *The Star of India*, Calcutta April 16, 1940
Editor's Comments: In the eyes of the public, Nawab Bahadur Yar Jung had not been arrested for being a Khaksar because he was a member of the upper class and the Muslim League. Meanwhile, a large number of Khaksars were being arrested just because they were members of the Movement. Even supporters and sympathizers of the Khaksar Movement were arrested and beaten. The public considered this attitude of the Punjab Government to be discriminatory toward the poor.

A Lahore Magistrate sentences a Khaksar (arrested on April 04, 1940) to six months of rigorous imprisonment for being a member of the Khaksar Tehrik.

A Khaksar is arrested in the evening in Lahore.

The Proceedings of the Inquiry Committee

J.T.M Bennett (Deputy Inspector General of Police, C.I.D.) testifies at the Government Inquiry Committee hearing at the Lahore High Court. In the course of his statement, Bennett informs the court that at the outbreak of World War II, Allama Mashriqi made an offer of 50,000 Khaksars to the British Government (to defend India from foreign aggression). Bennett also states that Beaty (Deputy Superintendent of Police) gave the order to fire on March 19, 1940.

The Tribune, Lahore while covering High Court proceedings writes " ...Among those whom witness [M. Bennett] arrested were two sons of the leader of the Khaksars." *The Tribune*, Lahore April 16, 1940
Editor's Comments: It is sad that the Government did not even spare Mashriqi's family. All this was done to put pressure on Mashriqi to disband the Movement.

At the proceedings at the Lahore High Court, Dr. Khalifa Shuja ud Din cross-examines F.C. Bourne, District Magistrate. F.C. Bourne states in front of the High Court Committee that he had heard of a contemplated march of the Khaksars at about 10:30 am on March 19. Upon hearing this, he had consulted the Premier (Sir Sikandar) and the Chief Secretary *before* the firing began.

At the Lahore High Court, F.C. Bourne also states that he did not see Gainsford being attacked by the Khaksars. He states that in his opinion, the firing was uncontrollable to some extent.

At the proceedings, E.W.C. Wace (D.I.G. Police) testifies that, three or four days prior to the March 19th incident, he had received information that the Khaksars were coming to Lahore and intended to hold a demonstration (against the ban on the Khaksar Tehrik). He also states that immediately after the firing, he telephoned the Inspector General of Police and asked him to call in military troops and reserve police.

1940 April 16

The police are active and maintain a close watch on the Khaksar activities in Lahore. Police fear that the Khaksars will hold demonstrations in the streets of Lahore.

The Punjab Government issues its conditions for removing the ban on the Khaksar Tehrik.

The Government of Punjab issues a communique:
There has been considerable speculation about the attitude of the Punjab Government regarding the rescinding of the order under the Criminal Law Amendment Act, 1908, declaring the Khaksars an unlawful association. The condition on which Government would be prepared to consider the rescission of the order have already been outlined in the Punjab Legislative Assembly, and it is desirable that they should be made clear to the general public. Briefly, Government must be satisfied that —
1.   The Khaksars will do nothing to disturb the public tranquillity or interfere with the maintenance of law and order, and will not attempt to defy the restrictions imposed in Notifications Nos. 24-15-B. DSB. and 2417-B, DSB, dated the 28th February, 1940 on the carrying of arms or articles capable of being used as arms in processions, or on drill of a military character with or without arms.
2.   The Khaksar Association will give satisfactory gurantees that its activities will be confined to lawful pursuits and genuinely social work.
3.   The movement will be under the control and direction of law-abiding and responsible persons.
As an earnest of their 'bonafides' the Khaksars who have come into the Punjab from other Provinces must leave the province, and other Khaksars now assembled in Lahore, Rawalpindi and elsewhere must disperse to their homes. When they have done so and when the Punjab Government are fully satisfied that the three conditions specified above have been fulfilled, the Punjab Government will be prepared to cancel the orders under the Criminal Law Amendement Act, 1908, declaring the Association unlawful.
Editor's Comments: To the Khaksar circle, this communique meant the following:
1.   Khaksars would not take part in politics.
2.   Leadership of the Khaksar Tehrik would go into the hands of the person who, according to the Government, was a law-abiding citizen. In other words, Mashriqi would be removed from the leadership of the Khaksars, and a person acceptable in the eyes of the Government would assume leadership.

The Sind Government denies issuing a circular to local bodies banning their employees from joining the Khaksar Tehrik.

A Khaksar is arrested in Lahore for being a member of the Khaksar Tehrik.

1940 April 17

At the Inquiry Committee's proceedings at the Lahore High Court, P.R.J. Morgan (Superintendent in charge of Additional Police force, Lahore Fort) and Disney (Inspector of Police, Lahore) are examined.

The Khaksar Tehrik is discussed in the Punjab Legislative Assembly. The Parliamentary Secretary states that the Government is taking precautions to ensure that the Khaksars do not participate in unlawful activities. He also states that the Government is considering compensating the family of the police officer who was killed as a result of the Khaksar-Police clash on March 19, 1940.

13 Khaksars are arrested in various parts of Lahore.

Khaksars demonstrate in Lahore. Police and the tear gas squad arrive on the scene. Tear gas bombs are used and five Khaksars are arrested.

Another batch of Khaksars demonstrate in Lahore. Five Khaksars are arrested.

Two more Khaksars are arrested in Lahore.

The Lahore police present the "Challan" of 248 Khaksars arrested soon after the clash on March 19, 1940. The accuseds are brought before the Magistrate in the court.

1940 April 18

The High Court Inquiry into the police firing on the Khaksars on March 19, 1940 resumes. Karam Ilahi, a constable of the Reserve Police Force, testifies that Beaty (Deputy Superintendent of Police) gave the orders to fire on March 19, 1940.

At the Lahore High Court, Inspector Disney testifies that Beaty gave the order to fire. According to Disney, Beaty shouted "Maro, Fire Karo" (Attack and Fire).

Various officials are examined at the Government Inquiry Committee's proceedings at the Lahore High Court.

Sir Sikandar Hayat Khan responds to questions about the Khaksar Tehrik in the Punjab Assembly. Sir Sikandar informs the members of the Assembly that the Khaksars are coming to Lahore to take part in demonstrations and to demand the removal of restrictions on the Khaksar Tehrik. He states that the Punjab Government is taking measures to stop their influx into Lahore.

Heavily armed police are deployed in Lahore and Rawalpindi to disrupt Khaksar demonstrations against the ban on the Tehrik. In Lahore, H.G. Russell (Assistant Inspector General of Police), P.R.J. Morgan (Superintendent of the Additional Police force), and other government officials are on high alert.

18 Khaksars are arrested in Lahore, including Muzaffar Ali, Fazal Hussain, and Ghulam Haider.

Khaksars demonstrate in Lahore. Police, including F.C. Bourne (District Magistrate) and Scroggie (Superintendent of Police), arrive at the scene. Six Khaksars are arrested.

Four other Khaksars are arrested at Ravi Road while entering Lahore.

Another batch of five Khaksars is arrested while demonstrating in Lahore.

Police lathi charge a batch of Khaksars. Five Khaksars are arrested. Police continue to watch the Khaksars in Lahore. Police also place pickets at various places in Lahore.

The police use lathis in a clash near Tibbi Police station in Lahore. They brutally injure two Khaksars, one of whom (Mohammad Kasim from U.P.) dies in the hospital later in the day.

A Lahore Special Magistrate is to conduct the hearing in the case of 248 Khaksars who were arrested in connection with Khaksar-Police clash on March 19, 1940.

15 Khaksars are sentenced to various terms of imprisonment in Rawalpindi. Five of these Khaksars are sentenced to three years of rigorous imprisonment while six others are sentenced to one year of rigorous imprisonment.

Khaksars demonstrate in Rawalpindi. Eight Khaksars are arrested.

A batch of Khaksars is arrested in Rawalpindi.

Two Khaksars are injured by police and are admitted to the hospital. One of them remains in precarious condition.

1940 April 19

The Government Inquiry Committee continues its proceedings at the Lahore High Court. Police witnesses are examined.

Three shopkeepers are examined at the Government Inquiry Committee's proceedings at the Lahore High Court. Thakur Partap Singh (Sub-Inspector of Gowalmandi Police Station) states that all the dead Khaksars had gunshot wounds. The proceedings are adjourned until April 22, 1940.

Barrister Mian Ahmed Shah meets Quaid-e-Azam in Bombay to discuss the ban on the Tehrik and the release of Mashriqi. Jinnah asks Mian Ahmed Shah to bring the Khaksar Tehrik under the Muslim League's flag. Sensing that Jinnah is uninterested in resolving the Khaksar issue with the Punjab Government, Mian Ahmed Shah decides to meet Sir Sikandar Hayat Khan himself.

Editor's Note: According to the book *Region and Partition: Bengal, Punjab and the Partition of the Subcontinent* (page 78), this meeting between Mian Ahmed Shah and Jinnah took place on April 29, 1940. However, according to *Khaksar Tehrik Ki Jiddo Johad Volume 2* (page 68), this meeting took place on April 19, 1940.

Editor's Comments: According to the Khaksars, they were disappointed at Quaid-e-Azam's indifferent attitude. They firmly believed that Quaid-e-Azam was not interested in Mashriqi and Khaksars' release and the removal of the ban. Quaid-e-Azam's only interest lay in bringing the Khaksars under the Muslim League. The Khaksars felt abandoned by the leadership of the Muslim League.

Fearing Khaksar demonstrations, police forces are increased in Lahore. Police remain vigilant throughout Lahore and a tear gas squad is kept ready.

Eight Khaksars are arrested in Lahore.

Two Khaksars, Mohammad Daud and Mustakin, are sentenced to six months imprisonment each in Lahore.

15 Khaksars from the North West Frontier Province are sentenced in Lahore. Five of them are sentenced to three years of rigorous imprisonment each under the Defence of India Act and six months of imprisonment each for being members of the Khaksar Tehrik. The sentences are to run concurrently. Six of the 15 are sentenced to one year of rigorous imprisonment each while the remaining four are released.

Khaksars demonstrate in Rawalpindi. Six Khaksars are arrested.

1940 April 20

Two more Khaksars, who were killed on March 19, 1940, are identified as Kher Muhammad and Hasmat Khan.

Khaksar Sultan Ahmad (from Calcutta, who was arrested at Lahore Railway Station on April 13, 1940) is convicted in Lahore and sentenced to six months of rigorous imprisonment for being a member of the Khaksar Tehrik.

1940 April 21

The Hindustan Times, Delhi reports that the Government has issued a ban in Jammu and Kashmir prohibiting military type drills (with or without arms).

Khaksars hold a demonstration at Dabbi Bazaar in Lahore.

The Additional District Magistrate in Rawalpindi sentences eight Khaksars to various terms of imprisonment. Two of them are sentenced to 18 months of rigorous imprisonment each. Five of the eight are sentenced to nine months and three months of rigorous imprisonment each under different charges. The sentences are to run concurrently. The eighth Khaksar is released.

Two people are arrested in Lyallpur (now Faisalabad) for being members of the Khaksar Tehrik. The Khaksar flags are also removed from their shops.

1940 April 22

Police Officer D. Gainsford (the Senior Superintendent of Police), who was involved in the Khaksar-Police clash on March 19, 1940, leaves for England.

The Lahore High Court proceedings resume, and several police witnesses are cross-examined. Fazal Hussain Shah (Foot Constable, Additional Police) informs the court that he heard Beaty order the police to fire on March 19, 1940.

The Khaksar counsel, Dr. Khalifa Shuja ud Din, states that Beaty (Deputy Superintendent of Police) fired his revolver at the Khaksars before the Khaksars advanced on him.

The Premier of Punjab, Sir Sikandar Hayat Khan, informs the Punjab Assembly that 695 Khaksars (349 of whom were from other provinces) have been arrested thus far (since March 19, 1940).

81 of the 695 arrested Khaksars have been convicted.

A Khaksar leader, Mohammad Sadiq, is arrested in Lahore.

Three Khaksars, Karim Bux, Faqir Mohammad, and Fazal Din, are convicted in Lahore and are sentenced to six months rigorous imprisonment each.

Khaksar Muhammad Shafi Kashmiri from Gujranwala is arrested in Lahore.

Police prevent Lahore Khaksars from demonstrating in Amritsar.

1940 April 23

The Inquiry Committee proceedings continue at the Lahore High Court. Police witnesses are cross-examined by Dr. Khalifa Shuja ud Din.

Women Khaksars demonstrate in Lahore. A large crowd gathers to watch the demonstration.

One Khaksar is arrested in Lahore.

The Special Magistrate in Lahore sentences six Khaksars to six months of rigorous imprisonment each for being members of the Khaksar Tehrik.

A Khaksar, Barkat Ali, is produced before the Special Magistrate and the court remands him until April 26, 1940.

Two Khaksars are convicted by the Additional District Magistrate in Campbellpur and are sentenced to six months and four months of rigorous imprisonment respectively.

The Isar Kareemi Press and the Saleemi Press are searched for allegedly publishing leaflets related to the Khaksar Tehrik. The printer of Isar Kareemi Press is arrested.

1940 April 24

The Government Inquiry Committee continues its proceedings at the Lahore High Court. Police witnesses are examined. Khan Sahib Khan Bahadur (Inspector, Provincial Additional Police) states that he had fired in the direction of Iqbal Manzil. A *Moharir* of the district police produces a register showing that 1,620 rounds were issued on March 19, 1940 to the police force under Beaty and 1,213 were returned.
Editor's Comments: The number of rounds fired was significantly higher than the number of dead announced by the Government. Thus, the actual number of dead was much higher than the Government had declared.

The Punjab and the Delhi Governments forfeit Allama Mashriqi's funds.
Editor's Comments: It is sad that the Government forfeited Mashriqi's funds and brought Mashriqi's family to the point of starvation. Mashriqi's son, Ehsanullah Khan Aslam was badly injured by the police on March 19, 1940 during the raid on the Khaksar headquarters in Ichhra, Lahore. Unfortunately, he could not get proper healthcare due to the family's lack of funds, and he died on May 31, 1940.

Khaksars parade in Anarkali, Lahore. Armed police and the District Magistrate arrive immediately. Police do not allow a Khaksar leader to address the public, but he manages to do so anyways. Nine Khaksars are arrested.

Six Khaksars are convicted in Lahore and sentenced to 18 months of rigorous imprisonment each.

The Special Magistrate in Lahore sentences five Khaksars (who were arrested on April 19, 1940) to 18 months of rigorous imprisonment each for taking part in drills and six months of rigorous imprisonment each for being members of the Khaksar Tehrik. The sentences are to run concurrently.

1940 April 25

The Government Inquiry Committee continues its proceedings at the Lahore High Court. F.C. Bourne (District Magistrate) and others are examined. Inayat Khan, a resident of Iqbal Manzil Tibbi Bazaar (a location that was near the place of the firing on March 19, 1940), testifies that after the firing began, some Khaksars took shelter in his building. According to Inayat Khan, police broke open the doors to the building, and he then heard three or four shots fired. He further states that he found bullet marks on the ground floor in the veranda and in a bathroom.

Khaksars parade in Lahore.

Another batch of six Khaksars parades in Dabbi Bazaar, Lahore.

A batch of six Khaksars is arrested near Tibbi Police Station in Lahore.

Additional police are posted in Gujrat to prevent Khaksar demonstrations.

1940 April 26

The Government Inquiry Committee concludes its examination of Government witnesses at the Lahore High Court. Lieutenant Colonel Ross Stewart (Civil Surgeon, Lahore) states that when a medical board examined Gainsford (Senior Superintendent of Police) on April 01, 1940, he was in fit condition to make a statement. Dr. C.F.H. Quick (Assistant Civil Surgeon) testifies that he did not perform a post-mortem examination on Khaksars killed on March 19, 1940 because he was not directed to do so. During cross-examination, Dr. Quick informs the court that a post-mortem examination cannot be held unless asked by the police. He states that he did perform a post-mortem examination for two police constables that were killed. The Inquiry Committee proceedings are adjourned until May 6, 1940.
Editor's Comments: Why wasn't a post-mortem ordered for all the Khaksars who were killed on March 19, 1940?

Police pickets in Lahore are strengthened in order to watch Khaksar activities. Khaksars parade in the streets of Lahore. The police follow the Khaksars around the city.

Khaksars demonstrate in Lahore. Six Khaksars are arrested.

17 Khaksars are sentenced in Rawalpindi. The sentences range from six months to three years.

1940 April 27

Khaksars hold a demonstration in Jallalpur Jattan near Gujrat and are arrested by the Superintendent of Police.

Abdul Rahman and four other Khaksars from U.P., who were arrested on April 18, 1940, appear in the court of the Special Magistrate in Lahore.

Bulaqi and five other Khaksars from Lucknow, who were arrested on April 25, 1940, are produced before the Special Magistrate in Lahore.

1940 April 28

A public meeting is held where people voice their concerns in regards to the manner in which police have been arresting Khaksars. *The Tribune* of April 30, 1940 would write:

"Unruly scenes were once again witnessed in a largely attended public meeting of the Muslims of Amritsar held last night in Khair Din's mosque, in order to lodge a vigorous protest against the manner of arrest of Khaksars made here yesterday...

At the outset a resolution deploring the manner in which the police had at first dragged the Khaksars from inside the mosque and then effected their arrests outside was passed."

Editor's Comments: Public sympathies remained with the Khaksars. The Khaksars were disciplined to remain patient and to not be hostile. Despite the fact that they were treated brutally at many instances, the Khaksars always upheld their principles.

Police keep an all night vigil in Amritsar to prevent Khaksars from demonstrating. Seven Khaksars (six from Lahore and one from Amritsar) are arrested.

Khaksars demonstrate in Lahore. Six Khaksars are arrested in Lahore. A large crowd gathers to witness the scene.

1940 April 29

The Khaksar activities are discussed in the Punjab Assembly. Adjournment Motion about the Khaksar demonstrations is ruled out.

The Khaksars hold a demonstration in Lahore.

In Amritsar, police search for Khaksars who had arrived from Lahore.

The seven Khaksars, who were arrested in Amritsar on April 28, 1940, are brought before the Additional District Magistrate.

Six Khaksars, who were arrested in Rawalpindi, are sentenced by the Additional District Magistrate in Rawalpindi to terms of imprisonment ranging from one year to three years of rigorous imprisonment.

1940 April 30

The Tribune, Lahore reports that Muslim members of the Punjab Legislative Assembly who sympathize with the Khaksars are to meet Sir Sikandar Hayat Khan to settle differences between the Khaksars and the Punjab Government. *The Tribune* writes, "Sheikh Sadiq Hassan, a prominent Khaksar Unionist member... says that he and over half a dozen other members [of Punjab Assembly] who believe that the Khaksars are a sincere class of people and would like to come to some sort of honourable settlement, are meeting the Premier at 3.30 p.m. tomorrow with a view to exploring ways and means to end the present impasse."

25 members of the Punjab Legislative Assembly meet Sir Sikandar Hayat Khan to bring a settlement between the Khaksars and the Punjab Government.

Khaksars take shelter in mosques in Jullunder. A police picket is placed outside one of the mosques. Police watch Khaksar activities closely in Jullundur and arrest one person for helping the Khaksars.

Khaksars demonstrate in Lahore. Five Khaksars are arrested after police refuse to let a Khaksar leader make a speech. Two other batches of Khaksars evade arrest in Lahore.

Police arrest one person for helping the Khaksars in Lahore.

Three supporters of the Khaksars are arrested in Lahore.

Ajaz (a Khaksar) and five other Khaksars (who were arrested on April 28, 1940) are produced before the Special Magistrate, who remands them to police custody for four days.

248 Khaksars are remanded for 15 days by the Special Magistrate.

May

1940 May 01

In the court of the Special Magistrate in Lahore, Barrister M.M. Aslam presents an application on behalf of the 248 Khaksars. The application requests that the counsel for Khaksars standing trial be engaged at the Government's expense and also that any documents to which the accused are entitled (statements of witnesses, copies of evidence before the Inquiry Committee, etc.) should be provided free of charge. It also requests better class of treatment for imprisoned Khaksars. The Special Magistrate promises to forward the application to the Government.

Four members of the Punjab Legislative Assembly, Sh. Sadiq Hasan, Khawaja Abdus Samad, Ch. Sahibdad Khan, and Ch. Shafaat Ali (who were a part of the deputation that met with Sir Sikandar Hayat Khan on April 30, 1940) meet with

Khaksars leaders at Golden Mosque, Lahore. They are trying to bring a settlement between the Khaksars and the Government of Punjab. The Khaksars inform the deputation that only Allama Mashriqi has the power to settle terms with the Government.

Khaksars intensify their activities and hold demonstrations in Lahore. 21 people are arrested; this includes four non-Khaksars who are arrested in Old Anarkali, Lahore, while bringing food for the Khaksars.

Khaksars demonstrate at Circular Road, Lahore. Eight Khaksars are arrested.

Khaksars demonstrate at Anarkali, Lahore.

Khaksars demonstrate at Kashmiri Bazar, Lahore. Six Khaksars are arrested.

Armed police are posted outside mosques in Lahore to arrest Khaksars as soon as they come out.

Four people are arrested in Lahore for supplying food to the Khaksars.

Five more Khaksars are arrested in Lahore at Katra Dulo Mosque. Police also confiscate their spades and uniforms.

A Khaksar is arrested outside a mosque at Yakki Gate, Lahore.

In Lahore, Muslims raise slogans against the Unionist Ministry. Three people are arrested.

There is an influx of Khaksars into Amritsar. Three Khaksars are arrested outside a mosque in Amritsar.

Khaksars plan to hold demonstrations in Amritsar. The police arrest 15 Khaksars in an attempt to prevent these demonstrations.

Three Khaksars are arrested at Lohgarh Gate in Amritsar.

16 local persons are arrested in Amritsar for helping the Khaksars.

Khaksars hold a demonstration in Lyallpur and a large number of people gather to watch the demonstration.

Khaksars hold a demonstration in Jullunder.

Two Khaksars, Dr. M. B. Mirza and Mushtaq Ahmad, are released on bail for Rs. 2,000 each.

Three supporters of the Khaksars (who were arrested on April 30, 1940) are remanded to judicial lock-up until May 09, 1940.

Four Khaksars (who were arrested in Shahdara, near Lahore) are tried in the court; the court reserves judgment.

1940 May 02

Prominent Frontier Khaksar leader, Mian Ahmed Shah (Bar at Law), leaves Bombay for Lahore in response to a telegram from Sir Sikandar Hayat Khan inviting him for a meeting.

Public provides support and is sympathetic to the Khaksars.

The Government considers imposing additional taxes on the inhabitants of areas providing shelter to the Khaksars.

Armed police pickets are posted in Lahore in light of the intensified activities of the Khaksars. The general public protests this measure taken by the police.

Police guard all mosques where Khaksars continue to take shelter.

Women help Khaksars taking shelter in mosques by providing them with food. The women hide the food in their burqas to bypass the police. Police consider employing women to check the activities of women in burqas.

A Muslim youth is arrested for attempting to take food for Khaksars in Golden Mosque.

A number of boys in Lahore hold a mock funeral procession in support of the Khaksars. The boys scream "Khaksar Zindabad" and chant anti-Police and anti-Punjab Ministry slogans. The police maintain a close watch over the demonstration.

Manzoor Elahi, a Khaksar, is arrested while securing signatures from the public in support of the Khaksars.

Khaksars again hold demonstrations in Lahore. Five Khaksars are arrested.

Nine Khaksars (who were arrested while parading in Anarkali Bazaar, Lahore) are put on trial in the court of the Special Magistrate in Lahore.

Three Khaksars are arrested in Lahore.

13 Khaksars (who were arrested on May 01, 1940) are remanded to police custody by the City Magistrate of Lahore.

The Special Magistrate in Lahore sentences a Khaksar (arrested on April 30, 1940) to six months of hard labor.

A Khaksar, Mohammad Alam, is convicted in Lahore.

Three Khaksars are sent to jail after being discharged from Mayo Hospital in Lahore. The Khaksars had been injured during the police firing on March 19, 1940.

Five Khaksars (who were injured on March 19, 1940) remain under treatment at Mayo Hospital.

The Tribune, Lahore reports that 16 supporters of the Khaksars have been arrested in Amritsar.

18 Khaksars (who were arrested on May 01, 1940) led by Mir Manzoor Mehmood Wali (Naib Hakim-i-Ala of the Khaksars in the Districts of Amritsar and Lahore), are produced in the court of the Additional District Magistrate in Amritsar. An application is filed on behalf of Mir Manzoor Mehmood Wali and Abdur Rehman Ghaznavi demanding better class treatment in jail. The 18 Khaksars are remanded to police custody until May 16, 1940.

Khaksars hold a demonstration in Lyallpur (now Faisalabad). Three Khaksars are arrested.

1940 May 03

Nawab Sir Shah Nawaz Khan of Mamdot, President of the Punjab Muslim League, pays warm tributes to the sincerity of Sir Sikandar Hayat Khan and asks the Khaksars to have full confidence in the Judicial Committee appointed by the Punjab Government to conduct the inquiry into the firing on the Khaksars on March 19, 1940.
Editor's Comments: The statement of Nawab Sir Shah Nawaz Khan disappointed the Khaksars.

Nawab Bahadur Yar Jang of Hyderabad addresses a meeting of Muslims. The meeting is held under the auspices of the District Muslim League. According to *The Hindustan Times*, Delhi of May 06, 1940, Nawab Bahadur Yar Jang "said that the Muslim League and the Khaksars were inseparable parts of the Muslim body. The former was their political institution and the latter their militia, and the co-existance of both was essential for the progress and prosperity of the Muslims of India."
Editor's Comments: Efforts to bring the Khaksar Tehrik under the umbrella of the Muslim League continued.

The Punjab Government issues a warning that if the Khaksars taking shelter in mosques do not surrender within three days, police will commandeer houses and shops near the mosques. Residents of these areas are also warned that anyone supplying food to the Khaksars may be prosecuted.

Editor's Comments: This was done to harass and prevent the public from supporting the Khaksars.

In Lahore, the City Kotwal issues an order to inhabitants in the vicinity of those mosques where the Khaksars are taking shelter. The order states that these inhabitants may be made to vacate their houses if the Khaksars do not leave the mosques within three days. Posters stating this are placed on walls around these neighborhoods.

Armed police are posted outside Niveen mosque and inside Ekki Gate in Lahore.

Police stationed outside mosques are instructed to fire if necessary.

The Punjab Government decides to employ women police to check veiled women who take food supplies to Khaksars in mosques. The female police are to be posted outside various mosques in Lahore where the Khaksars are taking shelter.
Editor's Comments: Prior to the Khaksar tragedy, females were not part of the police force.

Buses proceeding to Lahore are searched for Khaksars.

Khaksars hold a demonstration in Lahore. Eight Khaksars, seven of whom are from Gujranwala, are arrested.

Khaksars hold another demonstration in the afternoon in Lahore. Police order the Khaksars to surrender, but they refuse. Seven Khaksars are arrested.

A Khaksar is arrested under the Criminal Law Amendment Act for carrying clothes to fellow Khaksars in Golden Mosque, Lahore.

Police wait outside mosques to arrest Khaksars. In the afternoon, a Khaksar is arrested as soon as he emerges from Golden Mosque in Lahore.

In all, 19 arrests are made in Lahore on this day in connection with the Khaksar issue.

35 Muslims are "challaned" for sympathizing with the Khaksars. These Muslims are accused of raising slogans in favor of the Khaksars and denouncing the police and the Punjab Government.
Editor's Comments: The Government was even suppressing supporters of the Khaksar Tehrik.

Five Khaksars are put on trial in the court of the Special Magistrate in Lahore. The Khaksars' names are Hushmatullah Khan, Mohammad Yousaf, Shaukat Ali, Maqbool Beg, and Mohammad Dastgir. At the trial, a Police Sub-Inspector and two other witnesses (on behalf of the police) record their statements.

Khaksars gather at Jalalpur Jattan near Gujrat; police fear a demonstration and a Magistrate of Gujrat rushes to the area.

Eight Khaksars are arrested at Jalalpur Jattan.

1940 May 04

Some prominent Muslims, including K.L. Gauba (M.L.A.) and Begum Rashida Latif (M.L.A.), meet Khaksars in Lahore to discuss the prevailing situation. They also meet with police officers.

Begum Rashida Latif brings food for Khaksars taking shelter in a mosque in Lahore, but police do not allow her to deliver the food.

Police expand their activities and recruit more members in order to meet intensified Khaksar activities in Lahore. Armed police guard mosques in Lahore where the Khaksars are stationed. Police also install wire fences in front of mosques to control the activities of Khaksars taking shelter inside the mosques. Female police manhandle women bringing food for the Khaksars in the mosques.

Four women sympathizers of the Khaksars are arrested while bringing food for the Khaksars at the Golden Mosque in Lahore. People attempt to rescue the women from the police, but the police hit the rescuers with "lathis" and injure some of them.
Editor's Comments: The Government continued to crush the supporters of the Khaksar Tehrik, even if the Khaksars were to die of hunger. Even women were not spared.

At the Golden Mosque, police reinforcements arrive. Shops in the area remain closed.

Three women are detained by police at Unchi Mosque in Lahore. The women are accused of taking food for Khaksars inside the mosque.

One Khaksar is arrested in the morning in Lahore.

Seven more people are arrested in Lahore in connection with the Khaksar issue:
1. Two people are accused of possessing Khaksar literature.
2. One person is arrested for shouting slogans against the Punjab Government and the police.
3. Two others are arrested for taking food for the Khaksars.
4. Another person is arrested after an altercation with a police officer.
5. One woman is arrested for supporting the Khaksars.

Another Khaksar is taken into custody in Lahore after being discharged from Mayo Hospital (after recovering from injuries he sustained during the police firing on

March 19, 1940). Some Khaksars (who were injured on March 19, 1940) still remain in the hospital.

A deputation of shopkeepers protests the Government's warning (of May 03, 1940) to people living near mosques where the Khaksars are taking shelter. According to the warning, police can commandeer their houses or shops to prevent Khaksar demonstrations. The City Magistrate advises the shopkeepers not to help the Khaksars.

The bail application of a Khaksar is rejected in Lahore.

The Special Magistrate in Lahore sentences a Khaksar (who was arrested on April 23, 1940) to six months of hard labor.

The evidence of two constables is recorded in a case against five Khaksars in the court of the Special Magistrate in Lahore.

Ghulam Haider, a Khaksar from Agra, is sentenced to six months of rigorous imprisonment by the Special Magistrate in Lahore.

Khaksars demonstrate in Jullundur. Eight Khaksars are arrested and produced before the City Magistrate, who sends them to judicial lock-up.

1940 May 05

The Tribune, Lahore reports that according to orders issued by the Sind Government three years ago, Government servants in Sind are not allowed to join the Khaksar Tehrik.

The NWFP Government considers banning the Khaksars from leaving the NWFP province for Punjab. Those attempting to leave will be arrested. The ban is likely to begin on this day or on May 06, 1940.

Police intensify their blockade of mosques in Lahore in order to force the Khaksars to surrender. Police pickets are reinforced and barbed wire is placed at the approaches to mosques where Khaksars are taking shelter. Police search everyone entering the mosques to ensure that no food deliveries are made to the Khaksars. One Muslim supporter is arrested and Khaksar pledges are found in his possession. Shops remain closed in the area.
Editor's Comments: The Government hurled against supporters of the Khaksar Tehrik and did not care that the Khaksars might die of hunger.

Barrister Mian Ahmed Shah meets with Sir Sikandar Hayat Khan and presents the following demands:
1. Release Allama Mashriqi.
2. Release all imprisoned Khaksars.
3. Return transferred and non-transferred property to the Khaksar Tehrik.

4. Compensate the families of the Khaksars who were killed.
5. Remove the ban on the Khaksar Tehrik.
Sir Sikandar immediately rejects these demands.

1940 May 06

The Government Inquiry Committee resumes its hearings (regarding the police firing on March 19, 1940) at the Lahore High Court. Dr. Khalifa Shuja ud Din (Bar-at-Law, Counsel for the Khaksars) complains that Khaksar and non-Khaksar witnesses are being harassed. Dr. Khalifa Shuja ud Din alleges that anyone who takes interest in the Khaksars is being falsely involved in criminal cases, thus making it difficult to produce evidence.

Dr. Khalifa Shuja ud Din informs the Lahore High Court that he has met the Khaksars in Lahore Central Jail, Borstal Jail, and Mayo Hospital. He further informs the court that there were Khaksars who would have been willing to testify in court. However, they feel that the Government Inquiry is not only biased, but also that their testimonies would be used to implicate them in criminal court hearings. Dr. Khalifa Shuja ud Din further informs the court that the concerns of the Khaksars are genuine because some people who assisted in collecting evidence are being implicated in criminal cases.

Later, Dr. Mohammad Ayub is examined in court. Dr. Ayub Khan (Medical Officer of the Multan Central Jail) records his statement about the Khaksar-Police clash on March 19, 1940:
    "Witness [Dr. Mohammad Ayub]...drove to Hiramandi where he found the dead and wounded Khaksars scattered in the street. He saw one dead Khaksar in a drain...he heard a gun shot which was fired from the road into a window of a house [where some Khaksars had gone to take shelter from police fire]. The shot was fired immediately after a European officer had pointed towards the window. Immediately after the shot had been fired a *belcha* [spade] was dropped on the road from the window. Some policemen then climbed up the six-feet-high balcony of the house and from there threw down the Khaksars in the street. Later the police broke open the doors of the house and brought out about half a dozen wounded Khaksars. One of them died immediately afterwards. Those who were brought out had gunshot wounds...
    Proceeding, witness [Dr. Mohammad Ayub] said that some of the Khaksars, who were brought out from the house, were given a beating." *The Hindustan Times*, Delhi May 07, 1940
    Witness [Dr. Mohammad Ayub] says, "When I was in Spain I did not see such cruelty. I told Dr. Quick that it was brutal and dreadful." *The Tribune*, Lahore May 07, 1940

On May 07, 1940, the Inquiry Committee is to visit the scene of the occurrence.

Editor's Comments: Khaksars continued to be harassed. The statements of the witnesses reflect the cruelty that was inflicted on the Khaksars.

The trial of six Khaksars (who were arrested on April 25, 1940) is held in the court of the Special Magistrate in Lahore. The Police Sub-Inspector and Assistant Sub-Inspector testify in court. The six Khaksars are sentenced in Lahore to two years of rigorous imprisonment each.

In Lahore, two Khaksars are sentenced to six months of rigorous imprisonment each.

Eight Khaksars are put on trial in the court of the Special Magistrate.

13 Khaksars are produced before the Additional District Magistrate in Lahore.

Sympathizers of the Khaksars are arrested. Mohammad Saeed is arrested in Lahore for delivering food to the Khaksars taking shelter in mosques. He had tied loaves of bread around his legs to hide them from the police, but the police found them while searching him.
Editor's Comments: Just mere sympathy with Allama Mashriqi or the Khaksars had even become a crime.

The Khaksars demonstrate in Lahore.

Khaksars take shelter in another mosque in Lahore. Police pickets are posted outside the mosque.

Police maintain their blockade around three mosques in Lahore where the Khaksars are taking shelter.

1940 May 07

Sir Douglas Young and Ch. Niamat Ullah (Judges of the Government Inquiry into the Khaksar-police clash) — accompanied by Dr. Khalifa Shuja ud Din, Dr. Ayub Khan (witness), the Assistant Advocate General, and others — visit the scene of the firing. Dr. Ayub points out the balcony from which the Khaksars were thrown down. He also points out the Iqbal Manzil, from where the Khaksars were dragged out by the police.

Sir Douglas Young, Chief Justice and Head of the Government Inquiry Committee, laments the reluctance of witnesses to step forward and give evidence in the Lahore High Court.

The Government Inquiry Committee hears more evidence at the Lahore High Court. Malik Barkat Ali, Member Legislative Assembly, is examined in court. *The Tribune*, Lahore would write on May 08, 1940:
"Proceeding Malik Barkat Ali said that he had been on the spot on March 21…He went to Iqbal Manzil. There he saw a foot mark on the floor and it was nothing but blood. He then went to the courtyard which was besmeared with blood.

He went inside the room where he was shown bullet marks…He stated that he also went upstairs and saw patches of blood in the staircase. Then he went to the fuel shop close to which he saw a pool of blood. He also paid a visit to the shop of Shambhoo Nath and Jagan Nath, where the latter showed him bullet marks of six shots on the wall and four or five shots on the 'prats' (big brass plates)…Jagan Nath further told the witness [Malik Barkat Ali] that when firing ceased ten Khaksars were arrested by the police and he [Jagan Nath] actually saw five corpses of Khaksars lying inside the shop…He [Malik Barkat Ali] was then led to the shop of a milk-vendor, Milkhi Ram by name and shown bullet marks on the projection and walls.

He [Malik Barkat Ali] was taken to another place and shown bullet marks."

Police are posted near Attock border in NWFP to prevent any Khaksars from proceeding to Punjab to participate in demonstrations. Seven Khaksars have already been arrested under this order.

Editor's Comments: The Government made more arrangements to prevent entry of the Khaksars into Punjab. The Khaksars were trying to join their brothers for ongoing demonstrations for the release of Mashriqi and the Khaksars and removal of the ban on the Tehrik.

Islamia College students hold demonstrations and deliver food to Khaksars in mosques. They are arrested near Golden Mosque in Lahore.

Police submit a proposal to commandeer houses near three major mosques in Lahore where the Khaksars are taking shelter.

1940 May 08

A delegation of 70 leading Muslims of Lahore meets with Sir Sikandar Hayat Khan (Premier of Punjab) and urges him to remove the restrictions on taking food to the Khaksars in mosques. The delegation also asks the Premier to remove the barricades outside the mosques. The Nawab also attends the meeting. From the government side, the attendees include Major Khizar Hayat Khan and Mian Abdul Haye (both Ministers of the Punjab Government).

Khaksars parade in Lahore despite the ban.

Khaksars hold another demonstration in Lahore. Police maintain a close watch over mosques where the Khaksars are residing.

One Khaksar is arrested outside Golden Mosque in Lahore.

People attempt to throw food to the Khaksars from a house adjacent to Golden Mosque in Lahore, but the food falls short and is seized by the police.

Khaksars proceeding to Lahore are detained by police at Latambar.

Police remove the barbed wire entanglements that were placed around mosques in Lahore where the Khaksars are taking shelter.

The Government Inquiry Committee continues its proceedings at the Lahore High Court. A 16 year-old boy, one of the victims of the police firing on March 19, 1940, describes the happenings of that day. According to him, Khaksars who took shelter in a house were brought out and pushed over the balcony to the ground. The Judge asks the boy, "Were they [Khaksars] thrown gently or otherwise?" The boy replies, "You can judge for yourself." The boy further states that he heard reports of four or five shots in Iqbal Manzil where some Khaksars were taking shelter. The wounded Khaksars were brought out a few minutes later. *The Hindustan Times*, Delhi May 09, 1940

Quaid-e-Azam issues a statement:
"I have received numerous telegrams from influential persons from various parts of India and in particular from the Punjab during the last few days urging me to go to Lahore at once and negotiate with the Punjab Government a settlement regarding the Khaksar trouble.

I wish to inform the public and the Muslim Leaguers specially that I have no authority or power given to me by the Khaksar organisation or those who are the leaders now and guiding the movement. I have spoken to many of them, who came to see me, but none can speak with authority or give me the authority to bring about a just and honourable settlement with the Government.

The Muslim League at Lahore had to deal with the situation purely from the point of view and on the basis that Khaksars being a mainly Muslim organisation it was incumbent upon us to see that full justice was done to them and that the Punjab Government dealt with them fairly and justly. But the organisation has not so far cared to take the fullest advantage of our services, as they have acted and are acting independently of the Muslim League.

In order to refresh the public memory as to what the exact position was before the sessions of the Muslim League at Lahore, may I point out shortly that there were four questions raised:-
(1) The ban on Khaksar activities of a military and semi-military character which was already imposed upon them by the Punjab Government.
(2) The defiance of this ban, which was going on.
(3) The unfortunate clash between the Khaksars and the police culminating in the firing upon them, which resulted in a terrible loss of life and injuries on March 19, 1940.
(4) Order declaring the Khaksar organisation unlawful.
The Muslim League session by its resolution urged upon the Government to appoint an impartial and independent tribunal to enquire into the firing and the cause which led to the clash, which resulted in terrible blood shed. That enquiry is going on. The Muslim League also called upon the Government to withdraw the order by which the Khaksar organisation was declared unlawful as soon as possible. In the meantime it was expected that the Khaksars would cease the defiance of the ban and observe peace to enable us to examine the terms of the ban, which was directed against their alleged military or semi-military activities.

According to the declared creed of the Khaksars it was urged and pointed out, their aims and objects were religious and social service and hence any misunderstanding or apprehension on the part of the Government should be removed. But after the Lahore resolution was passed, it was difficult to find anyone on behalf of the Khaksars, who could either control or guide their members and give me the requisite authority and power to negotiate with the Government. On the contrary, the defiance of law and order continued and this has led to the situation getting from bad to worse.

I must point out that the Khaksar organisation is entirely independent of the Muslim League and it has no connection with it. The Muslim League cannot do anything in the matter as we have no control or supervision over the activities of the organisation nor have we got any authority or power to speak on their behalf and come to a settlement which would be implemented or fully carried out and adhered to.

In these circumstances with all my sympathies for the Khaksar organisation I feel helpless in the matter." *The Star of India*, Calcutta May 10, 1940 **Editor's Comments:** Quaid-e-Azam had not taken any concrete steps since the Muslim League passed a resolution on the Khaksar issue on March 24, 1940. As a result of this, Jinnah faced a lot of pressure from a large number of people, including influential personalities, from all across India to address the Khaksar issue. Quaid-e-Azam made this statement that sent shockwaves in the Khaksar circle. The Khaksars were highly disappointed in Quaid-e-Azam, and they felt that he was trying to avoid providing assistance to them on the pretext that he had not been given legal authority to intervene. The Khaksars felt that Jinnah could have helped them if he had really wanted to, and that he did not require any authority for helping out the Khaksars. At this point, almost one and a half months had passed since the Khaksars and all Muslims had desperately looked to Jinnah to resolve the Khaksar issue. That was when the Muslim League had passed a resolution (on March 24, 1940) that they would not rest until justice was done for the Khaksars. Despite this, no advancements had been made that would remedy the grievances of the Khaksar families whose loved ones had been killed, bring about the release of Mashriqi and the Khaksars under detention, or remove the ban on the Khaksars.

1940 May 09

Khaksars meet in Unchi Mosque in Lahore to discuss the current situation.

A number of Muslim leaders meet with Khaksar Salars in Lahore in an attempt to bring about a settlement between the Khaksars and the Government. The leaders include Maulana Zafar Ali (Member Legislative Assembly, Central) and Begum Rashida Latif (Member Legislative Assembly, Punjab). The Khaksars inform the Muslim leaders that they can only abandon their demonstrations and parades if they are advised to do so by Allama Mashriqi.

Maulana Zafar Ali (Member Legislative Assembly, Central) visits the Khaksars in Golden Mosque, Lahore. Maulana Zafar Ali informs the Khaksars that he sympathizes with them and would like to announce on the Khaksars' behalf that they would remain peaceful. The Khaksars ask him to march with them, but he refuses. The Maulana wants to make a speech, but the Khaksars do not allow him to do so.

A large number of men and women continue to bring food for the Khaksars who are taking shelter in mosques.

Editor's Comments: No effort from the Government stopped the public from helping the Khaksars. In fact sympathy for the Khaksars continued to grow.

The Special Magistrate frames charges against 47 Khaksars in Lahore who had been arrested on March 19, 1940 at the Khaksar headquarters.

The Lahore Magistrate sentences six Khaksars (for parading) to two years of rigorous imprisonment each for the first charge, six months under the second charge, and three months under the third charge. The sentences would run concurrently.

Khaksars parade in Lyallpur (now Faisalabad). Three Khaksars are arrested.

The Government is facing financial burdens in order to maintain peace. This is causing grave concern within the Government.

The Inquiry Committee

The Government Inquiry Committee resumes its hearings at the Lahore High Court. Dr. Khalifa Shuja ud Din informs the court that the Chief Justice's statement that witnesses should not be afraid seems to have motivated and encouraged some witnesses to come forward.

Dr. Khalifa Shuja ud Din also suggests to the Chief Justice that a letter be sent to Allama Mashriqi (in jail) inquiring whether Mashriqi permitted the demonstration by the Khaksars in Lahore on March 19, 1940. The court is informed that Allama Mashriqi is in Vellore Fort in Madras, and the Chief Justice decides to send a questionnaire to Allama Mashriqi. The Advocate General also wants to hear directly from Allama Mashriqi regarding this matter. The Inquiry Committee asks both Dr. Khalifa Shuja ud Din and the Advocate General to frame questions to be sent to Allama Mashriqi in jail.

The Inquiry Committee also examines three more witnesses.

First Witness on May 09, 1940
        One witness, Hafiz Mehar ud Din, states that he saw a Khaksar being dragged by a constable like a dead dog. He saw another Khaksar being dragged by two constables. He further describes how Khaksars taking shelter were brought out and beaten by the police. According to him, there were 30 or 40 dead or wounded Khaksars lying on the road near Iqbal Manzil. *The Hindustan Times*, Delhi of May 10, 1940 would report that Hafiz Mehar ud Din stated that "A Khaksar, who was

lying wounded, asked a police constable to give him a little water. The constable gave him an orange and while the Khaksar was putting his hand in his pocket to pay for the orange another constable of the additional police hit him on his head with the butt end of his rifle.

The Khaksar became unconscious and the orange dropped on the ground. Witness [Hafiz Mehar ud Din] then saw two wounded Khaksars being pushed down [by the police] from the balcony of house. When they fell down the police dealt them with lathi."

Second Witness on May 09, 1940

The Hindustan Times, Delhi of May 10, 1940 would report that another witness, Hafiz Feroze ud Din, stated that "The police were pursuing them [the Khaksars] and shooting them. At a water tap, six Khaksars with gunshot wounds were lying.

Witness further noticed some policemen firing into a sugar shop from where five or six bodies were later brought out by the police. Witness also saw some policemen kneeling down and firing at two Khaksars…crowds of spectators began to collect…the police dispersed them by tear gas. The wounded Khaksars who were lying near the water tap asked for water but nobody gave them water. Instead…the police gave them beating with the butt ends of their rifles…It was absolutely untrue that the Khaksars were chasing the police, added the witness." The witness informs the Chief Justice that he is prepared to make the above statement with the Holy Quran in his hand.

Hafiz Feroze ud Din also informs the court that there were six or seven wounded Khaksars in the middle of the road and also four who had fallen in the drain and had bullet wounds. According to the witness, after one o'clock, the dead and wounded Khaksars were removed in a lorry.

Third Witness on May 09, 1940

At the Lahore High Court, Mr. Rishi, a witness, describes the treatment of the Khaksars by the police. He recounts one of the same incidents that Hafiz Mehar ud Din had mentioned. *The Tribune*, Lahore would write on May 10, 1940 that according to Mr. Rishi, "The dead body was besmeared with blood. One policeman whistled to strike the Khaksar who was showing signs of life…There was another Khaksar close to him [Mr. Rishi] who asked for water. A policeman gave him an orange. The Khaksar wanted to pay the constable some coins in return, when another constable gave a blow with the butt-end of his gun on the head. The Khaksar fell unconscious again…He [Mr. Rishi] saw some policemen swinging two Khaksars, whose hands were bound, over the balcony of an adjoining house…and these Khaksars were swung down over the railings…A constable gave a lathi blow on the head of the unhurt Khaksar with the result that his brain was fractured"
Editor's Comments: The cruelty of the policemen was evident from the statements of the non-Khaksar witness.

1940 May 10

The Khaksars hold demonstrations in various parts of Lahore in the morning.

In Lahore, seven Khaksars are sentenced to two years of rigorous imprisonment each. A large crowd is present at the scene.

The Government Inquiry Committee proceedings continue at the Lahore High Court. Hafiz Mehrajuddin, a witness, informs the court that a person named Baggu had threatened a witness and asked him not to give evidence in front of the court.

Khaksars Suspend Demonstrations

The Government decides to remove police pickets and barbed wire barricades from the outside of mosques and allows food to be delivered to Khaksars in mosques. **Editor's Comments:** As a result of the intense public pressure, the Punjab Government was forced to yield to the people's demands.

Following the Government's decision, Z.A. Khan Lakhnavi (Commander of the Khaksars in Lahore), as a gesture of goodwill, orders the Khaksars in Lahore to suspend demonstrations for three days (from the afternoon of May 10, 1940 to May 13, 1940). Z.A. Khan Lakhnavi's instructions to the Khaksars are as follows: "The Punjab Government by removal of the restrictions over the food supply to the beseiged Khaksars and police barricades from the mosques have given an opportunity to the Khaksars to consider the possibility of conciliation between the Khaksars and the Punjab Government. Since the Khaksar stands for service to humanity and does not believe in aggression I, in view of the conciliatory step taken by the Government, order all the Khaksars in Lahore to desist from any kind of demonstration for three days. This is just to afford an opportunity to Government to consider that the Khaksar is ever ready for co-operation and conciliation. The Khaksar will not be found wanting should the Government be pleased to extend its hand of co-operation." *The Tribune*, Lahore adds, "There was no demonstration by the Khaksars after the issue of this order in the afternoon." *The Tribune*, Lahore May 11, 1940

1940 May 11

The Hindustan Times, Delhi reports that at the Government Inquiry Committee proceedings, a sensation is created in the court room when a witness complains that a man is terrorizing witnesses outside the courtroom. According to the witness, the man is telling witnesses that they will be implicated in a court case if they give evidence regarding the police firing on March 19, 1940. Another witness, Abdul Halim, tells the court that witnesses are being harassed. He states that the man outside the courtroom told him that the doctor who gave evidence before the Inquiry Committee would be involved in a serious case. Abdul Halim also states that the man told him that warrants of arrest have been issued against Hafiz Mehrajuddin, who had recorded his evidence in court the previous day. The man outside the court also tells Abdul Halim not to give evidence. The same man advised another witness, Aziz Din, not to give evidence and Aziz Din left the court without recording his statement. In regards to the March 19th incident, Abdul Halim states that a constable hit a Khaksar with the butt-end of his rifle. When the Khaksar turned around, another constable fired at him and the Khaksar fell down. Dr. Khalifa Shujauddin (the Khaksar counsel) informs the court that two witnesses who came to record their evidence had left after being terrorized. The Nawab of Mamdot is also examined. The Inquiry Committee adjourns its proceedings until May 13, 1940.

The Tribune, Lahore again reports of Jinnah's statement in which he said that "The Khaksar organization is entirely independent of the Muslim League and has no connection with it."

One Khaksar is sentenced to three months of rigorous imprisonment for being a member of the Khaksar Tehrik.

Five Khaksars are sentenced in Lahore to two years of rigorous imprisonment each.

Mohammad Zakar, a supporter of the Khaksars, is produced in court to stand trial.

Khaksars parade in Lyallpur (now Faisalabad). Three Khaksars are arrested.

A batch of Khaksars arrives in Amritsar from Jullunder. Police guard the exits of mosques to check for Khaksars.

A village Khaksar leader is arrested in Sind.

1940 May 12

Khaksars demonstrate in Amritsar and then take shelter in Mohammad Jan Mosque. Police guard Mohammad Jan Mosque in order to arrest the Khaksars who are taking shelter inside.

Police arrest a non-Khaksar in Amritsar on suspicion of being a Khaksar.

Five Khaksars march in formation in Amritsar.

1940 May 13

The Government Inquiry Committee resumes its hearings at the Lahore High Court. Captain Maghis ud Din testifies in front of the court. The captain states that he saw 15 dead and wounded in front of a shop in Hira Mandi. He also saw some wounded Khaksars lying next to the cast of Naugaza's tomb, five or seven Khaksars outside the mosque, and one dead Khaksar next to a water pump. He further states that he saw the police enter Iqbal Manzil and heard three shots upstairs after their entry. *The Tribune*, Lahore would report on May 14, 1940 that the Captain stated, "One Khaksar was held by two policemen. He was profusely bleeding. Another Khaksar was dragged by his hair. He was pushed and given a beating." The newspaper would further write that "the police, in his [Captain Maghis ud Din's] opinion, were out of control. If army were managing the situation, there, they would not have resorted to indiscriminate firing like that." At one point, the Chief Justice

questioned, "Was this firing, in your opinion, unnecessary?" The Captain replied, "Yes, My L:ord!" *The Tribune*, Lahore of May 14, 1940 would further report, "The captain stated that the firing was indiscriminate, uncontrolled and unnecessary…the police constables were excited and it appeared that to him [Captain Maghis ud Din] that they wanted to take revenge."
Editor's Comments: Another non-Khaksar witness explained the barbarity of the policemen on March 19, 1940.

At the same proceedings, the Advocate General submits to the Inquiry Committee that 57 Khaksars were injured and 32 died.

Five Khaksars are arrested in Amritsar. The Imam of M.A.O. College mosque is also arrested for assisting the Khaksars.

Five Khaksars are produced in the court of the Additional District Magistrate in Amritsar.

Another Khaksar is produced in the court of the Additional District Magistrate in Lahore.

Six Khaksars, including three students of Islamia College, are sentenced to two years of rigorous imprisonment each for parading. They are also sentenced to six months of imprisonment each for being members of the Khaksar Tehrik.

Five Khaksars are arrested in Lahore.

The Special Magistrate in Lahore issues further remand for 172 Khaksars who were arrested in connection with the Khaksar-Police clash on March 19, 1940.

The case against 248 Khaksars (resulting from the Khaksar-police clash on March 19, 1940) is postponed until May 27, 1940.

Two Khaksars, Saraj ud Din and Ghulam Muhammad, are convicted by the Lahore Magistrate and sentenced to two years of rigorous imprisonment each.

Khaksar Abdul Rashid of Ludhiana is arrested. He had come to Lahore to help the Government Inquiry Committee collect evidence on behalf of the Khaksars. He states that he had read posters that said that Khaksars who intended to help the Inquiry Committee would not be arrested.

The Special Magistrate accepts an application for better class treatment for Allama Mashriqi's son, who is in jail. The court also orders better treatment for a Khaksar who is the son of a Judge in the State of Hyderabad.
Editor's Comments: There was no justification for their arrests and the poor conditions under which they were kept.

1940 May 14

The Government Inquiry Committee continues its proceedings at the Lahore High Court. The Advocate General concludes his arguments. *The Hindustan Times*, Delhi of May 15, 1940 would report that Dr. Khalifa Shujauddin, arguing on behalf of the Khaksars, stated that "…most of the witnesses produced by the Government were policemen who actually took part in the atrocities. In the real sense they were accused persons. How could the Committee expect that they would tell the truth which would go against them? Counsel also drew the attention of their Lordships to the evidence of terrorising non-official witnesses." The newspaper would further report, "Referring to the incident of March 19, counsel [Dr. Khalifa Shujauddin] submitted that the Khaksars had collected in Lahore with the intention of devising ways and means to get the ban removed…According to the police evidence, the Khaksars attacked Mr. Gainsford near the Tibbi police station, but Mr. Bourne, District Magistrate, who was present at the spot, did not see Mr. Gainsford being attacked. The fact was that the mounted police charged the Khaksars..."

The Tribune, Lahore of May 15, 1940 would report that at the same proceedings, Dr. Khalifa Shuja ud Din said that "The theory of the right of self-defence [the police had argued that they had fired in self-defence on March 19, 1940] was a later concoction and an afterthought."

The Hindustan Times, Delhi reports that a deputation of Frontier Khaksars is to meet with the Governor of the North West Frontier Province today. The deputation is to discuss the ban on Frontier Khaksars traveling to Punjab. Their grievances include the unnecessary harassment and interrogation of Khaksars by Punjab Police, the detention of Khaksars traveling from the North West Frontier Province to Punjab, and the strict watch by police over Khaksar movements within the province. The deputation is to be comprised of Arbab Sher Akbar Khan (Salar-i-Khas, Frontier Province), Qazi Sabaud Din, Mohammad Sarwar Khan (Hakim-i-Alah, Assam), Habibullah Khan (Hakim-i-Alah, United Province), and Sardar Bahadur Khan (Member Legislative Assembly, Frontier Province).

The Khaksars wait for 3 days for the Punjab Government to resolve the Khaksar issue. However, when no action is taken by the Punjab Government, the Khaksars once again resort to demonstrating. They resume their demonstrations in Lahore after a four-day hiatus. Police pickets are posted outside mosques in Lahore where the Khaksars are taking shelter.

Khaksars parade in Lahore. Police attempt to arrest them, but fail to do so.

Charges are filed against three Khaksars in Lahore for taking food for Khaksars in mosques.

Eight Khaksars are tried in court in Lahore. The court reserves judgement.

Eight Khaksars are arrested in Amritsar.

Negotiations continue in order to bring a settlement between the Khaksars and the Government.

1940 May 15

The Last Day of the Inquiry Committee

The last day of the Government Inquiry Committee proceedings commences at the Lahore High Court. *The Tribune*, Lahore of May 16, 1940 would report that the "Chief Justice remarked that they had no reason to disbelieve the doctor, the dresser, the boy and Captain Maghis-ud-Din [witnesses who had supported the Khaksar version]."

The Government Inquiry Committee concludes its hearings at the Lahore High Court. Dr. Khalifa Shujauddin continues his arguments on behalf of the Khaksars. Dr. Khalifa Shujauddin states that after the main firing, the Khaksars dispersed. *The Hindustan Times*, Delhi of May 16, 1940 would report that Dr. Khalifa Shujauddin stated, "After this there was no occasion for firing. But if the policemen maintained that they fired inside the houses in self-defence the onus of the proof would be on them…there was clear evidence that the firing was excessive. Mr. Bourne, District Magistrate, had also stated in his evidence that he had heard reports of stray shots." The newspaper would further report, "Proceeding, counsel [Dr. Khalifa Shujauddin] analysed the injuries sustained by the Khaksars and submitted that 24 dead Khaksars had 50 injuries in all. Ten were in front, four in back and 26 on the sides. Counsel charged the police with ulterior motives in not having sent the bodies of the Khaksars for *postmortem* examination. He added that even in a cursory examination of the injuries of the dead Khaksars Dr. Quick picked out those injuries which he thought had proved fatal. That was deliberately done by the police. Eleven of the Khaksars who succumbed to their injuries in the hospital had 23 gun-shot wounds. Out of them four were in front, six in the back and 13 on the sides. There were 156 wounds on 67 injured Khaksars... Some of them had multiple injuries.

As regards injuries sustained by policemen…only four were discovered to be serious, while other injuries were merely abrasions.

Counsel then criticized the individual evidence produced by the police and finally submitted that nearly 400 cartridges were used by the police, but they were not accounted for in a satisfactory manner."

The Inquiry Committee concludes its hearings after holding 21 sittings and examining 57 witnesses (41 were on behalf of the Government while 16 others were summoned by the court). No witnesses were examined on behalf of the Khaksars. The Committee is expected to submit its report to the Government soon.

Khaksars demonstrate in Lahore.

Khaksars march in Lahore. Twelve Khaksars are arrested.

Four Khaksars are tried at the court of the Special Magistrate in Lahore. The case is adjourned for further hearing.

The Special Magistrate in Lahore sentences Farid Bagh and eight other Khaksars from U.P. to six months of rigorous imprisonment each. The Khaksars had been arrested on April 24, 1940.

The Special Magistrate in Lahore sentences Khaksar Mohammad Alam from Sialkot to six months of rigorous imprisonment.

A local Magistrate in Lahore sentences Riaz ul Haq and seven other Khaksars (who had been arrested on May 03, 1940) to two years of rigorous imprisonment on the first charge, six months on another charge, and three months on a third charge. The sentences were to run concurrently.

Eight Khaksars (arrested on May 05, 1940) are sentenced to two years of rigorous imprisonment each.

In Amritsar, Sheikh Mohammad Umar and eight other Khaksars are remanded to police custody for 14 days, until May 29, 1940.

In the court of the Additional District Magistrate in Amritsar, Khaksar Bashir Ahmad is remanded until May 26, 1940.

64 members of the Red Shirts are put on trial for attacking and injuring Khaksars in Akora (Peshawar District) on June 10, 1939.

The case against 25 Khaksars (arrested from the Khaksar headquarters on March 19, 1940) is withdrawn by the public prosecutor.

1940 May 16

Khaksars demonstrate and parade in Lahore. A crowd gathers to watch the demonstrations. Seven Khaksars are arrested.

In Lahore, Habib ur Rehman, a Khaksar from U.P., is sentenced to three months of hard labor. He was accused of delivering cigarettes to Khaksars taking shelter in mosques.

Another Khaksar, Mohammad Amin, is sentenced to two years of rigorous imprisonment by the City Magistrate in Lahore.

Eight Khaksars (who were arrested on May 01, 1940) are put on trial in the court of the Special Magistrate in Lahore. They are accused of parading in the streets of Lahore.

Islamia College students abstain from attending classes as a protest in support of the Khaksars. *The Tribune*, Lahore of May 17, 1940 would write:

"The Secretary of the Muslim Students Welfare Association, Islamia College, Lahore, in a communication says:

The Islamia College students assembled to-day in the College Compound. The meeting was held to protest against the policy of the Punjab Government towards the Khaksar movement.

They passed resolutions asking the Punjab Government to remove the ban on the Khaksar movement 'which is purely a social and peaceful body.' They demanded immediate release of Allama Mashriqi, the founder of the movement.

The College will remain closed for three days, Thursday, Friday and Saturday as a protest against the Government policy."

1940 May 17

A Khaksar deputation from the North West Frontier Province (NWFP) meets with the Governor to discuss the ban on Khaksars traveling to Punjab to participate in ongoing demonstrations. The deputation informs the Governor that Khaksars heading to Punjab for private business have been detained at Attock bridge. The deputation also tells the Governor that Khaksars simply moving from one place to another (and having to cross Punjab) have been interrogated and harassed. The deputation of Khaksars is comprised of Arbab Sher Akbar Khan (Salar-i-Khas, NWFP), Mohammad Aslam (Hakim-i-Alah, Bihar), Tahir Kheli (Hakim-i-Alah, Assam), Qazi Sabauddin, and Mohammad Sarwar Khan.

Khaksars demonstrate in Lahore. Three Khaksars are arrested.
Mir Manzoor Mahmood Wali (Hakim-i-Alah of the Khaksars in Amritsar) is re-arrested in Amritsar. After previously being arrested, his release was ordered by the Additional District Magistrate. However, as soon as he emerges from court, he is re-arrested.

Khaksar leader Abdul Latif (Hakim-e-Ala) from Bihar is arrested.

1940 May 18

Dr. Mohammad Ismail Nami, a Khaksar leader, sends a telegram to the Viceroy stating: "In spite of the deplorable and repressive attitude of the Punjab Government, I am authorized to state that the unconditional offer of Allama Mashriqi of 50,000 Khaksars [for the Defense of India from foreign aggression] to the Government at the present critical moment still stands."

Allama Mashriqi's son, Akram, and three companions are put on trial in the court of the Special Magistrate in Lahore. They were arrested on March 19, 1940.

Khaksars demonstrate in Lahore. Seven Khaksars are arrested.

15 Khaksars evade arrest in Lahore by taking shelter in a mosque.

Eight Khaksars are convicted and sentenced to various terms of imprisonment by the Special Magistrate in Lahore. Four of the accuseds are sentenced to two years of rigorous imprisonment each.

In Lahore, three Khaksars, Dost Mohammad, Mohammad Rehmat, and Abdul Shakoor, are sentenced to two years of rigorous imprisonment each.

A group of 12 Khaksars takes shelter in Juma Mosque in Rawalpindi. A large number of police officers gather outside the mosque to arrest the Khaksars.

1940 May 19

Khaksars hold demonstrations in various parts of Lahore in observance of "Khaksars Day." "Khaksars Day" is to remember those Khaksars who were killed or wounded during the police firing on March 19, 1940. Police pickets are stationed throughout Lahore to stop the Khaksar demonstrations. 43 Khaksars are arrested, including Muslim students from local schools and colleges.

1940 May 20

Students of Islamia School and Islamia College observe hartal and march through the streets of Lahore in sympathy with the Khaksars arrested on May 19, 1940. They also take out a mock funeral procession and raise anti-Government slogans. **Editor's Comments:** Sympathy with the Khaksars was worth witnessing.

Owing to the student demonstrations, traffic is blocked at various places in Lahore. Police arrive on the scene and lathi charge the demonstrators.
Khaksars from Bihar and Patna head for Lahore to take part in ongoing demonstrations.
Editor's Comments: Khaksars arrived from far-flung areas to show their support for Mashriqi and the Khaksars.

Khaksars demonstrate in Lahore. Five Khaksars are arrested.

A Local Magistrate in Lahore sentences four Khaksars to two and a half years of rigorous imprisonment each.

Four other Khaksars are sentenced to two years of rigorous imprisonment each and a fifth Khaksar is sentenced to three months of rigorous imprisonment.

In Lahore, three Khaksars are sentenced to two and a half years of rigorous imprisonment each.

In Lahore, another batch of nine Khaksars are sentenced to two years of rigorous imprisonment each.

15 Khaksars are produced in the court of the Duty Magistrate in Lahore for police remand. A large crowd gathers at the scene.

Allama Mashriqi's son, Akram, and three companions (who were arrested on March 19, 1940) are acquitted by the Special Magistrate in Lahore.

33 Khaksars are arrested from Wali Mohammad Mosque in Multan.

One Khaksar is arrested at Attock Bridge in NWFP while attempting to enter Punjab. He was proceeding to Lahore to take part in Khaksar demonstrations.

1940 May 21

In Simla, Sir Douglas Young (Chief Justice of the Lahore High Court) continues to work on the report of the Government Inquiry Committee (which inquired into the police firing on March 19, 1940). According to *The Hindustan Times* of May 22, 1940, the report is expected to be submitted to the Government within a week. Sir Douglas Young is also expected to return to Lahore upon completion of the report.

Khaksars hold demonstrations in Lahore. Many Khaksars are arrested.

Islamia School and Islamia College students hold a very large demonstration in Lahore in support of the Khaksars. The Muslims of Lahore announce another strike in support of the Khaksars is to be held the next day, May 22, 1940. The students ask shopkeepers in Lahore to observe a complete strike and keep their shops closed on May 22.
Editor's Comments: Continued support for the Khaksars was worth witnessing.

The City Magistrate in Lahore sentences ten Khaksars to two and a half years of rigorous imprisonment each for parading.

The Special Magistrate in Lahore sentences eight Khaksars to six months of rigorous imprisonment each for being members of the Khaksar Tehrik.

18 Khaksars from various parts of India are sent for trial in Amritsar.

1940 May 22

Muslims in Lahore observe hartal in support of the Khaksars. Islamia College and Islamia School students again abstain from attending classes. The Muslims march through the streets of Lahore. Begum Baji Rashida Latif, Member Legislative Assembly (M.L.A.), addresses the students. Police pickets are set up at strategic points in Lahore in order to control the protestors. At Wazir Khan Mosque, a public meeting is held and speakers demand the release of Allama Mashriqi and the removal of the ban on the Khaksar Tehrik.
Editor's Comments: A strike was held, despite the government's endeavors to crush supporters of the Khaksar Movement.

Shops remain closed and large crowds gather in different parts of Lahore. The people shout "Sikandar Government Murdabad" and other anti-Government slogans. They also raise pro-Khaksar slogans such as "Allama Mashraqi Zindabad." **Editor's Comments:** Continued support of Khaksars was worth witnessing.

Another big procession in support of the Khaksars is planned in Lahore for the evening. A Khaksar Salar announces in Lahore that the only man who could stop the front against the Government is Allama Mashriqi. The Government fears that the situation may grow out of control. *The Tribune*, Lahore, would write on May 23, 1940, "The situation in the city is now growing definitely worse and it is difficult to state what course the movement might take...With the increasing sympathy for the Khaksars, the movement is attracting new recruits."

Khaksars demonstrate in Lahore. 16 Khaksars are arrested.

15 Khaksars are arrested in Lahore.

Four Khaksars (who were injured by the police on March 19, 1940) are released from Mayo Hospital and immediately sent to Lahore Central Jail.

The trial of 47 Khaksars (who were arrested on March 19, 1940 from the Khaksar Tehrik headquarters) resumes in the court of the Special Magistrate in Lahore.

In Lahore, the Special Magistrate frames charges against five Khaksars.

Two Khaksars are convicted in Lahore and sentenced to six months of rigorous imprisonment for being members of the Khaksar Tehrik and parading in formation.

Seven Khaksars are produced before the City Magistrate in Lahore for police remand.

A Khaksar Salar addresses Muslims in Rawalpindi. He states that the Khaksar demonstrations will continue until all restrictions on the Tehrik have been removed and Allama Mashriqi has been released. Local authorities keep a close watch on the situation.

Another batch of Khaksars leaves Patna to join ongoing demonstrations in Lahore.

The Statesman, Calcutta reports that the NWFP Government has issued new instructions to the police regarding the exodus of Khaksars from the province. Khaksars are now required to obtain a permit in order to go to Punjab. They will be required to show this permit before crossing the border of NWFP into Punjab. These permits will not be issued if a Khaksar intends to participate in the ongoing Khaksar demonstrations in Punjab.

1940 May 23

In Simla, Sir Douglas Young (Chief Justice of the Lahore High Court) and Choudhri Niamatullah (a Judge of the Allahabad High Court) continue to prepare the Government Inquiry Committee's report on the Khaksar-police clash on March 19, 1940. Sir Douglas Young and Choudhri Niamatullah had come to Simla to prepare the report soon after completing the Inquiry Committee hearings in Lahore.

Maulana Zafar Ali Khan, Member Legislative Assembly (Central), sends a telegram to the Governor of Punjab stating: "Peace and contentment in Punjab, sword arm of India, essential in view of grave international situation. Khaksar movement with which Muslim opinion is in full sympathy rapidly gathering momentum…before position worsens and wave of unrest passes over entire Muslim Punjab skillful and sympathetic handling of situation is problem of the moment. Removal of unnecessary ban on Khaksars and release of their leader [Allama Mashriqi] will bring immediate peace. Trust Your Excellency's statesmanship will rise to its full status and tackle the situation by prompt intervention." *The Tribune*, Lahore on May 25, 1940

A Khaksar Salar addresses Muslims at Juma Mosque in Lahore. He states that the Khaksars will continue demonstrating until Allama Mashriqi is released and all restrictions on the Khaksar Tehrik are withdrawn. He also states that the Khaksars will not leave Juma Mosque unless they are ordered to do so by Allama Mashriqi.

Khaksars demonstrate in Lahore. Five Khaksars are arrested.

Khaksar Bashir Ahmed Kakezai is arrested in Lahore for parading in a Khaksar uniform.

In Lahore, J.T.M. Bennett (Deputy Inspector General, C.I.D. Police) appears in court as a witness in a trial against 47 Khaksars (who were arrested on March 19, 1940 from the Khaksar Tehrik headquarters). The Deputy Inspector General states that he proceeded to the Khaksar headquarters at around 4:30 pm (on March 19, 1940) and was accompanied by about 80 policeman and also soldiers from the Indian Army. He also called the tear gas squad and utilized them to seize Khaksar materials, search the headquarters, and arrest the Khaksars.

In the trial of 47 Khaksars (arrested on March 19, 1940 from the Khaksar Tehrik headquarters), a list of defense witnesses is filed in court. The list includes Nawab Bahadur Yar Jang, Salar-i-Azam of the Khaksar Tehrik. The court summons all of the witnesses, with the exception of Nawab Bahadur Yar Jang.

The trial of five Khaksars resumes in the court of the Special Magistrate in Lahore.

Seven Khaksars (arrested in Lahore on May 15, 1940 for demonstrating) are sentenced to two and a half years of rigorous imprisonment each. They are also sentenced to three months of rigorous imprisonment each for being members of the

Khaksar Tehrik. As the Khaksars are being taken from the court to the lock-up, a large crowd gathers. More police officers are called in to control the situation.

In Multan, three prominent members of the Fidayan-e-Islam Society are arrested for helping the Khaksars.
Editor's Comments: Public support for the Khaksars continued.

Seven Khaksars are arrested in Multan. Police guard all entry points into Multan and search lorries for Khaksars.
Editor's Comments: The police prevented Khaksars from entering Multan so that they could not hold demonstrations.

Khaksars demonstrate in Multan. Police create panic as they point their guns at the demonstrating Khaksars. Shops in Multan are closed.

A number of Khaksars (who came from Sind to join the demonstrations) are arrested in Multan.

1940 May 24

The Tribune, Lahore writes that, reports about the Khaksar situation are sent to Simla almost every day. The newspaper also writes that the Punjab Government keeps abreast of the Khaksar situation in several parts of the province through these reports.

A huge public meeting is held in Lahore to show sympathy with the Khaksars. A large number of students from local colleges and Muslim schools are present. At the meeting, the people request the Government to establish a memorial in memory of the Khaksars who were killed in Lahore on March 19, 1940. The people also burn copies of the *Civil & Military Gazette* and *Inqilab*. Eventually, the meeting becomes a procession and the people march through the streets of Lahore chanting slogans in favor of Allama Mashriqi and the Khaksars. The slogans include "Remove Khaksar Ban," "Release Allama Mashriqi," "Khaksar Zindabad," and "Who are you? …Khaksars!" The procession marches to Golden Mosque (where the Khaksars are taking shelter) and the people present a Guard of Honor to the Khaksars. Later in the night, speeches are delivered at Golden Mosque. The proceedings continue into the early hours of the morning of May 25, 1940.
Editor's Comments: The public burned copies of the newspapers because they felt that these newspapers were biased and were reporting against the Khaksars.

Khaksars demonstrate in Lahore. Five Khaksars are arrested.

19 Khaksars are convicted in Lahore and sentenced to two years of rigorous imprisonment each.

In Lahore, five Khaksars (who were arrested on May 23, 1940) are produced before the City Magistrate and are remanded to judicial lock-up.

A Local Magistrate in Lahore sentences 18 Khaksars (arrested on May 19, 1940) to two years of rigorous imprisonment each.

Upon arrival from Patna, 12 Khaksars are arrested at Lahore Railway Station. **Editor's Comments:** People continued to come in from far areas, at their own expense, to join the ongoing demonstrations. This showed their dedication to Mashriqi, the Khaksar Tehrik, and the cause.

Mohammad Ashraf, a Khaksar leader, is arrested in Rawalpindi.

1940 May 25

Sir Sikandar Hayat Khan leaves Simla for Lahore to discuss the Khaksar situation with local police and other officials.

Sir Douglas Young (Chief Justice of the Lahore High Court) and Chaudhuri Niamatullah (former Judge of the Allahabad High Court) complete the Government Inquiry Committee report regarding the police firing on March 19, 1940. The report is to be submitted to the Governor of Punjab on May 27, 1940.

In a speech at Juma Mosque in Rawalpindi, Maulvi Mohammad Ismail appeals to the Viceroy and the Secretary of State to remove the restrictions on the Khaksar Tehrik.

In Lahore, five minor boys are arrested for parading.

1940 May 26

Two Khaksars are arrested in Sheikupura.

1940 May 27

Sir Douglas Young returns to Lahore from Simla after he and Chaudhri Niamatullah signed the Government Inquiry Committee report regarding the Khaksar-police clash on March 19, 1940. The report is to be submitted to the Punjab Governor within a day or two.

The case of 173 Khaksars (arrested following the police firing on March 19, 1940) is taken up by the Special Magistrate in Lahore. The court allows the cases against 12 of the 173 Khaksars to be withdrawn. However, one of the 12 Khaksars is immediately re-arrested upon exiting the courtroom. The trial of 173 Khaksars is adjourned until May 29, 1940.

In Lahore, 17 Khaksars are sentenced to two years of rigorous imprisonment each on one charge and six months of rigorous imprisonment each for being members of the Khaksar Tehrik.

In Lahore, five Khaksars are sentenced to two and a half years of rigorous imprisonment each.

A batch of Khaksars from Haripur, NWFP enter Juma Mosque in Rawalpindi to join other Khaksars already staying there.

1940 May 28

The trial of seven Khaksars (arrested for parading in Lahore) is held in a court in Lahore. Six of the Khaksars are sentenced to two years and nine months of rigorous imprisonment each.

The City Magistrate in Lahore convicts five Khaksars and sentences them to two years of rigorous imprisonment each.

A Local Magistrate in Lahore sentences six Khaksars (arrested on May 21, 1940) to two and a half years of rigorous imprisonment each on one charge and three months of rigorous imprisonment each on a second charge.

The trial of four Khaksars (arrested on April 18, 1940) resumes in the court of the Special Magistrate in Lahore.

A Khaksar leader is prosecuted in Amritsar.

A batch of Khaksars from Hazara arrives in Rawalpindi to join the ongoing demonstrations.

1940 May 29

The Star of India, Calcutta reports that Barrister Mian Ahmed Shah (a Khaksar leader) wrote a letter to Maulvi A.K. Fazlul Haq (Chief Minister of Bengal) offering the services of the Khaksars of Bengal for the defence of India during World War II:

"With reference to your appeal published in the 'Amrita Bazar Patrika' dated May 24, for co-operation with the British Government in this hour of crisis, I, as the chief officer of the Khaksars of this province, place the services of the local Khaksars at the disposal of the Government, as already indicated to His Excellency the Viceroy in this behalf on May 18. The telegram sent to His Excellency in this connection by the present Chief Officer of the movement is as follows:

'His Excellency the Viceroy, Simla- In spite of the deplorable and repressive attitude of the Punjab Government, I am authorised to state that the unconditional offer of Allama Mashriqui of 50,000 Khaksars to the Government at the present critical moment still stands. - Mohammad Ismail Nami, Madarun Nizam of Khaksars.'

I assure you again that you will not find us behind any other association or movement in extending the fullest possible co-operation to the Government of India at this critical juncture. It now rests with the Government as to how to make use of

our services in conformity with the lines of co-operation on which Allama
Mashriqui, the founder of the movement, has made an offer of 50,000 for active
service

> - Yours, etc. MIAN AHMAD SHAH."

The Hindustan Times reports that the Government Inquiry Committee has sent its
report (regarding the police firing on March 19, 1940) to the Punjab Government.

Khaksars demonstrate at Dabbi Bazaar, Lahore. Police open fire and a large crowd
witnesses the scene. Dabbi Bazaar is closed. Police reinforcements arrive and police
pickets are also added at strategic points to control the situation. One of the injured
Khaksars dies at Mayo Hospital. Another injured Khaksar later died in Golden
Mosque on May 30, 1940.

Troops are called out in Lahore.

A Lahore Magistrate convicts eight Khaksars (arrested for parading) to two years of
rigorous imprisonment each.

The trial of 161 Khaksars (arrested following the police firing on March 19, 1940)
commences in front of the Special Magistrate in Lahore. The court is held in Lahore
Central Jail where a large crowd is present to witness the proceedings. The
Inspector of City Police testifies in court.

Five Khaksars are tried in the court of the City Magistrate in Lahore.

12 Khaksars, heading from Karachi to Multan (to join ongoing demonstrations), are
arrested at Khanpur Railway Station and produced before the Additional District
Magistrate.

In a meeting of Majlis-i-Naujawanan-i-Islam, Muslims pass a resolution asking the
Government of Punjab to withdraw the ban on Khaksars.

1940 May 30

Mohammad Saman, a Khaksar from Bhopal who was injured by the police firing on
May 29, 1940, dies at Golden Mosque, Lahore. A large crowd gathers outside the
mosque. Islamia College is closed and students organize a procession. Muslims
observe hartal in support of the Khaksars and in protest against the police firing on
May 29, 1940. Muslim and Hindu shops remain closed. At about 3:00 pm, the
funeral procession of the Khaksar who died at Golden Mosque earlier in the day
begins. The 20,000 mourners in the procession, including women in "burqas,"
shouts of "Khaksar Zindabad." When the procession arrives at the site of the police
firing on March 19, 1940, the mourners stop for 15 minutes and the Khaksars give a
salute. The procession also passes through Unchi Mosque near Tibbi Police Station
and Nila Gumbad Mosque, and Khaksars martyrs are saluted at both places.
Military and police keep a close watch on the situation. The procession takes 5

hours to reach Miani Sahib graveyard, which is a distance of three miles from Golden Mosque (where the procession began). Mohammad Saman is buried at Miani Sahib graveyard.

The Tribune, Lahore of May 31, 1940 would report that during the procession in Lahore, people shouted pro-Khaksar and anti-Government slogans. They continuously shouted "Release Allama Mashriqi," "Khaksar Zindabad," and "Shahidan Lahore Zindabad (Martyrs of Lahore Zindabad)." The police kept a close watch on the procession and the military moved in lorries alongside the procession.

In Lahore, police officials hold a conference to discuss the Khaksar situation. Armed police are kept ready and posted in Lahore. The military is also called and kept on standby.

As a result of the recent events in Lahore, the Special Magistrate adjourns the trial of 161 Khaksars until June 04, 1940.

Mohammed Hussain, a Khaksar leader, is arrested in Sheikhpura.

Khaksars are heading from Sind to Multan.

1940 May 31

Khaksars continue to travel from Sind to Multan to join the ongoing demonstrations in Punjab against the arrest of Mashriqi and the Khaksars and the ban on the Khaksar Tehrik.

A serious clash takes place between the police and the Khaksars at Khanewal Railway Station near Multan. The police board a train carrying Khaksars headed from Sind to Multan (to join ongoing demonstrations) and attempt to force the Khaksars off the train. A clash ensues and the police kill one Khaksar using a bayonet and injure many others. 28 Khaksars are arrested.

In Lahore, thousands of people observe hartal (strike) out of respect for the Khaksars killed as a result of the police firing on May 29, 1940. The people also raise pro-Khaksar slogans.

Almost all of the local Magistrates in Lahore try Khaksar cases in their courts.

In Lahore, seven Khaksars (arrested on May 29, 1940) are convicted and sentenced to two years of rigorous imprisonment each.

Another group of seven Khaksars (arrested on May 19, 1940 in Hira Mandi Bazaar) is tried in Lahore and sentenced to two and a half years of imprisonment each.

In Lahore, another batch of seven Khaksars (arrested at Lahore Railway Station upon arrival from Patna) is convicted and sentenced to six months of imprisonment each.

Five Khaksars (arrested at Lahore Railway Station upon arrival from Calcutta) are sentenced to six months of rigorous imprisonment each.

In Lahore, one Khaksar is convicted and sentenced to five months of imprisonment for being a member of the Khaksar Tehrik.

A Lahore Muslim is convicted to five months of hard labor for providing food to Khaksars taking shelter in a mosque.

Mohammad Akhtar, a Khaksar from Bihar, is tried in Lahore. He is accused of receiving a batch of Khaksars at Lahore Railway Station.

June

1940 June 01

Sir Sikandar Hayat Khan invites Agha Ghazanfar Ali Shah (a lawyer from Bulandshahr, United Provinces and Hakim-e-Ala of the Khaksar Tehrik) for a meeting (to be held on June 03, 1940 in Simla) to discuss the Khaksar situation.

Police pickets are relaxed and troops are withdrawn from Lahore.

Khaksars demonstrate in Lahore. 8 Khaksars are arrested.

1940 June 02

In Rawalpindi, students of Islamia College as well as other local students hold a demonstration in sympathy for the Khaksars. After marching through the main bazaars of the city, the students arrive at Juma Mosque where they hold a meeting. At the meeting, they pass a resolution demanding the removal of restrictions on the Khaksar Tehrik and the release of Allama Mashriqi.

Police in Rawalpindi arrest Mansabdar and another shopkeeper for helping the Khaksars.

Five more people are arrested in Rawalpindi in connection with the Khaksar issue. Mohammad Ashraf, a Khaksar leader, is re-arrested under the Criminal Law Amendment Act while four others are arrested for helping the Khaksars.

In Jhelum near Rawalpindi, the Additional District Magistrate convicts eight Khaksars. He sentences three Khaksars to two and a half years of rigorous imprisonment, one Khaksar to one and a half years of rigorous imprisonment, and four Khaksars to six months of rigorous imprisonment.

One Khaksar is killed and several others are injured by police after the police enter a railway compartment carrying Khaksars. 28 Khaksars are arrested.

Khaksars demonstrate in Lahore.

1940 June 03

In Simla, Agha Ghazanfar Ali (Hakim-e-Ala of the Khaksar Tehrik) meets Sir Sikandar Hayat Khan to discuss the Khaksar situation.
Editor's Comments: Sir Sikandar had invited Agha Ghazanfar Ali for this meeting on June 01, 1940.

In Lahore, Khaksar trials take place in the courts of three different Magistrates.

The trial of 47 Khaksars (arrested on March 19, 1940 in Ichhra) resumes at the court of the Special Magistrate in Lahore. *The Tribune*, Lahore of June 04, 1940 would report that Abdul Salam testified in court. According to him, the police threw tear gas grenades at the Khaksar Tehrik's headquarters in Ichhra. Abdul Salam also states that the police set fire to the tents set up at the headquarters of the Tehrik. He further testifies that a European police officer snatched a spade from a Khaksar leader and struck the back of the Khaksar leader's neck with the spade.

A Lahore Magistrate sentences ten Khaksars. Five are sentenced to two and a half years of rigorous imprisonment each while the other five are sentenced to two years of rigorous imprisonment each.

Police pursue Khaksars in Lahore but fail to arrest them.

Khaksar leader, Abdul Latif (Naib Hakim-e-Ala), is prosecuted in Amritsar.

Khaksars walk 70 miles from Dera Ismail Khan to join their fellow Khaksars in demonstrations in Rawalpindi. Five Khaksars are arrested upon arrival in Rawalpindi.

A large public meeting is held in Rawalpindi in connection with the Khaksar situation. A.A. Williams (Deputy Commissioner of Police) and Scott (Superintendent of Police) address the gathering. A.A. Williams informs the people that the Government does not intend to arrest Khaksars inside mosques.

The Superintendent of Police assigns a special staff to handle the Khaksars in Rawalpindi.

1940 June 04

The Hindustan Times, Delhi reports that the daughter of Fazlul Haq (Premier of Bengal) has expressed sympathy with the Khaksars and contributed an article to *Al-Islah*, the Khaksar newspaper.

The Hindustan Times, Delhi reports of an article in *Al-Islah* regarding Barrister Mian Ahmed Shah's interview of Jinnah. The newspaper states, "Mian Ahmed Shah, Barrister, during his conversation strongly pressed Mr. Jinnah to persuade Sir Sikandar Hyat Khan to lift the ban on the Khaksars. Mr. Jinnah is stated to have suggested to Mian Ahmed Shah that the Khaksars should rally round the Muslim League Flag."

Agha Ghazafar Ali (Hakim-e-Ala of the Khaksar Tehrik) meets with the Chief Secretary of the Punjab Government. *The Tribune*, Lahore of June 05, 1940 would report that Agha Ghazanfar Ali is to meet Allama Mashriqi. The newspaper would further write that Agha Ghazanfar Ali is to inform Mashriqi about his meeting with Sir Sikandar and seek Mashriqi's advice.

Khaksars hold a demonstration in Lahore. Police again arrive on the scene but are unable to arrest the Khaksars.

In the court of the Special Magistrate in Lahore, more evidence is recorded in the trial of 161 Khaksars. The case is adjourned until the next day, June 05, 1940.

The Additional District Magistrate in Lahore starts a magisterial inquiry into the police firing on Khaksars on May 29, 1940. A number of witnesses are examined. A local student states that the police lathi charged the Khaksars, and the Sub-Inspector in charge of the police stepped into a shop from where he fired shots at the Khaksars. He did not see any attack by the Khaksars against the police.

Khaksar leader Abdul Latif (Naib Hakim-e-Ala) is charged in Amritsar for being a member as well as an organizer of the Khaksar Tehrik.

1940 June 05

More evidence is recorded in the trial of 161 Khaksars in the court of the Special Magistrate in Lahore.

1940 June 06

Khaksars demonstrate in Lahore. 12 Khaksars are arrested.

1940 June 07

Khaksars demonstrate in Lahore.

In the court of the Special Magistrate in Lahore, more evidence is recorded in the trial of 161 Khaksars.

The Star of India, Calcutta reports that a condolence meeting was held in Patna for Khaksar martyrs who died as a result of the police firing in Lahore on May 29, 1940. There was a large crowd present at the meeting and a number of people spoke at the occasion. Speakers included Masood Ahmed Saheb (Former Member of the Central Legislative Assembly), who said that he found a large percent of the population to be in deep sympathy with the Khaksars. The following resolution was also unanimously adopted at the meeting:

"This public meeting of the Muslims of Patna requests Their Excellencies the Viceroy and the Governor of the Punjab to remove the ban and all other restrictions on the Khaksars' organisation.

The six demands formulated by the public of Lahore in this connection may be complied with as early as possible.

This meeting conveys condolence to the families of the martyrs two mujahids and one muavin on the passing away of those noble souls."

1940 June 08

The Hindustan Times, Delhi reports that the findings of the Government Inquiry Committee (to investigate the police firing on March 19, 1940) are to be discussed at the next meeting (to be held on June 15, 1940) of the Working Committee of the All-India Muslim League. The Inquiry Committee is expected to have concluded its work by June 15, 1940.

Eight Khaksars (arrested on June 02, 1940) are sentenced in Lahore. Four of them are sentenced to two years of hard labor each while three are sentenced to one year of imprisonment each. One Khaksar is ordered to pay a security of Rs. 300.

Sadrul Islam Khan sends a letter to Quaid-e-Azam to resolve the Khaksar issue. Many others have also written letters and sent telegrams to Quaid-e-Azam in this regard.

1940 June 09

The Government of Sind imposes a ban on Khaksars traveling by train to Punjab to participate in ongoing demonstrations.

1940 June 10

Five Khaksars are arrested in Rawalpindi.

Ten Muslim sympathizers of the Khaksars are arrested in Lahore.

1940 June 11

Police initiate a rigorous drive to arrest Khaksars. At about 2:00 am (in the middle of the night between June 10 and June 11), police (including British officers) raid all the mosques in Lahore where the Khaksars are taking shelter. Police officers leading the raids include Morton, Durrant, Bennett, and Deheaume. Large crowds gather at the mosques. Police use tear gas at a number of mosques to arrest the Khaksars. Morton (Superintendent of Police) opens fire, killing one Khaksar and seriously injuring another. The military is called in and posted at various places in the city. Throughout Lahore, the police kill one, injure 14, and arrest 300 Khaksars. The injured Khaksars are admitted to Mayo Hospital. Over 1,000 policeman participate in this operation.

In Lahore, hartal is observed in sympathy with the Khaksar who was killed and the others who were arrested by the police during the night. Crowds gather in front of various mosques to show their support for the Khaksars. The Khaksar who was killed is buried under police escort.

Shops remain closed in Lahore and large crowds gather. Police confiscate Khaksar materials including belchas.

As a result of the police raids on mosques, a public meeting is convened at Golden Mosque, Lahore. A procession of women is also to march to court arrest in the evening.

Khaksars continue their demonstrations in Lahore and more Khaksars take shelter in Golden Mosque, Lahore.

The Muslims of Lahore hold a meeting to protest the arrests of the Khaksars. *The Tribune*, Lahore would publish a photo on June 13, 1940 showing a Khaksar commander addressing the meeting and the people supporting the commander's words.

The public places posters on the doors of the Golden and Unchi Mosques in Lahore. The posters appeal to the people to assist the Khaksar Movement and to not let it die.

High Government officials, including District Magistrate F.C. Bourne, City Magistrate Sardar Abdul Samad Khan, and Senior Superintendent of Police A.J. Scroggie meet to discuss the Khaksar situation.

The Governor of Punjab declares Lahore City in a disturbed and dangerous state and issues the following Gazette Extraordinary:
　　　　Under Section 15 (1) of Act V of 1861, the Governor of the Punjab is pleased to declare that the area in the jurisdiction of Lahore City Kotwali is in a disturbed and dangerous state.
　　　　The Governor of the Punjab further directs that this declaration shall remain in force for a period of one year from the date of notification.
　　　　Under the provisions of Sec. 15 of the Police Act of 1861, the Governor of the Punjab is pleased to declare that owing to the misconduct of the inhabitants of the area known as Lahore City in the jurisdiction of Lahore City Kotwali, Lahore District, it is expedient to increase the number of Police.
　　　　This proclamation shall remain in force for a period of one year from the date the extra Police are actually entertained.

The Punjab Government issues a press note stating that they have posted additional police forces in Lahore (to stop the Khaksars from demonstrating) and that all Muslim residents in the City, except those who have not supported the Khaksars, will pay for the cost. A Naib Tehsildar (Government officer) begins designating the areas where residents shall pay this punitive police tax.

Police in Rawalpindi raid Juma Mosque and use tear gas to arrest Khaksars taking shelter there. 50 Khaksars are arrested. Police pickets are posted at strategic points throughout Rawalpindi.

Sir Sikandar Hayat Khan issues a press statement regarding the Khaksar Tehrik:
"Government are satisfied that there are definite indications of real connexions between the Khaksar movement and enemies of this country...
It is unfortunately not possible for the Government at least not at present to divulge information which they possess about certain organizations receiving inspiration and instruction from abroad, because Government cannot afford to disclose their sources and contacts." *The Statesman*, Calcutta, June 14, 1940
Editor's Comments: Sir Sikandar's statement, that the Khaksars had connections with the enemies of India, had no basis. These accusations were made only to grant legitimacy to the actions of the Government against the Khaksar Tehrik. He ignored Mashriqi's loyalties to his homeland, when Mashriqi offered the services of 50,000 Khaksars for the defense of India on October 04, 1939 soon after World War II broke out. Sir Richard Tottenham's statement in the Central Assembly further proved that Sir Sikandar's allegation had no substance. On September 23, 1942, Sir Richard Tottenham replied to a question in the Central Assembly, "The Government of India have never made this charge against the Khaksars, nor do they make it now" (*The Tribune* Sept. 24, 1942). Furthermore, if the Government had any evidence against Mashriqi, then why wasn't he tried under this charge?

1940 June 12

The people show their resentment towards the police. *The Tribune*, Lahore reports that the public threw stones and bricks at the police. The newspaper also reports that there are blood marks in mosques where clashes had occurred between the Khaksars and the police.
Editor's Comments: People protested, as they were concerned with Sir Sikandar's false accusation that the Khaksars were linked to the Nazis.

Hafiz Mehraj Din, a Muslim League Sub-Committee Secretary, is arrested in Lahore for being a sympathizer of the Khaksar Tehrik. He had also appeared as a witness during the Government Inquiry Committee hearings regarding the Khaksar-Police clash on March 19, 1940.

Documents containing plans about the Khaksar Tehrik in Lahore are allegedly confiscated from Hafiz Mehraj ud Din's possession.

District Officers in Lahore, including the District Magistrate and police, continue their conference to discuss ways to control the Khaksar Tehrik.

Police remain vigilant in Lahore and keep a close eye on Khaksars.

Military and armed police pickets remain in place in Lahore to curb Khaksar demonstrations.

Khaksar sympathizers are warned that if they help the Khaksars, they will face police charges.

50 Khaksars (arrested in Rawalpindi on June 11, 1940) are produced before the City Magistrate in Rawalpindi and remanded to police custody.

Muhammad Jan writes a letter to Quaid-e-Azam to resolve the Khaksar issue.

1940 June 13

Police raid houses in Lahore and arrest Khaksar sympathizers.

Two dozen Muslim homes are raided in Lahore and 30 Muslims are arrested.

11 Khaksar sympathizers are arrested in Lahore.

Khaksars leave Kundiga Mosque in Lahore. Police search houses near the mosque for Khaksars and make some arrests.

Police arrest sixteen Khaksars from Unchi Mosque in Lahore.

In Lahore, twelve Khaksars (arrested on June 05, 1940) are sentenced to two years of rigorous imprisonment each.

In Gujrat, police raid the Timble Bazaar Mosque and arrest five Khaksars who are taking shelter there.

1940 June 14

Khaksars demonstrate in Lahore. Police arrive on the scene and shops in the area are closed.

Seven Khaksars are arrested in Lahore.

200 armed policemen surround Golden Mosque in Lahore in an attempt to arrest Khaksars taking shelter there.

Khaksars from Patna arrive in Lahore to join ongoing demonstrations.

The Special Magistrate in Lahore frames charges against Khaksar Abdul Haye.

In Lahore, 274 Khaksars are remanded to judicial lock-up.

An injured Khaksar (wounded by the police on May 11, 1940) dies at Mayo Hospital.

16 Khaksars are arrested in Lahore.

Eight Khaksars, including Abdul Sabhan, are arrested in Lahore.

Siddiqui Ispahani Nooruddin from Calcutta sends a telegram to Quaid-e-Azam to resolve the Khaksar issue with the Punjab Government: "We appeal to you and the members of the Working Committee actively to intervene in Sikandar-Khaksar unfortunate dispute. Muslim feeling greatly agitated."

1940 June 15

Nawab Bahadur Yar Jang, President of the Muslim States League and a Khaksar leader, denies any Khaksar connection with the enemies of India. *The Hindustan Times*, Delhi of June 18, 1940 would report that "He [Nawab Bahadur Yar Jang] resented the suggestion of Sir Sikandar Hyat Khan, and thought, it was only a lame excuse to arrest the Khaksars and destroy the movement."

Police raid Bukhal Khan mosque in Lahore and arrest five Khaksars from U.P. and the Central Provinces.

One of the Khaksars injured, during the police raids on the mosques in Lahore on June 11, 1940, dies in the hospital.

The Tribune, Lahore reports that the City Magistrate is to conduct an inquest regarding the death of Khaksar Mohammad Azim.
Editor's Comments: Mohammad Azim was fatally wounded by police firing on the night between June 10 and June 11, 1940.

In Rawalpindi, the houses of three Khaksar Salars are searched. Khaksar literature and materials are confiscated. Police remain vigilant in order to quell Khaksar activities.

The Working Committee of the Muslim League

The Star of India, Calcutta would publish (on June 18, 1940) a telegram from Barrister Mian Ahmed Shah to Khawaja Sir Nazimuddin, Fazlul Haq, and Maulana Akram Khan Saheb, who were attending the Working Committee meeting of the Muslim League in Bombay. Jinnah and Sir Sikandar Hayat Khan were also in Bombay for the meeting. Mian Ahmed Shah's telegram stated: "Strongly challenge Sir Sikander Hayat Khan's mis-statement regarding 'Fifth Column,' and lame

excuse for justifying his action. Kindly see Working Committee is not misled. -
Mian Ahmad Shah."

The Working Committee of the Muslim League holds a meeting in Bombay at
Quaid-e-Azam's residence. Sir Sikandar Hayat Khan is present at the meeting.
Quaid-e-Azam presides over the meeting and the following resolution is passed:

RESOLUTION NO. 4
In view of the grave world situation and its possible repercussions on India
when every community will organizing its Volunteer Organizations for the
protection of its life and property the Working Committee of the All India Muslim
League is of the opinion that time has come when the Provincial Muslim Leagues
should exert every nerve to start, organize, and strengthen the Muslim National
Guard Corps and give them such training as will enable them to discharge their duty
in maintaining peace, tranquility and order in the country worthy of the best
traditions of Islam. The Committee earnestly appeals to the Muslims to join the
National Guards in large numbers under the banner of the Muslim League and
directs the Provincial Muslim League to submit monthly reports to the Honorary
Secretary to the All India Muslim League regarding the progress made and the steps
adopted for the training of the Muslim National Guards. It is also the considered
opinion of the Committee that the members of the Provincial Muslim League
Working Committees and the District Committees should offer themselves for
training at least once a week, with a view to give impetus to enlistment.
It is proposed to consider further the details of the scheme, but in the
meantime the Provincial Muslim Leagues shall act in accordance with the following
main principles:-
A. Aims and objects of the organisation:-
1. To train and discipline Muslims in coordinate activity for social, and physical
   uplift of the Muslims and to maintain peace, tranquillity and order in the
   country.
B.
1. The organisation shall consist of officers and guardsmen who will be willing to
   undertake a definite liability and responsibility to fulfill the aims and objects of
   the organisation herein before defined.
2. It shall be made up as follows:-
   a. Active Corps members
   b. Reservists Corps members
   c. Juvenile Corps
3. Active Corps shall consist of men who are capable of taking part in all the
   activities of organisation.
4. Reservists Corps shall consist of men who due to age, occupation or physical
   disability are not able to serve on the active corps.
5. Juvenile Corps shall consist of boys under sixteen years of age.
6. The Muslim National Guards shall be organised under the authority control and
   supervision of the Working Committee of each Provincial Muslim League
   subject to the final authority of the Working Committee of the All India
   Muslim League.

7. The Working Committee of each Province shall appoint properly qualified persons for the purpose of (a) organising the Corps (b) giving them training and (c) Officering them.
8. A Guardsman, on being declared eligible, shall sign the following pledge in duplicate on the prescribed form:-
Pledge. – I___Son of___solemnly swear by Allah, and the Holy Quran, that I hereby of my own free will surrender myself to the Muslim National Guards organisation. I shall unflinchingly obey my officers and shall remain faithful to the organisation and its aims and objects. So help me Allah Amin! Signature___
9. The Head Quarters of every Provincial organisations shall maintain a classified list of the vocation and profession of every guardsman under its command.
10. A guardsman shall not be a member of any other Political organisation except the Muslim League, or of any volunteer Corps.
11. It shall be impressed on all guardsmen that courtesy to all ranks and classes of society shall be observed.
12. Uniform:- 1. Khaki Coat or shirt, Khaki trousers and Khaki cap or turban. Or 2, Grey Coat or shirt, Grey trousers and Grey cap or turban. Provided however that every Province will have the option to select either of the two colours but shall keep and maintain the same colour and uniform throughout that Province.

Editor's Comments:
At the time of this meeting of the Muslim League, less than three months had passed since the massacre of the Khaskars on March 19, 1940. In the Khaksar circle, there were great hopes that the Muslim League would do its utmost to help obtain the release of Mashriqi and the Khaksars and the removal of the ban on the Khaksar Tehrik. However, the Khaksars were highly disappointed that no firm action was taken at this meeting. Instead, a resolution was passed to establish the Muslim National Guard Corps, which was essentially a copy of the Khaksar Tehrik; even the Khaki color of the Khaksar uniform was to be used by the Corps members. The important question then is why a parallel organization was needed instead of further strengthening the Khaksar Tehrik. In the Khaksar circle, this action provided further confirmation that there was some sort of conspiracy against the Khaksar Tehrik and that anti-Khaksar elements didn't want to tolerate the Khaksar Tehrik as an independent body.

1940 June 16

In Lahore, Yaqood ul Hassan is arrested for helping the Khaksars.

Five Khaksars (arrested on June 15, 1940) are produced before a Magistrate in Lahore, who remands them to police custody.

Women Khaksars demonstrate in Lahore and shout Khaksar slogans.

Khaksar women, led by a 10 year old girl, hold a demonstration in Lahore.

Eight Khaksars are arrested in Lahore.

Khaksars hold a mock fight in Cawnpore. A large crowd gathers to watch their activities.

1940 June 17

Barrister Mian Ahmed Shah (a Khaksar leader) issues the following statement:
"In order to justify his most drastic action against the Khaksars Sir Sikandar Hayat Khan, Premier, Punjab has been pleased to declare that his Government 'are satisfied that there are definite indications of a real connection between the Khaksar Movement and the enemies of this country.' The question is why should there be any connection whatsoever of the Khaksars with the enemies. If India is to remain a dependent country as in the present circumstances she has obviously no means to become absolutely free, I believe that the present regime under the British Government will certainly be better than any other form of Government that might be forced upon us by some new invader of India. No useful purpose will be served if either the Khaksars or another body be foolish enough to keep a clandestine connection with the enemies of the country. Of course, it is quite different to call the Khaksars the 'Fifth Columnists in the pay of Nazi-Germany' and then pounce on them with the utmost violence in order to totally crush them.
Correspondence is still going on between the Punjab Premier and myself with a view to patching up the present dispute as early as possible. Whatever conditions have been laid down by Sir Sikander as settlement terms have been accepted 'in toto,' yet no end of the trouble seems to be in sight. For instance, Sir Sikander writes:- 'Provided a responsible leader of the Khaksars would give an ssurance that the Khaksars would give up defiance of law and order and would in future confine their activities to genuinely social work and as an earnest of their 'bona fides' the Khaksars now assembled in Lahore and other places would return to their homes, Government would be prepared to rescind the notification of March 19[1940].'
In answer to this, I have stated as follows: 'I can give you this assurance with full authority from the "Idara-i-Alliya," provided the Government is also willing to put an end to the unfortunate trouble simultaneously (1) by lifting all restrictions on the movement, (2) by releasing Allama Mashriqi forthwith, (3) by setting aside all pending cases, also restoring whatever property has been confiscated or auctioned.
We never mean to deceive anyone when we honestly declare that we Khaksars are quite prepared to co-operate with the Government provided an honourable chance is given to us. Let the question whether we are 'Fifth Columnists or Sixth Columnists or Hindu-created Columnists in the pay of Nazi Germany' be put to the test. I am sure we will not be found less loyal than anyone else in India, especially at this critical moment when to stand by the British Government is to defend our own country, India, itself.
I earnestly appeal to the Government of India to kindly intervene and have the dispute in the Punjab honourably settled." *The Star of India*, Calcutta June 18, 1940, *The Hindustan Times*, June 19, 1940

A Khaksar is arrested inside Delhi Gate in Lahore.

Zahur ud Din, a Khaksar Salar, is arrested in Lahore.

Six Khaksars are arrested in Lahore.

Khaksars from the United Provinces (U.P.) demonstrate in Lahore. Eight Khaksars are arrested.

The Chief Secretary of the Government of U.P. sends a telegram to the Secretary of the Government of India (Home Department) regarding the ban on the Khaksar Tehrik.

1940 June 18

Khaksars demonstrate in Lahore. Four Khaksar women and a 10 year old girl are arrested. Seven male Khaksars are also arrested. *The Tribune*, Lahore would report on June 19-20, 1940, that the 10 year old girl who was arrested took out a letter from her pocket addressed to Sir Sikandar Hayat Khan and began reading it. The letter mentioned Sir Sikandar and the Khaksar issue. The police seized the letter.

Editor's Comments: This shows the public's backing for Mashriqi and the Khaksars.

Khaksar Paira Khan from Delhi is arrested after emerging from Golden Mosque in Lahore.

Khan Bahadur Abdul Quyum Khan and Agha Ghazanfar Ali Shah arrive in Vellore to discuss the Khaksar issue with Allama Mashriqi, who is in Vellore Jail.
Editor's Comments: The Government allowed Khaksars to meet Mashriqi because it was unable to curb the massive and continued resistance from the Khaksars and the public.

The Khaksar issue is discussed at a meeting of Hindus.

1940 June 19

Sir Sikandar issues a statement regarding the Khaksars and announces that a large number of additional police have been recruited to control the Khaksar situation.
Editor's Comments: Additional police were needed because the Government failed to overcome the resistance from the Khaksars and the public.

Special police are sent to Attock to prevent Frontier Khaksars from going to Lahore to participate in ongoing demonstrations.

Khaksars demonstrate in Lahore. Five Khaksars are arrested. Four shopkeepers are also arrested for helping the Khaksars.

Seven Khaksars and five women (including a ten year old girl) are tried in a court in Lahore. The court grants a remand.
Editor's Comments: Even women supporters were not spared from trial.

The trial of 161 Khaksars resumes in the court of the Special Magistrate in Lahore. The Inspector of Reserve Police, Disney, is examined. He states that he didn't see Mr. Beaty being hit, but he distinctly heard Mr. Beaty say "Maro, Fire Karo" (Attack and Fire).

The Commissioner, Patna Division issues a communique regarding the death of a Khaksar in Patna: Recently one Makhan Khan Sardar Azam, of Aurangabad Khaksar Movement returned from Lahore to Aurangabad. On the evening of June 13, he was assaulted and a case under Section 326 I.P.C. was instituted on his statement. Later, he succumbed to his injury and it created a panic in Aurangabad town. The District Magistrate and Superintendent of Police at once visited Aurangabad to control the funeral procession and the situation in the town. The arrival of these officers and of a force of armed police had a good effect. There was excitement and shops were closed, but nothing untoward happened. The evidence at present available indicates that the attack on Makhan Khan was due to a private grudge.

1940 June 20

Khaksar Pere Khan from the North West Frontier Province (NWFP) is arrested in Lahore for being a member of the Khaksar Tehrik.

In the court of a local Magistrate in Lahore, five Khaksars from the United Provinces (U.P.) (arrested on June 15, 1940) are sentenced to four months of rigorous imprisonment each.

Agha Ghazanfar Ali leaves for Punjab after meeting with Allama Mashriqi in Vellore Central Jail in Madras.

An inquest regarding Khaksar Mohammad Azim's death is held in the court of the City Magistrate in Lahore. A number of police witnesses are examined and the hearing is adjourned.

Maulvi Ahmad Ali, the Imam of Sheranwali Mosque (where the Khaksars had taken shelter), is arrested.

1940 June 21

16 Khaksars are tried in the court of a Lahore Magistrate. 15 are convicted and sentenced to two years of rigorous imprisonment each.

A Lahore Magistrate sentences 15 Khaksars (arrested from Unchi Mosque on June 14, 1940) to a total of five years of rigorous imprisonment each for different charges. The sentences are to run concurrently.

In the court of the Special Magistrate in Lahore, almost all prosecution witnesses are again cross-examined in the trial of four Khaksars arrested on April 18, 1940.

A Khaksar case is adjourned in the court of the Special Magistrate in Lahore.

In Lahore, the court issues a Warrant of Arrest against Allah Dad, a defense witness, in the trial of Karam Ullah Khan and four other Khaksars.

Khakars demonstrate in Lahore. Five Khaksars are arrested.

1940 June 22

Headed by F.C. Bourne (District Magistrate), Scroggie (Senior Superintendent of Police), de Heume (in charge of the tear gas squad), and K.B. Said Ahmad Shah (Superintendent of Police), police raid the Golden Mosque in Lahore. A tear gas squad is also present. Police block all exits to the mosque. 26 Khaksars are arrested. One of the Khaksars is from Lahore, four are from Calcutta, seven are from Hyderabad, three are from Nagpur, one each is from Patna, Rampur State, Gondol, Kathiawar, and Bijnaur, and the remaining Khaksars are from various districts of Punjab. Police also confiscate Khaksar materials from the mosque. Armed police are posted outside Golden Mosque. Punitive police are also to be stationed in Lahore beginning on July 01, 1940.

The Tribune would further report on June 23, 1940 that a heavy police force and armed reserves raided the Golden Mosque in Lahore on the night between June 21 and June 22, 1940. The police force included F.C. Bourne (District Magistrate), De Heume (Superintendent of Police and in charge of the tear gas squad), Scroggie (Senior Superintendent of Police), K.B. Said Ahmad Shah (Superintendent, C.I.D.), Disney (Reserve Inspector), Ross (Assistant Superintendent Police), K.S. Mir Afzal (City Inspector), and Morgan (Superintendent Additional Police).

Approximately 64 Khaksars are transferred from Lahore to Multan District Jail (where a large number of Khaksars are already present). The jail refuses to supply the Khaksars with meat, milk, and other necessities and the Khaksars go on strike.

The case against 161 Khaksars resumes in the court of the Special Magistrate in Lahore. Two more prosecution witnesses are examined. The case is adjourned until June 24, 1940.

In the court of the City Magistrate in Lahore, eight Khaksars are remanded to police custody until June 24, 1940.

Pera Khan, a Khaksar leader from the North West Frontier Province (NWFP), is convicted by a local Magistrate in Lahore and sentenced to four months of rigorous imprisonment.

A Khaksar leader from Bihar, Abdul Latif (Naib Hakim-e-Ala), is tried in Amritsar in the court of the Additional District Magistrate. Judgement in the case is reserved. According to *The Tribune*, Lahore of June 23, 1940, the court orders are to be announced on June 24, 1940.

1940 June 23

Khaksars demonstrate in Lahore. Zahur Din and five other Khaksars are arrested.

In the court of the Duty Magistrate in Lahore, Ali Ahmad Jan and 25 other Khaksars (who were arrested at Golden Mosque on June 22, 1940), are remanded to judicial custody.

A sympathizer of the Khaksars is arrested in Lahore.

1940 June 24

Six Khaksars are arrested from Unchi Mosque in Lahore.

The Special Magistrate in Lahore convicts 46 Khaksars (arrested on March 19, 1940 from the Khaksar Tehrik headquarters in Ichhra) and sentences them to three years of rigorous imprisonment each along with a fine of Rs. 250 each (if they default on the fine, then they must undergo an additional imprisonment of three months). They are convicted for being members of the Khaksar Tehrik.

In Lahore, six Khaksars (arrested on June 17, 1940) are sentenced to six months of rigorous imprisonment each for being members of the Khaksar Tehrik.

The trial of 12 Khaksars, including four Muslim women and a ten year old girl, commences in the court of a Lahore Magistrate. Police witnesses testify. The court frames charges against the 12 Khaksars and a bail application on behalf of the Muslim women is rejected.

The Additional District Magistrate in Amritsar convicts and sentences Khaksar leader Abdul Latif (Hakim-e-Ala) from Bihar to six months of rigorous imprisonment. Abdul Latif was arrested on May 17, 1940 and charged with being a member of the Khaksar Tehrik and organizing Khaksar activities.

Abdul Sabhan and seven other Khaksars (arrested on June 14, 1940) are convicted and sentenced to three months of rigorous imprisonment on each count. The sentences are to run concurrently.

Khaksars demonstrate in Delduar and Karatiya. Khaksars are also recruited in Kishoreganj. A recruiting center exists in Mymensingh town.

1940 June 25

In the court of the Special Magistrate in Lahore, more evidence is recorded in the trial of 161 Khaksars. One of the accused, Ghulab Khan, dies in Borstal Jail in Lahore.

275 Khaksars (arrested on June 10, 1940) are produced before the Special Magistrate in Lahore and remanded until July 05, 1940.

12 Khaksars from various places (including Bengal, Bihar, and Meerut) are arrested in Lahore.

Police clash with Khaksars at Golden Mosque in Lahore. Seven Khaksars are arrested. Two of the Khaksars are from Bihar, four are from U.P., and one is from Bengal.

The Star of India, Calcutta publishes an article by Khaksar Muhammad Akram Khan, Jalees (Hakim-i-Ala, Province of Sind, Karachi) entitled "A Rejoinder to Sir Sikandar's Canard." In the article, Muhammad Akram responds to Sir Sikandar's statement of June 11, 1940. Below are a few of the major points made by Muhammad Akram Khan in his article:

Sir Sikandar: "Government are satisfied that the Khaksars are in liaison with the enemies of this country."

Muhammad Akram: "...Khaksars have made history. The short span of their life is studded with social service, irrespective of caste and creed. We can with confidence challenge the powers that be to prove conclusively the alleged connections of Khaksars with enemy countries..."

Sir Sikandar: "Khaksars are the only party in the Punjab who have dared to defy Government orders, while all other volunteer organizations have faithfully submitted."

Muhammad Akram: "The organizations that are said to have 'submitted' were the creations of the 'cabal' manufactured to aggravate the situation and bring the matter to a head, so as to create a boogy...

The orders and the ban in question, sought to sap the very life and existance of the Khaksars. The orders were unjustified and uncalled for, and hence the grim resolve of Khaksars to defy and seek to right the wrong."

Sir Sikandar: "Khaksars claim to be a non-communal and non-sectarian organization, in actual facts it is not so."

Muhammad Akram: "The constitution of the Khasar Movement provides for entry of Hindus, Sikhs and others. A number of Hindus and Sikhs are Khaksars..."

Sir Sikandar: "Khaksars claim that their one and only mission is social service, yet their action belie their professions."

Muhammad Akram: "…If by social service we are to understand that a party should make high sounding speeches and consider and adopt a plethora of pious resolutions - the Khaksars have failed in that kind of activity. But social service means service of humanity, irrespective of colour, creed or label, then the Khaksars have created in the nine years of their life a noble record. In this short term they have rendered 60,000,000 acts of services. Is it sectarianism, to give Khaksar blood for hundereds of transfusions and thus save the lives of dying Europeans and Hindus. India knows it too well and none can deny the truth of our assertion. Even Sir Sikandar, at times, much before these troubled days, while receiving the Khaksar Guards-of-Honour, has acknoweledged and eulogised in the best terms, the services the Khaksars render, and has prayed for the blessings of God on the movement."

Sir Sikandar: "The Khaksars have openly abjured all alleged connection with the enemy. This new phaze can only be countenanced, if and when the Khaksars, give up their unlawful activities, go back to their homes, and help Government in war efforts."

Muhammad Akram: "The defence of India, is prime consideration with the Khaksars and when that moment arrives, the Khaksars will shed every drop of their blood for the protection of this country, and save her from the ravaging hand of the enemy."

Editor's Note: The entire rejoinder is not given here. Refer to the newspaper for full contents.

1940 June 26

The City Magistrate in Ahmedabad sentences Khaksar Chandbhai Dinmahmud to a fine of Rs. 50, or in default one month of simple imprisonment, for taking out a procession of Khaksars. The accused Khaksar opts to go to jail.

The trial of 160 Khaksars (one of the accused Khaksars died in Borstal Jail on June 25, 1940) continues in the court of the Special Magistrate in Lahore.

The Lahore City Magistrate sentences five Khaksars to two years of rigorous imprisonment each for demonstrating in Lahore.

1940 June 27

Quaid-e-Azam meets with the Viceroy in Simla. Khaksar issue is discussed. *The Tribune*, Lahore would report the news on June 28, 1940 under the heading, "Mr. Jinnah Meets Viceroy: Complete Secrecy Maintained."

Six Khaksars (arrested on June 22, 1940) are "challaned" in the court of a Lahore Magistrate and five are sentenced to four months of rigorous imprisonment each.

A Lahore Magistrate sentences five Khaksars to two and a half years of rigorous imprisonment each for parading.

Five Khaksars are convicted for parading in Lahore and sentenced to two years of rigorous imprisonment each in the court of a Lahore Magistrate.

In the court of the Special Magistrate in Lahore, prosecution witnesses are examined in the trial of 160 Khaksars. The case is adjourned until July 01, 1940.

In Ahmedabad, two Khaksars are convicted for taking out a procession. They are sentenced to a fine of Rs. 50 or one month of imprisonment.

1940 June 28

Khaksars hold demonstrations in Lahore. Six Khaksars are arrested.

Quaid-e-Azam issues a statement to the Press regarding the Khaksars:
"I have received a number of letters and was personally pressed by the Muslim public on my way to Simla from Bombay to intervene in the Punjab Government-Khaksar trouble. There is also an impression among the Muslim public and the rank and file of the Khaksars that the All-India Muslim League is not doing anything in the matter. I may reiterate that it is the declared policy of the All-India Muslim League to do all it can to help the Muslims wherever they may be and see that justice is done to them. I personally have not concealed my sympathy with the Khaksars generally and I would like to repeat that if the Khaksar leaders put their heads together and enable me with authority to serve them and follow my advice I shall be prepared to do all I can to find an honourable solution of the present impasse." *The Hindustan Times*, June 29, 1940

Editor's Comments: Quaid-e-Azam continued to face pressure from the Muslims of India to take steps to resolve the Khaksar issue. They expressed this verbally and also through letters and telegrams directly sent to Jinnah, and he admitted this in his statement on May 08, 1940. But again, Jinnah merely issued a Press statement clarifying his position and reiterated that he had no authority to take any action on behalf of the Khaksars. In the eyes of the Khaksars and their sympathizers, Quaid-e-Azam's words were seen as nothing more than sugar coated pills used to satisfy and calm the pressure that he was receiving from the Muslim community. Although Quaid-e-Azam sympathized with the Khaksars in his statement, he took no real and practical action to help the Khaksars. After his meeting with the Viceroy on June 27, 1940, Jinnah spoke to the Press, but he never disclosed whether he discussed the Khaksar issue with the Viceroy and if so what the details of that discussion had been.

Even though the Khaksars did not think that Jinnah needed their permission to bring about a settlement regarding the Khaksar issue, they still decided to send him a telegram officially granting him authority to resolve their issue with the Government. Thus, following Quaid-e-Azam's statement, Dr. Mohammad Ismail Nami, a Khaksar leader, sent him a telegram on July 03, 1940 giving Jinnah authority (as per his requirement) to negotiate on behalf of the Khaksars.

1940 June 29

Khaksars demonstrate in Lahore. Five Khaksars from Peshawar are arrested.

A Khaksar is arrested near Golden Mosque in Lahore.

1940 June 30

Khaksars hold a demonstration in Lahore. Four Khaksars are arrested.

Abdul Karim and four other Khaksars from the North West Frontier Province (NWFP) are produced before the Duty Magistrate in Lahore and remanded to police custody.

July

1940 July 01

Khaksar Mohammad Shafi is produced before the Additional District Magistrate in Amritsar and remanded for 13 days.

Two sympathizers of the Khaksars are arrested in Lahore. They are accused of giving shelter to Khaksars arriving from other cities.

Khaksars demonstrate in Lahore. Four Khaksars are arrested.

1940 July 02

Agha Ghazanfar Ali meets with Sir Sikandar Hayat Khan and mentions the results of his meeting with Allama Mashriqi.

Four Khaksars (arrested on July 01, 1940) are produced before the City Magistrate.

The inquest proceedings into the death of Khaksar Mohammad Azim resume in the court of the City Magistrate in Lahore.

Police raid a Khaksar house in Lahore. Two people are arrested. Police also confiscate Khaksar belchas.

Noor Khan (member of the District Board) is arrested for helping the Khaksars.

1940 July 03

Dr. Mohammad Ismail Nami (a Khaksar leader) sends a telegram to Quaid-e-Azam, authorizing him to negotiate on behalf of the Khaksars for an honorable peace with the Punjab Government: "Regarding your recent statement I, the present Head of the Khaksar Movement, delegate authority to you for honourable peace with the

Punjab Ministry including removal of ban of February 28, release of Allama Mashriqi and others, compensation to the survivors of those killed, refund of fine and return of property confiscated by the Government."
Editor's Comments: As per Jinnah's requirement, an authority was also issued.

In the court of the Special Magistrate in Lahore, hearing resumes in the trial of Karim Ullah and four other Khaksars accused of assaulting a police constable.

The City Magistrate in Lahore holds an inquest into the death of a Khaksar. The Khaksar died as a result of injuries sustained from one of the police raids on mosques in Lahore on the night between June 10 and June 11, 1940. *The Tribune*, Lahore would report on July 04, 1940 that during the inquest, a Civil Surgeon stated that the death of the Khaksar "was due to concussion, bruising and laceration of brain, attendant on fractured skull."

1940 July 04

Khaksars demonstrate in Lahore. Four Khaksars are arrested.

The trial of 159 Khaksars resumes in the court of the Special Magistrate in Lahore.

The Star of India, Calcutta reports that Barrister Mian Ahmed Shah has sent a letter to the Home Minister of Bengal assuring him help in maintaining peace under the prevailing circumstances in Bengal. Mian Ahmed Shah's letter states: "I as the Chief Officer of the Khaksars of this province put the entire services of the Khaksars at the disposal of your Government. The Government can make use of them in any way they like. I hope that the Khaksars, being well-organised and non-communal will prove of tremendous help to the Government. I emphatically assure you that we Khaksars will never fail to assist the Government whenever necessary."

The Star of India, Calcutta reports that Barrister Mian Ahmed Shah has issued the following statement:
"I very much regret to note that a section of the Hindus of Bengal has given expression to the fear that if the war situation develops in a particular way the Hindus of the Province will not be secure because of the Khaksar Movement gaining strength day by day. They appeal to the authorities to take necessary steps against the movement.
Let me, as a responsible Chief of the Khaksars of this province, assure my Hindu brethren that at any critical time the Khaksars will be the first to stand by the Hindus to render them all possible help. If the Khaksars would behave otherwise, they would betray their own principles, their motherland and also those who are sons of the soil. Instead of alienating sympathy let us embrace one another as brother bearing in mind that India can be saved only through Hindu-Muslim unity.
I also vehmently refute the change [charge] that the Khaksars Movement is encouraging Fascism."

1940 July 05

Khaksars demonstrate in Lahore. Four Khaksars are arrested.

The trial of five Khaksars resumes in the court of the Special Magistrate in Lahore.

In the court of the City Magistrate in Lahore, five Khaksars (arrested on June 30, 1940 for demonstrating) are sentenced to two years of rigorous imprisonment each.

230 Khaksars (arrested on the night between June 10 and June 11, 1940) are sent for trial before a Lahore Magistrate. Evidence is to be recorded on July 06, 1940.

1940 July 06

The trial of 159 Khaksars resumes in the court of the Special Magistrate in Lahore. Prosecution witnesses are examined. *The Tribune*, Lahore of July 7, 1940 would report that the witness "did not see any person firing at the police party."

Quaid-e-Azam replies to Dr. Mohammad Ismail Nami's telegram of July 03, 1940: "Your telegram. My advice suspend defiance pending negotiations. If your instructions obeyed by rank and file your authority cannot be doubted. Willing help find solution."

1940 July 07

Khaksars hold a demonstration in Lahore. Three Khaksars are arrested.

Dr. Mohammad Ismail Nami issues a statement to the press saying: "Peace negotiations have been taken up by Mr. Jinnah. To facilitate his efforts I order suspension of defiance of law and order by Khaksars in the Punjab till July 27 [1940]. Salar-i-Khas-Hind should take immediate steps to stop Khaksar activities." *The Statesman*, Calcutta, July 08, 1940, *The Hindustan Times*, July 08, 1940

Dr.Nami also sends the following telegram to Mr. M.A. Jinnah: "Advice accepted. Orders issued for suspending defiance of law till July 27 [1940]. Instruct Sir Sikandar Hyat Khan also to suspend arresting Khaksars."
Editor's Comments: As per Jinnah's demand, demonstrations of the Khaksars were also suspended.

1940 July 08

The trial of 159 Khaksars resumes in the court of the Special Magistrate in Lahore. Two more prosecution witnesses are examined.

Seven Khaksars (arrested on the night between June 10 and June 11, 1940) are tried in the court of a Lahore Magistrate. The case is adjourned.

Four Khaksars (arrested for demonstrating in Lahore) are convicted and sentenced to two years of rigorous imprisonment each.

In Lahore, three Khaksars (arrested on July 07, 1940) are produced before a Local Magistrate and remanded to judicial lock-up.

Frontier Khaksars organize a provincial camp near Attock.

In response to Dr. Mohammad Ismail Nami's instructions of July 07, 1940, Khaksars suspend their demonstrations until July 27, 1940. No demonstrations are held today.

1940 July 09

Inside a packed courtroom in Lahore, Abdul Majid and 19 other Khaksars (arrested following a raid at Sheranwali Mosque on the night between June 10 and June 11, 1940) are tried in front of a Local Magistrate. The court frames charges against the Khaksars.

A Lahore Magistrate sentences Mohammad Yaqoob and three other Khaksars from U.P. (arrested on July 02, 1940 for demonstrating) to two years of rigorous imprisonment each for one charge and four months of rigorous imprisonment each for another charge. The sentences are to run concurrently.

The trial of 159 Khaksars resumes in the court of the Special Magistrate in Lahore.

The trial of 12 Khaksars, including five women, resumes in the court of the Additional District Magistrate in Lahore.

The Additional District Magistrate in Multan sentences 78 Khaksars from Sind to six months of rigorous imprisonment each for being members of the Khaksar Tehrik.

28 Khaksars from Sind (arrested on June 01, 1940 at Khanewal Railway Station) are tried in Multan.

1940 July 10

The trial of 159 Khaksars resumes in the court of the Special Magistrate in Lahore.

The trial of Abdul Karim and 20 other Khaksars resumes in the court of a local Magistrate in Lahore.

The provincial Khaksar leader of Bihar orders the Bihar branches not to send any more Khaksar batches to Lahore, pending the negotiations between Quaid-e-Azam and the Punjab Government.

1940 July 11

Quaid-e-Azam responds to Dr. Nami: "I received your telegram of the 6th July suspending defiance of law by the Khaksars in Punjab till 27th July. I will communicate with you in the matter as soon as possible."

1940 July 12

The trial of 159 Khaksars resumes in the court of the Special Magistrate in Lahore. F.C. Bourne, Lahore District Magistrate, testifies in court.

14 Khaksars (arrested on June 11, 1940) are tried in the court of a Lahore Magistrate.

Three Khaksars (arrested on July 07, 1940) are "challaned" in the court of the Lahore City Magistrate.

1940 July 13

In Multan, Maulvi Mohammad Sadiq, Fazal Elahi, and Khair Mohammad (Khaksar Salars) are sentenced to six weeks of solitary confinement each for ordering Khaksars in the Multan District Jail to hold daily parades.

In Multan, 16 Khaksars from Sind are sentenced to three and a half years of rigorous imprisonment each.

In Multan, two Khaksars from Sind are sentenced to six months of rigorous imprisonment each.

A hotel keeper in Multan is put on trial for helping the Khaksars.

A hotel keeper in Multan is sentenced to one year of rigorous imprisonment for helping the Khaksars.

In Multan, the Additional District Magistrate sentences Khaksars in seven different cases to six months of rigorous imprisonment each. The cases are as follows: 16 Khaksars arrested at the Wali Mohammad Mosque (Multan), 12 Khaksars arrested at Khanpur Railway Station, five Khaksars arrested in Shamast-Barez (Multan), two Khaksars arrested from Joia Wali Mosque (Multan), one Khaksar arrested at Multan Cantonement, 17 Khaksars arrested from Bahawal Haq Khangah (Multan), and 26 Khaksars arrested at Khanewal.

The Additional District Magistrate in Multan sentences a Khaksar to one month of imprisonment. Another Khaksar is asked for a security of Rs. 300.

The trial of 159 Khaksars resumes in the court of the Special Magistrate in Lahore. Prosecution witnesses are examined and the case is adjourned for further hearing.

1940 July 15

A Khaksar is produced in the court of the Additional District Magistrate in Amritsar.

1940 July 16

The Hindustan Times, Delhi reports that the Khaksars took care of Mehta Ram Rakha Mal, a political prisoner who became ill while in prison. This is reported by Munshi Hari Lal, M.L.A.

Quaid-e-Azam writes a letter to Lord Linlithgow, Viceroy of India:
Dear Lord Linlithgow,
        With reference to our talk regarding the Khaksar situation in the Punjab, I have made one more attempt to find a satifactory solution and I am enclosing here with a copy of the statement that I issued from Simla and the subsequent development that is shown by the correspondence that has passed between me and Dr. Mohammad Ismail Nami of Calcutta.
        I am inclined to think from what information is available to me that he is next to the Mashraqi in the Khaksar organisation.
        He has accepted my advice and has suspended defiance till 27th July, but if necessary I will be able to persuade him for continuing this suspension pending our being able to find a satisfactory solution. I think we ought not to miss this opportunity at this juncture to bring the Khaksars round as the matter has now gone beyond the Khaksar organisation and there is a universal feeling among the Mussalmans all over India and particularly in the Punjab that they are being crushed by the Punjab Government at the bidding of Sir Sikander Hyat Khan.
        If you are inclined to take up the matter as I thought you were inclined, during the course of our conversation, I shall be glad to do all I can do to see that a reasonable solution is accepted by the Khaksars.
Yours sincerely,
M.A. Jinnah

1940 July 17

The Additional District Magistrate and the Superintendent of Police give orders to put Khaksars in cells in Multan.

1940 July 18

A Lahore court announces its verdict in the case of a Khaksar from Ahmedabad who was arrested on the night between June 10 and June 11, 1940.

Five Khaksars (arrested on the night between June 10 and June 11, 1940) including Khushal Khan, editor of *Insaf*, are tried in the court of a Lahore Magistrate. Further hearing is adjourned.

1940 July 19

37 Khaksars (arrested from Unchi Mosque on the night between June 10 and June 11, 1940) are tried in the court of a Lahore Magistrate. *The Tribune*, Lahore of July 20, 1940 would report that the "Assistant Sub-Inspector of Police, stated that the Unchi Mosque was raided on the night of the 10th June. The door was broken open and tear gas bombs were thrown in the mosque. There was a clash between the Khaksars and the police as a result of which one Khaksar died later on. In all 39 Khaksars were arrested one of whom was unconscious. They were removed to the Central Jail." The case is adjourned until the next day, July 20, 1940.

Questions regarding the Khaksar Tehrik are raised in the Bengal Assembly. *The Tribune*, Lahore of July 21, 1940 would report that "As to the steps the Government proposed taking for the control of the movement Sir Nazimuddin said that the whole question was under the examination of the Government."

In Rawalpindi, 10 Khaksars from Kohat (North West Frontier Province) are sentenced to six months of rigorous imprisonment each for being members of the Khaksar Tehrik.

1940 July 20

The trial of 32 Khaksars (arrested from Unchi Mosque on the night between June 10 and June 11, 1940) resumes in the court of a Lahore Magistrate.

20 Khaksars (arrested at Sheranwala Mosque on the night between June 10 and June 11, 1940) are "challaned." The case is adjourned without a hearing.

1940 July 23

84 Khaksars (arrested on the night between June 10 and June 11, 1940) are tried in the court of a Lahore Magistrate. The case is adjourned without a hearing.

11 Khaksars are tried in the court of a Lahore Magistrate. The case is adjourned for court orders.

The inquest hearing regarding the death of Khaksar Mohammad Azim resumes in the court of the City Magistrate in Lahore. The case is adjourned for further hearing.

In Rawalpindi, a court frames charges against Khaksar leader Khadam Hussain from the North West Frontier Province (NWFP).

1940 July 24

The trial of 84 Khaksars (arrested on the night between June 10 and June 11, 1940) resumes in the court of a Lahore Magistrate.

The Viceroy, Lord Linlithgow writes to Quaid-e-Azam:
Dear Mr. Jinnah,
Thank you very much for your letter of 16th July about the Khaksar movement. I have read it with much interest, but I do not see how I can intervene in this matter, which is primarily one for the Punjab Government. I now understand that Sir Sikander Hyat Khan has published the conditions on which he would be prepared to revoke the order which makes the Khaksar movement an unlawful association.
Yours sincerely,
LINLITHGOW

1940 July 25

The trial of 84 Khaksars (arrested on the night between June 10 and June 11, 1940) continues in the court of a Lahore Magistrate. Further prosecution evidence is recorded.

In the court of the Special Magistrate in Lahore, the trial of 159 Khaksars is adjourned without any proceedings.

Questions are raised in the Bengal Assembly about the Khaksar Tehrik. Sir Nazim ud Din (Bengal Home Minister) replies and again states that the Khaksar issue is under the consideration of the Government.

1940 July 26

The trial of 159 Khaksars resumes in the court of the Special Magistrate in Lahore. More prosecution witnesses are examined.

14 Khaksars (arrested at Mubarak Mosque on the night between June 10 and June 11, 1940) are tried in the court of a Lahore Magistrate.

The City Magistrate in Lahore sentences three Khaksars (arrested for parading on July 07, 1940) to two years of rigorous imprisonment each for parading.

Dr. Mohammad Ismail Nami (a Khaksar leader) extends his order to the Khaksars in Punjab to suspend their demonstrations and activities until August 10, 1940. The Khaksars are awaiting the result of Jinnah's efforts to bring a settlement between the Punjab Government and the Khaksars.
Editor's Comments: The Khaksars even extended the suspension of their demonstrations, hoping that Jinnah would bring desired results.

1940 July 27

The Hindustan Times, Delhi reports that Khaksar activities in Punjab are to remain suspended until August 10, 1940. According to the newspaper, "Mr. Ahmad Shah [a Khaksar leader in Bengal], in a statement to the Press, says that he has received orders from Dr. Mohd. Ismail Nami to the effect that the latter has not so far heard from Mr. Jinnah about the result of his peace efforts with the Punjab Government. He (Dr. Nami), therefore, orders extension of the suspension of the Khaksar activities in the Punjab till August 10."

1940 July 29

The trial of 159 Khaksars resumes in the court of the Special Magistrate in Lahore. More prosecution witnesses are examined.

Lahore District Magistrate, L. P. Addison, disposes of an application, which was filed on behalf of all of the Khaksars arrested on the night between June 10 and June 11, 1940. The application requests that these Khaksars' cases be transferred to another province. According to *The Tribune*, Lahore of July 30, 1940, nine Khaksar Salars appeared in court and: "…explained that the Government did not consider them to be its subjects but it gave them the name of 'fifth columnists.' Under the circumstances they apprehend that they would not get justice in this province.
      Sardar Sahib Bhag Singh, Prosecuting D.S.P., opposed the application on the ground that the Governor-General alone could pass orders on the application under Section 527, I.P.C." The court orders that the Khaksar application be forwarded to the Government. However, a second application to transfer the Khaksars' case from Lahore Magistrate Diwan Somer Nath's court is rejected.

The Star of India, Calcutta publishes a letter to the Editor from Barrister Abdun Nabi Khan. In his letter, Nabi Khan condemns the British attitude towards Allama Mashriqi: "…Allama Mashriqi and his movement have been condemned while the British are still begging for help from Mr. Gandhi and the Congress. Does it, therefore, mean that the British Government and the British people have chosen to prefer a sleeping partner to an active [one]…To my mind, Allama Mashriqi is one of the few leaders who had sufficient vision to foresee the events of to-day and the only one who had the courage to prepare for them while all the 'great' political organisations of India were, and still are, wasting time and energy in petty pickering. Sometimes I wonder why Sir Sikandar Hyat Khan, has banned the Khaksar movement in his province…Sir Sikandar Hyat Khan can be induced to modify his standpoint and consider the Khaksars' case sympathetically."

1940 July 31

The Special Magistrate in Lahore sentences Ahmad Dastgir and four other Khaksars to three years of rigorous imprisonment each.

August

1940 August 01

The trial of 12 Khaksars, including four women and an 11 year old girl, resumes in the court of the Additional District Magistrate in Lahore. F.C. Bourne, Deputy

Commissioner of Lahore, and Bashir Ahmad Saddiqi, a Khaksar leader, are examined in court. The case is adjourned until August 05, 1940 when Begum Shah Nawaz is to give evidence.

The Statesman, Calcutta reports that Sir Khwaja Nazimuddin (Home Minister) replied to questions about the Khaksar Tehrik in the Bengal Legislative Council. According to the newspaper, he informed the Assembly that the Khaksar Tehrik is a non-communal movement and that Hindus and Sikhs are also members of the Khaksar Tehrik. He further states that the issue of the treatment of the Khaksars in Bengal is under consideration by the Government.

1940 August 02

The trial of 159 Khaksars resumes in the court of the Special Magistrate in Lahore. 60 of the 159 Khaksars record their statements.

The inquest hearing in regards to the death of a Khaksar following a raid by police (on the night between June 10 and June 11, 1940) resumes in the court of the City Magistrate in Lahore. Adam, the Assistant Superintendent of Police at Amritsar, is examined in court.

Quaid-e-Azam writes a letter to the Lord Linlithgow, Viceroy of India:
Dear Lord Linlithgow,
 I am in receipt of your letter about the Khaksar movement, dated the 24th July 1940.
 I moved in the matter firstly, because Your Excellency showed concern about the Khaksar situation in the Punjab in the course of our conversation on the 27th June; and secondly, that in the earlier stages Sir Sikander Hyat Khan, in the course of our correspondence, indicated in the following words: 'It may be necessary to consult the Government of India also, and consequently it will take some time before final decision can be taken.' Lastly, I can cite more than one instance that the Viceroy and the Governor General have found a way to intervene when it was considered necessary.
 However, I am sorry if Your Excellency considers that in this case you do not see your way to intervene.
 I am glad that Your Excellency informs me that Sir Sikander Hyat Khan has published the conditions on which he would be prepared to revoke the order which declares the Khaksars an unlawful association. I am not aware of those conditions, but I have requested Dr. Nami to obtain a copy of those conditions and get in direct touch with Sir Sikander Hyat Khan.
Yours sincerely,
M.A. Jinnah
Editor's Comments: The Viceroy put the responsibility on the Sir Sikandar. Quaid-e-Azam applied no pressure and basically accepted Viceroy's non-intervention.

1940 August 03

The trial of 159 Khaksars continues in the court of the Special Magistrate in Lahore. 49 of the 159 Khaksars record their statements. The case is adjourned until August 05, 1940.

1940 August 05

The trial of 159 Khaksars resumes in the court of the Special Magistrate in Lahore. 46 of the 159 Khaksars record their statements.

The trial of five women Khaksars, including an 11 year old girl, resumes in the court of the Additional District Magistrate in Lahore.
Editor's Comments: Even a minor girl was not excused and was brought under trial.

1940 August 06

The trial of 159 Khaksars resumes in the court of the Special Magistrate in Lahore. 30 of the 159 Khaksars record their statements.

The trial of 26 Khaksars (arrested from Golden Mosque on June 22, 1940) begins in the court of a Lahore Magistrate.

The Government of India bans drills by non-official volunteer organizations in the entire India.

1940 August 07

Barrister Mian Ahmed Shah meets with R.F. Mudie, Chief Secretary of Punjab (upon his invitation), to discuss the Khaksar issue.

1940 August 08

In Lahore, Sir Sikandar Hayat Khan responds to journalists' questions. He gives the following terms for removing the ban on the Khaksar Tehrik:
1. Khaksar must limit their activities to social work only.
2. Khaksars should give an undertaking not to defy the Punjab Government's orders.
3. All Khaksars that have come to the Punjab from other areas should return to their homes.
The Tribune, Lahore of August 09, 1940 would report that "The question of the removal of the ban of the 28th February on parades in military formation, etc. did not arise now because the ban had now been imposed all over India."

1940 August 09

In the court of a Lahore Magistrate, charges are framed against 20 Khaksars arrested from Patolianwali Mosque.

The trial against 12 Khaksars, including five women, continues in the court of the Additional District Magistrate in Lahore. Mohammad Sadiq, defense counsel, describes the Punjab Government's ban on the Khaksar Tehrik as being vague and indefinite. *The Tribune*, Lahore of August 10, 1940 would report that "He [Mohammad Sadiq] stressed that membership of all-India body could not be made an offence by merely declaration of provincial Government."

Agha Ghazanfar Ali issues a Press statement.

The Star of India, Calcutta reports that Jinnah has advised Dr. Ismail Nami to get in touch with Sir Sikandar Hayat Khan in regards to settling the Khaksar issue. The newspaper further reports that Dr. Ismail Nami has appointed Dr. Sir Zia ud Din Ahmed, Nawab Bahadur Yar Jang, and Barrister Mian Ahmed Shah to settle the issue with the Punjab Government.
Editor's Comments: When Quaid-e-Azam asked Dr. Nami to talk to Sir Sikandar himself, it was understood that Quaid-e-Azam was withdrawing from conducting direct and active negotiations with Sir Sikandar Hayat Khan and the Central Government. The Khaksar circle viewed this as an indication that Jinnah and the Muslim League had abandoned the Khaksars. It was believed in the Khaksar circle that Jinnah never put in serious effort to get the matter resolved. With no results from Quaid-e-Azam, the Khaksars had to rely on their own efforts.

1940 August 10

The trial of four female Khaksars concludes in the court of the Additional District Magistrate in Lahore. The court reserves judgement until August 13, 1940.

Police remain vigilant in Lahore, watching for any Khaksar activity.

The Khaksars had suspended their activities until today in order to give Jinnah time to negotiate with the Punjab Government. As desired by Jinnah, the Khaksars had stopped their demonstrations, but Jinnah made no effort to exert any pressure on the Government to redress the grievances of the Khaksars or for the release of Mashriqi and others.

1940 August 11

The Hindu Mahasabha demands immediate withdrawal of the Government's ban on military uniforms by members of non-official volunteer organizations.

1940 August 12

The Star of India, Calcutta reports Dr. Ismail Nami's statement:
"Mian Ahmed Shah Bar-at-Law and Nawab Abdulla Khan Director of 'Hamdam' Lucknow is still busy with peace efforts and they will not be able to complete their work by August 10 [1940].

At the request of Mian Ahmed Shah the truce time has been extended till August 25 [1940].

With the permission of the Government of India, Mian Ahmad Shah accompanied by two other Khaksars is proceeding to see Allama Mashriqui Sahib in Vellore Jail.

'Salar-e-khas Hind' should see that all the activities of the Khaksars in the Punjab remain suspended, till August 25 [1940]."

In the court of a Lahore Magistrate, 26 Khaksars (arrested from Golden Mosque on June 22, 1940) are sentenced to six months of imprisonment each.

The Statesman, Calcutta reports that "Moslem League quarters here [Lucknow] have been informed that Mr. Jinnah's intervention with the Punjab Government has not been successful. "

The Statesman, Calcutta reports that Raja Ghazanfar Ali (Parliamentary Secretary, Punjab Government) went to Lucknow and Allahabad to assess the sentiments of Muslim League leaders in U.P. in regards to the Khaksar issue.

The Statesman, Calcutta reports that Barrister Mian Ahmed Shah (a Khaksar leader) recently met with the Chief Secretary of the U.P. Government to discuss the Khaksar issue. The newspaper further reports that it is understood that Mian Ahmed Shah has been granted permission to see Allama Mashriqi in jail.

1940 August 14

The trial of 159 Khaksars resumes in the court of the Special Magistrate in Lahore.

1940 August 15

Barrister Mian Ahmed Shah (Bar at Law and a Khaksar leader) meets Allama Mashriqi in Vellore Central Jail to discuss the Central Government's ban on the Khaksar Tehrik. The meeting would take place over three days.

1940 August 20

13 Khaksars are tried in the court of a Lahore Magistrate.

R.B. Ghaznavi (a Khaksar Salar in Peshawar) expresses hope that an agreement will be reached between the Khaksars and the Punjab Government.

1940 August 21

Barrister Mian Ahmed Shah (Barrister and a Khaksar leader) issues a statement regarding the Central Government's ban on prohibiting drills by volunteer organizations:

"I met Allama Mashriqui Saheb in the Vellore Central Jail on August 15 and discussed with him for three days the situation arising out of the all-India ban imposed by the Central Government prohibiting drills, etc. by various volunteer organizations as well as the Khaksars dispute with the Punjab Ministry. After consultations with Allama Saheb, *Adara-Alliya-Hind* and *Madarun-nizam*, I make the following statement with full authority that till the duration of the present European war:

a) The Khaksars shall obey the ban imposed by the Central Government wherever enforced by any Provincial Government and shall cease to drill.

b) There is no objection to their going to their weekly meetings or to the mosques together or one behind the other, but they must not do this in a way which gives the character of military drill or formation to their movement. Similarly, they shall continue to do their social work and daily programme in their mohallas with the above restrictions.

c) *Belchas* may, of course, be carried, but they must not drill with them.

d) The uniform will be slightly altered to make it less like military uniform by the removal of shoulder straps and flaps to the pockets.

e) There may be periodical Khaksar rallies with the permission of *Idara-ulliyia* but the above restrictions have to be strictly observed.

I hope that the difficulties in the way of the Khaksars in Delhi, Punjab and the Frontier Province will be removed very soon. I also wish to come to an agreement with the Punjab Government on the lines of that reached by me with the U.P. Government last November." *The Hindustan Times*, August 22, 1940

Editor's Comments: The Government was facing acute pressure due to World War II and was thus seeking Mashriqi's cooperation desperately. Keeping in view this desperation, Mashriqi again came forward to help the Government by extending cooperation for the duration of the war.

1940 August 22

The trial of 39 Khaksars (arrested from Unchi Mosque on the night between June 10 and June 11, 1940) continues in Lahore. Prosecution evidence is recorded and further hearing is adjourned.

1940 August 24

In the verdict of the trial of 159 Khaksars (arrested in connection with the Khaksar-Police clash on March 19, 1940), the Special Magistrate in Lahore commits 149 of the Khaksars to Sessions. Of the remaining ten Khaksars, one escapes from police custody and the other nine are discharged.

1940 August 27

The trial of 83 Khaksars (arrested from Golden Mosque on the night between June 10 and June 11, 1940) resumes in the court of a Lahore Magistrate. The case is adjourned for further hearing.

Barrister Mian Ahmed Shah meets with Sir Sikandar Hayat Khan. They are to meet again on September 03, 1940.

1940 August 28

Barrister Mian Ahmed Shah advises the Khaksars to follow the Central Government's restrictions on volunteer activities. He also states that hopefully the ban on the Khaksar Tehrik could be removed after his meeting with Sir Sikandar Hayat Khan on September 03, 1940.

247 defense witnesses are filed on behalf of 149 Khaksars who had been committed to Sessions on August 24, 1940 by the Special Magistrate in Lahore.

The Special Magistrate in Lahore sentences a Khaksar (arrested in Ramgali on March 21, 1940) to five years of rigorous imprisonment.

1940 August 29

The Additional District Magistrate in Lahore announces the verdict in the trial of 12 Khaksars, including four women and an 11 year-old girl. The male Khaksars are sentenced to a total of two years and three months of rigorous imprisonment on multiple charges. The women Khaksars are ordered to keep peace and order for one year or face six months of simple imprisonment. The 11 year-old girl is acquitted on all charges.

1940 August 30

Khaksar Mohammad Sharif (Naib Hakim-i-Ala, Punjab) is produced before the Special Magistrate in Lahore. Sharif was re-arrested, after having been released, for being a member of the Khaksar Tehrik.

September

1940 September 01

The Hindustan Times, Delhi reports that a conference of Khaksar leaders is to take place on September 03, 1940 in Lucknow. The conference is to plan out the future of the Khaksar Tehrik. The newspaper further reports that Abdulla Jan (Nazami-i-Ala) and Arbab Sher Akbar Khan (Salar-i-Khas) have left for the conference.

The Tribune, Lahore reports that the Punjab Government has decided to remove the ban on the Khaksar Tehrik. The Government of India has decided to do the same in the Delhi Province. A notification regarding this decision is to be issued by the Chief Commissioner.

1940 September 02

The Punjab Government issues a Press Note regarding the removal of the ban on the Khaksar Tehrik:

It is announced that with effect from to-day (the 2nd of September, 1940) the Punjab Government have withdrawn the Notification of March 19, 1940 by which the Association known as the Anjuman-i-Khaksaran was declared to be an unlawful association under Section 16 of the Indian Criminal Law Amendment Act, 1908.

The Punjab Government have further withdrawn with effect from to-day another Notification of March 19, 1940, by which the premises known as Idara-i-Aliya in the village of Ichhra, near Lahore, were notified for the purposes of Section 17-A of the Indian Criminal Law Amendment Act, 1908.

Editor's Comments: With renewed demonstrations (after suspension) and renewed Khaksar activities against the Government, the authorities realized that the ban had to be removed.

1940 September 03

A conference of Khaksar leaders is held in Lucknow to review the Khaksar-Government issue.

1940 September 04

Several batches of Khaksars (arrested from various mosques on the night between June 10 and June 11, 1940) are tried in the court of a Lahore Magistrate. The case is adjourned for defense evidence.

1940 September 05

The Hindustan Times, Delhi reports that Allama Mashriqi has issued a statement through Agha Ghazanfar Ali Shah (deputed by the Punjab Government to meet Mashriqi in jail). According to the newspaper, Mashriqi stated:

"The terms now put forward are not such that I cannot agree to them. In fact one of the terms is a request from the Punjab Government that the Khaksars will help them in every way during the war. This is rather amusing after we have been called Nazis and naturally takes away the blame from us. The other is that I did not give any order for the Lahore clash on March 19 [1940] nor did the Khaksars gather under my directions on that day, which is literally true as I was not there and do not know even now how the clash happened. The third is that the Khaksar movement will stick to genuine social service as its fundamental aim. This, no Khaksar can possibly object to. The fourth is that the Khaksar will not object to the orders of February 28 [1940] for the duration of the war. Agha Ghazanfar Ali tells me…that the Premier has agreed to lift the ban on the movement immediately after these terms are agreed to by me. I agree to all these terms in order to end this situation at such a critical moment."

The newspaper adds, "Allama Mashriqi reiterates his offer of the services of the 250,000 Khaksars to the Viceroy for the defence of India and says in spite of all that has been done against the Khaksars, I do not wish to add to the troubles of the British Government owing to the grave situation with which they are confronted at present."

1940 September 07

Sir Sikandar Hayat Khan (Punjab Premier) and Barrister Mian Ahmed Shah (a Khaksar leader) discuss the release of imprisoned Khaksars following the Government's removal of the ban on the Khaksar Tehrik.

1940 September 08

Khaksar leaders meet with Sir Sikandar Hayat Khan to discuss various topics, including the release of Khaksars following the Government's removal of the ban on the Khaksar Tehrik. The Khaksar leaders present at the meeting are Barrister Mian Ahmed Shah (Bar at Law), Haji Subhan Ullah (Hakim-i-Alah of U.P.), Arbab Sher Akbar (Hakim-i-Alah of NWFP), and Sheikh Wali Ullah (from Lucknow).

1940 September 10

The Session Judge of Lahore rejects a Khaksar plea (against the Punjab Government's order prohibiting drills by the Khaksars).

1940 September 13

Police search a Khaksar leader's house in Tangail, Bengal and seize a Khaksar photo album.

In the Bengal Assembly, Sir Nazim ud Din (Home Minister, Bengal) responds to questions regarding the Khaksars. He states that a Government officer had joined the Khaksar Tehrik.

1940 September 15

In Karachi, two Khaksars are sent to trial before the Magistrate.

1940 September 23

The Additional District Magistrate in Rawalpindi sentences 49 Khaksars (arrested in June 1940) to terms of imprisonment ranging from one day to one year.

The Punjab Government states in a communique that belchas are included in their notification of July 04, 1940, which banned a person from carrying any arm or article capable of being used as an arm in a procession.

1940 September 24

The case against 37 Khaksars continues in the court of a Lahore Magistrate. Two European police officers give evidence.

Quaid-e-Azam meets with the Viceroy and Sir Sikandar Hayat Khan in Simla.

1940 September 27

A local Lahore Magistrate frames charges against 39 Khaksars who were arrested from Unchi Mosque, Lahore on June 12, 1940.

1940 September 28

Dr. Nami, a Khaksar leader, asks the Khaksars not to defy the ban on drills of a military nature. He issues the following statement to the press: "The ban of the Punjab Government dated February 28, 1940, was considered to have merged into the ban of the Central Government, dated August 5, 1940, but now it has been specifically withdrawn. Therefore, the question of its defiance does not arise at all. As regards the ban imposed by the Central Government, it has already been finally decided that it is not to be defied, wherever imposed, although efforts to secure the release of the Allama and all Khaksars, whether convicted or under-trials, would continue." *The Tribune*, Lahore September 29, 1940

1940 September 30

The Statesman, Calcutta reports that the release of Mashriqi and the Khaksars and other matters were discussed at a recent meeting (in Lucknow) of Khaksar leaders from various parts of India.

October

1940 October

A Khaksar conference is held in Delhi. At the conference, the Khaksars pledge to uphold the Tehrik's ideology.

1940 October 08

Frontier Khaksar leaders urge the Deputy Commissioner of Peshawar to remove the ban on Khaksars traveling to Punjab. The Deputy Commissioner forwards their case to the Provincial Government.

1940 October 14

The Government decides to withhold its previous decision to release the Khaksar prisoners.

1940 October 15

The Government decides to release only those Khaksar prisoners who had been convicted or charged for non-violent offenses.

1940 October 17

Barrister Mian Ahmed Shah writes a letter to the Chief Secretary of U.P. stating that he should be allowed to see Allama Mashriqi in Vellore Jail. He also complains of the Government's withholding of Allama Mashriqi's pension.

1940 October 23

The Tribune, Lahore reports that the Punjab Government has ordered the release of 300 Khaksar prisoners. Prisoners from other provinces are to be released in their hometowns.

1940 October 31

Sir Maurice Garnier Hallett (Governor of U.P.) sends a confidential letter to Lord Linlithgow (Viceroy of India) stating that "the offer of cooperation is primary and entirely genuine and that the proposal for the release of the Allama [Mashriqi] is secondary and mainly important as a condition necessary for successful cooperation."
(Muhammad 1973, 78).

November

1940 November 04

The Sessions trial of 149 Khaksars begins in the court of the Sessions Judge in Lahore.

1940 November 06

The Star of India, Calcutta publishes Agha Ghazanfar Ali Shah's (a Khaksar leader) statement to the press:
"I have come to Lahore only with one object, namely, to endeavour to secure the liberation of Allama Inayatullah Khan Mashriqui from jail. I was given to understand that although it is the Government of India which will ultimately consider the question of the release of the Allama, yet being their concern, the Government of the Punjab must initiate it or make the necessary gesture. Mohd

Sharif Khan, in charge of the Idara Aliya Hindia, Ichhra, and myself are moving the Punjab Government for this purpose and we may possibly interview the hon'ble [honorable] the Premier for that end.

As regards other Khaksar prisoners, they are being set at liberty. It is also possible that the Government of the Punjab might drop the pending cases and give general amnesty to the Khaksar prisoners in view of the liberal offer of the Allama for 50,000 volunteers...I affirm with all the emphasis at my command that whatever has happened between the Khaksars and the Punjab Government was due to a very grave misunderstanding augmented and utilised for their own selfish ends, by mischief-mongers..."

1940 November 08

The case against 149 Khaksars resumes in the court of the Sessions Judge in Lahore. Among the witnesses examined on this day is F.C. Bourne, Home Secretary to the Punjab Government and former Deputy Commissioner.

1940 November 20

The trial of 149 Khaksars resumes in the court of the Sessions Judge in Lahore. J.T.M. Bennett (Deputy Inspector General, C.I.D.) is examined in court.

December

1940 December 03

The Sessions Judge in Lahore pronounces his judgement in the trial of 149 Khaksars. He convicts 19 Khaksars and acquits 130. He sentences the convicted Khaksars to transportation for life under section 302 read with 140, four years of rigorous imprisonment each under section 307 I.P.C. read with 140, two years of rigorous imprisonment each under section 54(4), and two years of rigorous imprisonment each under rule 58(2) of the Defence of India Rules. The sentences are to run concurrently. The court also orders all confiscated Khaksar equipment, spades, and uniforms to be destroyed.

1940 December 08

Lord Linlithgow writes to Sir Maurice Garnier Hallett (Governor of U.P.):
"I feel no doubt whatever on the material that I have seen that the Khaksar movement is in fact a dangerous organisation of a communal character; while even if it may be prepared in its own interest to support government in present circumstances, it is in fact the nearest approach in India to a well organised private army. It is only a few months since we publicly recognised the danger of such organisations, and any move on our part which may be interpreted as amounting to the acceptance of active help from the Khaksars as an organisation would...I am certain...be most unwise...Although the movement is at the moment quiescent — thanks to the action taken against its leaders — it is, as I suggest above, still

potentially violent in character; and I do not think it is going too far to suggest that this attempt at negotiation is dictated under a threat more or less veiled of a renewal of violent activities."

Editor's Comments: This letter is a clear reflection of how fearful the British Government was of the Khaksars.

1941-1942

1941

1941 January 01

A meeting of Khaksar leaders is held in Delhi to discuss the Government's attitude towards the Khaksars. The Khaksars consider a number of different options, including starting a civil disobedience movement to settle their issues with the Government. However, they ultimately decide to await the Government's decision regarding the release of Mashriqi and the Khaksars.

1941 January 06

Sahibussiyadat Qazi Abdulha Sadarunnizam, his staff, and other prominent Khaksar leaders reach Lahore. Sadarunnizam refuses *salami* (welcoming reception) until Allama Mashriqi is released. They go to the graveyards where they salute and pray for the Khaksars that were killed during the March 19, 1940 massacre at Lahore. They also visit the Khaksars in jail. They demand Allama Mashriqi's and other Khaksars' release. Sadarunnizam opens Idara-i-Aliya (Khaksar Tehrik headquarters) at Lahore.

1941 January 11

The Star of India, Calcutta reports that, under the guidance of Barrister Mian Ahmed Shah, Sahibussiyadat Qazi Abdulha Sadarunnizam and other prominent Khaksars are awaiting in Lahore for the return of the Premier of the Punjab.

1941 January 23

The Star of India, Calcutta reports that Dr. Sir Zia ud din Ahmed, Nawab Bahadur Yar Jang, and Maulvi Sanaullah have been asked by the Khaksar leaders to mediate with the Central and Punjab Governments to obtain Allama Mashriqi's release.

1941 January 25

Khaksars provide volunteer services in Rawalpindi. They save a house that is on fire.

1941 February 03

Efforts to reorganize the Khaksar Tehrik continue.

Eight Khaksars are detained in Lahore and then later released.

1941 February 13

Three Khaksar leaders, Qazi Abdul Baqi, Mir Manzoor Mahmud (Hakim-i-Alah, Punjab), and Haji Mohammad Islam Chisti (Naib Hakim-i-Alah, Punjab), are arrested at the Khaksar Headquarters in Ichhra.

1941 February 14

Mahmud Minto and Mohammad Sadiq, two Khaksar leaders, are arrested in Rawalpindi. The District Magistrate in Rawalpindi rejects their bail applications.

1941 February 15

The Sessions Judge in Rawalpindi rejects the bail application presented by Jan Mohammad, Barrister, on behalf of Mahmud Minto (a Khaksar leader arrested on February 14, 1941).

1941 February 26

The Khaksars decide to resume their activities. A Khaksar Camp is held at Lyallpur (now Faisalabad) where the martyrs of March 19, 1940 are paid rich tributes and accorded a gun salute. At the camp, the Head of the Khaksar Tehrik issues instructions to hold Khaksar Camps throughout India.
Editor's Comments: The Khaksars resumed their activities because the Government had not released Mashriqi and the other imprisoned Khaksars. Following the orders issued at Lyallpur camp on February 26, 1941, Khaksar Camps were held throughout the country in memory of the martyrs of March 19, 1940.

1941 March 07

Sir Richard Tottenham (Additional Secretary, Home Department) writes a secret letter to J.D. Penny (Secretary to the Government of Punjab) regarding the Khaksar Tehrik.

1941 March 10

Mashriqi writes a letter from jail to Professor Rafiq of Aligarh Muslim University. In the letter, Mashriqi states: "My last days are nearing. It will be alright if I receive a reply and I am released. Otherwise I am going to die...I am not going to change my decision nor do I repent for it. I am happy because I am going to lay down my life..." At the conclusion of his letter, Mashriqi writes, "Again gird up your loins. Do not let my face be blackened. Save the honour of Islam...We will all return home happily, else my dead body will reach you." (Muhammad 1973, 85; Zaman 1987, 77).

1941 March 11

The Tribune, Lahore reports that Khaksars leaders from all over India are to meet in Aligarh.

1941 March 15

The Chief Commissioner of Delhi writes to the Home Department suggesting that although the elimination of the Khaksar Movement is not impossible, it is certainly difficult. Therefore, the policy should be to curtail the Tehrik's growth with an objective to completely wiping it out.

1941 March 17

Barrister Mian Ahmed Shah writes letters to the Government of India and to Sir Sikandar Hayat Khan appealing to them to release Mashriqi, who is seriously ill in Vellore Jail.

1941 March 19

Khaksars pay homage to their brethren who were killed on March 19, 1940. Khaksars salute the deceased Khaksars and lay wreaths at the site of the massacre on March 19, 1940. Muslim shopkeepers in Lahore raise black flags as a sign of mourning for the Khaksars. A large police force watches over the situation.

The Chief Secretary of the Government of Bihar writes the following to Sir Richard Tottenham: "It [Khaksar Tehrik] is a purely sectarian organization of a confessedly militaristic type; and one of its proposed aim[s] is to work for the seziure of power…it seems unnecessary to aim at the total extinction of the movement. But the release of Allama Mashriqi and other leaders without a reason…would merely enable the movement to revive with renewed vigour and would be interpreted as either a machiavellian design or a sign of weakness." (Muhammad 1973, 87-88). **Editor's Comments:** According to *Khaksar Tehrik Ki Jiddo Johad Volume 2* by Sher Zaman (page 78), the message further stated that the Government should keep the elimination of the Tehrik in mind.

The Chief Secretary of the U.P. Government writes a secret letter to the Home Department stating that it would be impossible "to extinguish the Khaksar Movement without a display of ruthlessness and that would not be tolerated by public opinion in the case of a body the external professions of which are religious and social service and which had the sympathy of the great body of Muslims…" (Muhammad 1973, 79, 88). **Editor's Note:** This information is also available in *Khaksar Tehrik Ki Jiddo Johad Volume 2* (page 78) by Sher Zaman.

1941 March 20

Maulana Zafar Ali Khan moves an adjournment motion in the Central Assembly alleging the unwarranted interference of Delhi police in the lawful activities of the Khaksar Tehrik.

1941 March 21

Sir Reginald Maxwell (Home Member) makes a statement in the Central Assembly regarding Maulana Zafar Ali Khan's adjournment motion of March 20, 1941.

1941 March 24

26 Khaksars (arrested at Khanewal after arriving from Sind to take part in ongoing demonstrations) are sentenced in Multan. One of the 26 Khaksars, Khair Mohammad, is sentenced to three years of imprisonment for one charge and six months of imprisonment under another charge (the sentences are to run concurrently). The remaining 25 Khaksars are sentenced to one year of imprisonment for one charge and six months of imprisonment for a second charge (the sentences are to run concurrently).

Barrister Mian Ahmed Shah meets Sir Sikandar Hayat Khan.

1941 March 25

J.D. Penny (Chief Secretary of the Punjab Government) writes a secret letter to Sir Richard Tottenham (Additional Secretary of the Government of India, Home Department). In this letter, he recommends resisting the movement to the end.

1941 April 15

Barrister Mian Ahmed Shah writes to Sir Sikandar Hayat Khan urging him to use his offices to secure Mashriqi's release.

1941 April 21

Word of Allama Mashriqi's deteriorating health in Vellore Jail continues to spread among the public.

1941 May 02

"Mashriqi Day" is observed in the entire India. Muslims demand Mashriqi's release at Badshahi Mosque (Lahore) after Friday prayers.

1941 May 22

Dr. Sir Zia ud Din Ahmed writes to Sir Richard Tottenham (Additional Secretary of the Government of India, Home Department): "From what I have been able to see, the release of the Allama or even a gesture which may ultimately lead to his release will create very good impression among all the persons interested in the Khaksar Movement." (Muhammad 1973, 73-74).
Editor's Note: In his book *Al-Mashriqi: The Disowned Genius* (page 150), Syed Shabbir Hussain reports the date of this letter as May 02, 1941. Whereas, in *Khaksar Movement In India*, by Shan Muhammad (page 73-74), this date is listed as May 22, 1941.

1941 June

Mohammad Ahmed Kazmi presents a resolution in the Central Assembly regarding the release of Allama Mashriqi. However, no action is taken on the resolution. Quaid-e-Azam and Liaquat Ali Khan do not attend this session of the Central Assembly.

1941 June 01-02

Khaksar leaders from all over the country meet in Peshawar. They decide to hold protests against the Government's attitude toward the Khaksars.

1941 June 03

S.M. Zauqi writes a letter to Quaid-e-Azam from Dhan Mandi, Ajmer. In the letter, he states: "...I wish the League, the Seerut, and the Khaksars could be amalgamated into one Grand Whole — the League to look after the political work, the Seerut to do the social reconstruction and economical uplift, and the Khaksars (rather difficult body to be brought round) to do the work where physical exertion is needed..." (Pirzada 1977, 392).

1941 June 04

Police arrest a local Khaksar leader in Bombay. Bombay police also arrest Khaksar leaders Dr. Mohammad Sadiq, Sheikh Mohammad Azim, and Mohammad Miskin. Police seize Khaksar literature from these Khaksars' homes.

1941 June 05

The Khaksar Tehrik is declared to be unlawful in various parts of India, including Bombay, Bengal, C.P., and Bihar.

Police raid various places in Lahore and arrest 75 Khaksars.

In Lahore, police keep a night-long watch on Khaksar activities and seize Khaksar materials, including belchas.

Aziz Din, a Khaksar leader, is arrested in Multan. Police keep a close watch on the Khaksars and a large police force is stationed near Wali Mohammad Mosque.

Another Khaksar is arrested in Multan.

The Government of India issues a communique banning the Khaksar Tehrik in the entire India.

Editor's Comments: In the Khaksar circle it was viewed that the ban was removed on September 02, 1940 so as to break the momentum of the ongoing demonstrations and public outcry. If the Government was sincere toward the Khaksar Movement, it would have released Mashriqi and all other Khaksars. However this was never done and instead the ban was imposed.

1941 June 06

The Tribune, Lahore publishes the headline "'Khaksar Menace Will Be Dispelled' — Govt. of India's Declaration — 'No Repetition of Disturbances Will Be Risked.'"

The Sind Government takes precautions in an attempt to prevent any activities by the Khaksars.

60 Khaksars are arrested in Lahore. At the time of the arrests, a crowd forms, and people shout "Khaksar Zindabad."

13 Khaksars (headed to Lahore to participate in ongoing demonstrations) are arrested in Jullundur.

Four Khaksars are arrested in Amritsar. Two of the Khaksars were heading to Lahore to participate in ongoing demonstrations.

Mohammad Yunus and Mohammad Shafi, two Khaksars, are arrested in Amritsar.

Khaksar arrests in Peshawar continue.

19 Khaksars (arriving in New Delhi to join ongoing demonstrations in Punjab) are arrested in New Delhi.

4 Khaksars are arrested in Patna.

In Nagpur, 17 Khaksars (arriving from Madras to participate in ongoing demonstrations) are arrested.

1941 June 07

Khaksar arrests continue in various parts of India.

The Tribune, Lahore reports that Governments in many parts of India, including North West Frontier Province, Delhi, and Sind, have declared the Khaksar Tehrik to be unlawful.

The Khaksar Tehrik is declared an unlawful organization in Kashmir, the United Provinces (U.P.), Ajmer-Merwara, and Baluchistan.

14 Khaksars (arrested on June 06, 1941 at the New Delhi railway station after arriving from Ajmer and Rampur to join ongoing demonstrations) are produced before the Additional District Magistrate in New Delhi. The Khaksars are remanded to police custody until June 09, 1941.

In Bihar, armed police search the office of Khaksar F.M. Shamsi. Files of *Al-Islah* (the official Khaksar weekly) are seized.

1941 June 08

The Khaksar Tehrik is declared an unlawful organization in Hyderabad.

Police arrest a Khaksar in Bihar. Thousands of people, including Muslims and Hindus, shout "Zindabad" in support of the Khaksar.

Police continue to search Khaksar leaders' residences in Rawalpindi. Police arrest Khaksar Salars, Mir Hussain Shah and Arkhan, and confiscate Khaksar materials from their houses.

1941 June 09

The Tribune, Lahore reports that the Khaksar Tehrik is declared an unlawful organization in British India. The Khaksars' activities remain under close watch by the police.

14 Khaksars (arrested on June 05, 1941) are convicted and sentenced to imprisonment until the rising of the court.

Khaksar leader, Mohammad Yunus, is arrested in Muzaffarpur (Bihar) and sent to jail.

One Khaksar is arrested in Lahore.

Five Khaksars are arrested in Lahore following police raids.

1941 June 10

The Government of India receives daily reports regarding the arrests of Khaksars. The Government also considers taking action against *Al-Islah*, the Khaksar newspaper.

The Khaksar Tehrik is declared unlawful throughout Travandore.

Dr. Zahur Ahmed, a Khaksar Salar and former college professor, is arrested in Rawalpindi City while leading Khaksar volunteers to Lahore to participate in ongoing demonstrations.

Seven Khaksars are arrested in Rawalpindi City for allegedly planning to march to Lahore to participate in ongoing demonstrations. Police also seize Khaksar materials and literature.

1941 June 11

One Khaksar is arrested in Lahore.

The Khaksar Tehrik is banned throughout the entire Mysore State under the Mysore Public Security Act.

Khaksar leader Rahimbaksh Ghaznavi is arrested in Peshawar.

1941 June 12

The Deputy Commissioner of Peshawar issues a poster denying that Khaksar Ilahi Baksh was beaten to death by the police.

26 Khaksars, who had been released from jail following an appeal to the Lahore High Court, are re-arrested in Multan.

Four Khaksars are arrested in Peshawar.

1941 June 13

Khaksar arrests continue in Lahore.

Two Khaksars are arrested in Lahore.

Arbab Sherakbar Khan, a Khaksar leader of the North West Frontier Province, is arrested in Peshawar.

1941 June 14

Sardar Khan, a Khaksar leader from Haripur, is arrested in Peshawar.

1941 June 16

The houses of Khaksars are searched in Peshawar and Khaksar materials are seized.

26 Khaksars (re-arrested in Multan on June 12, 1941) are released.

1941 June 17

Khaksar Abdul Gani is arrested in Lahore. Police maintain a close watch on the Khaksars throughout Lahore and its suburbs and also guard the mosques.

1941 June 20

The Tribune, Lahore reports that Frontier Khaksar leader Barrister Mian Ahmed Shah arrived at an agreement with the Deputy Commissioner of Peshawar and that all Khaksars facing trial in Peshawar have been released. However, the release of convicted Khaksars remains subject to the result of an appeal.

1941 June 21

Quaid-e-Azam replies to Zauqi's letter of June 03, 1941. He says, "…I certainly agree with you that the Seerat [Committee] and the Khaksars should work as members of the Muslim League under one flag and one platform." (Mujahid 1981, 90).

1941 June 24

A Khaksar Salar, Abdul Rauf (arrested on May 31, 1941), is "challaned" in the court of the City Magistrate in Lahore.

1941 June 27

Khaksars continue to take shelter in Khadan mosque in Nagpur. They pray for Allama Mashriqi's recovery from illness and also for his release. Police pickets are posted outside the mosque.

Khaksar arrests continue in Nagpur.

1941 July 08

In the court of the City Magistrate in Lahore, charges are framed against Khaksar leader Abdul Rauf (arrested on May 31, 1941).

1941 July 18

Seven Khaksars are arrested in Vellore and remanded to police custody. They are charged for moving about with Khaksar uniforms and badges.

1941 July 25

The Tribune, Lahore reports that all Khaksars convicted in the Frontier Province under the Criminal Law Amendment Act have been released.

1941 August 24

Barrister Mian Ahmed Shah writes a letter appealing to the Viceroy to release Mashriqi and the Khaksars and to remove the ban on the Khaksar Tehrik. He reiterates the Khaksars' loyalty to India and also states that they are not an obstacle in the Government's war effort.

1941 September 11

Sir Richard Tottenham (Additional Secretary of the Government of India) writes to Barrister Mian Ahmed Shah that "even membership of the Khaksar organization is now technically an offence. It follows that those who resort to active support to the movement render themselves all the more liable to the penalties of the law." (Muhammad 1973, 80).

1941 October 16

Mashriqi begins fasting in Vellore Jail. He decides that he will fast until death unless he and all his followers are released.
Editor's Comments: Mashriqi had been in jail since March 19, 1940 without a trial.

1941 October 24

The Chief Secretary of the Government of Madras writes a telegram to the Secretary of the Government of India (Home Department).

1941 October 25

Sir Sikandar Hayat Khan meets with Quaid-e-Azam.

1941 October 28

The Central Assembly rejects Mr. Kazmi's adjournment motion to discuss the "banning of Khaksar volunteers by the Government of India and thereby hampering the development of indigenous organizations which are a necessity for the defence of the country in times of war." *The Dawn*, Delhi November 2, 1941

1941 November 09

At a large public meeting in Madras (presided over by Maulana Abdul Latif Farukhi), people express great concern in regards to the health of Allama Mashriqi, who continues to fast in Vellore Central Jail. A resolution expressing this concern and demanding Allama Mashriqi's release is passed at the meeting. Attendees at the meeting include Bulusu Satyamurthi and other Congressman who were recently released from Vellore Central Jail.

1941 November 10

Dr. Pattabhi Sitaramayya, who had been in Vellore Central Jail with Mashriqi, discloses that Allama Mashriqi has been fasting in jail since October 16, 1941 and would continue to fast until death unless the Khaksars (including Mashriqi) are released and the restrictions on the Khaksar Tehrik are removed. In an effort to obtain his and the Khaksars' release and the removal of the ban on the Khaksar Tehrik, Mashriqi had written a letter to the Government on June 22, 1941. Dr. Sitaramayya reports that in the letter, Mashriqi stated that his case must be settled. Also, Mashriqi complained about the loss of his second son (Ehsanullah Khan Aslam) and the imprisonment of his first son. Mashriqi also asked for the release of all his money. Mashriqi informed the Government in his letter that if their reply was not satisfactory, then he would begin fasting until death starting from July 22, 1941. Not having received any reply from the Government, Mashriqi originally began his fast on July 22, 1941, but was persuaded to stop the fast until he had received a reply from the Government. On October 16, 1941, Mashriqi received a reply (dated September 12, 1941) from the Government. However, the Government refused to release Mashriqi and the Khaksars or remove the ban on the Khaksar Tehrik. Thus, Mashriqi began fasting in jail on October 16, 1941. Dr. Sitarayamayya also reports that Mashriqi is not allowed any interview with any person and even an application for an interview filed by his wife and son was rejected. Mashriqi is treated like an ordinary prisoner. Mashriqi is allowed to spend money from his own funds, but he does not receive any allowance from the Government.

Editor's Comments: The Government was hiding the fact that Mashriqi was fasting in jail and his health was deteriorating.

1941 November 13

Khaksars go on a hunger strike in front of Assembly Chambers in Lahore to show their support for Allama Mashriqi, who continues to fast in Vellore Central Jail. The Khaksars demand Mashriqi's release and state that they will not give up the hunger strike until Mashriqi is released. Six Khaksars are arrested.

Editor's Comments: This was a remarkable example of the Khaksars' support for Mashriqi. The Government's atrocities toward Mashriqi helped increase the Khaksars' support for Mashriqi. The moment the Khaksars came to know that Mashriqi was fasting, they followed suit.

The Central Assembly disallows an adjournment motion (moved by Mr. Kazmi) regarding the poor health of Allama Mashriqi (who continues to fast in Vellore Jail) and the ban on the Khaksar Tehrik. *The Dawn*, Delhi would report on November 16, 1941:

"The Chair asked [Mr. Kazmi] if it was a religious fast.

Mr. Kazmi reported that it was a fast undertaken in protest against the treatment meted out to him [Allama Mashriqi].

The Chair: What treatment?

Mr. Kazmi said it was for the Government of India to explain to the House whether it was or was not a fact that the fast was on account of the treatment meted out to him [Mashriqi].

The Chair suggested that the mover should tell the House what the nature of the treatment was.

Mr. Kazmi said, that certain demands were made by Allama Mashraqi and the Government of India did not concede them. It was for the Government of India to show that the demands were unreasonable."

1941 November 14

A Khaksar meeting is held in Lucknow. At the meeting, it is decided that on November 15, 1941, the Khaksars should observe fast and prayers should be held for Allama Mashriqi's release.

1941 November 19

Dr. Sir Zia ud Din (Vice Chancellor of Aligarh Muslim University) meets with Sir Richard Tottenham (Additional Secretary of the Government of India, Home Department) to discuss the Khaksar issue and demand the release of Mashriqi and the Khaksars. Dr. Sir Zia ud Din also informs Sir Tottenham that letters pouring into his office show that the Muslims are highly resentful towards the Government's actions against the Khaksars.

1941 November 23

Dr.Sir Zia ud Din (Vice Chancellor of Aligarh University) writes a letter to the Secretary of the Government of India (Home Department) stating, "It is now the 22nd day of the fast. On account of the changed conditions there exists no point to detain Allama Mashriqi in jail…I request you to communicate the decision of the Government of India to me at an early date."

After having been released from Vellore Jail, Gadde Rangiah Naidu (Member Legislative Assembly [M.L.A.]) speaks to the Press about Mashriqi. According to *The Dawn*, Delhi:

"The Allama, he [Naidu] said, ever since his [Mashriqi's] arrest and imprisonment was making representations to the Government regarding himself and the movement…He even went to the extent of offering 50,000 Khaksar[s] to the British Government as soon as war broke out. But the Government heeded not his appeals…The Khaksar movement was banned in all the provinces…

Two months ago, Mr. Naidu proceeded, the Khaksar leader sent an important representation (final one) to the Government refuting the undesirable motives attributed to himself and his followers and demanding the release of all

Khaksars throughout India, in default of which he intimated that he will go on a penitential fast unto death…

…by the middle of October he received the Government's reply. It was a big No. The Government refused to consider any of his representations. And on October 16 [1941], Allama Mashriqui commenced his fast unto death…

Mr. Naidu in conclusion said that Mr. Mashriqui…has become very weak. He [Mashriqi] was confined to his room. He had also very much reduced in weight and voice has become feeble.

Asked whether they (the other detenus) did not request Mr. Mashriqi to desist from undertaking such a course, he said, 'we did, but to no purpose. He was determined and as a last resort he had taken this step."

The Dawn, Delhi writes an editorial regarding Mashriqi's imprisonment. The newspaper states:

"It is more than a year-and-a-half now that Allama Inayatullah Khan Al-Mashriqi of the Khaksar movement in India, is rotting without trial behind prison bars at Vellore [Jail] in South India. How long more he will be detained in jail nobody knows. Nor has he or the public been told of the nature of his crime, if any…

Well-known for his impatience with politics, the Allama is a well-read practical man who has held positions of trust with the Government of India. Resigning his job with the Government he plunged heart and soul into the task of rebuilding Muslim society strictly according to the Quran and started organising the Musalmans for social service, irrespective of race or creed. The Khaksar movement, which he started, is not confined to Muslims alone, and the movement by its universal appeal drew members at the very outset from almost all creeds and races in India — Hindus, Sikhs, Christians, non-Brahmins and Muslims, etc…

…Allama Mashriqi 'whose indefinite incarceration and detention without trial is causing grave concern not only to the members of Khaksar organisation but to the Musalmans generally.' Instances are not wanting of Hindu leaders having been let out on humanitarian ground. Why cannot they set free a Muslim leader for the same reason."

The Dawn, Delhi reports, "The release of Allama Mashriqui…was urged at a public meeting held recently…The following resolution was moved by Mr. Allapichai.

'This meeting of the citizens of Madras learns with deep concern the news of the fast from the 16th October of Allama Inyatulla Khan Mashriqui, the founder and leader of the Khaksar movement detained in the Central Jail, Vellore, and appeals to the Government of India to release him immediately.'"

1941 November 26

A secret report reveals that the Khaksars held a meeting in Delhi in November 1941 to discuss ways to obtain Mashriqi's release. At the meeting, it was unanimously decided to offer the arrest of two Khaksars daily who, upon reaching jail, would begin fasting until Mashriqi was released. As agreed at the meeting, the Khaksars began offering themselves voluntarily for arrest. While offering arrest, the Khaksars shouted slogans such as "Allama Mashriqi Zindabad," "Hukumat-i-Bartania Barbad Ho," "Khaksars Zindabad," and "Allama Mashriqi Azad Ho."

Editor's Comments: This was another remarkable example of the Khaksars' support for Mashriqi. The Khaksars stayed determined and continued to put up resistance in any manner that deemed fit, causing a lot of difficulty for the Government. All of these factors helped Muslims to come to a common platform to seek freedom. However, with Mashriqi in jail and the ban on the Khaksar Movement, the Muslims had no other choice but to unite under the Muslim League flag. With each passing day, the Muslim League continued to grow stronger.

1941 November 27

Students of Government College, Lahore, observe fast in protest against the Government's treatment of Mashriqi. Evening prayers for the health and release of Allama Mashriqi are also held at the college mosque.

1941 December

Barrister Mian Ahmed Shah, Sher Zaman, and Abdul Samad Khan visit Mashriqi in jail. Mashriqi informs them that he has already submitted proposals to the Central Government and that he would not stoop before the Government for justice.

1941 December 05

The Government of India informs Mashriqi that the only way for him to obtain his release from jail is to disband the Khaksar Tehrik.

1941 December 11

A public meeting is held in Ahmedabad. The following resolution is passed demanding the release of Allama Mashriqi:

This public meeting of the Muslims of Ahmedabad draws the attention of the Government of India to the fact that prolonged and indefinite incarceration and detention without trial of Allama Mashriqi is causing grave concern, not only to the members of the Khaksar organization but to the Muslims in general. In view of the changed situation, this meeting urges upon the Government of India to reconsider their policy and release Allama Mashriqi without delay.

This meeting urges upon the British Government and the Government of India that no further steps be taken or adjustments be made in future, even within the framework of the present constitution without the approval and consent of the All-India Muslim League, and warns the Government that any action in this connection, without the approval of the Muslim League will be deeply resented by the Muslims and the responsibility for the consequences that may ensue will be entirely that of the Government.

1941 December 18

Hassan writes to Jinnah "Yesterday in the Assembly when Fazlul Huq said that he was at heart 'Khaksar', there were shouts from the Muslim League benches: 'No, you are a traitor; you are a quisling.' Again, when he went on to say that he expected such a demonstration, there were cries from our benches: 'Guilty conscience', the man was absolutely non-plussed. The great joke came when he addressed us and said: 'Rely on me to do the best', there was such jeering and derisive laughter from our benches that the hideous fox was completely dumbfounded." (Zaidi, *M.A. Jinnah: Ispahani Correspondence*, 230).

Four Khaksars are arrested in front of the Punjab Government Secretariat in Lahore while protesting the Government's attitude towards Allama Mashriqi.

1941 December 19

Mashriqi sends a letter from Vellore Jail to the Government of India.

The Tribune, Lahore reports that Khan Khushal Khan Jadoon (a Khaksar leader who had been in Muzaffargarh Jail since March 1940) is suffering from Tuberculosis (T.B.). His sickness results in great anxiety in Khaksar circles.

1941 December 21

Barrister Mian Ahmed Shah sends the following letter to Sir Richard Tottenham:
     "His [Mashriqi] condition as I have seen him is dangerously serious and nothing remains in his body except tissues. He cannot walk even two steps without leaning on something, nor can he talk even five or six sentences at a time. I am afraid he may break down any moment and finish…Moreover, the cell in which he has been put appears from its very size to be one in which convicts condemned to death are usually kept. If he were, therefore, to die, say, within a fortnight, this sort of solitary, dark and unairy cell will certainly shorten his lingering life by a few days.
     From what I have seen of the Allama, I may say that he is nearing his death. Therefore, very urgently I point out that his letter of 19th instant may be immediately favourably considered and his release ordered without any further loss of time."

1942

1942 January 13

The Tribune, Lahore reports that as a result of Muslim appeals to the Government, Allama Mashriqi is likely to be released within the next few days.
Editor's Comments: Mashriqi's fast in jail and the public pressure forced the Government to release Mashriqi from jail in the coming days.

1942 January 15

The Tribune, Lahore reports that the Government is considering releasing Allama Mashriqi.

1942 January 19

Mashriqi is released from jail, but his movements remain restricted to the Madras Presidency*. The ban on the Khaksar Tehrik also remains in place.
Editor's Comments: *Under British rule, most of south India was integrated into a region called the Madras Presidency. In 1956, the Madras Presidency was disbanded and Tamil Nadu was established.

1942 January 25

The Dawn, Delhi publishes Mashriqi's press statement:
"I started fasting from October 16, 1941 in defence of the religious Islamic principles of active brotherhood, Godly actions, amity with all, prayers, bodily health, social service, etc., on which the Khaksar organisation is based, also for the release of the remaining Khaksar prisoners. Government of India had already before this released several hundred prisoners in May and June last and had also intimated to me the full and unconditional release of my personal money amounting to several lakhs, also had asked me to apply for the release of my invalid pension amounting to several thousands. On the 51st day of my suffering the Government of India informed me that only circumstances in which my permanent release would be considered, would be if I were to issue a public pronouncement to the effect that the movement was to be abandoned and the entire Khaksar organisation wound up and if I were at the same time to order my followers to act accordingly. This position was impossible and I continued suffering…

While not relinquishing the right of every people to improve their bodily health and spirit by innocent physical excercises I felt however that the military side of the Khaksar organisation is a source of embarrassment to the Government during the war and I herewith order the Khaksars to discontinue altogether for the duration of the war, the display of uniforms or badges, the carrying of Belchas or any other weapons and marches or drilling of any description, either in public or in private. With regard to the remaining features of the organisation viz., prayers, social service, gatherings, etc., I propose to ask the selected Khaksars to meet me after my release and I shall have full and free consultation with them. I also propose to settle with the Government of India our relations with them in details after this consultation. I hope that the Government will release all the remaining Khaksars after this settlement is made. I ask the Khaksars therefore to remain perfectly peaceful and calm in the meanwhile.

On the expiry of the eightieth day, viz., January 4, 1942, after the Government became amenable I discontinued my fast with the extremest gratitude to the almighty Lord that I have passed through the ordeal successfully."

1942 February 12

After his release from Vellore Jail, Mashriqi sent a number of terms to the Government of India.

Editor's Note: For terms, see *Allama Mashriqi and Dr. Akhtar Hameed Khan: Two Legends of Pakistan* (pages 197-200).

1942 February

Mashriqi issues the following statement:
"The Government did not allow anybody to know about my fast till the 19th day. After that, news was not allowed to be published in the Press for another eleven days till the information leaked out. On the 32nd day started my serious afflictions. Telegrams were arranged from many persons asking me to give up fast. On the fiftieth day I was taken on stretcher from the Vellore Jail to a damp dingy cell in Madras. The purpose was to frighten me either to give up fast or die. For the first time I received a communication from the Government on the 51st day, that is on December 5, 1941, asking me to disband the Khaksar Movement and there was no other way of release. I sent back the reply that Khaksar Movement was not my property that I could do with it whatever I liked, nor can it be discontinued. I sent a detailed letter to the Government on 19th December asking the Government to accept the offer after which I would discontinue fast. The Government accepted the offer but spent another fifteen days in debating it and then decided on January 16 to release me. However, my movements were restricted to the Madras Presidency. On 12 February, as desired by the Government, I, in consultation with other Khaksars, sent a communication regarding our future relations with the Government but was informed after a week, 'you ask for a charter, but we have not to enter into any agreement with you.' In short the Government has gone back shamefacedly on all conditions…Quran is the charter of the Movement. Whatever was considered objectionable by the Government (drill) I have already stopped temporarily. No permission is needed for namaz and social service. I direct the Khaksars to fearlessly follow their new programme and rest assured that no Government can put restrictions on it."

1942 March 02

Jinnah meets with Sir Sikandar Hayat Khan in Delhi.

1942 March 23

Mashriqi sends the following telegram to Sir Stafford Cripps:
"The British Government have sent you to rectify the wrongs and to
reconciliate and secure the co- operation of India at this late hour. I put before you
the unparalleled tyranny of the Government on the Khaksars and ask redemption. I
committed the crime of offering to the Viceroy on October 6, 1939, when every
political party was irreconcilably hostile, 50,000 Khaksars unconditionally for the
defence of India to the last drop of their blood and of also publishing a pamphlet
exhorting everybody to help the British to the utmost. The result was that the
pamphlet was confiscated, I was jailed, the organisation was banned, 2,000
Khaksars were arrested, forty Khaksars were murdered in cold blood, my house
where women inmates observed purdah [conservative way of life for women,
consisting of dress covering full body and no interaction with men outside
immediate family], was thrice raided, my eldest son aged sixteen years was jailed,
my women and children were thus thrown to winds, my other son aged thirteen
years was murdered, my entire money amounting to several lakhs of rupees was
confiscated, my family of twelve persons was starved, my daughter was refused
dowry, I was forced to pay Rs. 1,000 towards personal expenses in jail, I was
threatened with lashes and was locked, tortured and kicked by the Superintendent
and was solitarily confined, even smoking was disallowed, my servants were
removed during the fast, my invalid pension of Rs. 300 a month which was in
arrears and amounted to Rs. 12,000 was confiscated, my wife, children, brother and
friends were not allowed to interview me—until after twenty-two months' detention
without trial I secured my release on death-bed after fasting for 80 days, and I am
still ordered to remain in Madras till a settlement.
Can you hope to reconcile India or secure her co-operation when your
men commit such wrongs on persons of my position? I have now offered the
Government most accommodating terms of a settlement, as prearranged, but I am
getting evasive reprimands in reply. My case is explained chronologically in the
following communications:—April 1, 1940 (ten pages), May 18, 1940 (two pages
with enclosures), May 24 (Telegram to the Viceroy), June 23 (three pages), August
23 (to the Viceroy, three pages), December 7 (to the Viceroy, six pages), May 14,
1941 (five pages), July 22 (nineteen pages), February 12, 1942 (three pages), March
16 (four pages).
Immediate lifting of the ban and release of the prisoners is essential to
removal of extreme bitterness throughout India, as also adequate recognition of the
political importance of the Khaksars in any future constitution. Considering the
terrible price paid for showing unconditional practical loyalty, I now join the
Muslim League, the Congress and the Mahasabha in most emphatically demanding
complete independence for India."

1942 March 28

Mashriqi sends the following letter to Quaid-e-Azam:
Dear Mr. Jinnah,

I understand that a copy of my telegram to Sir Stafford Cripps has been sent to you. I can see what he has to offer, but he can very well utilize our communal differences to his own account.

If you can at this moment manage, at least, to present the united demand of complete independence, I have already declared that I am with the Muslim League, the Congress and the Hindu Mahasabha, and shall do whatever you ask me to do unitedly.

I have written to this effect to Messers Azad [Maulana Abul Kalam] and Savarkar [V. D. Savarkar, Chief of Hindu Mahasabha] also.

Editor's Comments: Though his movements were restricted to the Madras Presidency after his release from Vellore Jail, Mashriqi continued his efforts for the freedom of India.

1942 April 03

The Khaksar Tehrik officially rejects the Cripps proposals.

Mashriqi sends telegrams to Quaid-e-Azam, Abul Kalam Azad, Mahatma Gandhi, Jawaharlal Nehru, Veer D. Savarkar, and Dr. Pattabhi Sitaramiyya. The telegrams state:

"Khaksar organization rejects Cripps' proposals in entirety, considers them meaningless, unreal, while enemy actually India's doors unless every party is unhesitatingly and fully armed in order to defend India utmost, also unless an Indian Defence Minister, capable of galvanizing India utmost, is immediately appointed."

A meeting of the representatives of the people of the Hazara District is held under the chairmanship of Mohammad Sarwar Khan Tahirkheli. At the meeting, a resolution is adopted and is sent to the Viceroy, the Governor of the North West Frontier Province, and Sir Stafford Cripps. The resolution adopted unanimously is as follows:

This representative meeting most emphatically demands from the Government that all legal restrictions imposed upon Allama Inayat Ullah Khan Almashraqi (now interned in Madras Presidency) and the Khaksar movement be removed forthwith and the Khaksar prisoners and detenues be released immediately. It was further resolved that in view of the present political problems facing India and the much-needed public cooperation at this juncture facilities to be provided for a very early interview between Sir Stafford Cripps and the Allama.

1942 April 10

Following the Khaksar Tehrik's lead, the Muslim League and Congress reject Cripps' proposals.

1942 April 11

Allama Mashriqi sends the following telegram to the Presidents of the Muslim League, Congress, and the Hindu Mahasabha: "Your rejection of the Cripps proposals is the happiest augury to a united and peaceful India. Accept heartiest congratulations. I fully undertake the responsibility of securing by negotiation complete independence for India from the British Government within six months, provided the Congress, the League and the Mahasabha unitedly demand independence now, and of also non-communally organising for the safety of civil population everywhere. I offer immediately half a million Khaksars for service, irrespective of caste or creed. I have wired similarly to other presidents. Deliberate profoundly. Do not miss this critical opportunity."

1942 April 12

The Dawn, Delhi reports that the Aligarh Muslim University Union unanimously passed the following resolution:
This meeting of the Muslim University Union urges on the Government the necessity of removing immediately the restrictions imposed on Allama Iniautullah Khan Mashraqi and of lifting the ban on the Khaksar movement. At a time of national crisis when political prisoners of all shades of opinion have been released it is unfair, in the opinion of this house, to restrict movements of Allama Mashriqi.

1942 April 21

Rajagopalachariar sends a letter to Allama Mashriqi.
Editor's Note: See letter in *Al-Mashriqi: The Disowned Genius* by Syed Shabbir Hussain (page 157).

1942 April 22

Allama Mashriqi sends the following message to Rajagopalachariar:
        "Mr. Saeed Ahmed told me now, after your letter was received, that you desired to discuss the present deadlock and a way out of it by my mediation, if possible.
        If you can let me know the details of your proposals, I shall be able to let you know exactly what I can do in the matter. I am also very keen that the present deadlock be resolved as early as possible."

Rajagopalachariar sends the following message to Mashriqi:
        "I am very grateful for what you have said. My opinion is that Allama Sahib should have a long talk with Maulana Abul Kalam Azad in person. Also that Allama Sahib should use his influence with Mr. Jinnah, make him shed his fear of a National Government in India, postpone all questions of the future and make a united demand for immediate National Government for India. This will lead to complete independence and unity.

If nothing else can be done, Mr. Jinnah may be induced at least to say definitely on what conditions he can agree to join the Congress in forming the National Government at once.

This can easily be done by Allama Sahib."

K. Srinavasan, editor of the newspaper *The Hindu* (Madras), requests Allama Mashriqi to settle the present deadlock between the Muslim League and Congress.

1942 April 26

Mashriqi calls a Khaksar meeting to discuss the following proposal by the Muslim League: "Upon Allama Sahib agreeing to join the All-India Muslim League and declaring to that effect and requesting his followers to join the Muslim League, which is the only authoritative and representative political organisation of the Musalmans in India, the President of the League will be glad to have the prominent Khaksars associated with the executives of the Provincial Leagues and Allama Mashriqi will be welcomed to join the Working Committee of the All-India Muslim League." At the meeting, it is decided that the Khaksars would extend full co-operation to the Muslim League.

Editor's Comments: Despite the Khaksars' full intent to cooperate with the Muslim League, an agreement between the two parties did not materialize due to their differing political ideologies.

1942 April 28

Allama Mashriqi sends the following telegram to Maulana Abul Kalam Azad: "Ex-Premier Rajagopalachariar, in his message of 22nd [1942], suggests my long talk with yourself, also my urging Mr. Jinnah to put united demand for National Government. Editor Srinivasan also suggests my mediation between Congress and Muslim League. Prepared making effort. Can you meet?"

Allama Mashriqi sends the following telegram to Jinnah: "Ex-Premier Rajagopalachariar also Editor Srinivasan suggest, in their messages of 22nd [April, 1942], my mediation between League and Congress concerning united demand National Government. Moment critical, Unity essential. Do you agree mediation?"

1942 April 30

Allama Mashriqi sends the following telegram to C. Rajagopalachari, who resigned from the Congress Working Committee: "I heartily congratulate you on your bold step towards India's emancipation. The whole Khaksar organisation is entirely with you in the matter of promotion of Hindu-Muslim unity at this critical and eventual juncture."

1942 May 05

Allama Mashriqi sends the following telegram to Jinnah: "My telegram dated 28th April unreplied. Can you state minimum conditions for united demand for National Government? Do you approve active cooperation of Khaksars with Rajagopalachariar."

1942 May 10

The Dawn, Delhi publishes a letter to the Editor stating that Muslims are demanding the removal of the ban on the Khaksar Tehrik and the release of Khaksar prisoners.

1942 May 11

Jinnah sends the following reply to Mashriqi's telegram of May 05, 1942: "Your telegram 5th May [1942]. My appeal to Khaksars is to join and support wholeheartedly League policy at this critical juncture. Not possible discuss terms united demand as requested by means correspondence."

1942 May 12

Mashriqi sends the following telegram to Quaid-e-Azam: "Your telegram 11th May [1942]. Assure you Khaksars unflinching support every endeavour Muslim League for India's complete independence, Muslim-Hindu unity, united demands, united private protection of evacuees. Fix date discussion terms united demand New Delhi."

Allama Mashriqi sends the following telegram to Maulana Abul Kalam Azad: "My telegram twentyseventh unreplied. Viewing Quaide-Azam's yesterday's reply prepared discussing Jinnah verbally terms united demand provided you give minimum amenable fundamental conditions. Your proposal of selecting five representatives both sides unwieldy, unhelpful."

1942 May 13

Maulana Abul Kalam Azad replies to Mashriqi: "Your telegram 12th May [1942]. Please refer to my Allahabad statement. There can be no other method in such matters."

1942 May 16

Allama Mashriqi sends the following telegram to Jinnah: "Reference my telegram twelfth May [1942]. Abulkalamazad, Jawaharlal reaching Madras. Can you accept my humble invitation? Fix near date."

Mashriqi sends the following telegram to Maulana Abul Kalam Azad: "Your telegram 13th May [1942]. Allahabad statement cannot fructify without fundamental personal understanding. Yours and Jawaharlal's proposal reaching Madras opportune. Endeavouring Jinnah come. Wire date arrival together."

1942 May 27

Allama Mashriqi sends the following telegram to Quaid-e-Azam: "My telegrams twelfth and sixteenth May unreplied. Abul Kalam Azad agrees to appointment single representative both sides, complains your silence concerning his Allahabad proposal. Remember my solemn undertaking of securing for India complete independence within six months in my telegram of 11th April. Agree meeting Madras. Time precious, critical."

Allama Mashriqi sends a telegram to Maulana Abul Kalam Azad.

Allama Mashriqi sends the following telegram to Mahatma Gandhi and Jawaharlal Nehru: "Appealing at this eventful juncture to your foresightedness to reflect over advantage of Congress League settlement. Maulana Abulkalam Azad agrees to single representative both sides. Should meet Quaideazam Madras personally. Remember my telegram 11th April also repeated warnings given to you in 1928 which went unheeded. Time precious. Make Maulana agree."

The Star of India, Calcutta reports a letter from a Khaksar.

The Government of Punjab writes the following to the Central Government: Khaksars "were a dangerous organisation which would be far better ended than mended." (Muhammad 1973, 90). "The suggestion of release of Mashriqi is unrealistic" (translated from Urdu). (Zaman 1987, 78).

1942 June 07

In an article in *The Dawn*, Ahmad Dastagir writes about the Khaksar Tehrik. He states that the Khaksar Tehrik was founded by "the renowned author of *Tazkira* [Allama Mashriqi]… on the basis of Islamic principles. Its motto was *discipline*, its line of action *social service*, and its aim *peace* — the essence of Islam and every other religion. The organisation spread to every corner of India, Burma, Bahrein and South Africa." Dastagir further writes that the Khaksar Tehrik is a non-political, non-communal party. Besides Muslims, it is comprised of many Hindus, Christians, and Sikhs. The Tehrik is based on the development of individual and collective character, the improvement of physical and spiritual health, and the elimination of all controversies (sectarianism) through social service (regardless of caste, color, creed, religion), firm discipline, and all-embracing love. According to Dastagir, "The [Khaksar] mission caught the imagination of the people and millions flocked to it." Dastagir adds, "Everywhere a Khaksar was loved, honoured and trusted. Through endless toil and steady work the movement spread and was established firmly in every corner of India." The Khaksars provided comfort wherever it was needed. In many instances, the Khaksars saved the lives of their countrymen, even at the risk of their own lives. During the Shia-Sunni clash in Lucknow in 1939,

20,000 Muslims were imprisoned and hundreds were wounded; thousands of families starved. "The Khaksars who could not stand all this bloodshed, who stood for peace and love, had to come forward." Thus, Allama Mashriqi came to Lucknow to resolve the issue. In another instance, at the start of World War II, Allama Mashriqi offered 50,000 Khaksars to the Government for the defense of India. Despite all of the Tehrik's work for the uplift of humanity, the Government still tried to crush the movement. Dastagir states, "How the Khaksars were killed in the streets of Lahore, the Allama arrested, his and other leaders' properties confiscated, Allama's invalid pension withheld, thousands of Khaksars persecuted, Allama's elder son [Ikramullah Khan Anwar] imprisoned, the younger one [Ehsanullah Khan Aslam] murdered in cold blood by being tear-gassed is too tragic a tale to be told." *The Dawn*, Delhi June 07, 1942

1942 June 10

Allama Mashriqi sends the following telegram to Maulana Abul Kalam Azad, Mahatma Gandhi, and Jawaharlal Nehru: "Corresponding Quaideazam further. Probability his agreeing single representative near. Please name Congress representative immediately."

Allama Mashriqi sends the following telegram to Jinnah: "Implore your immediate attention League-Congress settlement. Pray agree Abul Kalam Azad's proposal single representative. Fix personnel, time, place. Myself responsible utmost satisfaction."

1942 June 12

Abul Kalam Azad sends the following letter to Allama Mashriqi from Camp Wardha:
My dear Inayatullah,
There seem to be no reason why the League should not have responded to my offer, if she was desirous of any settlement.
My offer is still there. The number of representative is of little importance, it may be five, three, or even one only. If the League be prepared to hold talks in response to my offer, she should say so. No sooner than she expresses her willingness to do so, I would call the working committee and get the representatives or representative nominated...
Yours sincerely,
A.K.Azad

Jawaharlal Nehru sends the following letter to Allama Mashriqi from Wardha:
Dear Mr. Inayatullah Khan,
Thank you for your telegram which I have received today. I do not quite understand it. As you know we shall gladly do everything in our power to bring about a friendly settlement between the Congress and the Muslim League, as well as other organizations. The obvious way to bring this about is for representatives to discuss the matter. That is why the Congress President, Maulana Abul Kalam Azad,

suggested some time ago that such representatives might be appointed on behalf of the Congress and the League. The number of the representatives is immaterial, though probably it will be better if there were several on each side. Before the Congress can take definite steps in the matter, it should know whether the Muslim League is agreeable to the suggestion made. From creation speeches made by the Muslim League leaders, it would appear that they are not agreeable. Your telegram is vague and it is difficult for any step to be taken till we have more definite and direct knowledge of the Muslim League attitude.

Your sincerely,

Jawaharlal Nehru

Dr. Hajee Aslam Chisti (a Khaksar leader) meets with Quaid-e-Azam today and delivers his message to Mashriqi. Quaid-e-Azam's message to Mashriqi states that Quaid-e-Azam will not be ready to negotiate until the Congress withdraws the Allahabad Resolution.

1942 June 18

Allama Mashriqi sends the following telegram to Maulana Abul Kalam Azad and Jawaharlal Nehru: "Your letter twefth. Quaideazam prepared to negotiate after withdrawal Allahabad Resolution. Technically reasonable. Please arrange expeditiously."

1942 June 19

Allama Mashriqi sends the following telegram to Jinnah: "Abulkalamazad and Jawaharlalnehru both write expressing unequivocal immediate friendly settlement. Prepared calling working committee meeting for selection representative after your agreeability. Your insistence in message through Haji Aslam Chisti withdrawal Allahabad Resolution mere technicality. Unnecssary. Yourself responsible delay. Beseech immediate agreement."

1942 June 24

Mashriqi sends the following letter (from Madras) to the Chief Secretary:

Dear Chief Secretary,

The treatment meted out to me by the Government of India puts to shame all canons of propriety, justice, and fair play. How much such treatment can benefit Government directly or indirectly baffles my imagination. I wrote to you on the 16th May telling you in as resentful a language as possible that I was most perfidiously treated and asked you to get the matter settled by the 22nd May. On the 18th May I received a surprise letter from Sir Zia-ud-Din Ahmad to the effect that 'the government of India took a very generous view of the whole situation and they would naturally like that the Khaksars may take part in the general defence of the country in the manner you decide.' He added, 'I think a small band of Khaksars may perhaps help in this direction also (i.e. the establishment of the Pioneer Defence Corps) and while in this corps they may keep their individuality and may also use their uniforms.' He said that he had written this letter 'after a long talk with the Additional Home Secretary.' I promptly extended my hand of friendship and wrote to the Government of India the same day. On the 19th May I received a letter from Sir Ricahrd Tottenham to the effect that 'the matter (i.e. the settlement of the Khaksar question) is engaging the careful attention of the Government of India and their orders will be communicated to you as soon as possible.'

Having received nothing for twentyfive days more, I telegraphed as follows to the Home member on 19th June:

Reference Sir Richard Tottenham's letter 15th May received 19th May promising communication orders soonest, also my letter 16th and 18th May embodying Sir Zia-ud-Din's suggestions concerning the participation of Khaksars in the general defence of India. Please expedite settlement Khaksars ordered to prepare for general defence.

No response came and I telegraphed to Sir Reginald Maxwell and Sir Sultan Ahmed again on the 15th June as follows:

Most respectfully submit altogether unbecoming for the great Indian Government to torture myself also friendly Khaksars for five months for settlement. Original promise one month 50 days passed since submission draft of instructions to Khaksars, 30 days since Sir Richard Tottenham's promise of earliest consideration, 150 since submission terms 12th February. My two family members terribly ailing for the last eleven weeks from climate effects. Request settlement.

One month and ten days have passed today since the letter of Sir Tottenham cited above and still no settlement is in sight and no reply has been given to the above two telegrams even. In the meantime Sir Zia-ud-Din again wrote on the 18th June as follows: 'The Government of India have very great sympathy with you and their decision will mostly depend upon the replies they get from the Provincial Government'; while the Law Member writes to one of his friends as follows, 'I had a talk with the Home Member only this morning (i.e. 8th June) and while he is very sympathetic and all of us are prepared to settle this matter immediately the Punjab is again creating obstacles.' How Punjab or any Provincial Government can create obstacles when Government of India have very great sympathy with us and even wish us to take part in the general defence of the country in the manner I decide, also what occasion there is now to consult the Provincial Government after five months have passed since start of the settlement, surpasses my understanding.

I request you to let me know without delay how the matter stands. Government of India should have scrupulously kept their word of effecting a satisfactory settlement with us within their own appointed time, viz. one month. Today is the 157th day, and it makes one ashamed to utter these words. Not the slightest modification nor amendement nor objection has been made to anything that I have put forward during these 157 days concerning the future programme of Khaksars, nor any counter suggestion to any effect has come forward suggesting what Government desires. I have also unequivocally expressed my desire to join the war effort in accordance with what Sir Zia-ud-Din has said after a settlement is made with us. I do not know in what other way I can assure Government of our bonafides. The extra-ordinary dilatory methods of the Government only show that Government do not know how to make friends nor know how to make up mind. I have remained in contact with the Government matters long enough to say that what

has been done with the Khaksars during the past two and a half years, and most especially during the past last five months, is most unwise, is most preposterous and most distinctly harmful to the interests of the Government. I expect a most prompt reply from you please.
Yours sincerely,
Inayatalluah Khan

1942 June 25

Allama Mashriqi sends the following telegram to Quaid-e-Azam: "Congratulations Jinnah Rajagopalacharia Meeting. Fervently urge tangible results."

1942 June 28

Jawaharlal Nehru sends the following letter to Mashriqi from Allahabad:
Dear Mr. Inayatullah Khan,
         I have received your telegram in which you say that Mr. Jinnah desires the withdrawal of the Allahabad resolution before he can negotiate. Presumably this refers to the recent resolution of the All-India Congress Committee relating to the unity of India. That resolution merely confirmed the position for which the Congress has stood for 57 years now. Anyway nobody can withdraw it except the All-India Committee. Personally I would be against any change in that resolution as I think the Congress position relating the unity of India is sound. Mr. Jinnah's suggestion that this resolution should be withdrawn is on a par with a suggestion I might make that the Muslim League resolution about Pakistan should be withdrawn. Such suggestions do not help either way. If people are prepared to talk over matters, they do not put forward conditions which in themselves are tantamount to decisions. The suggestion I made in Bombay and elsewhere was that people holding different views on this subject should, while adhering to their views, agree to cooperate on the basis of achieving independence of India and the transfer of full political power to the representatives of the Indian people. Further, they can cooperate then in the defence of a free India. After that they can consider the other questions that divide them and come to an understanding. This course of action does not commit anyone or compel him to give up his own particular point of view.
Yours sincerely,
Jawaharlal Nehru

1942 July 02

Dr. Pattabhi Sitaramiyya (a prominent Congressman) interviews Allama Mashriqi at Mashriqi's residence in Madras. They discuss the political situation in India as well as the issue of Hindu-Muslim unity.

1942 July 05

The Dawn, Delhi writes, "The Khaksar Movement is primarily concerned with the maintenance of peace: the main plank of its programme is the service of people, irrespective of caste, creed, race or religion. Its membership is open to all communities; in fact all communities are represented in the organisation…therefore, it is the duty of the Central Government to recognise the worth of this organisation and withdraw all the restrictions…"

1942 July 06

Mashriqi sends the following telegram to Jawaharlal Nehru:
"Pandit Jawaharlal Nehru, Wardha,
Your letter twentythird June received. Allahabad Resolution cannot be considered as reiteration of the Congress creed. It is more a provocateur antidote to Rajagopalachariar's resolution on Pakistan. Please remove last obstacle put by Jinnah. Also think deeply and practically over plan of Indian independence devised by me and communicated to [Dr.] Pattabhi Sitaramiyya."

1942 July 07

The Star of India, Calcutta reports that Jinnah was given a Guard of Honor by the Khaksars in Bhopal.

1942 July 08

In response to Mashriqi's telegram of July 06, 1942, Jawaharlal Nehru sends the following letter (from Wardha to Mashriqi in Madras):
Dear Mr. Inayatullah Khan,
            I have received your telegram. I think I have already made our position clear to you. The Congress ever since its inception has been based on the national unity of India. Without that idea of unity, the Congress fails in its purpose and might as well be wound up. The resolution passed by the All-India Congress Committee in Allahabad in effect stated that the Congress should not agree to the break-up of that unity. This resolution may or may not have been necessary, but in effect it merely confirmed the old Congress position. To annul that resolution is to state to the world that the Congress is prepared to consider the division of India into two parts. That would be against the fundamental Congress position.
            Apart from this, however, the Congress has stated that while it stands by the unity of India and considers any division fatal for all concerned, still it cannot think in terms of compelling any territorial unit to remain in an Indian union against its declared emphatic will.
            I have already told you that constitutionally speaking it is beyond my power to upset a resolution passed by the A.I.C.C. only the A.I.C.C. or the full Congress can do that.
            I think the position is quite clear. What I suggested to you previously was that the Congress and the Muslim League, as well as others, need not give up their particular positions or objectives but may still cooperate together for the independence and defence of India. What they must all decide is that they will not look up to British Government for help in furthering their particular claims as this is

derogatory to the dignity of any Indian or any group in India. It is for us to settle these matters among ourselves without invoking foreign authority.
Yours sincerely,
Jawaharlal Nehru

1942 July 11

Khaksar Nur Mohammad Karbalai (Hakim-i-Ala, Multan) is arrested by police in Multan and produced before a Lahore Magistrate. Police also search his house and seize Khaksar literature.

Mashriqi sends the following letter to Rajagopalachariar:
Dear Ex-Premier,
Your resignation from the Congress is a clear proof that you will have Hindu-Muslim unity at any cost. I congratulate you on this rare courage in upholding your convictions.
I sent Mr. Allah Bukhsh Syed the other day to find out from you the outcome of your visit. I did not see your point in not telling him what transpired between you and Quaid-e-Azam Jinnah. I have already got, and hope to get something more tangible from both sides but it requires more application. Unless you have something up your sleeve which if disclosed to me would prejudice the Hindu Muslim cause, I trust you will help me to the utmost. I hope you are well.
Yours sincerely,
Inayatullah Khan

1942 July 14

Rajagopalachariar replies to Mashriqi's letter of July 11, 1942.

1942 July 23

Mir Abdul Kadir, a Khaksar leader from Sind, is arrested in Tandobago near Karachi.

1942 July 24

Allama Mashriqi appoints Mir Ali Ahmed Khan Talpur (Hakim-i-Ala, Sind) and Arbab Sher Akbar Khan (Hakim-i-Ala, North-West Frontier Province and Kashmir) to meet with the Punjab Premier, Sir Sikandar Hayat Khan.

The Government of India considers removing the ban on the Khaksar Tehrik.

1942 July 28

Allama Mashriqi sends the following telegram to Maulana Abul Kalam Azad, Khan Abdul Ghaffar Khan, Mahatma Gandhi, Rajagopalachariar, Jawaharlal Nehru, Rajendra Prashad, and Dr. Pattabhi Sitaramiyya. He sends a copy to Jinnah, the

Former Speaker of the Madras Assembly, and Sardar Vallabhai Patel. The telegram states: "I am in receipt of Pandit Jawaharlal Nehru's letter of July 8th. My honest opinion is that civil disobdeience movement is a little pre-mature. The Congress should first concede openheartedly and with handshake to Muslim League the theoretical Pakistan, and thereafter all parties unitedly make demand of Quit India. If the British refuse, start total disobdeience. Country emasculated in the midst of war, also unprepared. Real dynamic and vitalizing incentive necessary for successful termination of the struggle."

Editor's Comments: Syed Shabbir Hussain, in his book *Al-Mashriqi: The Disowned Genius*, writes "The telegram…was hailed by the Muslim Leaguers with a shower of telegrams to Allama Mashriqi, appreciating the timely advance of the Pakistan issue and more especially valuing the safe warning given to the Congress for starting a lonely struggle…At any rate the net result of the telegram was that an open talk started in Bombay concerning the desireability of Mahatma Gandhi meeting Mr. Jinnah at once, and steps were actually taken to that effect on 4th and 5th August." (Hussain 1991, 170).

1942 August 05

Allama Mashriqi sends the following telegram to Jinnah, Abul Kalam Azad, Mahatma Gandhi, and Jawaharlal Nehru: "Beseech God's sake Mahatma Gandhi settle Quaideazam Jinnah before launching civil disobdience movement. Reaching despite illness and detention. Wait."

Editor's Note: August 05, 1942 is an approximate date for this telegram.

1942 August 07

Additional Secretary, Home, sends a letter to Allama Mashriqi.

1942 August 13

The Government of India sends a message to Mashriqi threatening to arrest him.

1942 August 19

Allama Mashriqi sends a letter to the Additional Home Secretary (in reply to his letter of August 07, 1942).

1942 August 20

Dr. Sir Zia ud Din writes a letter to Sir Richard Tottenham stating that the re-arrest of Mashriqi would be unwise.

1942 August 30

The Dawn, Delhi writes that despite the fact that the ban on the Communist Party has been removed, "The Khaksars continue suffering from the restrictions that were imposed on them two years ago and their leader is rotting in detention at Madras, even though he has been released from jail."

Editor's Comments: Mashriqi's movements were restricted to Madras Presidency.

1942 August 31

Allama Mashriqi sends a copy of his letter (which he sent to the Additional Home Secretary on August 19, 1942) to Sir Sultan Ahmed.

1942 September 07

The Allahabad Muslim League adopts a resolution urging the removal of the ban on Allama Mashriqi and the Khaksar Tehrik and suggests that the All-India Muslim League Executive make the necessary effort to ensure that the Government rules favorably on this point.

1942 September 11

The Star of India, Calcutta reports that the Muslim citizens of Calcutta held a meeting, which was chaired by K. Nooruddin (Member Legislative Assembly). The meeting demanded the release of Allama Mashriqi and the removal of the ban on the Khaksar Tehrik. The following resolution was passed:

"This meeting of the citizens of Calcutta resolves unanimously that the Government of India be moved to remove the ban on the Khaksar organisation in India and that the accredited leader of the movement Allama Inayetullah Khan Mashriqi be released.

This meeting appeals to the Qade Azam and the Working Committee of the Muslim League to move the Government of India to remove the ban on the Khaksar movement and to release Allama Mashriqi."

1942 September 13

The Dawn, Delhi prints an article about the Khaksar Tehrik under the heading "What Khaksars are about?"

1942 September 23

The Central Assembly discusses a resolution (moved by Sir Raza Ali) regarding the Khaksars. Allama Mashriqi's restricted movements, the arrested Khaksars, and the ban on the Khaksar Tehrik are discussed in the Central Assembly. Sir Raza Ali contrasts the treatment given to Congressman and communists versus that received by the Khaksars and questions why the Congressman and communists had been released but the Khaksars had not. He also questions why the inquiry report (prepared by Sir Douglas Young, Chief Justice of the Lahore High Court, and Chaudhri Niamat Ullah, Former Judge of the Allahabad High Court) regarding the massacre on March 19, 1940 had not been published. Home Secretary Sir Richard

Tottenham also comments on the Khaksars. *The Tribune*, Lahore would report on September 24, 1942:

> "A reference had been made [in the Assembly] to the charge that the Khaksars were or might be fifth columnists in touch with the enemy. 'The Government of India,' he [Sir Richard Tottenham] declared, 'have never made this charge against the Khaksars, nor do they make it now.'
>
> ...Secondly, Sir Richard said that it was difficult to withdraw the ban on the Khaksars in certain parts of India and not in others. The Khaksars were an all-India organisation and it would be awkward if they were dealt with differently in different parts of the country...
>
> Sir Zia ud Din states that if Sir Tottenham has any evidence that the Khaksars were fifth columnists, then he should show it to a few members of the Muslim League and if they are convinced, then the issue would be dropped. Sir Zia ud Din further states that Allama Mashriqi should be invited to Delhi in order for any two members of the Executive Council to interview him and get firsthand information.
>
> Mr. M.A. Kazmi objects to a ban on any organization simply on the grounds that military drill is a part of their training. He states that at this time (as a result of World War 2), volunteer organizations should be encouraged to train people in guerilla warfare and military discipline."

The Eastern Times would further report on September 25, 1942, that in the same sitting, Khan Bahadur Piracha asked why the Government had treated the Khaksars differently from other organizations, such as those sponsored by the Hindu Mahasabha or the Sikhs.

At the Central Assembly: closing, Sir Raza Ali congratulates the Home Secretary for stating that there was nothing to show that the Khaksars were in league with the enemy. Sir Raza Ali states that the Khaksars should be treated at the same level as Congress volunteers and others. After devoting the entire day to discussion of a resolution regarding the Khaksars, the Central Assembly passes the resolution (sponsored by Sir Raza Ali) without any division (the Government benches remain neutral). The resolution urges the removal of the restrictions on Allama Mashriqi and the lifting of the ban on the Khaksar Tehrik as well as the release of Khaksars detained under Regulation 3 of 1818 and the Rules of the Defence of India Act.

1942 September 25

Agha Ghazanfar Ali Shah issues a press statement: "The Central Legislative Assembly has passed almost unanmiously the resolution that the ban upon the Khaksar Organisation be lifted and Allama Mashriqi's movements may not be restricted. The Government have remained neutral, which means that they have been convinced of our *bona fides*. If the Government lifts the ban and permits freedom to Allama Mashriqi they will not only have no chance to repent but may have occasion to congratulate themselves upon this move." *The Eastern Times*, Lahore September 26, 1942

1942 September 26

The Eastern Times, writes in its editorial "Muslims all over India, but especially in the Punjab, will have a sigh of relief that at last a beginning has been made in the matter of the Khaksar movement...If memory does not fail us, the Punjab Government expressed the opinion at the time action was taken against the Khaksars in march 1940 that they were Nazi fifth-columnists. Sir Richard Tottenham, replying to the debate on behalf of the Government, repudiated the charge categorically and said, 'The Government of India have never made this charge against the Khaksars, nor do they make it now.' This unqualified and authoritative rehabilitation of the Khaksars should effectively remove the shadow that has hung over the movement for so long."

1942 September 30

Dr. Sir Zia ud Din's sends the following letter to Jinnah from Aligarh: "...I went twice to your house, but you were engaged and myself fell ill during the last four days of my stay so much so that I had to deliver my speech on the Khaksar question with a temperature of 102. There were several points I wanted to discuss with you..." (Pirzada 1977, 408).

1942 October 14

A Khaksar prisoner escapes from lock-up in Lahore.

1942 October 20

The Eastern Times, Lahore, reports, "A widely signed representation on behalf of the Muslims of Jhang District has been sent to Sir Sikandar Hayat Khan" urging him to remove the ban on the Khaksar Tehrik. The newspaper also reports the following quote: "As a Muslim, as a member of the Muslim League and as a representative of the public and the Province, which is the sword arm of the country, it devolves upon you to spare no effort and to *use every influence to have the restrictions withdrawn*."

1942 October 23

Al-Elan, a U.P. newspaper, writes: "The Government of India may well labour under the delusion that they can end the Khaksar movement through a policy of complete taciturnity which they have been adopting for some time past. The paper reminds the Government that no movement has fizzled out in this way; on the other hand it has gained momentum gradually. The efforts made by the Government of India in 1940 to crush the movement have failed, because instead of weakening it, it has in fact considerably strengthened the movement much as the Khaksars have, by making valuable sacrifices, become hardly soldiers imbibed with an unconquerable spirit of achieving their goal."

Al-Flah, another newspaper from U.P., gives a warning to the Government to remove the restrictions on the Tehrik such as those on carrying spades and conducting drills. The newspaper further states that the Government of India is working under the false notion that it can eliminate the Khaksars through its policy of silence, which it has adopted for quite some time. In 1940, the Government had made several attempts to crush the Khaksar Movement but failed. Instead the Tehrik gained even more strength. After seeing the loss of precious lives, the Khaksars became more determined soldiers and acquired a stronger spirit to achieve their goals.

1942 October 30

Allama Mashriqi receives an enthusiastic welcome upon arrival at the Juma Mosque in Madras. *The Eastern Times* of November 01, 1942 would report that the Khaksars presented Mashriqi with a Guard of Honor. According to the newspaper:
"Allama Mashriqi, addressing the Khaksars and a large gathering of Muslims assembled in the Juma Mosque, made an appeal for unity and discipline. He asked his audience to follow the Islamic principles. He laid special emphasis on daily prayers.
[He asked] the Khaksars to organise themselves into a strong body and work for the cause of Islam and humanity. He asserted that 40 lakh persons had joined his movement and they carried the red badge on their shoulders."
Editor's Note: Mashriqi's movements were still restricted to Madras on this date.

1942 November 11

The Eastern Times reports that a number of students from Aligarh University have enrolled in the Khaksar Tehrik.

1942 November 19

In an interview, Sir Ghulam Hussain Hidayatullah (Premier of Sind) states that he has recommended to the Central Government to remove the ban on the Khaksar Tehrik.

1942 December 12

Allama Mashriqi sends a telegram to Sir Sultan Ahmed, who is acting as a mediator between the Government of India and Mashriqi. Mashriqi states that if the ban on his movements (Mashriqi's movements were restricted to Madras) is not removed before Christmas, he will leave for Lahore. Furthermore, if anyone tries to stop him from proceeding, he would resist until death.

1942 December 26

After attending the marriage of his children, Sir Sikandar Hayat Khan dies in Lahore.

1942 December 28

The Government of India issues a communique stating that the ban on the Khaksar Tehrik and the restrictions on Allama Mashriqi have been lifted.

In order to ease any further internal difficulties for the Government of India (for the duration of World War II), Allama Mashriqi issues a statement saying:

"I am glad to give the news to all that the Government have agreed to lift in general the ban on the Khaksar organisation, cancel restrictions on my residence in the Madras Presidency and have asked me to issue orders to the Khaksars all over British India in accordance with the terms put forward by me in April and September and the announcement of January 16.

On January 16, 1942, after 80 days' fast in defence of the religious principle on which the Khaksar organisation was based and for the release of the remaining Khaksar prisoners, I issued a statement to the Press from jail, which the Government of India pronounced as acceptable.

In that statement I gave instructions to the Khaksars to abandon for the duration of the war the display of uniforms or 'akhuwwat' badges carrying of any 'belchas,' or any other weapons, and marches or drilling of any description. I now reaffirm those instructions which are to be observed both in letter and spirit by all Khaksars and are to be interpreted as meaning that, for the duration of the war, daily and weekly social service may be performed by Khaksars in an individual capacity, but there are to be no drills, no carrying of implements, no wearing of uniforms or badges.

I further direct that, in view of the political situation, both inside and outside India and in order to help as much as possible in the war effort to save India from becoming worse politically through aggression by the Axis Powers, future activities of Khaksars are to be of such a nature as not to cause the least anxiety to the authorities anywhere, as long as the war lasts.

I am convinced that the programme of a Khaksar at this eventful moment is to make himself ready for selfless service irrespective of caste or creed, and to be of utmost use to all. Any orders issued to Khaksars, which are inconsistent with these present instructions are to be regarded as cancelled." *The Eastern Times,* Lahore December 30, 1942, *Bombay Chronicle* December 29, 1942

1942 December 29

Allama Mashriqi states that since the Government of India has removed the restrictions on his movements, he will be leaving for Lahore on December 31, 1942.

1942 December 31

The Star of India, Calcutta reports that Allama Mashriqi will leave for Lahore today. Mashriqi asks the Khaksars to observe Friday January 01, 1943 as the day of thanksgiving to Almighty God for lifting the ban on the Khaksar Tehrik by the Government of India. He also makes a special request to the Khaksars to pray on January 08, 1943 for the release of 14 Khaksars transported for life and simultaneously asks the Government of India to release them and other prisoners forthwith.

The Tribune, Lahore publishes the following statement by Allama Mashriqi in which Mashriqi pays a tribute to Sir Sikandar Hayat Khan (who died at midnight on December 26, 1942): "People have been under the impression that the last three years of suffering of the Khaksars have been due to some animosity between Sir Sikandar and myself for the last many years. I must remove this impression. As far as I can see, Sir Sikandar did with the Khaksars what he considered right valiantly and without fear of any blame and this is a grand quality. I pray for him. The only appeal I can make to his successor is that he may release the 14 Khaksars condemned to transportation for life as early as possible."

Editor's Comments: Mashriqi's greatness was evident from his statement. He appreciated Sir Sikandar on his death, despite the fact that he had suffered so much at the hands of this person.

1943-1944

1943

1943 January 01

The Bombay Chronicle reports that the Sind Government has removed the ban on the Khaksars.

A day of thanksgiving is observed by Khaksars all over India to express thanks to God for the release of Allama Mashriqi and the removal of ban on the Khaksars.

1943 January 02

Allama Mashriqi arrives in New Delhi (from Madras) after the Government removed the restrictions on his movements. He addresses a large crowd that has gathered to welcome him at the Delhi railway station. Mashriqi asks the Khaksars to work for Hindu-Muslim unity, stating that neither community can obtain freedom for itself or for the country if it is fighting the other.

Allama Mashriqi addresses Khaksars while passing through Jhansi, en route to Lahore. *The Hindustan Times*, Delhi of January 05, 1943 would report that "He [Mashriqi] pleaded with the Muslims for religious tolerance, broadmindedness and magnanimity. The Muslims ruled for 1,000 years only because they treated non-Muslims with consideration, loved them and shared their sorrows and troubles, he observed. The Muslim Empire showed signs of decay when Muslim Rulers became intolerant towards non-Muslims and conservatives in their religious outlook. 'I want Khaksars to preach the gospel of Hindu-Muslim unity which is a living force and without which no liberation is possible. Those leaders who preach ratio communalism are not your leaders. You must discard them and throw them overboard.'"

1943 January 03

Allama Mashriqi arrives in Lahore and receives a hero's welcome. On this day (January 03, 1940), Mashriqi arrives at Lahore Railway Station as a free man and he is accorded an enthusiastic reception. He addresses a huge crowd and thanks God that he is able to address the public after three years. He further states that India is enslaved today because Indians have gone astray from the path of truth and righteousness. He again asks for unity among all communities, regardless of religion. He concludes by stating that there is nothing secret about the Khaksar Movement, which has spread throughout India within 12 years.

In his book *Al-Mashriqi: The Disowned Genius*, Syed Shabbir Hussain further describes Mashriqi's arrival in Lahore. He states that Mashriqi arrived in Lahore at 10:00 pm and was welcomed with a 51-gun salute. Hussain also states that "In his brief speech to the 'Muslim and non-Muslim Brethren' he [Mashriqi] said that Khaksars had always remained – and wished to remain – aloof from the 'dirty Indian politics which is aimed at clash between the Hindus and the Muslims' and then added: 'There is no bigger and more powerful weapon for subjugated and weak nations to take up than service and virtuousness. Rulers have always feared righteous actions. Jesus Christ was crucified because of his extemely virtuous deeds."

1943 January 04

The Government of Orissa removes the ban on the Khaksar Tehrik.

The Bombay Chronicle reports that the C.P. Government has removed ban on the Khaksars.

1943 January 06

The Government of the North West Frontier Province issues a Gazette Extraordinary withdrawing the ban on the Khaksar Tehrik.

1943 January 08

Khaksars observe public prayers in mosques throughout India to express thanks to God for the release of Allama Mashriqi and the removal of the ban on the Khaksars. As per Allama Mashriqi's instructions, the Khaksars also offer special prayers for the release of imprisoned Khaksars, including those sentenced to transportation for life.

Allama Mashriqi addresses a huge gathering at Badshahi Mosque in Lahore. *The Star of India*, Calcutta of January 09, 1943 would report:
"The need for communal unity at the present critical times through which India was passing was stressed by Allama Mashriqui, the Khaksar leader, addressing a thanksgiving meeting organised under the auspices of the Anjuman-i-Khaksaran at the Badshahi Mosque this afternoon.
Allama Mashriqui emphasised the non-political and non-communal character of the Khaksar movement which, he said, was primarily designed to promote social service. The need for a band of selfless social workers, he pointed out, was never greater than at the present time when India was threatened with aggression from a ruthless enemy like the Japanese. He however, made it clear that in accordance with the orders of the Government of India the Khaksars were free to perform social service individually only and not as an organised body.
The Khaksar leader recalled the attempts made by the Congress as well as the Muslim League during the past three years to win over the Khaksars and announced that the separate identity of the movement would be maintained although they were ready and willing to render service to both the organisations.
About half a dozen Hindu and Sikh Khaksars also made speeches repudiating the allegation that the Khaksar movement was intended to crush Hindus and Sikhs."

1943 March 01

The Star of India, Calcutta reports "Much interest now centers round Allama Mashriqi as Muslim circles here are of opinion that Allama can no longer sit idle and watch the situation. There is already a move to bring Mr. Jinnah and Allama on a common platform or at least make an effective collaboration between them possible. It is also said that Allama does not favour the amalgamation of Khaksar organisation with Muslim League but will support closer co-operation whenever possible."

Editor's Comments: The public wanted a close collaboration between Allama Mashriqi and Quaid-i-Azam, however, there were forces among the British, the Congress Party, and within the Muslim League which prevented this cooperation. The forth coming attack on Jinnah on July 26, 1943 was the result of a conspiracy against a possible collaboration and to defame Mashriqi and finish him politically.

1943 March 19

"Khaksar Day" is observed in India in memory of the martyrs of March 19, 1940.

1943 March 25

The Bahwalpur State Police raid the Khaksar headquarters and remove the flag from the building.

Khaksars hold a grand rally in Poona. Khaksar leaders make speeches and explain the objectives of the movement.

1943 April 15

The Bombay Chronicle reports that Mashriqi has sent a telegram to Nawab Bahadur of Murshidabad, the President of the Hindu-Muslim Unity Association. The newspaper also states that Mashriqi welcomed the move to bring unity among various communities in Bengal. Mashriqi assured the Nawab of his full cooperation.

1943 June 05

Mashriqi sends the following telegram to Quaid-e-Azam: "Gandhiji's letter to you [Jinnah] to meet him is indeed a prelude to the achievement of Pakistan as well as India's independence. Your attitude towards the matter is extremely perturbing. Request to reconsider the significance of the invitation."

Mashriqi issues a statement. In the statement, he asks the Khaksars to send letters (between June 15 and July 15, 1943) to Jinnah and the Viceroy so that a Jinnah-Gandhi meeting could be held.

Editor's Comments: Thousands of letters would be sent to Jinnah and the Viceroy between June 15 and July 15, 1943. Letters to the Viceroy were meant to ask him to facilitate the meeting between Quaid-e-Azam and Gandhi.

1943 June 23

The Madras Provincial Khaksar organisation passes a resolution regarding the political state of affairs in India. *The Bombay Chronicle* would report on June 25, 1943 that they passed a resolution "deploring the present grave political and economic situation in the country and requesting Mr. Jinnah to meet Mahatma Gandhi and find a way out of the present deadlock…By another resolution the meeting expressed the view that the present rigid attitude of the Government was responsible for prolonging the deadlock and it urged the Viceroy to change his attitude and allow Mr. Jinnah and Mahatma Gandhi to meet and come to an agreement."

1943 July 15

Mashriqi writes a letter to Dr. Sir Zia ud Din stating issues that need to be settled with the Government of India. Mashriqi also sends a copy of the letter to Jinnah. According to Mashriqi, the issues are:
1. The Punjab Government put the ban on *Al-Islah* of Rs.1000/- which it has not lifted since although the ban was put in November 1942 for the reason that the Khaksar Organisation was at that time an unlawful association.
2. The remaining prisoners (fifteen in number or perhaps more) have not been released. They have been condemned to transportation for life on account of clash of 19th March 1940, in which according to reliable versions more than 75 Khaksars were killed. The Government set up afterwards an Enquiry Committee headed by the Chief Justice of Lahore and spent Rs. 17000/- on it, but no report of it was published. Afterwards these Khaksars were tried and transported. In their telegram of 9th January 1941, the Government of India while transmitting the conditions of my release after the termination of my fast of 80 days, stated that prisoners will be released after a settlement has been made by me with them, although they qualified that statement by saying that this did not apply to violent prisoners. If by the term 'violent' prisoners Government meant these unfortunate fifteen who had absolutely nothing to do with violence and were the ramnants of that party of Khaksars who were literally riddled with bullets on March 19, 1940, then indeed there were no prisoners to be released regarding which a solemn promise was made by the Government of India in writing.

    An absolutely non-violent prisoner, Prof. Abdul Azeez, has come out of the prison only a few weeks back after serving his full imprisonment term of two years. A detenu-Bashir Ahmed Siddiqui-is still under the orders of Government not to leave his province and another is detained in a district. The prisoners are treated in the most inhuman fashion as third class criminals and absolutely no amenity of any kind is given to them.
3. My 'invalid' pension of 300/- p.m. for 13 months prior to my detention on March 19, 1940, was withheld by Government simply because it was lying in the Treasury of Lahore by chance and I had not drawn it on account of pressure of other work. This is an instance of injustice unparalleled in the history of any

tyranny. I have made three representations and failed every time without Government giving any reason.

My 'invalid' pension for the 22 months I was in jail was not paid to me. A fresh order was issued arbitrarily by Government ordering the renewal of my pension with effect from the 1st of January, 1942, i.e. from a date 19 days before my release from the Madras jail. No reason was given as to why the pension for these 19 days was given. Over and above my detention for 22 months in jail, I was detained in Madras for 11 months and 10 days. No compensation was given to me for this detention after my release. Three days after my arrest on March 19, 1940, I put forward a representation to Government saying that as no charge had been brought forward against me, I should be compensated at the rate of at least Rs. 3000/-p.m. for the period I would be detained, as this was the pay I would have got in the ordinary course of Government service if I had continued in that service. The Government after several reminders replied on 2nd June 1942 to the effect that 'as far as they are aware the Allama was not deprived of any legitimate income of any importance by reason of his detention, and that they are, therefore, unable to consider his demand for a family allowance.' This reply is manifestly wrong and absurd as in the first place I was not only deprived of my legitimate pension during the 22 months of detention in jail and that the pension of 13 months prior to that period was also confiscated, but that the profit of several thousands of rupees p.m. which accrued to the Khaksar organisation through the sale of literature and the utilisation of my services to the organisation also stopped for the whole period of 33 months and 10 days that I was under detention both inside and outside jail. Three thousand rupees per month is only a very poor compensation in lieu of my services and the sale of literature and books and I claim the sum of exactly one lakh of rupees for that period at that rate. This should be paid to me without further delay. If Government desires I can submit the income from the sale of literature for a period immediately previous to my detention and the post office authorities may be asked to certify the correctness of it.

In addition to this the sum of about 1000/- was paid by me to the jail authorities for my personal expenses in jail. This sum should be returned to me.

I was not given any railway fare for my return from Madras to Lahore after my release, although Government while taking me from Delhi to Vallore got a cabin (five seats second class) reserved for me. This second class fare (five seats) should be given to me under the rules.

Over and above all these charges which amount to one lakh one thousand three hundred seventy five rupees, the sum of Rs. 12000/- with interest confiscated from pension should be refunded to me, the total sum thus coming up to nearly 113375/- rupees.

4. There is a long list of articles, properties and other things in the form of properties moveable and immoveable as well as rights and privileges which have been confiscated by Government during the time the organisation was banned. Legally and morally these articles should now be returned. Their value comes to several lakhs of rupees and these should now be returned without the slightest hitch.

1943 July 19

Sir Richard Totthenham, the Additional Secretary of the Government of India, sends a letter to Mashriqi. He warns Mashriqi that if the Khaksars do not stop their activities, the Government will re-impose the ban.

1943 July 22

Allama Mashriqi issues the following statement (he also sends a copy of the statement to Jinnah):

It appears that the Government of India would not let the Khaksars live or give to them even what is allowed to all others. The ban was raised on December 28 last after a terrible struggle of three years on clear and definite conditions put in my statement which the Government of India reproduced in their communique of that date, but these conditions were repudiated on January 25.

Since then the Government of India have threatened again and again that I shall be re-arrested and the ban on the Khaksars re-imposed unless the red symbol on the arm of the Khaksars is abolished, the gatherings of the Khaksars forbidden and their social service rendered individually. After the writings of the 3rd March last, I handed over to the Government of India for issue an announcement dated the 9th March to the effect that, being unable to go further, I suspend the Khaksar Organisation throughout India, but this announcement even the Government of India was not pleased to accept.

The latest warning of the 19th July is that, if within a fortnight from that date, the red symbol is not removed from the arm of every Khaksar in India and the display of belchas, drills, marches, also collective service inside camps not abolished, the Government of India will declare the Khaksars to be an unlawful association again. This is called the final warning.

I have always been more in favour of Khaksars being distinguished from non-Khaksars by their useful and noble deeds, their real humility, their sincere social service, their soldierly discipline, alert posture, and Godly qualities than by round or square symbols on their bodies but Government wants to take away from us what it allows to every other organisation in the country and is essential for keeping ordinary discipline. On the other hand, in order to prove my good will, I do not wish to embarrass Government as far as possible. I, therefore, under protest order Khaksars all over India to remove red symbols from their arms at once and without the slightest feelings of ill-will against Government. This will be for the duration of the war only and during that period every Khaksar is required to work so as to get himself distinguished by his noble deeds so that no colour mark is required at all to distinguish him. Every Khaksar, henceforth, is also ordered to keep a small copy of his Holy Book (Quran, Geeta, Granth, Bible) always with him for the improvement of his spiritual powers. Khaksars all over India must leave wearing head-dress altogether to show that they are humble and humiliated and cover their heads with ordinary white handkerchiefs when required at the time of prayers.

As regards camps, I order that absolutely no military display of any kind, viz, that of belchas, military uniforms, drills, marches, should henceforth take place even inside camps which must be exclusively reserved for congregational prayers, religious and social lectures and sports. No camps also are to be held anywhere in India for the purpose of doing social service at fairs or melas for the duration of the war.

After August 2, every Khaksar will disobey these orders at his own risk and Government may arrest him. No further orders will be issued to Provincial leaders or centres of the Organisation by the Idara-i-Aliyya but Provincial leaders must issue instructions to their sub-centres and so on at once. I am entirely satisfied with the enormous work done by the Khaksars all over India in connection with Jinnah-Gandhi meeting at my orders and I expect prompt obedience of these orders without a murmur.

Editor's Note: News of this statement is also reported in *The Hindustan Times*, Delhi of July 25, 1943.

1943 July 26

The Hindustan Times, Delhi reports that the Khaksars have sent many letters and telegrams to Jinnah urging him to meet with Gandhi. The newspaper further reports that similar letters have been sent to the Viceroy. Resolutions were also passed at three Khaksar meetings (one of which was attended by a large number of Hindus).

Attack on Jinnah

Rafiq Sabir Mazangavi uses a knife to inflict minor injuries on Quaid-e-Azam. The Khaksars visit Jinnah at his bungalow to sympathize with him. Rafiq Sabir Mazangavi is alleged to be a Khaksar without any investigation (the Bombay High Court Judge would later rule that Mazangavi was not a Khaksar). Mashriqi and the Khaksars are shocked to learn that Mazangavi is accused of being a Khaksar, and they view the allegation as a deep conspiracy against the Khaksar Tehrik.

Khaksar leaders condemn the attack on Jinnah. Dr. Mohammad Sadick (Naib Hakim-e-Ala) states, "We went to Mr. Jinnah's bungalow as soon as we learnt that a cowardly attack was made on his person by a Muslim who said that he was a Khaksar. We congratulate the Qaid-e-Azam on his escape, and strongly condemn that man who has done such a mean action which is absolutely against the Khaksar principles. We cannot believe that such a person could be a Khaksar." *The Bombay Chronicle*, Bombay July 27, 1943

Allama Mashriqi condemns the attack on Jinnah: "Quaid-e-Azam Jinnah is the most revered leader of the Mussalmans at this moment and all hopes are centered in him. I may differ from him in his methods of getting something for the Mussalmans but I have always considered him as a most essential person at this moment. I cannot believe the allegation that the assailant is a Khaksar from Lahore as no Khaksar of the name Mohamed Rafiq exists in Lahore excepting Mohammad Rafiq Ghauri, who is [at] present in Lahore, nor a Khaksar would ever think of such a thing. But the crime whosoever has done it is most dastardly and mean. I would simply say that, my personal sympathy apart, the young devil who has tried issues with an old man of the personality of Mr. Jinnah has done the greatest disservice to the immediate task before the Khaksar Organisation concerning which I was about to say something very substantial. The culprit must be brought to book but I would appeal to Qaid-e-Azam as well as everyone in India not to give this incident the slightest political tinge for the sake of the most important things that are happening and the most immense results involved. I would have taken it as a mere accident if the thing had happened with me and perhaps would not have cared to give it to the press or even get the culprit arrested, on account of the vital issues before the country." *The Star of India*, Calcutta July 27, 1943

Quaid-e-Azam's Secretary, Mr. Syed, gives the following statement to the Associated Press regarding the attack on Jinnah:

"Mahmood Rasikh [Rafiq Sabir Mazangavi], stated to be a Khaksar, came to Mr. Jinnah's residence at about 1-30 p.m. today. The Pathan watchman asked the visitor whom he was and what he wanted. On being informed that he wanted to see Mr. Jinnah, the watchman brought him to my room. I asked him why he wanted to see Mr. Jinnah and he said that he had come from Lahore to discuss with Mr. Jinnah about the League and other matters. I told him that Mr. Jinnah was busy and that he should fix an appointment to meet him. The visitor took a paper and wrote on it in Urdu that he wanted to see Mr. Jinnah to discuss some important matters and that he would be grateful if he met him.

While we were discussing the possibility of getting Mr. Jinnah to agree to see him immediately, Mr. Jinnah chanced to come into the room to take a file. Mr. Jinnah asked me who the visitor was and what he wanted. I told Mr. Jinnah the purpose for which the visitor had come. Mr. Jinnah then told the visitor that he was busy and that he should arrange an appointment. The visitor was not, presumably, willing to do this and he picked up a quarrel with Mr. Jinnah, in the course of which he drew out a knife and attempted to stab him in the neck. Mr. Jinnah caught his hand and thus prevented the knife striking him in the neck. The assailant, however, succeeded in inflicting minor injuries on Mr. Jinnah's chin and left hands. The Pathan watchman and myself overpowered the assailant and with great difficulty we snatched away the knife from his hands. The Police were immediately summoned and the assailant was handed over to them.

Mr. Jinnah was bleeding in the face and his left hand. The wounds are slight and Mr. Jinnah is now resting." *Star of India*, Calcutta July 27, 1943

1943 July 27

Rafiq Sabir Mazangavi (Jinnah's assailant) is produced before the Chief Presidency Magistrate in Bombay, who remands him to police custody.

Linlithgow (Viceroy of India) sends a private and a secret letter to Amery. "Jinnah was yesterday attacked...I made enquiries about his condition at once and have sent him a telegram of sympathy." (Mansergh 1973, 127).

1943 July 28

Regarding Quaid-e-Azam's injury on July 26, 1943, his secretary states, "There is no need for any anxiety as he [Jinnah] is progressing very favourably." *The Hindustan Times*, Delhi July 29, 1943

1943 August 05

The Criminal Investigation Department (CID), Lahore, makes a secret report regarding the activities of the Khaksars.

1943 August 17

Linlithgow (Viceroy of India) writes from Delhi to Sir Bertrand James Glancy (Governor of Punjab). Linlithgow shows his discontentment for continued Khaksar resistance and suggests that he will take harsh actions against the Khaksars if they do not seize their activities.

1943 August 18

Al-Hilal newspaper writes that the Punjab Police (that had gone to Bombay to investigate the attack on Jinnah) stated in its investigation report that Rafiq Sabir Mazangavi was the Propaganda Secretary of the Muslim League and his real name was Mohammad Sadiq. (*Al-Islah* 1997, 59).

1943 August 26

Mashriqi appeals to Jinnah to meet with Gandhi in order to reach a Hindu-Muslim settlement so that the independence of India could be obtained.

1943 September 02

The second edition of Mashriqi's *Muqalaat* is published.

1943 September 07

The trial of Jinnah's assailant, Rafiq Sabir Mazangavi, begins in Bombay in the court of Oscar Brown, the Chief Presidency Magistrate. The court records Jinnah and his secretary's (Syed Ahmed Syed Yaqub) statements. Below is Jinnah's statement:

"I live at Mount Pleasant Road in a bungalow with no name. Mr. Syed is my Secretary. His office is on the ground floor of my house. I work on the ground floor. I have a Pathan watch-man at the gate. Anybody who wanted to see me was allowed to come in if I was free. I willingly saw people. Recently I was getting threatening letters apart from the Khaksars. I was, therefore, obliged to be a little more careful. I told my Secretary and watchman that anybody who called without appointment should be taken first to the Secretary before I saw him.

I got a copy of the instructions and orders issued by Allama Mushriqi, leader of the Khaksar organisation in the first or second week of June. Thereafter, I received telegrams, postcards and letters daily, both in Bombay and in Sind and Baluchistan during my tour in June and July and on my return till the incident on July 26. All of these letters ordered me to see Mr. Gandhi at once and contained an insinuation that I was in the way of the freedom of India and a tool in the hands of British Imperialism.

On July 26, I was working in my study on the ground floor. I was engaged on something very important. At 1-30 p.m. I got up and went to my Secretary's room for a particular file. I saw the accused there. He was sitting and writing at my Secretary's table. On seeing the accused, I asked who he was. The Secretary said that he was a visitor who wished to see me. The accused said it was urgent business and he must see me at once. This was inspite of the fact that my Secretary had already told him that I was engaged on an important matter at the time. I was standing by the edge of the table. The accused stood up. He had a paper on which he had written something. I told him that I was very sorry that I could not see him at once. I told him to write out whatever he had to say. I assured him that I would look into the matter and would be glad to see him the following day or the day after to fix up some time. My mind was on the matter I was attending to. I moved to leave the room. Suddenly, in the twinkling of an eye, the accused sprang at me and gave me a blow with his clenched fist on the left side of my jaw. I reeled back a little. Simultaneously, the accused whipped out a knife and held it in his clenched hand." When the Magistrate questions whether it was an open knife, Jinnah responds:

"Yes, it was an open knife. The accused wanted to strike at my throat. The accused took it out from his vest. The knife was open already. My instinct of self-defence made me parry the blow with the knife which the accused aimed at my neck. Fortunately, I seized the accused's wrist and broke the momentum of the blow. The knife only reached my chin and made a small cut. I forced back the accused's hand holding the knife and seized his other hand. A scuffle ensued. It was all a matter of a few seconds. My Secretary rushed up and my watchman came up and seized the accused. I received an injury on my left hand. In the struggle my coat also received a cut on the left shoulder.

The Secretary and the watchman pulled the accused away from me. I let go the accused's hand. My Chauffeur also came on the scene and disarmed the accused by taking away the knife. I was bleeding from my cuts. I went up to my room and sent for Dr. Masina. He dressed my injuries. The police were informed and they arrived. They took charge of my coat, waistcoat, trouser, shirt, and collar. The police also took charge of the knife. My statement was recorded. I did not know the accused before.

Between the time of the attack on me and the arrival of the police, the accused said it was a misfortune that he had failed in his mission. He said he had done this because I had refused to carry out the orders of Allama Mashriqui to meet Mr. Gandhi. He said that I was in the way of the freedom of the country and that I was a tool of British Imperialism. The accused was holding forth this way because it had been suggested to him by someone that he was a hired assassin." *The Bombay Chronicle*, Bombay September 08, 1943

Editor's Comments: Jinnah's statement in the Court was highly deplored in the Khaksar circle, because his statements put the blame on Mashriqi and the Khaksars without real reason. Mashriqi's request to not turn this into a political scandal was ignored. This was seen as a conspiracy to destroy Mashriqi and the Khaksars politically. It is important to note that in his verdict on November 04, 1943, Justice Blagden of Bombay High Court refused to accept that Rafiq Sabir Mazangavi was a Khaksar and did not accept Quaid-e-Azam's assertion.

1943 September 08

The trial of Quaid-e-Azam's assailant is resumed in the court of Oscar Brown, the Chief Presidency Magistrate of Bombay. Dr. Masina and other people record their statements. *The Bombay Chronicle* of September 09, 1943 would report that "A large crowd thronged the Court...among the crowd were some European ladies also. An unusual feature was that by the side of the Magistrate to his left sat a European Honorary Magistrate on the Bench watching the proceedings with keen interest." The case is postponed until September 14, 1943.

1943 September 13

A meeting is held in Jamia Masjid in Delhi. Liaqat Ali Khan presides over the meeting. Professor Inayatullah Lahori, the editor of *Pakistan* newspaper (a Muslim League paper published in Delhi), addresses the session and admits that Rafiq Sabir Mazangavi was not a Khaksar, but a Muslim Leaguer. Lahori says, "I state with regret that Mr. Jinnah's attacker was from amongst us and has been working for the Muslim League for a long time. It's even more regrettable that Mazangavi belongs to the same area where I come from. When I see that this is the same Rafiq Sabir Mazangavi whom we used to consider one of our valuable companions, I bow my head in shame." (translation from Urdu). (*Al-Islah* 1997, 26).

1943 September 14

Rafiq Sabir Mazangavi's trial is further postponed until September 18, 1943.

1943 September 16

Allama Mashriqi issues a statement ordering the Khaksars to help 600,000 Bengali men, women, children, and destitutes, regardless of caste, color, creed, or religion, until the situation returns to normal:

"Hitherto my orders to Khaksars invariably have been not to collect subscriptions for any purpose and to perform only those social services which involve no expenditure of money, but I must change them now if Bengal is to be saved. I order that 25 lakhs of Khaksars should by the end of September make six lakhs groups of four Khaksars each and the head of lack group should write a postcard, asking one the following seven persons in Bengal to send one famished person, male or female, young or old, to their address for support: (1) Sir Nazimuddin, Premier, (2) Mr. Fazlul Haq, ex Premier, (3) Abdur Rashid Qureshi

Hakim I. Aala, 31/109 Lower Chitpur Road, Calcutta, (4) My son Akhtar Hameed Khan, I.C.S. Netrokona, Mymensingh, (5) Nawab of Murshidabad, Calcutta, (6) Prof. Humayun Kabir. Ballygunge, Calcutta, (7) Tahira Begam, 31/109 Lower Chitpur Road, Calcutta. I have telegraphed these seven persons to send famished persons to Khaksars and have requested the Bengal Premier to arrange their transit free of railway charges.

I order that every group must make itself ready to support one person until hunger and death disappear from the land. Khaksars are permitted to take legitimate human work from capable refugees with the written permission of the local Salar. They must keep female refugees under the care of their wives, mothers or sisters. No refugee should be molested, or given food against his religious convictions, nor any Khaksar should interfere with his religion, while Hindu as well as Muslim Khaksars should take part in this movement irrespective of caste or creed.

To the Khaksars of Calcutta and elsewhere where famine prevails and people are dying, I order that every single Khaksar or a batch of two should go to every rich man in the city, get bundle of leaves or two seers of rice or flour or other eatables from him, and distribute these things there and then to the dying men and women. He must not touch any hard cash." *The Bombay Chronicle*, Bombay September 17, 1943

1943 September 18

The Hindustan Times, Delhi of September 19, 1943 would report that "Rafiq Sabir Mazangavi, the alleged assailant of Mr. M.A. Jinnah, was committed to take his trial at the current criminal sessions of the Bombay High Court by the Chief Presidency Magistrate."

1943 September 23

The Star of India, Calcutta reports, "In August 1940 Government issued notification banning the performance of military drill and the wearing in public of dress resembling a military uniform. As explained in a Press Note issued at the time, this action was designed to prevent [t]he growth of private armies and to stop militaristic activities on the part of non-official volunteer organisations that could only result in disturbing the public peace and interfere with the security of the country, says a Press Note.

It has now become necessary to supplement these notifications by taking powers to prevent secret gatherings at which breaches of the orders may occur and to ensure that any proposal on the part of a political or communal organisation to hold a camp or parade is brought to the notice of the authority locally responsible for the maintenance of law and order — that is to say the District Magistrate or the Commissioner of Police in Presidency towns. The new powers take the form of an addition to Rule 58 of the Defence of India Rules and a general order made thereunder, which are published today.

There is nothing in this order which interferes with any legitimate activity, it merely reinforces Government's determination to suppress with complete impartiality the dangerous tendencies which are inseparable from any concerted attempt by non-official political or communal organisations to usurp the functions that are proper to the State and to the State alone."

1943 October 24

The Dawn, Delhi reports that the Working Committee of the Bombay Provincial Muslim League has passed a resolution requesting the Council of the All-India Muslim League to disassociate itself from the Khaksar Tehrik.

1943 November 01

The trial of Jinnah's assailant, Rafiq Sabir Mazangavi, commences before Justice Blagden and a common Jury at the Criminal Sessions of the Bombay High Court. The court records evidence from Jinnah, his secretary (Syed Ahmed Syed Yaqub), the Pathan watchman, and the doctor (Dr. Dinsnaw Masina).

1943 November 02

The trial of Quaid-e-Azam's assailant, Rafiq Sabir Mazangavi, continues in the court of Justice Blagden. Rafiq Sabir Mazangavi cross-examines Jinnah. *The Bombay Chronicle* would report on November 03, 1943:
"Eighteen letters received by Mr. Jinnah after 5th June threatening him if he should refuse to see Mr. Gandhi were put in as exhibits by Mr. Jinnah and read out in court by his counsel.
The accused having dispensed with the services of his counsel proceeded in person to cross-examine Mr. Jinnah. On being asked whether these threatening letters could have been written by persons other than Khaksars, Mr. Jinnah replied that that was a matter of opinion. In reply to further questions from the accused Mr. Jinnah stated that he did not remember the accused having handed him a letter at Lahore in 1935 when he went there in connection with some dispute relating to a mosque and stated that there was no personal enmity between him and the accused."

1943 November 03

The trial of Jinnah's assailant, Rafiq Sabir Mazangavi, continues and the court is crowded with people. Jinnah is present and is cross-examined by Mazangavi. However Justice Blagden does not allow Mazangavi to raise certain questions to the witness (Jinnah). The accused states that he is a member of the Muslim League and therefore he is entitled to ask the questions to the President (Jinnah) of the Muslim League. However, Jinnah states that he does not know if the accused was ever propaganda secretary of the Lahore District Muslim League. Mazangavi further states in court, "There is no dispute between me and Mr. Jinnah over any property or a woman. I looked upon Mr. Jinnah as a leader and I went to his bungalow on July 26, 1943 thinking he was a leader." *The Bombay Chronicle* of November 04, 1943 would further report Mazangavi's statement:
"*Mr. Jinnah, he [Mazangavi] said was a big man, but knew nothing of the sufferings and difficulties of the Muslim masses and it was with the idea of*

acquainting him with such affairs that he went to Mr. Jinnah's bungalow on July 26.

The watchman took him [Mazangavi] to the Secretary's room where he was offered a seat. The Secretary asked him what he wanted, and he said he had come to tell Mr. Jinnah 'his tale of woe.' The accused was given paper and was asked to write out whatever he wanted to discuss with Mr. Jinnah.

While writing, Mr. Jinnah entered the room. The accused stood up, and so did the Secretary and he saluted Jinnah. The Secretary told Jinnah the purpose of the accused's visit. 'After hearing the Secretary, Mr. Jinnah asked me to get out of the room', said the accused. 'Jinnah spoke to me in English and pointed to the door evidently asking me to leave the room. I requested him in Urdu entreating him as representative of the Prophet, he should give me a hearing. Jinnah again asked me to the leave the room. Then I told him, 'We are persons who have made you leader. If you don't allow me to speak to you then to whom else could I go.' Jinnah, the accused continued, caught hold of his wrist and pushed him. The accused freed himself. The Secretary tried to push the accused out but he gave a jerk and the Secretary fell down. Jinnah again made for him and hit him on the head. Meanwhile, he was given a punch-back on his head. The accused turned round and saw it was the watchman. The accused gave him a fist blow and the watchman reeled down. Jinnah hit him again and the accused retaliated by delivering a fist blow. Jinnah fell down near the doorway. By then, the accused was overpowered.

Asked by the Court if he had anything to say, the accused wanted to know whether blood stains on the knife were those of Mr. Jinnah's blood or somebody else's blood. The court: 'Here is a point for the prosecution to consider in the future cases.'"

1943 November 04

In front of a packed courtroom, Justice Blagden of the Bombay High Court sentences Jinnah's assailant, Rafiq Sabir Mazangavi, to five years of rigorous imprisonment. However, Justice Blagden refuses to accept that the assailant is a Khaksar. Anti-Khaksar elements are highly disappointed, as Jinnah was unable to prove that Rafiq Sabir Mazangavi is a Khaksar.
Editor's Comments: *Al-Islah* reports that Justice Blagden stated in his verdict that Jinnah, Jinnah's attorney, and witnesses all had failed to prove that Rafiq Sabir Mazangavi was a Khaksar. (*Al-Islah* 1997, 59). Despite the fact that Quaid-e-Azam himself was a reputable attorney, he could not prove that Rafiq Sabir Mazangavi was a Khaksar. Keeping in view the decision of Justice Blagden of Bombay High Court, there is no justification to report Rafiq Sabir Mazangavi as a Khaksar. This is a clear misrepresentation and a distortion of the facts.

1943 November 05

Mashriqi instructs the Khaksars to help the people suffering from the Bengal famine. The Khaksars would immediately respond and arrive in Bengal.
Editor's Note: This is the approximate date for this event.

1943 November 07

Zamindar newspaper, Lahore states in an article that Rafiq Sabir Mazangavi was not a Khaksar. (*Al-Islah* 1997, 7, 31).

1943 November 14-15

Quaid-e-Azam presides over a meeting of the All India Muslim League Council in New Delhi. Ch.Khaleeq-uz-Zaman moves a resolution to ban Muslim Leaguers from joining the Khaksar Tehrik. A number of Leaguers speak in favor of the resolution. I.I. Chundrigar asks the Khaksars to leave the Tehrik and join the Muslim League. Gazdar states that, until recently, they had considered the Khaksars a useful body. But he also states that the Khaksars today are following a policy hostile to the League. In regards to Jinnah's comments, *The Bombay Chronicle* of November 15, 1943 would report:
    "[Jinnah stated that the] Khaksars in the past had confined their activities to religious and social matters...The moment they came into politics they were a separate body. 'Are you or are you not satisfied that the Khaksars by their recent writings and actions have adopted a political policy and that this policy is hostile to the Muslim League?'
    'You cannot owe allegiance to two organisations at one time.'"
Hamid Nizami opposes passing the resolution because he feels that it will divide the Muslims. M.Ashraf also concedes that the whole Khaksar Tehrik organisation should not be condemned. Ultimately, the resolution prohibiting Muslim Leaguers from joining the Khaksar Tehrik is passed.

Following are two of the resolutions passed at this meeting:

RESOLUTION NO.2
    This Council of the All India Muslim League strongly condemns the dastardly and insane assault made on the person of Quaid-i-Azam Mr. Muhammad Ali Jinnah in Bombay and thanks Almighty God that He saved the life of our beloved leader.
    This Council of the All India Muslim League extends its sincere congratulations to the Quaid-e-Azam on his providential escape and prays that he may be spared long to guide the hundred million Muslims of India under his great leadership to their cherished goal of Pakistan.
Editor's Comments: On November 04, 1943 at the Bombay High Court, Justice Blagden refused to accept Rafiq Sabir Mazangavi to be a Khaksar. Thus, this resolution has no mention of Mazangavi and does not declare him to be a Khaksar. Keeping this in mind, I urge writers not to quote Mazangavi as a Khaksar, as this would be a distortion of the history of Pakistan.

RESOLUTION NO.5
    The Council of All India Muslim League, after careful and earnest consideration, has come to the conclusion that the Khaksar organization which was originally a purely social and religious organization, has shown by its writings and

actions that it is now pursuing a general policy which is hostile and antagonistic to the policy of the All India Muslim League. In the circumstances, the Council resolves that no member of the Muslim League should hereafter join or continue to remain as a member of the Khaksar organization.

Editor's Comments: This resolution clearly shows that the Muslim League did not want any other Muslim organization to play a political role in India. It should be noted that despite Mashriqi's political differences with Jinnah, the Khaksar Tehrik never imposed restrictions on its members against joining the Muslim League. There were many Khaksars who were also members of the Muslim League. In fact, the Khaksar Tehrik encouraged this in order to bring unity among the Muslims.

It is sad to note that the Muslim League did not realize that such decisions were harmful for the Muslim cause. Throughout history, such decisions have weakened the Muslims and have given strength to Muslim opponents.

1943 November 17

Zamindar newspaper, Lahore, writes an editorial criticizing the Muslim League's descision to prohibit Leaguers from joining the Khaksar Tehrik.

1943 November 18

At a Khaksar Camp in Calcutta, Maulvi Mohammad Usman (a prominent Muslim leader) appreciates the Khaksars' services for famine-stricken people in Bengal.

1943 December 03

Begum Ummatul Islam addresses the Khaksars at the Khaksar Camp in Calcutta. She lauds the Khaksars' services for the famine stricken people of Bengal.

1943 December 25

Zamindar newspaper, Lahore praises the services the Khaksars made toward the people affected by the Bengal famine. It states that the Khaksars' help will always be remembered. The glorious services of the Khaksars to save and support the famine-striken Bengal will always be remembered with a great sense of pride in Indian History and all of humanity.

1944

1944 March 01

Khaksars, sentenced to imprisonment for life, begin fasting in jail. They pledge to continue fasting until death unless they are released.
Editor's Comments: These Khaksars had been in jail since 1940.

1944 March 03

Mashriqi sends a telegram to the Viceroy of India, Sir R. Maxwell (Home Member), and other important people. In the telegram, Mashriqi informs them that the Khaksars who were sentenced to imprisonment for life are fasting in jail. He adds that two of the Khaksars, Badshah Gul and Karam Din, are in critical condition. Mashriqi further states that in January of 1942, the Government had promised him that all Khaksars imprisoned for nonviolent crimes would be released. However, in spite of eight requests, the Government has been unresponsive. He adds that eight Khaksars from Ajmer have also been arrested for congregating to say their prayers, in spite of repeated assurances by the Government that there are no restrictions on praying collectively. Mashriqi states that the situation is grave and asks the Government to secure the release of these prisoners.

1944 March 09

Mashriqi sends to Quaid-e-Azam his telegram of March 03, 1944 (sent to the Viceroy, Sir R. Maxwell, etc.) regarding the Khaksars fasting in jail.

1944 March 11

The Deccan Times, Madras reports, Khaksars are fasting in the Punjab jails and are in critical condition. The Frontier Muslim Association and prominent Muslim Societies and individuals have sent telegrams to Liaquat Ali Khan, Maulana Zafar Ali Khan M.L.A. (Central), Raja of Mehmudabad, and Nawab of Mamdot, requesting them to demand from the Punjab Government and the Central Government the early release of these captives.

1944 March 18

Mashriqi writes the following letter to Quaid-e-Azam from Lahore:
Dear Mr. Jinnah,
      I have learnt just this minute that you are in Lahore and attending some occasion. Events of the past some months have made you cause a breach between the Khaksars and the Muslim League and I have yet to know if I am to blame for that. My conviction is that Mussalmans and Hindus must come to an understanding at this critical moment, in order to gain Pakistan as well as independence for India; but you in your fury are losing these precious moments amidst despair and inaction.

I am open to conviction if you can convince me otherwise. You told Khaksars in Quetta that I should have written to you or met you if I thought you were mistaken. I have persistently written and do write again. I shall be pleased to meet you if you come to Ichhra, but if my humble invitation does not suit you I do not feel at all small if I come over to you.

Please let me know per bearer as I think we must come to an agreement. I hope you are well.

I am & c.

Inayatullah Khan

1944 March 19

Quaid-e-Azam sends the following reply to Mashriqi's letter of March 18, 1944:

Dear Mr. Inayatullah Khan,

I am in receipt of your letter of the 18th of March, late last night, and I regret very much indeed to note that you have thought fit to accuse me for having caused the breach between the Khaksars and the Muslim League and further you convey and insinuate that I am, to use your own expression, 'in my fury' opposed to Hindu-Muslim understanding under any circumstances. There is no truth whatsoever in these allegations that you make against me, and you should know that there is no justification for it. I have repeatedly made my position clear by my statements and speeches that have been broadcast in the press.

However, as you say you are open to conviction, may I draw your attention to the fact that now, the All-India Muslim League has appointed a Committee of Action, in whom are vested all the powers of organising the Muslim League, and request you to get in touch with the chairman, Nawab Mohamed Ismail Khan, whose address is Mustafa Castle, Meerut, U.P. or the convener Nawabzaba Liaquat Ali Khan whose address is, 8B, Hardinge Avenue, New Delhi as they are free from accusations and reflections that you have cast on me both in this letter under reply and by your previous writings and statements that you have issued to the press heretofore; and I hope that in that atmosphere they may be able to convince you that the policy and the principles and the programme of the League are in the best interest of Muslim India. I am informed that the full Committee of Action is going to meet at Delhi on the 25th instant. I am releasing this letter to the press as I notice that you have already published yours without waiting for my reply.

Yours sincerely,

M.A. Jinnah

Editor's Comments: A "breach" between the Khaksars and the Muslim League was a result of actions on the part of the Muslim League. First, not only was Rafiq Sabir Mazangavi (Jinnah's attacker) alleged to be a Khaksar, the Muslim League never came forward to correct this misconception when Justice Blagden ruled that Mazangavi in fact was not a Khaksar. Secondly, within a few days of Justice Blagden's decision, the Muslim League passed Resolution No. 5 at a meeting on November 14-15, 1943 which stated "Council resolves that no member of the Muslim League should hereafter join or continue to remain as a member of the Khaksar organization." Actions such as these were a source of friction between the Khaksars and the Muslim League.

Mashriqi replies to Jinnah's letter of March 19, 1944. He states:

Your reply to my letter of last night, received after much persuasion after sixteen hours, settles that I am not to blame for not meeting you for an understanding between the Mussalmans and the Hindus, or even between the Mussalmans themselves. My assertion, therefore, that you made an attempt to cause the breach between the Khaksars and the Muslim League stands true. Please reconsider the position in which you have involved yourself by this refusal. I can assure you that the Khaksar is not against the Muslim League in spite of everything that has happened.

Your reference to the 'Committee of Action' as having been given powers to organise the Muslim League is most amusing as this means that you consider the Muslim League to be a disorganised body so far. I assure you that the disorganisation is solely due to your inaction and despair, also, if I may add, to the expectant sentiments you arouse at the shows you make in public and the high words you give to them. I can respectfully assure that the Mussalman public is tired of all this.

I have asked you to reconsider your decision not to meet me, but I confess here that I shall be one of your lieutenants if you show real action. As regards your 'Committee of Action' I shall certainly give my best attention to it if it shows any action.

As a last word I can only say that if you, as the Quaid-i-Azam of the Mussalmans of India do not show any real action in the matter of Hindu-Muslim understanding or in getting Pakistan for the Mussalmans, I shall be compelled to the conclusion that the Mussalmans of India must leave you alone and try their luck elsewhere.

With best expectations that I shall get a more prompt reply.

Editor's Comments: Despite the actions of the Muslim League, Mashriqi was willing to act as Quaid-e-Azam's lieutenant as long as public interest was served.

1944 March 20

The Bombay Chronicle reports the correspondence between Allama Mashriqi and Quaid-Azam.

1944 April 28

Mashriqi addresses the public at Shahi Mosque, Lahore.

1944 May 09

Allama Mashriqi sends a telegram to Gandhi: "Your release delightful. Pray speedy recovery. Requesting Qaid-e-Azam Jinnah to make appointment for meeting you as soon as possible in response to your last year's request. Shall accompany him if necessary. Please wire condition health for possible interview."

Allama Mashriqi urges Quaid-e-Azam to meet with Gandhi in order to settle the dispute between the All-India Muslim League and Congress. In his communication to Jinnah, Mashriqi states: "Mahatma Gandhi's release has made the situation suddenly most delightful and easy. I implore you with all the humility at my disposal to grasp the opportunity most firmly and start talks with him at once. I have to-day telegraphed to him and await with interest future developments in this direction as well as your friendly gesture to me that you will agree to meet him. As the Mahatma is not in good health, it will be a matter of extreme courtesy to go and see him on his sick bed and no question of prestige can be involved if the step is taken now. In case you ask me to accompany you, I shall be ready to go."

1944 May 11

Mashriqi again urges Jinnah to settle his differences with Gandhi, keeping in mind the crucial period facing the nation in regards to India's independence.

1944 May 15

Gandhi replies to Mashriqi's telegram. Gandhi thanks Mashriqi and writes, "My last year's request to Qaid-i-Azam Jinnah still stands, and I will be ready to discuss the question of Hindu-Muslim understanding as soon as I get better."

1944 May 16

The Bombay Chronicle reports that Allama Mashriqi has summoned prominent Khaksar leaders in order to consult with them about the Jinnah-Gandhi talks. The newspaper also reports that Mashriqi may go to Kashmir to personally request Jinnah to meet with Gandhi.

1944 May 17

The Bombay Chronicle reports that "Enquries in informed quarters make it increasingly clear, as forecast exclusively by the Orient Press and now confirmed by Gandhiji himself in his telegram to Allama Mashriqui, that as soon as Gandhiji is restored to health his first task would be to see Mr. Jinnah."

1944 May 23

The Free Press Journal publishes news of Mashriqi's statement. Below is an excerpt from Mashriqi's statement:
"As regards the letter of the Mahatma, I must confess that his words 'why should not both you and I approach the great question of communal unity with a determination to solve it to both parties satisfaction,' came as a complete surprise to me. The only 'if' with Mr. Jinnah hitherto had been that Mahatma Gandhi did not agree to talk to him as representative of the Hindus and no words than those quoted can express more clearly that 'change of heart' which Mr. Jinnah demanded last year...
Mr. Jinnah has not replied to my letter of 9th instant yet, although he acknowledged the receipt of it on the 13th. I am making a telegraphic request to him

to expedite his reply as the Khaksars are determined not only to see that this eventful and momentous meeting between the two political leaders does take place but that the conversations reach a successful issue.

The Mahatma has already telegraphed to me that he is too ill to move about or carry on serious conversation and this renders it imperative that Quaid-e-Azam should see Mahatma at once on his sick bed in order to open up the way to conversation and create an amicable atmosphere. If Churchill can meet healthy Stalin on Russian soil for the good of his people Mr. Jinnah can surely meet Mahatma Gandhi for the sake of Pakistan...

I make another public appeal to Quaid-e-Azam to descend from the heights of Kashmir for deciding the destiny of India without delay as I feel sure that the Mussalman public will get enraged if he shows inaction and despair at this critical moment. Understanding between the Hindus and Muslims must take place at all costs and the Khaksars are determined to see that it is carried on to a successful issue."

1944 June 20

The Tribune, Lahore reports, "It is learned that Allama Mashriqi, the Khaksar leader, is proceeding to Kashmir to meet Mr. Jinnah with a view to persuading him to meet Gandhi for a League-Congress rapprochement. After meeting Mr. Jinnah he will see Gandhiji at Poona."

1944 June 21

The Free Press Journal reports that Mashriqi is to meet Jinnah and Gandhi to bring a Muslim League-Congress settlement.

1944 June 24

Ghulam Qadir Hakimwala meets with G.M.Syed and discusses the Khaksars.

1944 June 27

The Bombay Chronicle reports that "Inquries made by the Orient Press from the Khaksar Circles reveal that Allama Mashriqi has sent orders for Provincial Khaksar Organisation asking them to keep ready for proceeding to Poona and to meet Gandhiji in deputation, for exerting his influence on him to come to terms with Muslims in order to bring about communal harmony."

1944 June 30

Bahar ul Ummal, a publication from Lucknow, states that Rafiq Sabir Mazangavi was the Propaganda Secretary of the Muslim League.

1944 July 02

The Deccan Times, Madras reports, Allama Mashriqi has written a letter to Gandhi asking him to send a fresh invitation to Quaid-e-Azam in order to bring about Hindu-Muslim understanding.

1944 July 30

Quaid-e-Azam arrives in Lahore.

1944 August 01

Mashriqi sends the following letter to Jinnah from Lahore:
Dear Mr. Jinnah,

After anxious and patient moments of the last few weeks when I finally wrote to you, I have my most sincere appreciation that you have come forward to alter the destiny of India to something better, however little, and I assure you again that I, along with every Khaksar that is in the land, will work with you in the full spirit of loyalty and friendship for the achievement of Pakistan, and consequently, the independence of India.

I deliberately ask my pardon for the harsh words spoken both in public and in my letters to you, as I feel intensely delighted over the words you uttered in Rawalpindi that you were working for the freedom, not only of 10 crores of Muslims but of 30 crores of non-Muslims as well. I can only say that the utterance will stand out as a pledge of your sincerity to India in the grave talks that are coming. Mr. Gandhi is to be congratulated no less for the bold and frank letter that he has written and I am sending a telegram of profound thankfulness to him today. I am also writing to him but these moves have already cleared the tense atmosphere that existed and I assure you that Hindus and Muslims are more ready for an understanding today than they were ever before.

I have purposely refrained from saying anything concerning the formula put forward by the ex-Premier of Madras, chiefly because you were silent, but also because, as I told you, I was determined to bring the matter of your meeting with Mr. Gandhi to a tangible conclusion. You are shrewd enough to see through it yourself, but as far as the Khaksars are concerned no stone will be left unturned in order to bring your conversations with Mr. Gandhi to the successful conclusion that every soul in India demands. May God help you and Mr. Gandhi as well.

On this serious occasion in the history of India I am proposing to order a batch of Khaksars to reach Bombay and shall if possible, reach Bombay myself for the purpose of begging you and Mr. Gandhi with folded hands to reach a suitable settlement satisfactory to both parties. I have no doubt that a settlement is bound to be reached with these good beginnings on both sides and that you as well as Mr. Gandhi will appreciate the reaching of this mixed batch of Hindu as well as Muslim Khaksars at the time of your conversations. I am writing to M. Gandhi also to the same effect.
Yours sincerely,
Inayatullah Khan

Editor's Note: A portion of this letter is also published in *The Tribune*, Lahore of August 02, 1944 and *The Deccan Times,* Madras of August 13, 1944

1944 August 14

Mashriqi sends a letter to Mahatma Gandhi.

Mashriqi sends the following letter to Jinnah from Lahore:
My Dear Quaid-i-Azam Jinnah,
I send you herewith an exact copy of the letter I have written to Mahatma Gandhi to-day. The same is to you word by word with the exception of the second paragraph which relates to him and may interest you.
Most unwholesome and unbecoming words were attributed to you by the distinguished messengers who undertook to take my letter of 30th July last personally to you, but I cannot believe that you uttered these words against me even in fury. My disgrace anywhere by anybody is for the good of my people and is therefore acceptable to me with good grace and without the slightest feeling of bitterness against anyone. After that letter I assure you again that not a word of bitterness has entered my heart.
With these frank words I request you to come to a settlement with the Mahatama under all circumstances, and if you think that a settlement has become impossible on the conditions that you present, please have patience to inform Dr. Rafique or his assistants near Crawford Market, so that they may take steps at once to see the Mahatma and request him with folded hands to come down to an agreement. You may rest assured that the Khaksars are determined to have these conversations come to a tangible conclusion and this can only be if you do not break away abruptly and leave a loophole somewhere. I am sure that we shall prove loyal to you in your difficulties and I may at the same time warn you, if you do not already know it, that there are hundred and one difficulties in the way of actually getting Pakistan or the independence of India even after you two come to an agreement. The time is very precious indeed and the British would like it to be whiled away as long as it suits their purpose.
With these brief remarks I wish you glorious success in your efforts.
Your sincerely,
Inayatullah Khan

1944 August 15

The Bombay Chronicle reports that the Khaksar Tehrik has appointed Professor Rafique, Head of the Science Department of Aligarh Muslim University, to help form favorable public opinion and facilitate a Jinnah-Gandhi meeting. The newspaper further reports that Professor Rafique has left for Bombay to talk to prominent leaders.

1944 August 18

The Bombay Chronicle reports that the Jinnah-Gandhi meeting (scheduled for August 19, 1944) has been postponed because Jinnah has a fever. As a result of Jinnah's fever, Gandhi cancels his scheduled trip to Bombay.

1944 August 21

Dr. Rafique Ahmed, who is in charge of the Khaksar Camp in Bombay issues the following statement: "The purpose of the arrival of Khaksars in Bombay on the eve of the Gandhi-Jinnah meeting is to create by their example of brotherhood and selfless service the right atmophere for a lasting Hindu-Muslim understanding. It is hoped that Hindus, Muslims, Parsees and other communities will extend their full co-operation in this difficult but most necessary task." *The Dawn*, Delhi August 21, 1944

1944 August 22

The Eastern Times reports that a Khaksar leader in Bombay sent a telegram to Allama Mashriqi stating that no more Khaksars are needed in Bombay, as the number is already more than enough for the Jinnah-Gandhi talks. The newspaper further reports that the Khaksars prayed at the mosque for Jinnah's health.

The Free Press Journal reports that Allama Mashriqi is arriving in Bombay (to ensure a settlement between Jinnah and Gandhi).

1944 August 25

The Tribune, Lahore reports that Jinnah is to meet with Gandhi in the next week. The newspaper also reports that 4,000 Khaksars have arrived in Bombay and continue to hold meetings and address gatherings to stress the urgent need for a Hindu-Muslim settlement and to ensure a successful conclusion to the Gandhi-Jinnah talks.

1944 August 27

Syed Allah Bakhsh (Head of the Political Department of the Khaksar Central Organisation) issues the following statement to the Press:
"In certain quarters of the Press it is attempted to suggest that the Khaksar movement is a quasi-Nazi organisation.
Let me make it clear once more that the Khaksar movement is based on the precepts of religion and is far above any racial economical or biological philosphies of life. All that the Khaksars want is the prevalence of religion, truth and justice. All that they are armed with is their selfless social service irrespective of all religions, self discipline and high individual character. The tremendous sacrifices that they had to perform in connection with the Bengal famine relief is a proof of their ideas.

It is needless to say that no Fascists organisation could ever show even a fraction of this sacrifice and virtuous action.

Armed with the aforesaid moral weapons they came to Bombay and are conquering it. During the week they have been in Bombay its broad-minded and sympathetic citizens have been very kind and have greeted the Khaksars with friendly smiles and sympathetic enquiries. I am glad to say that there has been no indication whatsoever that their coming was resented by anybody." *The Free Press Journal,* Bombay August 29, 1944

1944 August 29

The Eastern Times reports that about 4,000 Khaksars are in Bombay. The Khaksars arrived in Bombay to facilitate the Jinnah-Gandhi talks. The newspaper further reports that the Khaksars met with different political leaders and visited other areas in order to create a favorable atmosphere for the success of the talks. Areas visited by the Khaksars include Ahmedabad, Ahmednagar, and Poona.

1944 August 30

The Eastern Times reports that in case the Jinnah-Gandhi talks fail, the Khaksars plan to hold a Round Table Conference of various parties in order to evolve a formula for Hindu-Muslim unity.

1944 September 03

The Deccan Times, Madras reports that 4,000 Khaksars from various parts of the country have arrived in Bombay. They are meeting leaders of different parties to create a congenial atmosphere for the success of the Jinnah-Gandhi talks.

1944 September 09

As a result of Mashriqi's efforts, a Jinnah-Gandhi meeting takes place at Bombay.

1944 September 25

Eight Khaksars from Lahore are sentenced to terms of imprisonment ranging from one to two years.

1944 September 27

The Gandhi-Jinnah talks fail.

1944 September 28

Mashriqi issues a statement regarding the failure of the Jinnah-Gandhi meeting. According to Mashriqi:
"I do not see any failure when both leaders have been in conference for nearly three weeks and departed. The real difficulty is that neither Mahatma Gandhi nor Mr. Jinnah wishes to get out of the rut of dead theoretical politics, created round them by long years of cries for independence, on to the smooth road of living practical politics leading to immediate freedom. I must admit how ever that the Qaid-e-Azam has realised this difficulty considerably more than Mr. Gandhi and that is what makes me more hopeful of an early settlement. Our next step can only be to go on striving and I have now resolved to meet Mahatma Gandhi at the earliest opportunity available to me." *The Eastern Times,* Lahore October 01, 1944
Editor's Note: News of this is also published in *The Free Press Journal,* Bombay September 30, 1944 and *The Bombay Chronicle*, Bombay September 29, 1944.

Mashriqi asks the Khaksars to return from Bombay to their homes.

1944 October 03

Allama Mashriqi sends a letter to Viceroy Wavel after the failure of the Jinnah-Gandhi talks.

1994 October 07

Viceroy Wavel replies to Mashriqi's letter of October 03, 1944.

1944 October 30

Syed Allah Baksh Shah (Head of the Political Department of the Khaksar Tehrik) issues a press statement:
"It is now one month since the Gandhi-Jinnah talks broke down. The aftermath of frustration and dismay is over. Now is the fittest time to start our work afresh...
It is for us to see that when Mahatma Gandhi and Qaid-e-Azam meet again they meet in a definitely better atmosphere, in an atmosphere that will guarantee the immediate promulgation if [of] the decisions they arrive at.
The task before us is stupendous. There are many obstacles, visible and invisible. But the greatest among them is the dread of the imaginary 'third power.' We must believe that false dread. We must prove that when people determine to unite, no 'third power', imaginary or real, in fact no power on earth can stop them from doing so. And by the help of God we shall prove it."
Syed Allah Baksh Shah also instructs Khaksar leaders throughout India to strive for "Unity in Action" and to bring co-operation between leaders of both the Hindu and Muslim communities. *The Bombay Chronicle*, Bombay October 31, 1944

1944 December 15

Sir Tej Bahadur Sapru writes a letter to Sir Maharaj Singh: "…Khaksar deputation which saw you also came to see me. I told them…I was, and would be, in sympathy with any movement which had for its object a settlement of communal differences…I sympathize with Allama Mashriqi on this point…I have asked him to favor me with his views or suggestions…" (Hooja, 424).

1944 December 18

Mashriqi informs the Press that he sent telegrams to Jinnah and Gandhi urging them to meet again for a settlement. Mashriqi further states: "I shall continue to press these two leaders [Jinnah and Gandhi] to come to a settlement but if in spite of the best efforts of everybody they do not come to a settlement by the end of February, 1945, I propose to release for publication the constitution agreed to by all parties in the land as required by the British Government and shall present that Constitution as the basis of negotiation with the Government soon after that date." *The Tribune,* Lahore December 19, 1944

1944 December 19

The Sind Observer, Karachi reports that Allama Mashriqi has sent telegrams to Mahatma Gandhi and Jinnah asking them to meet again to arrive at a communal settlement. The telegrams read as follows.

Mashriqi's telegram to Jinnah says: "With folded hands I request you to meet Mahatma Gandhi again as promised to the whole India public before you separated last September. I have requested Mahatma Gandhi to send you fresh invitation but being as anxious as Mahatma for settlement, it equally devolves on you to invite him."

Mashriqi's telegram to Gandhi says: "Over seven months have passed since your release from jail and eleven weeks since you and Quaid-e-Azam parted unsuccessfully. Your attention to irrelevant matters in these precious moments is most distressing. Please take it as India speaking when I say with folded hands that you should meet Quaid-e-Azam again immediately and send a fresh invitation. India is getting unified automatically and I undertake to present you an agreed constitution soon after settlement is reached between you both, pray give me opportunity to explain."

On December 24, 1944, *The Deccan Times*, Madras would also publish Mashriqi's telegram to Jinnah: "With folded hands I request you to meet Mahatma Gandhi again as promised to the whole Indian public before you separated last September. I have requested Mahatma Gandhi to send you fresh invitation but being as anxious for settlement it equally devolves on you to invite him. Please rest assured that the whole of India, irrespective of parties, is ready for unification for the purpose of presenting an agreed constitution before the British Government and as already most encouraging replies are being received by me. I undertake to put that constitution before you soon after you settle. Pray give me opportunity to explain further."

Allama Mashriqi writes from Lahore to Sir Tej Bahadur Sapru (President, Non-party Leaders Conference) in Allahabad:
Dear Sir Tej Bahadur,
…You will have noticed that I have appealed again to Jinnah and Gandhi to meet each other and am engaged in the meantime in getting an agreed constitution between the main elements of India's national life…considering that your work also appears identical with ours in many respects it may occur to you to coordinate your work with ours, so that we may not be running on parallel lines…I honestly think that the Hindu-Muslim problem can be solved in the way it has hitherto been attempted. At any rate my most sincere wishes are with you. With best wishes, I am, Yours sincerely,
(sd/. Allama Mashriqi)

1944 December 23

Mashriqi asks Jinnah and Gandhi to resolve their political differences by February 1945 (in order to attain independence). Mashriqi states that if they fail to reach an agreement by that time, then he himself will release a constitution agreeable to all parties. According to Mashriqi:
"On October 3, I wrote a straightforward letter to Lord Wavell, telling him what I thought of Cripps' Offer and asking him to help in solving the tangle. The Viceroy gave a straightforward reply indicating that India should help herself to what had already been offered in the pronouncements made by him and a close study of his pronouncements has revealed that an agreed constitution on the lines of what is required by the British Government is possible to attain without reference to Hindu-Muslim differences on the question of Pakistan or no Pakistan. In fact Dr. Khare, an Executive Member of the Viceroy's Council, gave a press statement to that effect a few days after my letter to the Viceroy. I am therefore confident that our efforts are not only in the right direction, but that the only way which now remains in order to make the Congress and Muslim League come to terms is to make the elements of India's national life come to an agreement. Mahatma Gandhi and Quaid-i-Azam Jinnah will only then, come to terms under duress.
The Khaksar organisation has felt the existence of more or less 75 parties in the country and is already in communication with a large number of them. The replies I am receiving for the purpose of presenting a united India before the British Government are extremely encouraging. Every party seems bent on finishing the job as the end of the war is in sight and chiefly because Mahatma Gandhi and Quaid-i Azam Jinnah have come to no settlement. I am confident now in the spring of next year the Khaksar organisation should be able to present a united India before the bar of the world.
I have already sent telegrams to the two leaders imploring them with folded hands to resume their talks and relieve India from the agony of suspense. I shall continue to press these two leaders to come to settlement to the best of my power but I announce here that if in spite of the best efforts of everybody they do

not come to actual settlement by the end of February 1945, I propose to release for publication the constitution agreed to by all parties in the land as required by the British Government and shall present that constitution in negotiable form to the Government soon after that date."

1945-1947

1945

1945 January 26

Allama Mashriqi sends the following letter to Gandhi from Lahore:
My dear Mahatma Gandhi,

My humble submissions and incessant wailings do not apparently make you feel ruffled…

Quaid-e-Azam, in his Ahmedabad statement, has courageously come forward to say that he is ready to meet you again. It is, I humbly submit, your turn now to outdo him and come to a settlement within few hours.

…your agreement will at any rate stir India and this may prove useful. I am also daily succeding in getting various elements of India's national life united and the British will have to think twice before they pay a deaf ear to what I am going to present them. I have already told you that I am ready to take you and Quaid-i-Azam in full confidence in case you desire.

I, therefore, request you not to lose a further moment. I told Sir Tej Bahadur [Sapru] also, when he was in Lahore lately, that I consider your evidence in his Committee inopportune at this moment and that I had already written to you to that effect. I also complained that he ought to have consulted Mr. Jinnah as he consulted you beforehand. He gave cogent reasons, but the matter of Conciliation Committee has got spoiled now.

I send a copy of this letter to Quaid-e-Azam also and send a copy of my letter to him. With best wishes, I am,
Yours sincerely,
Inayatullah Khan

Mashriqi writes the following letter to Quaid-e-Azam from Lahore:
My dear Qaid-i-Azam Jinnah,

I must congratulate you on your Ahmadabad Press statement to the effect that you are ready to meet Mahatma Gandhi again. The courage with which you initiated the move has created fresh hopes and I hope the attempt at solution this time will be from an entirely different angle and that you will mean business and business alone on this occasion.

I have to-day written a fresh strong letter to Mahatma Gandhi, of which I send you a copy. I have every reason to believe that the Mahatma will respond to my request to him to send you a fresh invitation, but as you are the initiator this time you must have sent your Press statement to him by now, if not please send it to him now.

As regards other matters I have sufficiently explained them in my letter to the Mahatma, and I hope I shall not be accused of having done anything behind the back of either of you, or hidden anything from one which I said to the other. You may rest assured that I have no sinister motives and that the only thing I wish is that you two come to a settlement.

I request that this settlement be by the end of February. I have already told you and Mahatma Gandhi that I am ready to take you in full confidence concerning the Consititution that the Khaksar Organisation is preparing if you so desire.

I am also sending you a copy of my recent statement concerning Sir Tej
Bahadur Sapru.
With best wishes
Yours sincerely,
Inayatullah Khan

1945 January 30

Maulvi Haji Khair Mohammad Nizami, a Khaksar leader, is arrested upon his return
from Saudi Arabia (where he had gone to perform Haj). He was convicted for three
years imprisonment during the Khaksar agitation.

1945 February 23

Questions are raised in the Punjab Assembly regarding the imprisoned Khaksars.
The Parliamentary Secretary to the Punjab Premier informs the house that there are
fifteen Khaksars still in jail, ten of whom are serving long-term detentions. When
asked whether the Punjab Government intends to release any of the Khaksars, he
replies that the intentions of the Government cannot be disclosed. In reply to Sheikh
Sadiq Hassan's question about Khaksars on hunger-strike, the Parliamentary
Secretary evades the issue by stating that this is a new question and fresh notice is
needed.

1945 February 27

Mashriqi writes to Gandhi asking him to reach an accord with Jinnah. He states that
Gandhi's silence in response to Mashriqi's letter of January 26 is highly
disappointing. If Gandhi does not agree to reach a pact with Quaid-i-Azam by
March 31, then Mashriqi will command 10,000 Khaksars to proceed to Savagram
and begin fasting until death.

1945 March 12

Mashriqi writes to Gandhi.

1945 March 25

Mashriqi sends a telegram to Gandhi asking him to invite Jinnah for a meeting.

1945 March 26

Khaksars parade in Lahore. Police raid a number of locations in the city and arrest
12 Khaksars.

1945 March 28

Six Khaksars are arrested for parading in Lahore.

1945 April 06

Mashriqi sends telegrams to Churchill, Amery, and the Viceroy.

1945 April 26

Mashriqi writes a letter to Gandhi. Mashriqi asks Gandhi "to leave deliberating on how the next meeting with Mr. Jinnah is going to take place and meet him [Jinnah] as he is not in the best of health." Mashriqi further empasizes that the Mahatma should "simply go to him [Jinnah] for enquiring about his health." Mashriqi appeals to him to "leave all ideas of personal smallness before the good of the country."

Allama Mashriqi writes a letter to Jinnah stating: "I have requested him [Gandhi] to come to you to enquire about your health and this will open up the way for another meeting." Mashriqi appeals to him to "leave all ideas of personal smallness before the good of the country."

1945 June 22

Mashriqi delivers a speech in Shahi Mosque, Lahore regarding the *Khaksar Constitution of Free India.*

1945 July 03

Allama Mashriqi sends the following telegram to Jinnah, Gandhi, Maulana Abul Kalam Azad, Nehru, Pattabhi Sitaramiyya, and Patel:
"I pray Mahatma Gandhi and Quaid-i-Azam Jinnah both to think that their disagreement at this critical moment in the history of India will be most shameful and unbecoming.
I claim unreservedly that settlement between the two parties is impossible unless both leaders think in terms of the whole of India and every element of people in the country, and not only in terms of their own parties, especially because Congress and League are invited to speak on behalf of all India. Strongest possible representations have reached me on behalf of backward and neglected classes of both Hindus and Muslims and other communities against Congress and League monopolising all seats for themselves. I have, therefore, urged the Viceroy that two seats each be reserved for Congress, League, Hindu Mahasabha (including Arya Smaj, Dev Smaj, and Brahmu Smaj), and Non-Muslim League Sunni Muslims. Also one seat each be reserved for Hindu Backward Classes, Muslim Backward Momins, Shiah Muslims, Dravidians, Christians, Sikhs, and Scheduled Classes. This will make fifteen seats in all. I strongly urge both great leaders for equitable treatment towards all parties. The claims of Congress as well as Muslim League that they represent the whole of India, or even all Hindus and all Muslims, are absolutely untenable. I shall present to Mahatama and Quaide-e-Azam both the Constitution agreed by seventy five parties representing the voice of over three hundred million people of the contry as soon as Congress and League come to settlement. Pray

consider the consequences of disagreement, as Khaksars will then strive to the last drop of their energies for upholding the cause of weak parties."

1945 July 10

Allama Mashriqi sends telegrams to the Viceroy, Quaid-e-Azam, Raja of Mahmoodabad, Liaquat Ali Khan, the three Muslim Premiers, and members of the Muslim League Working Committee.

1945 August 08

The Tribune, Lahore reports that Khaksar Abdul Aziz is on a hunger strike in Lahore Central Jail. The newspaper further writes that Nawab Sir Kakhdum M. Hussain Qureshi (M.L.A. [Central]), Maulana Sharaful Haq (Secretary, Majlis-i-Ahrar), Syed Saeed Ahmad (Municipal Commissioner), Sardar Gopal Singh (President, Congress Workers' Assembly), Malik Amrit Lal Patney (Advocate, Senior Vice President Municipal Committee), and Sardar Nanak Singh (Pleader, President Sikh Association) have sent letters to the Premier and the Finance Minister of Punjab asking for the Khaksar's release.

1945 September 03

The Khaksar Hakim-i-Ala, Bengal issues a statement saying that the Khaksar Headquarters have decided to work out a solution that is acceptable to all Indian political parties. He further states that the decision was taken because all other conferences (including the Simla Conference) failed to achieve the desired results and because the British made it clear that they will not grant freedom to India until all major political parties are in agreement and present a joint demand.

1945 September 06

Gandhi writes from Poona to Mashriqi:
"… I have now read the same [your letter] and I had your telegram also about it. My personal opinion is that there should be no distribution of seats but that elections should be on a basis of adult suffrage and only one electorate. But mine is a voice in the wilderness. Therefore, I am afraid, it will not count among divided counsellors." (Gandhi 1980, 231).

Gandhi writes to Dastagir:
AHMED DASTAGIR SAHEB,
As promised I am sending a letter to you for Allama Saheb. I had your letter. You can come over whenever you wish to. Today I have Allama Saheb's letter and a copy of his earlier letter. As desired by him, I have written to him also.
Mohan K. Gandhi

1945 September 07

The Civil & Military Gazette, Lahore reports that Khaksar Abdul Aziz has died in jail in Multan. The newspaper further reports that in protest of the death of Aziz, Mashriqi sent telegrams to the Premier and Ministers of the Punjab Government and to the Home Member of the Government of India. Abdul Aziz had been serving a sentence of life imprisonment since 1940 in connection with Khaksar protests against the restrictions placed on the Tehrik by the Government.

1945 September 09

Mashriqi talks about the *Khaksar Constitution of Free India* in front of a huge crowd at Shahi Mosque, Lahore.
Editor's Comments: It took a tremendous effort of almost one year to produce this constitution. People from all walks of life, including High Court Judges, law experts, university professors, politicians, trade experts, and scholars, took part in the preparation of this constitution. This constitution was necessary because the British refused to grant freedom unless all communities in India reached a mutual settlement. This constitution was also known as the *Constitution of Free India, 1946* or *Mashriqi's Constitution.*

1945 September 16

Mashriqi states in an interview that he wishes to see Indian Muslims united on one platform. According to Mashriqi:
"We must work out some formula for compromise between different parties before the bitterness becomes too great for national considerations, and I have already asked my Khaksars throughout India that greater and intensive efforts should be made to smooth out these antagonisms by meeting leaders of different political parties including Abdul Ghaffar Khan.
I also wrote to Mr. Jinnah in this connection, but I have not received any reply as yet. I am even now prepared to join the Muslim League provided it definitely recognises some reasonable share for the poor masses and does not retain all the powers exclusively for certain main leaders. The first step in this direction should be to reorganise the League on more democratic lines and the League President and the Working Committee should be elected directly through a general election all over India."
The Dawn, Delhi September, 20, 1945

1945 September 25

The Tribune, Lahore reports that the release of Khaksar prisoners was urged at the meeting of the All-India Jamiat Ulema held on September 18 and September 19, 1945. The newspaper further reports that the resolution passed by the All-India Jamiat Ulema stated:

"This meeting of the Council of the A.I. Jamiat Ulema, therefore, recommends to the Punjab Government that such prisoners from the Khaksars also along with other politicals should be released.

The meeting hopes that the Punjab Government will thereby be able to make good for the mistakes which the pro-Muslim League Government of the past did in that respect."

Mashriqi issues the following statement:

"Last August I proposed to Mr. Jinnah that in order to make Muslim League representative of Musalmans in any sense he should agree to my most modest proposal of giving, out of 40%, only ten percent to poor Musalmans and 5% to Shiahs, leaving 25% to Khan Bahadurs and other well-to-do individuals who overwhelm the Muslim League, otherwise, I told him, the Khaksars will help the poor Musalmans to fight for their rights, as they constituted more than 95 percent of the Muslim population. I made a similar appeal to Mr. Gandhi on behalf of the poor and depressed and suppressed Hindus.

...I still adhere to the statement I made in Peshawar that I as well as all the Khaksars will join the Muslim League only if Mr. Jinnah allows us into his fold, as then he will not be able to have everything for the flatterers round him and for himself alone. I only wish him to ponder over the fate that awaits him and his League in the next elections.

I appeal to Mahatma Gandhi publicly to think again over the reply he has given to me concerning the future fate of eighteen crores of supressed Hindus. I am grateful to him for the reply that he has given to me in Urdu with his own hand, and this shows his conciliatory spirit, but if in Free India power is to be the monopoly of a few individuals, it is best that we remain under the British rule until parties come to know the true meaning of democracy. I feel sure I am voicing the feelings of a large majority of Hindus also in this matter."

Editor's Note: A portion of this statement is also reported in *The Tribune*, Lahore of September 26, 1945.

1945 September 26

Mashriqi issues another statement in response to Jinnah:

"I have seen the statement of Mr. Jinnah of September 24, issued from Quetta, today in which he virulently attacks me and another gentleman, attributing to me baseless things and using almost obscene language. My speeches everywhere are written and Mr. Jinnah will not find a word of personal attack on him. I am not responsible for what the press has written against him in my name. But if Mr. Jinnah wants to secure the sympathy of the public for himself by using such vile language, not fit for a gentleman, he may rest assured that the Mussalman public is not with him and wants to do away with all the rubbish he created around himself.

I have already told Mr. Jinnah our one condition of joining the Muslim League, and we are not
going to have any more humbug from him about his leadership of the Mussalmans. My speeches strictly confine themselves to the unrepresentative character, the tyrannies and the hypocracies of the Muslim League as at present constituted, and

we shall not allow that the word Muslim be exploited by the so-called Muslim Leaguers at any rate in the coming elections.

Ninety-nine per cent of the Mussalmans are groaning under the tyranny of Mr. Jinnah's self-made leadership and the way in which he justifies the Muslim League to be the sole representative of the Mussalmans is most shameful and preposterous. After we have cleared the Muslim League of these elements the Mussalmans will heave a sigh of relief and then alone the Muslim League will represent the Mussalmans. It is until now only a clique of Khan Bahadurs and Nawabs." *The Tribune*, Lahore September 27, 1945

1945 September 28

The Civil & Military Gazette, Lahore publishes outline of the *Khaksar Constitution of Free India*.

1945 October

The Khaksar Constitution of Free India is published.

1945 October 05

The Tribune, Lahore reports that the Khaksars have decided to form a Parliamentary Board in Bengal for the upcoming general elections.

The Civil & Military Gazette, Lahore reports that the leaders of the Punjab Muslim Majlis urged the Premier of Punjab to release the Khaksar prisoners who had been arrested in 1940. The newspaper further reports that the Premier responded, in a letter to Mufti Mahomed Naeem (President of the Punjab Muslim Majlis), that he is considering the matter.

1945 October 06

Mashriqi sends Jinnah a copy of the *Khaksar Constitution of Free India* (prepared by the Khaksar Tehrik).

1945 October 07

Allama Mashriqi addresses Khaksars and the public at Aitchison Park in Amritsar. During his speech, Mashriqi explains the *Khaksar Constitution of Free India*. Muslim Leaguers attempt to disturb the gathering by attacking Khaksars and members of the public with lathis. They also rush to the stage, smashing a number of tables and chairs. Khaksars and members of the public receive various injuries, including head injuries.

1945 October 08

Mashriqi states, "The Muslim League seems to be employing gangs of vagabonds everywhere in order to make noise and create disturbance in our meetings and as they follow exactly the same technique everywhere, it is evident that the whole thing is pre-planned." *The Tribune*, Lahore October 11, 1945

1945 October 09

Mashriqi addresses the public at Jamia Mosque in Delhi.

1945 October 11

Dr. Mohammad Alam (M.L.A. Advisor to the Punjab Government) writes to the Premier of Punjab urging him to ask the Central Government to release all non-violent Khaksar prisoners and remove all restrictions on the Khaksars and the Khaksar Tehrik newspapers (*Al-Islah* and *Bahrul-Amal*).

1945 October 13

Allama Mashriqi addresses Khaksars and the public in front of Jumma Masjid in Delhi. Muslim Leaguers again attempt to disrupt the gathering by smashing bulbs and throwing stones at the stage.

1945 October 16

Khaksars are attacked and injured (while preparing for a public meeting in Lucknow near Aligarh Muslim University) by some Aligarh University students who support the Muslim League. The Khaksars shift the venue of the meeting to Jumma Masjid where Allama Mashriqi addresses a large crowd.

1945 October 18

The Vice Chancellor of Aligarh University apologizes to Allama Mashriqi for an assault (on October 16, 1945) by university students that injured a number of Khaksars as they were preparing for a public address by Allama Mashriqi. Mashriqi asks for a compensation of Rs. 2,000 to be paid to the injured Khaksars.

1945 October 19

Allama Mashriqi addresses over 100,000 people in Delhi. Slogans are raised in support of the Khaksars. Anti-Khaksar elements again attempt to disrupt the meeting.

1945 October 20

Mashriqi meets with Khaksar leaders in Calcutta, Bengal to discuss the coming election. Mashriqi also meets with N.R. Sarkar (former Commerce Member, Government of India). Professor Humayun Kabir and Shamsuddin Ahmad of the Krishak Proja Party also meet with Mashriqi to discuss the Khaksar constitution.

1945 October 28

Allama Mashriqi leaves Patna for Madras via Nagpur. During his stay in Patna, Mashriqi met with Khaksar leaders from all over the province as well as leaders from various Muslim organizations (including the Muslim Independent Party and Jamiat-Ul-Momin) to discuss the political situation in India.

The Deccan Times, Madras reports, "As an organiser he [Allama Mashriqi] was first rate; his supremacy was supreme there. He created militant spirit in an otherwise dull youth. He preached the message of action in the world that thought only in terms of idealism. Muslim India stood by him and promised him all support."

The Deccan Times, Madras reports, "...He was considered as one of the biggest of Muslim leaders and his Movement was looked upon as the sword arm of Muslim India for the achievement of its goal. Based on the Quranic ideals and militant action, his [Allama Mashriqi] organisation spread like wild fire, commanding awe in the government ranks and admiration among Indians. He inspired old and young alike. The Khaksar ideals were so attractive that they drafted into their fold some of the best brains in the country. KAZI ABDUL BAQI of U.P. renounced his lucrative practice at the bar and rallied round the banner of the ALLAMA [Mashriqi]. The late NAWAB BAHADUR YAR JUNG was the Khaksar Chief of Hyderabad. The Movement gathered momentum day by day; branches shot up in every district and it grew up to be one of the most powerful organisations in the country."

1945 October 29

Quaid-e-Azam issues a press statement asking the Muslims not to attend meetings of the Khaksar Tehrik.

1945 November 01

Gandhi writes to Mashriqi:
ALLAMA SAHEB,
I have received the printed constitution you have sent. I have gone through it. Though great pains have been taken in drafting it, I have doubts about its usefulness...
Yours,
M.K. Gandhi

1945 November 17

Mashriqi addresses students at Ismail Yousaf College in Bombay.

Gandhi writes to Mashriqi:
ALLAMA SAHEB,

I got your letter and two Khaksar officials also came and saw me. I was very
happy…On the 20th we have to catch a train for Wardha but still I have told the
Khaksar officials that you may come at 3 p.m. I shall wait for you then. If you want
any change in the time, please send a message to me at the Birla House.
Yours,
M.K. Gandhi

1945 November 18

The Deccan Times, Madras reports, "Born of a well-to-do Pathan family of Amritsar
in the year 1888, Inayatullah Khan had an exceptionally brilliant academic career
both in India and England. He became the Vice Principal and later on Principal of
Islamiah College, Peshawar, But in whatever capacity he served, he showed
unflinching enthusiasm in serving his community… *Tazkira*…gave to the world a
new interpretation to the Quranic philosophy. The book won world-wide tributes
and in 1925, the Nobel Prize Committee even asked for its translation in one of the
Primary European languages. This request, however, was not complied
with…Einstein expressed…appreciation of the book, when they met Allama
Mashriqi in 1926. Encouraged by this favourable reception, he published another
book *Isharat* through which he issued a call to his nation for action…

The dynamic personality of the leader and the militant character of the
organisation soon attracted a large number of Muslim Youths. Within five to six
years, Khaksar Movement spread to all parts of India…

The Khaksar organisation grew from strength to strength… The
happenings in the Punjab [March 19, 1940 massacre] and U.P. [Shia-Sunni clash in
1939 in Lucknow, in which Mashriqi and the Khaksars played a great role in
bringing peace, and many Khaksars were killed by the police.] gave to the Khaksars
the rank of martyrs. They commanded the love and respect of every Muslim heart.

The Allama was arrested…After about two years he was released but was
not allowed to leave Madras presidency. During the two years the situation in India
changed completely. There was a great awakening among the Muslims. They rallied
round the [Muslim] League, which gave to them in Pakistan, a goal to fight and die
for. Though they still retained their love and respect for the Khaksars… "
Editor's Comments: The Khaksars played a vital role in mobilizing the Muslims
and the massacre of the Khaksars on March 19, 1940 greatly enhanced the
following of the Muslim League. The Khaksar Tehrik brought Muslims together to
rise for the freedom of India.

1945 November 19

Gandhi writes from Birla House to Mashriqi:
ALLAMA SAHEB,
I have your letter…The biggest problem is the condition you have laid down. I cannot speak on behalf of the Congress. I can speak for myself and I think I have already conveyed my view to you that though you have taken great pains in drafting the constitution, it is not workable…I cannot agree with you on your constitution…I am afraid we shall not be able to agree at the forthcoming meeting. I had thought and I still think, that whatever the outcome of our meeting might be, we should meet and at least try to understand each other's point of view. Your letter gives me no such hope.
Yours,
M.K. Gandhi

1945 November 20

Gandhi writes from Birla House to Mashriqi:
"ALLAMA SAHEB,

I have your letter… What I had told you was never meant for the Press and so far as I am concerned I would like to say that whatever we have been writing to each other should not be sent to the Press…"

1945 December 18

Allama Mashriqi addresses a very large public meeting in Karachi.

Allama Mashriqi addresses a public congregation organised by the Karachi Municipal Corporation. During his speech, Mashriqi calls for unity. He further states that the Khaksars are working on a formula that will be suitable for all Indians.

1946

1946 January 01

Gandhi writes from Contai to Mashriqi.

1946 January 13

Mashriqi arrives at the Muslim League public meeting to announce his support and solidarity with the Quaid-e-Azam in front of the masses. Mashriqi seeks Jinnah's permission to address the public. However, Jinnah denies it and leaves the gathering. The Muslim Leaguers attack Mashriqi and knock him unconscious.

1946 January 31

The Civil & Military Gazette, Lahore, publishes a list of the candidates supported by the Khaksar Tehrik for the upcoming election. It includes candidates from the Muslim League, the Unionist Party, the Ahrar Party, and independents.

1946 February 22

Mashriqi addresses a public gathering of 50,000 people in Bankipur (Patna).

1946 March 17

The Deccan Times, Madras reports, Allama Mashriqi suggests to Muslim leaders that all Muslim parties, including the Khaksar Tehrik, be amalgamated into the All-India Azad Muslim League. He wrote to various Muslim leaders including Fazlul Haq, Prof Humayun Kabir, Malik Khizar Hayat Tiwana, etc.
Editor's Comments: Mashriqi believed that this would strengthen the power of the Muslims.

1946 March 20

The Tribune, Lahore reports:
"Mr. Fazl-ul-Huq [former Premier of Bengal and Leader of the Opposition in the last Bengal Legislative Assembly] makes the charge that Muslim Leaguers are 'using all sorts of force and violence and making a fair election impossible'...
Mr. Fazl-ul-Huq says: 'On the 16th [March 16, 1946] League hooligans fell upon peaceful Khaksars drinking tender coconuts at noon at Kadamtola, police station Backergang. Enquires now reveal that a murderous assault was made on the Khaksars, and that attack included sacrilegious handling of the holy Quran in the possession of the Khaksars...Six Khaksars, who received serious wounds, were removed to the local emergency hospital. The condition of two is precarious. Missing victims include...one Khaksar.'"

1946 March 22

Al-Islah publishes a letter to the editor, written by Rafiq Sabir Mazangavi (Jinnah's attacker).

1946 March 23

Mashriqi writes to Jinnah about the attack on him by Muslim Leaguers (at Islamia College, Lahore on January 13, 1946). Mashriqi complains of "the treatment meted out to me by thousands of hooligans after you hurriedly left the meeting of January last when I arrived in order to do my utmost for the purpose of creating unity among the Musalmans." Mashriqi further states, "I have not the slightest ill-feeling against you or the Muslim League that you have created." He also informs Jinnah that the Muslims have suggested that all political parties in India should join hands for seeking freedom and he invites Jinnah for the same purpose. He assures Jinnah that if he agrees to join hands, they can move mountains. (Hussain 1991, 221; Zaman 1987, 203).

1946 March 24

Mashriqi writes a letter to Quaid-e-Azam. In the letter, he informs Quaid-e-Azam of his terms for joining the Muslim League. Mashriqi's terms are as follows:
1.   The Muslim League must ensure equal rights for the rich and the poor.
2.   All appointments in the Muslim League must be kept open and not reserved for the privileged class of Muslims.
3.   The Muslim League must seek independence for the entire India with the joint support of the Muslims and Hindus.
4.   The creation of Pakistan must provide protection to all Muslims in the entire India.
Editor's Comments: According to Sher Zaman's book *Sir Syed, Jinnah, Mashriqi* (page 71), Mashriqi had sent an invitation to the Muslim League leaders to attend a conference of the Muslim political parties in India (to be held on April 07-08, 1946). The purpose of the conference was to combine all the parties to create the All-India Azad Muslim League. However, Liaquat Ali Khan suggested that instead of creating the All-India Azad Muslim League, Allama Mashriqi should join the Muslim League and also convince other parties to come under the Muslim League flag.

The Muslim League was not willing to lose its identity but was asking other parties give up their own identities. If a party is genuine in seeking cooperation of others, then its proposal should reflect willingness to cooperate. Mashriqi was willing to cooperate and sent the aforementioned conditions for joining the Muslim League.

1946 April 01

Quaid-e-Azam writes to Mashriqi.

1946 April 06

Mashriqi writes to Quaid-e-Azam.

1946 April 07-08

A meeting of the Muslim political parties of India is held in Delhi. Mashriqi proposes to combine the parties to create one political party under the name "All-India Azad Muslim League." Mashriqi also offers to abolish the Khaksar Tehrik in favor of the wider interests of the Muslims of India.

1946 May 04

Ten Khaksars are arrested in Rawalpindi under the Defence of India Rules.

1946 May 11

In Lahore, the Minister for Jails orders the release of Badshah Gull (a Khaksar leader) who had been sentenced to imprisonment for life in March of 1941. Badshah Gull had been on a hunger strike in jail for almost 18 months and was brought before the Minister on a stretcher. The Minister persuaded him to break the hunger strike and seeing Badshah Gull's health condition, ordered his release.

1946 May 22

Allama Mashriqi states that the Khaksars are going to fight for Pakistan and makes an unconditional offer of the Khaksars to Quaid-e-Azam in the following press statement:
"If Mr. Jinnah is perfectly sincere about Pakistan I offer once more the services of the Khaksar organisation to him unconditionally and am ready to join hands with him in this effort...
If Mr. Jinnah agrees I shall throw the whole force into the matter unstintedly and every Khaksar will be ready to lay down his life for the cause of the country.
To begin with I propose to issue orders to Khaksars all over India to celebrate vigorously from June 9 to June 16 a 'Mourning Week' in honour of Pakistan which has been buried alive by the British so ruthlessly. I shall await Mr. Jinnah's reaction and then start." *The Star of India*, Calcutta May 23, 1946

1946 May 28

Mashriqi sends a telegram to Jinnah offering full support for attaining Pakistan. According to Mashriqi: "Reference my Press statement twenty second unequivocal cooperation Muslim League attainment of Pakistan also celebration ninth sixtenth June mourning week. Please wire cooperation concurrence."

1946 June 06

Allama Mashriqi issues a press statement:
    "The Khaksars are prepared to sacrifice blood and undergo any amount of hardship provided Mr. Jinnah is earnest about his mission of Pakistan. But his continued silence in not acknowledging my offer proves that Mr. Jinnah is not at all sincere about Pakistan...
    Although I have postponed orders for a mourning week for Pakistan from June 9 to June 16 my unconditional offer to place the entire services of the Khaksar organisation for attaining Pakistan still stands." *The Eastern Times,* Lahore June 09, 1946
Editor's Comments: Mashriqi had sent repeated communications to Quaid-e-Azam offering his unconditional support in attaining Pakistan. Quaid-e-Azam's silence prompted Mashriqi to issue the aforementioned public statement and postpone Mourning Week.

1946 June 21

Al-Islah publishes another statement by Mashriqi stressing the need for unity among Indians in order to obtain freedom.

1946 June 29

22 Khaksars are arrested in various parts of Lahore for parading. They are produced before the courts and remanded.

1946 July 02

The Tribune, Lahore reports that Khan Badshah Gull (a Khaksar leader who was arrested following the police firing on March 19, 1940) died of tuberculosis. He had contracted tuberculosis while in prison and was released on May 11, 1946 due to his poor health. The Khaksar's body was brought to Peshawar and buried following a large procession mourning his death.

1946 July 14

Mashriqi issues a statement to the Khaksars.

1946 August 08

Five Khaksars (who were arrested on July 24, 1946) for parading are sentenced to two months of rigorous imprisonment each and a fine of Rs.100 each by a Lahore Magistrate.

1946 August 30

In his Eid address in Bombay, Quaid-e-Azam appeals to Khaksars, Ahrars, and Muslim nationalists to join the Muslim League.

1946 September 03

Rais Fatimi (a Khaksar leader) leads a delegation of Khaksars to meet with Rafi Ahmed Kidwai (Home Minister, Government of U.P) in order to discuss the searches of Khaksar houses and the ban on the carrying of belchas. The Home Minister refuses to lift the ban on carrying belchas in Lucknow.

1946 September 07

The Eastern Times reports that a large number of Khaksars have arrived in Meerut and continue to distribute pamphlets to the public. The newspaper further reports that the police have confiscated the Khaksars' belchas.

1946 September 09

Allama Mashriqi writes a letter in response to Quaid-e-Azam's appeal to the Khaksars to join the Muslim League:

"To tell you the truth I am convinced that consciously or unconsciously you and the Mussalmans are being used by the Britishers against the independence of India. I also do not believe in the satisfaction that Mr.Gandhi or Congress feels at their entry into the Interim Government.

If therefore, you can convince me by your writing to me that you mean to achieve Pakistan as a part and parcel of the independence of the whole of India and will work with Mr. Gandhi on this clear basis against British plans. I shall throw the whole force of the Khaksar organisation with you and we shall die in thousands. I also undertake that the Hindus as well as the Congress will concede Pakistan if you clearly agree to wrest India from British hands. I shall in that case work willingly with you to the last ditch.

In case you do not agree to work on this clear condition, please stop 'badnaming' the Khaksars by these fa'lse appeals any more as we have resolved to work out our own destiny alone. I shall await your reply with interest."

18 Khaksars are arrested near Meerut for parading.

1946 September 10

Khaksars continue to arrive in Meerut. 18 Khaksars (arrested outside Kamboh Gate, Meerut City on September 07, 1946) are produced before the City Magistrate and sent to jail.

1946 December 11

Approximately 300 Khaksars are arrested in Hyderabad (Sind) under Section 144 Cr. P. C. Their belchas and other equipment are also confiscated.

1946 December 24

The Eastern Times reports that the Government of Sind has agreed to release 200 Khaksars who had come to Karachi during the Assembly elections.

1947

1947 January 18

Allama Mashriqi meets with Dr. Shafaat Ahmed Khan (former Member of the Interim Government) to discuss the current political situation.

1947 February 26

In Lahore, six Khaksars are arrested for parading and carrying belchas.

1947 March

Allama Mashriqi calls for 300,000 Khaksars to assemble in Delhi.

1947 March 07

A discussion takes place between Gandhi and the Khaksars. The Khaksars offer their help in connection with the Hindu-Muslim riots of Bihar.

1947 March 30

Allama Mashriqi arrives in Peshawar to consult with Frontier Khaksar leaders and study the political situation.

1947 April 11

The Eastern Times reports that Allama Mashriqi is to arrive in Lucknow on April 14, 1947. The newspaper further states that Major General Dost Mohammad Khan and Col. Ehsan Qadir will accompany him.

1947 May 03

13 Khaksars are arrested in Lahore while making speeches at a public meeting. Police disperse the crowd that had gathered for the meeting. Police pickets are also posted in the area.

1947 May 07

The Pakistan Times reports that "Allama Mashriqi is reported to have placed his views on the rehabilitation of Muslim refugees in the Province before the Bihar Government. He has expressed his views against levying of fines on affected villages, it is learnt, and has suggested instead the levying of a cess-tax of rupee one per adult, to be known as the Bihar Relief Tax to meet a portion of the heavy expenses involved in undertaking relief and rehabilitation measures."

1947 May 10

Khaksars parade in Lahore in observance of "Bahadur Shah Day." Many Khaksars are arrested.

Mashriqi addresses the public at Banqipur, Putna.

1947 May 13

Allama Mashriqi issues a statement demanding the rehabilitation of Bihar refugees. According to Mashriqi: "We remain firm in this demand until Government actually concedes it. I am also satisfied that the Bengal Government has actually spent rupees eighty lakhs on the Noakhali refugees and that about 75 per cent of the refugees have come back and resettled. No resettlement worth the name has taken place in Bihar so far." *The Dawn*, Delhi May 15, 1947

1947 May 14

Mashriqi addresses over 50,000 people at a gathering at Banqipur, Patna.

1947 May 24

A discussion is held between Gandhi and the Khaksars.

1947 May 29

Mashriqi issues a statement asking the people to start a revolution against the British Government.

1947 May 30

M.Yunus writes from Patna to M.A. Jinnah, and encloses his correspondence with Mashriqi (see enclosures 1-4 below):
My dear Quaid-i-Azam,
I am enclosing my recent correspondence with Allama Inayetullah Mashriqi, the Khaksar leader, regarding the rehabilitation scheme in Bihar.
Yours sincerely,
M.Yunus

Enclosure 1

Inayetullah [Allama] Mashriqi to M.Yunus
                    KHAKSAR RELIEF AND REHABILITATION H.Q.,
                    CAMP PATNA,
                    29 May 1947
My dear Yunus,

The Government has accepted almost all the demands that the Khaksar Organisation had made with respect to the rehabilitation of Bihar refugees and the work of constructing thousands of houses will now begin.

In January last, Sir Shafaat Ahmed Khan, when he met me at Ichhra and we discussed the problem, was particularly keen on telling me that you had written to him that you were very interested in relief work and that your "joining" the Muslim League was not so much on account of leaning towards the League as on account of their claim to do relief work. He also suggested that you should be asked to cooperate in the work that the Khaksars will undertake. I am, therefore, asking you to join as a member of the Relief Committee to which I am entrusting the task of rehabilitation before I leave Patna. A meeting of this Committee is going to be held today at 6 p.m. at the above address. Please attend it.

I hope you are quite well now.

Yours sincerely,

INAYETULLAH

Enclosure 2

M. Yunus to Inayetullah [Allama] Mashriqi

DAR-UL-MALIK, FRASER ROAD, PATNA,
29 May 1947

My dear Mr. Inayetullah,

Many thanks for your letter No. 42488 dated 29th May 1947. You have been kind enough to inform me that the Government has accepted almost all the demands that the Khaksar Organisation had made with respect to the rehabilitation of the Bihar refugees and the work of constructing thousands of houses will now begin. Its feasibility would depend on the nature of your demands and of your scheme, copies of which you have not been pleased to send me, and I shall be obliged if you will kindly do so to appraise in proper perspective the value of the rehabilitation scheme...

I am grateful to you for asking me to co-operate in the work that the Khaksars will undertake for relief work...

Yours sincerely,

M.YUNUS

Enclosure 3

Inayetullah [Allama] Mashriqi to M. Yunus

KHAKSAR RELIEF AND REHABILITATION H.Q.,
CAMP PATNA
29 May 1947

Dear Mr. Yunus,

I have your letter. On the back you will find the conditions that have been accepted. There are some others which they are likely to accept gradually. At any rate, the work should start at once as people in Bengal and Sind are suffering terribly and it is absolutely impossible to rehabilitate them anywhere except on their own lands, otherwise four lakh (people) will perish and lose all honour. The condition in the camps is simply terrible.

You must come forward individually or otherwise. The funeral is of the Biahris themselves, perpetrated through the dirty politics of the present day, and if the Biaris themselves do not do it, it will be a regrettable thing. In a humanitarian work one should leave all politics. I shall explain to you further if you come this evening at 6 p.m. I have given invitation to Mr. Jafar Imam through Syed Abdul Aziz who says he cannot joint as his condition is worsening unfortunately. If you can ask him to joint today's deliberations I shall be pleased.

Yours sincerely,
INAYETULLAH

Enclosure 4

PATNA,
29 May 1947

PRESS STATEMENT BY ALLAMA MASHRIQI

'Nearly five months' persistent haggling with the Bihar Government on the matter of resettlement of nearly 4 lakhs of Bihar refugees, I am glad to announce, has made the Government come to the conclusion that the problem has got to be tackled. My demand that one thousand rupees per adult be given at a flat rate for reconstruction of houses has not been met in full on financial grounds, but the final proposals which Mahatma Gandhi has placed before the Bihar Government concerning the conditions on which the Khaksar organisation would or should take up the work of rehabilitation, are as follows:

1. The Government will grant Rs.1,000 for every house rebuilt.
2. In addition, a rehabilitation grant of Rs. 500 for a family of 5 members will be made.
3. Building grants of more than Rs. 1,000 will be made in special cases.
4. Special grants of Rs. 1,500 or more will be given even to those who do not wish to resettle in Bihar on the recommendation of the Khaksar Organisation, (this being Mr. Gandhi's verbal suggestion may be taken to be the opinion of the Government).
5. Interest-free loans repayable in 5 yearly instalments will be given to artisans and agriculturists for the purchase of seeds and implements.
6. Free Education will be provided for refugees who settle.
7. Work will be given by the Government to those adults who need it.
8. During the recuperation period, free rations will be provided to those people who help in the work of reconstruction of houses by the Khaksar Organisation.
9. Orphanages and widows' homes will be provided for and built wherever recommended.

I have asked the Khaksar Negotiating Committee to start work on these lines at once as well as to keep up the negotiations with respect to the remaining demands. The work of rebuilding 10,000 houses in Bihar that we contemplate is a tremendous work and it is primarily for the Biharis and not the Khaksars to complete it. I am, therefore, setting up a strong Committee of Bihari intelligentsia and have invited Mr. Yunus, Mr. Jafar Imam, President Muslim League, and the ailing Syed Abdul

Aziz and others to join it most vigorously. A capable Rehabilitation Officer and an efficient paid staff will be and is being appointed. The whole scheme will be headed by the *Hakim-i-A'la* of the Relief Camp and his staff. I invite freely the help of every feeling person in India in this grand humanitarian scheme.

1947 June 02

The Mountbatten Plan is announced.

1947 June 09

The All-India Muslim League Council holds a meeting at the Imperial Hotel in New Delhi to make a decision regarding the acceptance of the Mountbatten Plan. Khaksars and other Muslims hold large protests outside the hotel to urge the Muslim League not to accept a truncated Pakistan. The Khaksars want other areas such as Ajmere, Delhi, and Agra to be a part of Pakistan. They are also opposed to the division of Punjab and Bengal. The Khaksars, who attempt to enter the hotel, are beaten up by the Muslim League National Guard. The Muslim League National Guard also uses lathis to remove the Khaksars from inside the hotel and from the room where the meeting is being held. Many of the Khaksars are picked up and thrown out of the hotel. The Muslim Leaguers also call police, who open fire, use tear gas, and arrest a large number of Khaksars.

Editor's Comments: This event has been distorted in many history books to suggest that the Khaksars were against the creation of Pakistan and that they tried to attack the Muslim League leaders. However, the reality is that the Khaksars were only opposed to the *truncated* Pakistan, which the Muslim League wanted to accept. The Khaksars' only crime was that they protested against the unjust Mountbatten Plan, which gave a truncated Pakistan to the Muslims (who had ruled India for almost 1,000 years). The Hindus were much happier than the Muslims as they were able to attain a majority of the land as a result of the Partition Plan, whereas the Muslims had lost a major share of the land they had once ruled. It is the basic right of the citizens of a nation to be able to protest against any injustice or leaders who are making wrong decisions. To turn the story around and accuse the Khaksars of being against Pakistan is highly deplorable.

The Star of India would report on June 10, 1947, "the New Delhi police this morning took into custody a number of 'Khaksars' and other Muslim demonstrators who paraded the vicinity where the Muslim League Council held its sessions raising slogans against the Plan and demanding a 'complete Pakistan.'"

1947 June 10

In Patna, police open fire on a Khaksar procession. Five Khaksars are killed and some are injured. The Khaksars had taken out the procession in observance of "Bahadur Shah Day."

Police raid a Khaksar Camp at Patna. 24 Khaksars are arrested and some others are injured (including one with bullet wounds).

Police search another Khaksar Camp at Lodikatra near Patna. The police remain on full alert to control the Khaksars.

In Delhi, the Muslim League Council holds a secret session. *The Tribune*, Lahore of June 11, 1947 would report:
"The session being secret, strict watch was kept on those who were going in. Mr. Jinnah's tactics in having a 'purdah' session was motivated to keep a wet blanket on the dissentient voices raised from the Leaguers from the Muslim minority provinces — east Punjab and Bengal — against the [Mountbatten] plan.
Khaksars, whose existence seems to have been forgotten suddenly highlighted the session against 'langra (lame) Pakistan,' their description of the truncated variety. Police removed them [the Khaksars] quickly…"

1947 June 11

Allama Mashriqi is arrested in Delhi. Strong preventive measures are taken by the Government to ensure that Mashriqi doesn't organize a movement against the Mountbatten Plan. Mashriqi is later released to avoid any demonstrations from the Khaksars.

The bodies of five Khaksars (who were killed by police in Patna on June 10, 1947) are taken out in a procession. Syed Makhdoom Shah Banori (the Ahrar leader), Major General Shah Nawaz, Colonel Mahboob Ahmed, Balram Dubey, Shah Uzair Munimi, and others follow the funeral procession.

Khaksar arrests continue in Delhi.

1947 June 14

Approximately 24 Khaksars are arrested in Jullundur.

1947 June 17

Khaksar drills and parades are banned in Agra.

In Lahore, Allama Mashriqi issues the following statement to the Press: "The report that I have received today concerning the massacre of Khaksars at Patna on the occasion of the 'Bahadur Shah Day' on June 10 last, surpasses in cruelty and arrogance of all human imagination. Four Khaksars were left to die in a hospital with no one to attend to them. The Khaksars were absolutely innocent, their procession peaceful and symbolised Hindu-Muslim unity. It is certain now that the Bihar Ministry, because they were compelled to accept the demand of Rs. 1,500 per family of the Khaksars, through the intervention of Mahatma Gandhi, retaliated on them as soon as I left Patna. We put forward this demand for 50,000 refugees and

10,000 houses that we shall reconstruct. I hold the Congress responsible for the killing of 50,000 Bihari Muslims. I appeal publicly to Pandit Nehru to stop this wholesale murder of Mussalmans by Congress agents in the interests of public peace." *The Pakistan Times*, Lahore June 18, 1947

1947 June 27

A Khaksar meeting is held at Idara-i-Aliya to discuss the Khaksar Camp in New Delhi.

1947 June 28

Mashriqi sends the following letter to Nehru:
Dear Pandit Jawaharlal Nehru,
           Please refer to my letter No.43636 dated the 17th June to you concerning the shooting of five Khaksars by the Bihar ministry and the subsequent events. I have now received the report of interviews the Khaksar deputation had with you and others, also you letter of 26th June to Nawab Muhammad Hussain Khan in which you put down the result of your enquiries from the Bihar Government and say that 'certain Khaksars attacked the police with belchas and also fired upon them, killing two, etc.' The story of the Bihar Government is, I venture to say, purely ficticious and is calculated to justify the wild doings of the ministry in your eyes. It is most regrettable that lies are passed as truths from responsible persons…
           …I request you again in the name of good neighbourly relations between the Hindus and the Muslims and the future good of India not to treat the matter lightly as the Khaksars are agitated over my supposed inattention towards the matter and persons who were murdered were very well to do men. The deputation is awaiting your decision at Delhi and has proposed that a sum of Rs. 20,000 should be paid to the relatives per person through the Khaksar Organisation, that all arrested Khaksars should be released, that no obstacle should be put by the Bihar ministry in the way of rehabilitation as agreed to by Mahatma Gandhi with the Khaksar Negotiating Committee and that amicable relations with the Bihar ministry should be re-established.
           These are not tough conditions in face of what has happened. It is only good relations between the two communities that can save India now. I would ask you and other Congress leaders to think more calmly about the events that are happening. I am disappointed with the hot words about the future treatment of the Congress with the Muslims spoken in the interviews of some Congress leaders with the deputation.
With best wishes,
Yours sincerely

Mashriqi sends the following letter to Gandhi from Lahore:
Dear Mahatma Gandhi,
           A serious tangle has occurred in our relations with the Bihar minstry owing to the killing of several Khaksars in Patna on 10th June and the arrest of several Khaksars etc. I referred the matter to Pandit Jawaharlal but he has told the

deputation that met him that the matter was a minor one in the face of what has happening eleswhere and he seems to have treated it lightly.

I have now asked the deputation to turn to you and appeal to you for making amends. I trust you will do the best you can. You can see the responsibility on my shoulders in the matter especially when these Khaksars tried their utmost to promote good relations among the two communities in Bihar for several months together at great personal inconvenience.

I am sending you a copy of the letter I have written to Pandit Sahib today in order to give you an idea of what has happened. The Khaksars are agitated over the affair and I hope the matter will be amicably settled very soob. Please do the needful as much as you can immediately.

With best wishes,

Yours sincerely.

1947 June 30

Khaksars gather in New Delhi for a rally scheduled to begin in the evening (Allama Mashriqi had asked in March 1947 for 300,000 Khaksars to assemble in Delhi). Police adopt strict measures, prevent the Khaksars from holding the rally, and arrest a large number of Khaksars. A ban on holding demonstrations or taking out processions continues to remain in place in Delhi. Delhi remains under Section 144. **Editor's Note:** See editor's comments on July 04, 1947.

The Dawn, Delhi would report on July 02, 1947, "Khaksars were not allowed to hold their rally which was scheduled to take place today [June 30, 1947] in Delhi."

1947 July 01

A delegation of Khaksars meets with Gandhi to discuss the police firing on the Khaksars on June 10, 1947 in Patna. The delegation demands that the Bihar Government pay Rs. 20,000 as compensation for each Khaksar who was killed. The delegation also demands the release of the Khaksars who were arrested following the police firing. Gandhi assures the Khaksars that he would request the Bihar Government to consider the matter. The Khaksars had also met with Pandit Nehru regarding this matter.

1947 July 02

The Tribune, Lahore reports that the Khaksar publicity chief, Shaukatullah, has stated that if the Khaksar rally which is to be held in Delhi on July 03, 1940 fails to draw 300,000 volunteers, then Allama Mashriqi would disband the entire Khaksar Tehrik. He further stated that 70,000 to 80,000 Khaksars had already arrived in Delhi and that the program is to include flag hoisting, a mass rally, and a public address. According to Shaukatullah, many Khaksars have already been arrested. **Editor's Note:** See editor's comments on July 04, 1947.

1947 July 04

Allama Mashriqi disbands the Khaksar Movement. *The Tribune*, Lahore would report on July 05, 1947 that Mashriqi stated:
"About three and a half months ago I announced that if three lakhs of Khaksars would not have rallied in Delhi there would be no revolutionary power left in the movement and, therefore, it would be necessary to disband it. Now with the establishment of Pakistan, which has been bestowed upon the Muslims by the British, the last hope that ten crores of Muslims who have been divided into various parts would continue their struggle for freedom has been lost. I, therefore, disband the movement."
Editor's Note: The date of July 04, 1947 for the disbandment of the Khaksar Movement is taken from Sher Zaman Khaksar's book *Khaksar Tehrik Ki Jiddo Juhad Volume 2* (page 325).

Al-Islah publishes Mashriqi's statement regarding the disbandment of the Khaksar Movement. "Ah! After 17 years of intense and honest struggle to which I gave the best part of my life and resources, the nation has not been able to develop qualities which could enable it to re-establish its authority in India."

Editor's Comments: According to the Khaksar circle, the figure of Khaksars who had already arrived in surrounding areas of Delhi was much greater than 70,000 to 80,000. Many had reached the outskirts of Delhi but were facing difficulty in entering the city owing to rigorous government restrictions. There was a continuous influx of Khaksars from across the country, however continued arrests and massive government checks and restraints were hindering them from reaching the venue.
　　According to the Khaksar circle, Mashriqi had called 300,000 Khaksars to assemble in the city so that they could forcibly take over Delhi in order to remove the injustices in the partition plan toward the Muslims. He knew that these injustices were well planned and were a result of vested motives. Mashriqi was against the division of India and believed in the brotherhood of all communities. However, he had observed events closely as they had been developing over time and felt that he was left with no choice but to protect the Muslim interest. The idea of partition had not only taken the land that was once ruled by Muslims but had created hatred between the Muslims, Hindus, Sikhs, etc.; the riots were a result of this hatred. He was sorrowful that the leaders were ignoring the repercussions of this division. Today's circumstances of the sub-continent speak of his vision.
　　As a result of mass arrests, etc., 300,000 Khaksars were unable to assemble in New Delhi. Thus, Mashriqi decided to disband the Khaksar Movement. This was a not an easy decision for him, and he was highly saddened and disheartened when he made the decision to dissolve the Khaksar Movement. Mashriqi had spent the best part of his life working toward his goal and had faced a lot of personal sufferings. However, he came to the understanding that the Muslims were not yet ready to change their lives and lacked the spirit that was needed to revolutionize their lives.
　　Mashriqi's message to disband the Khaksar Movement was announced in Delhi in front of hundreds of thousands of people. Upon hearing this, the public

cried, as people were completely shocked and saddened. They chanted slogans such as, "Dehli is Ours," "Lal Fort is Ours," "Allama Mashriqi Zindabad," "Khaksar-e-Azam Zindabad," and "Khaksar Tehrik Zindabad." Khaksars and the public pleaded to Mashriqi to reconsider his decision. Khaksar men and women continued to stay in Delhi, despite the disbandment, in the hope that Mashriqi would withdraw his decision under pressure. People sent thousands of messages requesting Mashriqi to reconsider, but Mashriqi did not withdraw his decision.

1947 July 05

Following the disbandment of the Khaksar Tehrik, Salar-i-Ala of the Muslim League National Guard asks the Khaksars to join the Muslim League National Guard forthwith.

1947 July 06

The Pakistan Times publishes an editorial regarding the Khaksar Tehrik. The newspaper states: "The Khaksars began and rose in the early Thirties — the period of blackest economic and spiritual depression throughout the world. The period was particulary black for the Indian Muslims who appeared to have fought and lost all their battles from the Mutiny to the Khilafat, with precious little left to hope or fight for."

1947 July 09

Khaksars raise slogans for the release of all Khaksars arrested in Delhi and Patna. 17 Khaksars are arrested in Delhi. Police use tear gas to disperse the Khaksars and the public.

1947 July 24

Even after the disbandment of the Khaksar Movement, many of the Khaksars remain in Delhi. Police open fire on the Khaksars at a mosque in Delhi. Some Khaksars are injured and many others are arrested.

1947 July 26

Gandhi writes to Sardar Patel regarding the Khaksars.

1947 August 06

Gandhi writes a letter to Vallabhbhai Patel regarding his meeting with the Khaksars.

1947 August 11

Sardar Patel writes to Gandhi regarding the Khaksars.

1947 August 18

The Radcliffe Award is announced. Muslims lose many other areas that were supposed to be a part of Pakistan.

1947 October

Mashriqi sends a telegram to Gandhi.

1947 October 09

Nehru writes a letter from New Delhi to Vallabhbhai Patel:
My dear Vallabhbhai,
     Dr. Zakir Husain mentioned to me that he had received information about the ill-treatment of Muslim prisoners in the jail here. According to report they are being manhandled, are beaten severely and are kept in solitary confinement...
     Many of these prisoners are the old Khaksars...
     I am told that among the Khaksar prisoners there is Allama Mashriqi's son Asghar Inayatullah, aged eleven years. If this fact is correct, the boy need hardly be kept in prison. His sister is in the Jamia.
Yours sincerely,
Jawaharlal Nehru

1947 October 16

The Pakistan Times publishes the headline "Pakistan opposed to mass migration of Indian Muslims." The newspaper also publishes Liaquat Ali Khan's statement.

1947 October 31

Islam League is formed.

1947 December 07

Mashriqi gives a warning to inform the nation and the Government about a brewing conspiracy between Gandhi and Lord Mountbatten regarding the Kashmir issue.

Khaksar Movement in Pictures

Allama Mashriqi — a great scholar, thinker, philosopher, and visionary.

Allama Mashriqi, a freedom fighter.

First batch of Khaksars near Lahore. Mashriqi is in front row on the right. Mashriqi, a world-renowned scholar from Cambridge University picked up the spade, a tool of the poor man, to revolutionize the lives of the masses.

The Khaksars came out on the streets to wake the nation from a deep slumber.

Mashriqi (first row middle) leads and directs the nation to rise. Mashriqi believed in equality. Here he parades with fellow Khaksars.

A Khaksar holds the Movement's flag with pride and leads the contingent.

Mashriqi goes to Khaksars and delivers his message. He does not require a fancy stage to address his people.

Mashriqi does not require expensive setup to address his people. Here he stands on an ordinary table and talks to Khaksars.

Mashriqi delivers a speech at Badshahi Mosque, Lahore (1936). Mir Ali Ahmad Talpur (dressed in tie and coat) is sitting directly to the right of the person holding the microphone.

A crowd listens intently to Mashriqi.

People gather to listen to Mashriqi speak.

Mashriqi witnesses Khaksar activity at a Khasar camp. He is standing on the right with his children.

Khaksar Salars at a Khaksar Camp.

Khaksar leaders at a Khaksar Camp.

Khaksars determined to bring freedom to their country.

A smartly dressed Khaksar batch.

Khaksar parades generate great enthusiasm among the public.
(Photo courtesy of Khaksar Sher Zaman)

Khaksars mobilize the public for freedom.

Khaksars stand proudly in formation.

Khaksar marches were a great source of instilling the spirit of freedom among the masses.

Khaksars lined up in a formation.

Khaksars standing in formation.

Khaksars parade in protest through the streets of Lahore on March 19, 1940. Many of these Khaksars became victims of the brutal Khaksar Massacre on that day.

Khaksars determined to uphold their flag. A large number of people witness Khaksar activities.

A smart turn out of Khaksars, standing in formation at a Khaksar Camp. Public witnesses Khaksar activities. Such camps were held in different parts of India at various times. These camps were not only a source of training but also a great source of motivation for the public to rise for freedom.

Another view of a Khaksar Camp. Khaksars sit in a disciplined manner, while listening to a speaker.

A large number from the public have gathered to enroll in the Khaksar Movement.
This was a regular affair at Khaksar Camps.

A view of a Khaksar Camp.

Public witnesses Khaksar activities.

A view of neatly lined up Khaksar Camps.

A scene of a mock war.

Injured Khaksars are treated at a Khaksar Camp. No injury could stop the Khaksars from striving toward their cause.

A view of a mock war.

A scene showing war training.

Mock war training of Khaksars continues.

Khaksars praying.

Khaksars perform community services on a daily basis. They engaged in services of all kinds and toward others, regardless of religion, color, caste or creed. This was a source of building the nation and bringing love and unity among the people.

Khaksars were always engaged and were ready to perform any duty may it be for the cause of community service or the message to rise for freedom, unity, or brotherhood.

A group photo of the robust Khaksars.

Smartly dressed Khaksars standing outside their camp.

A Muslim Khaksar is on the left and a Sikh Khaksar is on the right. The Khaksar Tehrik did not discriminate against anyone based on religion, caste, color, or creed, and many non-Muslims were part of the movement.

Some Prominent Personalities
&
the Khaksar Movement

Quaid-e-Azam visits Mashriqi in Karol Bagh on October 16, 1939.
From left to right: Liaquat Ali Khan, Allama Mashriqi, Quaid-e-Azam, Barrister
Mian Ahmed Shah, Dr. Sir Zia ud Din.

Mashriqi expected no disparity among the Khaksars. Nawab Bahadur Yar Jung (Salar of Hyderabad) is sitting second from left in the first row with the Khaksars.

Pir Elahi Buksh (Chief Minister of Sindh Province) greets Mashriqi.

Premier of Punjab, Sir Sikandar Hayat Khan (in the background, wearing a sherwani and shalwar [long Indian style coat and pants]) at a Khaksar Camp.

Khaksar Massacre
&
Mashriqi's Offer to Fight for Pakistan in the News

LATE MORNING EDITON

The Tribune

SUBSCRIPTION RATES

VOL. LX. NO. 77 — LAHORE, WEDNESDAY, MARCH 20, 1940 — PRICE:—ONE ANNA

SERIOUS CLASH BETWEEN KHAKSARS AND POLICE

HERR HITLER'S PEACE PROPOSALS

ELEVEN POINTS.

TERMS HANDED OVER TO POPE

New York, March 19.

A Reuter dispatch to the "New York Times" says that Herr Hitler's peace proposals which Herr von Ribbentrop gave to the Pope are understood to be the following points:

(1) General, simultaneous and immediate disarmament on land, sea and in the air.

(2) Return to a four-power pact which would divide areas of influence in Europe and inaugurate an anti-bolshevist policy with the idea of liberating Russia, by armed if necessary, from Communism.

(3) Recognition of absolute religious freedom after the emigration of all Germans Jews under the direction of Britain to Palestine, of Italy to Ethiopia and of France to Madagascar.

(4) Absolute freedom of trade and access to raw materials, close contacts with the United States for economic co-operation and facilitation of German and Italian emigration.

(5) Restitution within twenty years of German colonies or equal colonial compensation at least commensurate for German emigration in determined areas in Africa.

(6) Reconstruction of an independent Poland, composed primarily of a central area which once [...] million people; Gydnia to be a free Polish port; free trade to the Poles through Danzig; Polish frontier to be determined by the basis of a plebiscite controlled by an international commission; military problems of Poland and the whole Danube basin would be solved by usual transmigration of peoples.

(7) Czecho, Slovakia and Hungary to constitute a tripartite state allied to the Reich for 25 years with Germany enjoying certain privileges in industry and communications.

(8) Austria to remain in the Reich.

(9) A Danube Federation to be constituted as a sort of Customs Union in signaling the question of large and small States, the federation to comprise Germany, Italy, Yugoslavia, Roumania, Bohemia, Slovakia and Hungary.

(10) The status quo in the Balkans to be guaranteed.

(11) Free customs transit for Italian goods through Tibet; free passage of the Suez Canal for the expansion of the Commission in 1945; new statute for Italians in Tunis.

(12) [...]

SEVERAL OFFICERS WOUNDED

FIRE OPENED

26 KILLED : 70 INJURED

CURFEW ORDER PROMULGATED AT LAHORE

BAN PLACED ON KHAKSARS

Lahore, March 19.

A crowded locality within the jurisdiction of the Tibbi Police Post was the scene of a clash between the Khaksars and police force. The police had to resort to firing.

According to information that some 300 Khaksars were lurking in an enclosure and intended to march forth in mass formation. The S.S.P. and the City Magistrate arrived on the spot at once. The Khaksars are alleged to have resorted to violence as a result of which serious police officials received injuries. The police opened fire.

Now, the police force has completely cordoned off the scene of battle.

Enquiries reveal that 313 Khaksars wearing their uniform and carrying their Belchas who marched in military formation through Hiati Gate a little before noon, came into conflict with the local police near the Tibbi Police Station. As a result of the attack on the Police and the firing to which the Police resorted afterwards a large number of casualties are reported to have taken place.

Among the injured persons are Mr. P. C. Bourne, District Magistrate, Mr. D. Gainsford, Senior Superintendent of Police, Lahore and Mr. Beaty, Deputy Superintendent of Police, Lahore. The injuries received by Mr. Gainsford and Mr. Beaty are serious. Both the Police officials were serious and both of them are now lying in the Victor Albert Hospital. Both the Police officials were stated to have been attacked with Belchas and severely injured on the face and the arms.

Mr. Bourne received an injury on the face. One Sub-Inspector has also been injured.

The Khaksars were [...] the District Magistrate, the City Magistrate, Sardar Abdul Samad Khan, Mr. D. Gainsford, S.S.P., Mr. Beaty, D.S.P., and about 25 policemen armed with lathis. It is stated that the Khaksars were stopped and ordered by the District Magistrate not to proceed further and Beaty [...] it is certain locality. A military force is now guarding the city. Bazaars in certain localities are closed.

25 Killed ; 70 Injured.

ALLAMA MASHRAQI TO BE ARRESTED?

WARRANTS ISSUED

Lahore, March 19.

It is understood that warrants of arrest against Allama Mashraqi, leader of the Khaksars and his Lieutenants have been issued under orders of the Punjab Government.

Allama Mashraqi is stated to be in Delhi.

CURFEW ORDER PROMULGATED

CARRYING OF ARMS PROHIBITED

Lahore, March 19.

The District Magistrate of Lahore has promulgated an order under section 144, Cr. P. C. prohibiting the carrying of firearms, knife, sword, kirpan, belcha, lathi or any other article capable of being used as an arm for a period of two months in the streets and public places within the limits of the Lahore Municipality.

The District Magistrate has also promulgated a Curfew Order requiring people within the limits of the walled city of Lahore to remain indoors between the hours of 7 p.m. and 5 a.m. with effect from today.—A.P.I.

Belchas and one of the first persons to be attacked was the Senior Superintendent of Police, who was at the head of the party. He was attacked and Belchas fell on his face. In the clash that ensued several policemen were injured. More Police were at once called from the Fort nearby. The Khaksars remained defiant and injured more policemen. The Police opened fire and when the first shots were heard the Khaksars began running in all directions. The Police were able to arrest 16 of them only and they are now in custody.

The Inspector-General of Police, the D.I.G. of Police and other officers arrived at the spot immediately after this the Police combed the whole locality called the Tibbi area and took Baton Bhakkupurian, and took into the Tibbi area and [...] Baton Bhakkupurian and took into custody some Khaksars who were found there. The injured and the dead men were removed to the Mayo Hospital by the Police.

NO PRESIDENTIAL PROCESSION

BUT CONGRESS SESSION WILL BE HELD

Lahore, March 19.

The Reception Committee [...]

INDIAN NATIONAL CONGRESS MEETS

Open Session

RAIN UPSETS ALL ARRANGEMENTS

THOUSANDS OF PEOPLE WAIT IN KNEE-DEEP WATER

Ramgarh, March 19.

There was renewed stir in the Congress from early this afternoon for the opening sitting of the plenary session of the Indian National Congress.

The wooded hills around were agog with long trails of men and women converging on the Congress Nagar to witness the session.

A large portion of the volunteer corps was on duty busily at the gates of the vast amphitheatre where the session opens and as early as 2 p.m. the amphitheatre was gradually filling up. It provided the best galleried arrangement for the vast gathering every one of whom could see the huge dais on the western side for the President, leaders and members of the Reception Committee, while loud speakers carried the leaders' voice to every corner of the ground.

With its artistically designed gates, one in Buddhist and another in Moghul styles, the open air ground was a picture of simplicity and grandeur. A small well was given to the decorations by the plastic moulds on the wall of the dais, representing a farmer ploughing his field, a woman spinning with a charka and another grinding corn.

At 4 p.m. the sky was completely overcast and it threatened to rain any moment.

To anxious crowds watching the sky for signs of the clouds clearing away, a low-flying aeroplane provided diversion and Adibasis and other aboriginal tribes evinced the keenest interest in this symbol of civilisation from low countries beyond their hills.

Rain Breaks Out

Fifteen minutes before the open session of the Congress was due to commence this evening, a deluge of rain descended on Congress Nagar and the session had to be postponed.

Throughout the day clouds had delayed over Amphitheatre. As the sanguine crowds flocked to the great open amphitheatre where the session [...] at the commencement of the session up [...] when the rains started finally the clouds broke, and in a few minutes the gathering in the amphitheatre and the whole Congress [...]

[...] hills neighbouring Ramgarh. At the first few drops fell, the amphitheatre, who had some prepared with umbrellas raised them and volunteers rushed to the aid of many women and children who were without protection. The wetting did not damp the spirits of the crowd for above the hiss of the rain were heard frequent cries of Mahatmaji ki jai.

After a few minutes the people realised that there was no prospect of the storm abating and in small groups they hurried away to shelter, while others, already drenched, realised that they had under them the means of protection and covered themselves with bunches of the bugla grass which was spread on the ground.

Session Opens

When after several minutes, the first violence of the rain relented slightly, Maulana Abul Kalam Azad, Babu Rajendra Prasad and Pandit Jawaharlal Nehru, who had been walking to take part in the presidential procession to the amphitheatre, waited for the weather to clear, entered the arena. Babu Rajendra Prasad and Maulana Abul Kalam Azad, then addressed those who remained in the arena.

The addresses of the Chairman of the Reception Committee and the President were formally read before the House and taken as read.

Pandit Jawaharlal Nehru formally moved the resolution on the political situation, adopted by the subjects Committee, and Acharya Kripalani seconded it.

Maulana Azad then announced that the session was adjourned since the weather did not permit its continuance.

It is proposed that the matter should be held at 9 o'clock in the morning in the Subjects Committee, pandal; and the opening [...]

[...] Volunteers will be held in the open air, Mahatma Gandhi will not let his cottage when the rain [...]

Mahatma Gandhi [...]

[...] Mahatma [...] Gandhi [...]

(See page 2)

LATE MORNING EDITION

The Tribune

SUBSCRIPTION RATES

VOL. LX. NO. 78   LAHORE, THURSDAY, MARCH 21, 1940   PRICE—ONE ANNA

ALLAMA MASHRAQI ARRESTED

ENGAGEMENTS ON WESTERN FRONT

SHARP FIGHTING

GERMANS SUFFER HEAVY LOSSES

Paris, March 20.
Patrol engagements have been the only noteworthy incidents on the Western Front during the past 24 hours. In the Saar sector a German reconnoitring detachment fell into a French ambush. Sharp fighting followed and though the Germans succeeded in extricating themselves, they suffered losses and abandoned material. In the area west of the Vosges German patrols were repulsed and left a few prisoners in the hands of the French.

A Copenhagen message says: According to an Esberg telegram two 'planes of unknown nationality flew over the Danish Peninsula, Holmsland Klit 60 miles from Sylt, dropped bombs, but it is not known whether any damage was done. Ten minutes later two bombs fell near Hvide and Sande. Windows of houses were shattered.—Reuter.

NOT A SUPPORTER OF PEACE AT ALL COSTS

DUCE'S POSITION

London, March 20.
The official commentator of Rome Radio said that the Duce was not a supporter of peace at all costs. The opinion that peace plans are being continually elaborated in Rome is purely arbitrary. The Government cannot devote its entire energy to working out peace plans.

MR. SUMNER WELLES LEAVING FOR AMERICA

Genoa, March 20.
Mr. Sumner Welles arrived here and immediately boarded the liner "Conte di Savoia" which is expected to sail at 11-00.

FRENCH CABINET

Paris, March 20.
News of the resignation of the Government came as a surprise to the public, but not to the Deputies who took part in the secret session. They realised that the vote had placed the Government in a difficult position.

MR. JINNAH LEAVES NEW DELHI FOR LAHORE

New Delhi, March 20.
Mr. M.A. Jinnah, President Muslim League, left this evening for Lahore by a special train for the annual session of the League. A number of League members of the Assembly and other delegates, including a number of members, left by the same train.

'He Will Be Kept Under Detention'

Raids In Different Places

KHAKSARS TAKEN INTO CUSTODY IN LARGE NUMBERS

LAHORE CITY QUIET: SITUATION UNDER CONTROL

New Delhi, March 20.
Allama Mashraqi, leader of the Khaksars, was taken under detention late last night by the Delhi police under section 46 of the Defence of India Act. It is learnt that he is still kept in Delhi and a decision will be taken during the course of the day whether to continue to keep him in Delhi or send him outside.

It is believed the order of detention was issued by the Government of India.

A *United Press* message states: Allama Mashraqi was taken under detention at about 11-30 p.m.

It is reported the Senior Superintendent of Police and the D.B.P. with a posse of armed force went to the house of the Allama in Qarol Bagh, a suburb in Delhi, and served on him an order of detention by the Central Government which stated that there were reasons to believe that Allama Mashraqi was about to act in a manner prejudicial to the efficient prosecution of war and public order.

The order, which was signed by the Secretary to the Home Department of the Government of India, was under Section 46 of the Defence of India Act.

The Allama came out of the house and accompanied the police to the jail. A small batch of Khaksars and Allama's lieutenants gave him a salute as he drove off alone with the police officers. The Khaksars have been declared by the Chief Commissioner, Delhi, as an unlawful association.

Security Demanded From "Al Islah"

It is understood orders have been passed by the Local Government demanding security from "Al Islah," the official organ of the Khaksars, which was recently transferred from Lahore to Delhi.

The notification issued by the Chief Commissioner, Delhi, says: "In exercise of the powers conferred by Section 19 of the Indian Criminal Law Amendment Act, the Chief Commissioner of Delhi, being of opinion that the Association commonly known as the Anjuman-i-Khaksaran interferes with the maintenance of law and order, and constitutes a danger to the public peace, hereby declares the said Anjuman-i-Khaksaran to be an unlawful association.

In exercise of the powers conferred by section 17-A, of the same Act the Chief Commissioner of Delhi is pleased to notify No. 16287 Pair Road, Karol Bagh, Delhi, as a place which is in his opinion used for the purposes of unlawful association, namely, for the purposes of the Anjuman-i-Khaksaran."—A.P.I.

LAHORE CITY QUIET

No Further Demonstrations

Lahore, March 20.
The city was quieter this morning. The commotion that was caused by yesterday's happening had decreased considerably owing to the prompt measures taken by the authorities... Owing to and constitutes

NO BAN ON MUSLIM LEAGUE

RESTRICTIONS ON KIRPANS REMOVED

Lahore, March 20.
The District Magistrate, Lahore, issued the following order on Wednesday afternoon—

(1) In my order of the 19th of March, 1940 passed under section 144 of the Criminal Procedure Code, prohibiting any gathering or assembly of five or more persons in any street, etc. within the limits of the Lahore Municipality, the following proviso shall be added:—

"Provided that this order shall not apply to gatherings or assemblies formed in pursuance of the legitimate objects of the Conference of the All-India Muslim League now opening at Lahore, to any procession duly licensed under the Police Act."

(2) In my order of the 19th of March 1940 passed under section 144 of the Criminal Procedure Code, forbidding the carrying of firearms, etc. in the streets and public places within the limits of the Lahore Municipality, the word "Kirpan" should be deleted.

... curfew order the eight was quiet and no outward incidents were reported.

Business in the city this morning was normal and no incident was reported from any part of the city.

The apprehension, that the Khaksars might hold a demonstration again to-day, has been falsified. There has been no trouble at all any where in the city or at the suburbs.

Police Keeping Strict Watch

The police are keeping a strict watch over the city and the situation at the moment is under control.

From enquiries made by the *Tribune* representative at the Mayo Hospital it is learnt that 3 Khaksars, who were admitted into the Hospital yesterday, died during the night, bringing the total number of the dead to 29.

Mr. Gainsford, the Senior Superintendent of Police, and Mr. Beaty, the Deputy Superintendent of Police, who were injured seriously and are now lying in the Albert Victor Hospital, are stated to be progressing satisfactorily. A medical attendant informed the *Tribune* representative that "the condition of both of them is very much better" and they both passed "a fair night." Mr. Gainsford, it is however stated, is not yet out of danger.

The Sub-Inspector, who was injured, is also improving.

K.B. Mir Abdul Hai, Inspector of Police, who was also among the injured, was not admitted to the hospital and he is now on duty.

The total number of arrests so far made by the Police is stated to be 287. This includes 40 to 50 persons, who were taken

(See page 10.)

MR. JINNAH'S APPEAL TO KHAKSARS

"KEEP PEACE"

LEAGUE LEADER DEPLORES LOSS OF LIFE

New Delhi, March 20.
Mr. M.A. Jinnah, President of the All-India Muslim League in a statement to the Associated Press says:—

"I am deeply grieved to hear the tragic account of the incident in Lahore last evening regarding the clash between the Police and the Khaksars, resulting in terrible loss of life and injury on both the sides. I hope the Khaksars will carry out the instructions issued by their leader, Mr. Inayatullah Mashraqi published in the newspapers of this morning. As one who has always been so kindly treated by the Khaksars, I appeal to them most earnestly to keep peace and not precipitate matters by delaying law and order. It is difficult to say anything till I am in possession of full facts of the situation."

Mr. Jinnah added that according to his information there would be no change in their programme of holding the session of the All-India Muslim League at Lahore. "I am leaving by the special train at 7-30 this evening as already arranged."—A.P.I.

AIR RAIDS ON SYLT ISLAND

British Bombers In Action

WHOLE OF WEST COAST OF GERMANY ATTACKED

HINDENBURG DAM HIT

London, March 20.
A communique issued by the Air Ministry says: The attack on the air base at Hornum started at 20.00 and was still in progress at 02.00. The first aircraft to participate has already returned in safety and the Captains report accurate bombing of their objectives.

"The Air Force attacked and severely damaged the German air base at Hornum on the Island of Sylt to-night. This is one of the shore bases from which enemy aircraft operate against British naval forces and merchant shipping. This action follows the attack upon our own shore bases in Orkney."

It is learnt in London that the raid on Hornum was carried out by a strong force of bombers which attacked singly in relays—and maintained almost continuous assaults on the seaplane base from soon after dusk until the early hours of the morning.

A vast quantity of bombs was dropped and early reports indicate extensive damage done to hangars, workshops and slipways.

The first aircraft to search the Island identified the target by the aid of bright moonlight. Later as successive waves attacked, fires started by the first bombs, provided a guide to the position of the seaplane base.

By 3-30 all aircraft due to back by that time had safely landed and the preliminary reports of the pilots are being analysed. Typical of these was the report from the Captain of one of the first aircraft to reach Hornum: "One bomb was observed to burst between the hangars. Three bombs were observed just north of hangar. Two bursts observed between the base and the slipway."

The Captain of another aircraft stated that an enemy fighter was driven off by the accurate fire of his rear gunner.

Second Raid

It is understood that 2 more R.A.F. aeroplanes flew to Sylt about 8 a.m. for the purpose of taking photographs to assess the precise damage done during the raid.

The Air Ministry communique issued later announces: "The tanks on Hornum were over a period of about 7 hours. All our aircraft have returned safely with the exception of one, which is overdue and must be presumed lost. Information is

(See page 10.)

The Tribune (Lahore), March 21, 1940

Editor's Comments:

Allama Mashriqi's detention for a significant period of time directed the Muslims that no solution other than freedom would be acceptable. Mashriqi was the only prominent leader at the time who suffered the most at the hands of the rulers of India. The sufferings of Mashriqi did not go to waste and resulted in independence.

KHAKSAR TROUBLE : LAHORE CONFERENCE

Police continues its actions against the Khaksar Movement, while the Muslim League Session is in progress. The photo on the left depicts the use of tear gas by the police to arrests Khaksars. The photo on the right shows the Muslim League Session.

REGD NO C3040

Star of India

INCORPORATING THE 'CALCUTTA EVENING NEWS' AND 'BENGALEE'

VOL. XIV. NO. 234.   CALCUTTA, THURSDAY, MAY 23, 1946   SIX PAGES—1¼ ANNAS

TALKS ON INTERIM GOVERNMENT

Hitler In Argentina?

London, May 22.—It is rumoured that Joan Weisse—Hitler's double, who was recently found in an Argentine sanatorium—is really Hitler.

It is said that he now undergoing plastic surgery operations in Germany and was forced to flee to submarine before operations to change his face had been started, and that it was pure conceit that prevented him from shaving off his moustache.—(Globe).

Political Security Prisoners Released

With the release of a batch of five civil security prisoners in Bengal there have been set at liberty. There are, however, about 60 long-term political prisoners, including those of the Chittagong Armoury Raid still in jails.—(A.P.I.)

Khaksars To Fight For Pakistan

ALLAMA MASHRIQI'S OFFER TO MR. JINNAH

Lahore, May 22.—An offer to place the services of the Khaksar organisation at the disposal of Mr. M. A. Jinnah unconditionally for the achievement of Pakistan is made by Allama Mashriqi, leader of the Khaksar organisation in a statement to the Press.

New Half And Quarter Rupee Nickel Coins

New Delhi, May 22.—By a notification published in the Gazette to-day the Central Government has authorised the minting and issue of half and quarter rupee coins in pure nickel.

Further Cut In Forces' Ration

Nehru And Azad Meet Viceroy

CONGRESS LIKELY TO ACCEPT PROPOSALS

New Delhi, May 23.—The meeting between the Viceroy and the Congress President, Maulana Abul Kalam Azad, and Mr. Jawaharlal Nehru this morning lasted 90 minutes. At the end of the meeting Maulana Azad indicated that this morning's discussions covered a wide field in connection with the setting up of a provisional Government.

Certain proposals had been placed before him and Mr. Nehru by the Viceroy which he would place before the Congress Working Committee at its meeting this afternoon, whereafter he would communicate the Working Committee's decision to the Viceroy.

Arab Rulers' Meeting

Farouk To Speak For Ibn Saud?

Recall Of Ala Demanded

Charge Of Creating Further Ill-will

Russian Comment On Cabinet Mission's Plan

London, May 22.—The first Soviet comment on the new proposals for India was made to-night.

Mr. Jinnah's Views On Mission's Plan

Full Text Of Statement

Simla, May 22.—The following is the full text of the statement issued by Mr. M. A. Jinnah, President of the All-India Muslim League.

Communists Capture Tungan

Shanghai, May 22.—Government communiqué.

The Star of India (Calcutta), May 23, 1946
Editor's Comments:
Mashriqi's offer to Quaid-e-Azam to fight for Pakistan is also reported in the media.

Khaksar Tehrik Mobilized the Nation for the Freedom of Pakistan

Khaksar Tehrik Mobilized the Nation for the Freedom of Pakistan

Covering Allama Mashriqi's role in seeking freedom requires a separate book. However, I am highlighting a few points here to shed some light on his role toward the independence of the sub-continent that resulted in the creation of Pakistan. To provide a better understanding, I have divided the Khaksar struggle into phases.

Establishment Phase of the Khaksar Tehrik

The Khaksar Tehrik (Movement) was an unusual and spectacular movement that was founded in the Indian sub-continent in 1930. Allama Mashriqi founded this Movement to revolutionize the lives of masses and bring freedom to India. Here, I present an overview of the foundation of the Khaksar Tehrik.

Self-help

If one studies the philosophy of the Khaksar Movement, s/he will find that the foundation of the Khaksar Tehrik was built on a self-help basis. Mashriqi knew that a self-help basis would be the best formula to reach his goal. In other words, he instilled in the people a notion that they must step forward and take action themselves to change their lives. Mashriqi served as the driving force and used his exceptional organizational and motivational skills to direct the nation towards their ultimate goal to obtain sovereignty. He set the very first example by abandoning the luxuries of life, a tough choice in itself, and becoming a commoner. He accepted a hardy and rugged life and devoted his personal resources for the cause.

In Mashriqi's prescription, it was wrong to use public money for the promotion of a party or to meet the expenses of the party's leaders. Thus, he rejected the idea of collecting public funds for this purpose. All Khaksars, including Mashriqi, bore their personal expenses themselves, may they be for community service or mobilizing the public for the cause. The Khaksar Tehrik did not have a membership fee. The fact that Mashriqi was able to mobilize such a large number of devotees without any membership fee was an unparalleled phenomenon.

Basic Ideology

It is equally consequential to study the basic ideology of the Khaksar Tehrik, which was based on the 24 fundamental principles of the Khaksar Tehrik and the 14 points that Mashriqi decreed later on. All these points clearly explain the crux of the Khaksar Movement. However, here I have highlighted some of the key components:

1. Purify oneself (Khaksars were expected to be men of solid character, a basic ingredient of a strong nation)
2. Not fear anyone except God (this removed inferiority complexes)
3. Uphold soldierly qualities (four million Khaksars were a very well-disciplined and a robust group of people)
4. Become the ruling power (this inspired Khaksars and supporters to rise for freedom)
5. Support equality (this demolished the walls between the rich and the poor. It gave the commoner a sense of pride, confidence, and self-esteem. Allama wanted to eradicate exploitation of the poor and ensure justice for all regardless of status or position)
6. Believe in and take action (Khaksars were expected to take action rather than merely talk about it, and they proved to be men of action)
7. Ensure unity (harmony and unity prevailed among the Khaksars, and this was what they demonstrated and preached. The resistance of the Khaksars after the ban on the Movement provides evidence of this unity)
8. Remove prejudices and sectarianism (the Khaksar effort brought peace in the Shia-Sunni riots in Lucknow in 1939 and the fact that non-Muslims were part of the Khaksar Tehrik serve as proof that the Khaksars were against prejudice)
9. Provide community service to everyone regardless of religion, caste, color or creed (Khaksars provided countless community services to Muslims and non-Muslims. This was an important factor in nation building and bringing brotherhood, love, and affection among all. Community service is the most significant component in winning the hearts of the people)

The Khaksar Tehrik's ideology was very well conceived. Mashriqi's message to take action and to become the ruling power was well received by the masses. Mashriqi emphasized that no community could rule unless it was better than its rulers. Thus, in Khaksar Tehrik's principles lies the philosophy of the Movement. It discharges the nation from the shackles of slavery and leads them to self-rule.

The doctrine of the Khaksar Tehrik has great depth and provides insight for obtaining desired results. Its ideology and political ideas, such as revival of Muslim eminence, need to be examined in depth in a separate comprehensive study. The opponent's designs to eliminate the Khaksar Movement also require a thorough examination of the motivation.

Mobilization Phase of the Khaksar Tehrik

The tenets on which the Khaksar Tehrik was based point to Mashriqi's vision. Without a doubt, Mashriqi was a visionary. His message was so appealing to the masses that within a few years of Tehrik's existence, the Khaksar Movement generated over four million Khaksars and attracted millions as its supporters and sympathizers. Mashriqi proved his genius and emerged as one of the superb organizers in the Indian sub-continent. His movement spread to every corner of India and offices were opened in other countries.

Among his followers, Mashriqi successfully instilled a sense of personal sacrifice, community service, brotherhood, equality, simplicity, dedication to the cause, and more. The Khaksars became an organization of fearless men. They adopted strict discipline and soldierly lives. Millions of Khaksars dressed in immaculate uniforms and carried their shining spades on their shoulders; they marched proudly and in an organized fashion on streets across India. They rehearsed mock wars, and their mock wars and parades became a source of motivation for everyone.

The general public took keen interest in the Khaksar activities and its ideology. The determined Khaksars successfully spread Mashriqi's message to the masses and brought an uprising among the Muslims and the non-Muslims. Once the feeling to become the ruling power was instilled amongst the people, it was very difficult for anyone to eject this idea from their minds. This feeling of uprising eventually directed them to demand independence of India.

By the late 1930s, it seemed that the entire India was under the Khaksar Tehrik's grip. The Khaksar Movement became the largest Muslim party deeply rooted in the masses. Indeed, Mashriqi successfully woke the people from a deep slumber.

Resistance Phase of the Khaksar Tehrik

The Khaksar Tehrik's real power was revealed during the conflict with the Government of U.P. In 1939, riots between the Shias and Sunnis were taking place in Lucknow. Based on the philosophy of the Khaksar Movement to remove all sectarianism and prejudices from the society, Mashriqi demanded from the Government of U.P. to stop these riots in order to avoid devastation of the two Muslim sects. When his demand did not bring desired results, he and a large number of Khaksars from various parts of the country arrived in Lucknow and brought peace between the two sects.

This triggered alarm among all parties such as the British, the Muslim League, and the Congress. They realized that the power of Mashriqi's Khaksar Movement could be directed for any purpose with one order. This generated a sense of fear among all anti-Khaksar elements. To eliminate this threat, anti-Khaksar elements pounced on the Khaksar Movement, and the Government imposed a ban on the Movement in early 1940. The Government was unaware of the fact that the desire (to rise and become the ruling power) that Mashriqi had instilled in the Khaksars and among the masses could no longer be suppressed. Despite government directives against the Khaksars, the people's desire to seek independence became stronger.

After the Government's ban on the Tehrik, the resistance movement began and proved to be one of the toughest fights in India in the 20th century. The time had come when the entire nation wanted nothing short of freedom. Mashriqi and the Khaksars without a doubt fought valiantly against the atrocities that were inflicted on them.

Final Phase of the Khaksar Tehrik

Mashriqi was released from Vellore Jail on January 19, 1942, but his movements were restricted to Madras Presidency. Despite his restricted movements, Mashriqi again started working aggressively for the freedom of India. He mobilized the Khaksars to deliver his message among the masses that nothing short of freedom is acceptable. Upon the arrival of Sir Stafford Cripps in Delhi, Mashriqi sent him a telegram on March 23, 1942 and demanded complete independence of India. Meanwhile, millions of Khaksars and supporters of the Khaksar Tehrik continued to deliver Allama Mashriqi's message to the people to unite and rise for freedom. Mashriqi's actions included statements to the public and correspondence with various Muslim and non-Muslim leaders. Soon after December 28, 1942, when restrictions on his movements were lifted, he began to make many public speeches and took on even more rigorous activities.

Mashriqi also made an effort to bring reconciliation among the Muslims and the non-Muslims, so that they could unite and overthrow the foreign rulers. A Jinnah-Gandhi meeting on September 09, 1944 was a result of this effort. During the Jinnah-Gandhi meeting, Khaksars in all of India tried to convince both sides of the importance of a Muslim-Hindu understanding in order to get rid of the British rulers. At the time of Jinnah-Gandhi meeting, 4,000 Khaksars (as reported in the newspapers) came to Bombay from different parts of India to create an atmosphere of understanding between the two major communities. When Quaid-e-Azam and Gandhi failed to resolve their issues, Mashriqi drafted a constitution (*Khaksar Constitution of Free India*) acceptable to all communities. Many scholars, intellectuals and learned men from various religions and backgrounds took part in drafting this elaborate document. Mashriqi also made an effort to bring all Muslim parties on one platform. He proposed to merge all parties including the Khaksar Movement into one new party, but the Muslim League refused to merge. Instead, the League stated that it would be better if all Muslim parties came under the flag of the Muslim League. The Muslim League's decision not to compromise with and to ignore the Khaksar Tehrik resulted in loss of many areas, which would have been part of Pakistan.

Pakistan Appears on the Globe

It is noteworthy that within seven years of the Khaksar tragedy, Pakistan appeared on the world map. The Muslim League, though established in 1906, had played no consequential role in uplifting or bringing the masses together. There was no connection between the rich leaders of the Muslim League and the commoners. The fact is that the Muslim League gained strength after March 19, 1940. The Muslim League has claimed to achieve this strength after passing the Pakistan Resolution on March 24, 1940. It must be remembered that merely passing resolutions or statements cannot mobilize people. Instead, it is the atrocities against and murders of innocent people that mobilize the public. In this case, Mashriqi and the Khaksars were victims of all brutalities. And it is the spirit of freedom that Mashriqi instilled in the masses from 1930 to 1940 that eventually brought desired results.

Though pro-Muslim League historians have ignored the sufferings of Mashriqi and the Khaksars' resistance and their mobilization of the masses, no one can eliminate the facts of history. Giving full credit to the Muslim League for the independence of Pakistan is highly unjustifiable and is a distortion of facts. Anti-Khaksar writers have used anti-Khaksar material to prove their point of view. In case of Muslim League, the League's material is being used to prove their point of view and even the obvious negatives in the partition have either been covered up or justified. I urge the learned writers not to ignore the Khaksar material in their works.

Both parties, the Khaksar Tehrik and the Muslim League, achieved Pakistan, regardless of the fact that the parties had different ideas for Pakistan. The Khaksar efforts were directed towards establishing the entire India as Pakistan but the Muslim League worked for the division of India to create a separate homeland.

Since the Khaksars wanted the entire India to be Pakistan, this was one of the reasons that British preferred negotiations with Muslim League and, for vested reasons, they recognized the Muslim League as the sole representatives of the Muslims. The Muslim League capitalized on this recognition. The League ignored the Khaksar Tehrik, without realizing that this would harm the Muslim interest. If the Muslim League had accepted Mashriqi's offer of cooperation, the map of

Pakistan would certainly have been different. But the League ignored these offers for vested interests. As a result, the Muslims lost many areas and suffered under the partition plan. Muslims must learn from these mistakes or face consequences like the entire Muslim world is facing today.

Closing Words

It is a known fact that no freedom has been achieved without the sacrifices of human lives and in the process people have had to face brutalities. In the fight for liberty, leaders and followers are imprisoned and go through the sufferings associated with any independence. Mashriqi and the Khaksars suffered the most and paid the price for independence. History is witness to fact that the Mashriqi and the Khaksars' services for mobilizing the masses and resistance that resulted in obtaining autonomy are unparalleled. Pakistan's history is distorted and incomplete as it fails to acknowledge and discuss the struggles of Allama Mashriqi and the Khaksars.

May God bless Pakistan and its people.

Bibliography

Abbreviations
n.d.—No Date
n.p.—Publisher Unavailable/Place of Publication Unavailable

Ahmad, Waheed, Editor. 1978. *Jinnah – Linlithgow Correspondence (1939-1943)*. Lahore, Pakistan: Punjab Educational Press.

Ahmad, Waheed, Editor. 1992. *Quaid-i-Azam Mohammad Ali Jinnah The Nation's Voice Towards Consolidation*. Karachi, Pakistan: Quaid-i-Azam Academy.

Ahmad, Waheed, Editor. 1996. *Quaid-i-Azam Mohammad Ali Jinnah The Nation's Voice, Vol. II: United We Win*. Karachi, Pakistan: Quaid-i-Azam Academy.

Al-Islah (Khaksar weekly).

Bahar ul Ummal (Lucknow, India).

Bhatti, Mohammad Azmat Ullah. n.d. *Al-Mashriqi*. Lahore, Pakistan: Al-Mashriqi Research Academy Gujrat, Pakistan.

The Bombay Chronicle (Bombay, India).

The Bureau of National Reconstruction. n.d. *Struggle of Independence Photograph Album 1905-1947*. Lahore, Pakistan: BNR Government of West Pakistan.

The Cambridge Daily News.

Chronology of Pakistan Movement March 23 1940-August 14, 1947. Islamabad, Pakistan: Pakistan Publications.

The Civil & Military Gazette (Lahore, Pakistan).

Editor's Collection.

The Daily Chronicle (London, England).

The Daily Mirror (London, England).

Dawn (Delhi, India).

The Deccan Times (Madras, India).

The Eastern Times (Lahore, Pakistan).

Evening News.

The Free Press Journal (Bombay, India).

Gandhi, Mahatma. 1980. *The Collected Works of Mahatma Gandhi* (LXXXI, Jul. 17, 1945-Oct. 31, 1945). New Delhi, India: The Director, The Publications Division.

Gandhi, Mahatma. 1980. *The Collected Works of Mahatma Gandhi* (LXXXII, Nov. 1, 1945-Jan. 19, 1946). New Delhi, India: The Director, The Publications Division.

Gandhi, Mahatma. 1983. *The Collected Works of Mahatma Gandhi* (LXXXVII, Feb. 21, 1947- May 24, 1947). New Delhi, India: The Director, The Publications Division.

Gandhi, Mahatma. 1983. *The Collected Works of Mahatma Gandhi* (LXXXIX, Aug. 1, 1947- Nov. 10, 1947). New Delhi, India: The Director, The Publications Division.

The Hindustan Times (Delhi, India).

Hooja, Rima. *Crusader For Self-Rule: Tej Bahadur Sapru & The Indian National Movement - Life and Selected Letters*. Jaipur, India: Rawat Publications.

Hussain, Syed Shabbir. 1988. *The Muslim Luminaries*. Islamabad, Pakistan: National Hijra Council.

Hussain, Syed Shabbir. 1991. *Al-Mashriqi: The Disowned Genius*. Lahore, Pakistan: Jang Publishers.

Hussain, Syed Shabbir. 1994. *Kashmir Aur Allama Mashriqi*. Islamabad, Pakistan: World Affairs Publications.

Indian Student (London, England).

Indus Times.

Jawaharlal Nehru Memorial Fund. 1986. *Selected Works of Jawaharlal Nehru* (Second Series, Volume Four). New Delhi, India: JNMF.

Jawaharlal Nehru Memorial Museum and Library. 1988. *Jawaharlal Nehru Correspondence 1903-47: A Catalogue*. New Delhi, India: Vikas Publishing House PVT Ltd.

Malik, Iftikhar Haider. *Sikandar Hayat Khan (1892-1942): A Political Biography*. Islamabad, Pakistan: National Institute of Historical and Cultural Research.

Malik, Ikram Ali, Compiler. 1990. *Muslim League Session 1940 & the Lahore Resolution (Documents)*. Islamabad, Pakistan: National Institute of Historical and Cultural Research.

Mansergh, Nicholas, Editor. 1973. *Constitutional Relations Between Britain and India, The Transfer of Power: 1942-7* (Volume IV The Bengal Famine and the New Viceroyalty 15 Jun. 1943-31 Aug. 1944). London, England: Oxford University Press.

Mashriqi, Allama (Khan, Inayat Ullah). n.d. *Khitabat Au Muqalaat*. Compiled by Ghulam Qadeer Khawaja. Lahore, Pakistan: Al-Faisal Nashiran Au Tajaran Kutab.

Mashriqi, Allama (Khan, Inayat Ullah). n.d. *Qaul-i-Faisal: Yani Khaksar Tehrik Kay Gharz Au Maqqasid Ki Muqammal Tashrih*. Rawalpindi, Pakistan: Farog-e-Islam Foundation.

Mashriqi, Allama (Khan, Inayat Ullah). 1952. *Armughan-i-Hakeem*. Lahore, Pakistan: Al-Tazkirah Publications.

Mashriqi, Allama (Khan, Inayat Ullah). 1952. *Dahulbab*. Lahore, Pakistan: Al-Tazkirah Publications.

Mashriqi, Allama (Khan, Inayat Ullah). 1955. *Human Problem (A Message to the Knowers of Nature)*. Lahore, Pakistan: Al-Tazkirah Publications.

Mashriqi, Allama (Khan, Inayat Ullah). 1977. *Muqalaat Aur Doosri Tehreerain Volume 3*. Lahore, Pakistan: Idarah-i-Talimat-i-Mashriqi.

Mashriqi, Allama (Khan, Inayat Ullah). 1979. *Maulvi Ka Ghalat Mazhab*. Reprint, Lahore, Pakistan: Al-Tazkirah Publications.

Mashriqi, Allama (Khan, Inayat Ullah). [1924] 1980. *Tazkirah Volume 2*. Lahore, Pakistan: Al-Tazkirah Publications.

Mashriqi, Allama (Khan, Inayat Ullah). 1980. *God, Man, and Universe*. Edited by Syed Shabbir Hussain. Rawalpindi, Pakistan: Akhuwwat Publications.

Mashriqi, Allama (Khan, Inayat Ullah). 1987. *Quran and Evolution: Selected Writings of Inayat Ullah Khan Al-Mashriqi*. Edited by Syed Shabbir Hussain. Islamabad, Pakistan: El-Mashriqi Foundation.

Mashriqi, Allama (Khan, Inayat Ullah). 1993. *Man's Destiny*. 2nd ed. (Revised and Enlarged). Edited by Syed Shabbir Hussain. Islamabad, Pakistan: El-Mashriqi Foundation.

Mashriqi, Allama (Khan, Inayat Ullah). [1924] 1997. *Tazkirah Volume 1*. Lahore, Pakistan: Al-Tazkirah Publications.

Mashriqi, Allama (Khan, Inayat Ullah). [1926] 1997. *Khitab-e-Misr.* Lahore, Pakistan: Al-Tazkirah Publications.

Mashriqi, Allama (Khan, Inayat Ullah). [1931] 1997. *Isha'arat.* Lahore, Pakistan: Khaksar Hameed ud Din Ahmed (son of Allama Mashriqi) c/o Al-Tazkirah Publications.

Mashriqi, Allama (Khan, Inayat Ullah). [1960] 2001. *Beh Baha Takmillah Volume 1.* Lahore, Pakistan: Al-Tazkirah Publications.

Maztar, A.D. 1985. *Khaksar Tehrik aur Azadi-yi-Hind: Dastavezat.* Islamabad, Pakistan: Kaumi Idara Brai Tehkik Tarikh Au Sikafat.

Muhammad, Shan. 1973. *Khaksar Movement in India.* Delhi, India: Meenakshi Prakashan.

Mujahid, Sharif Al. 1993. *Quaid-i-Azam Jinnah: Studies in Interpretation.* Reprint, New Delhi, India: Low Price Publications.

Mujahid, Sharif Al, and Yousuf Saeed, Editors. 1981. *Quaid-i-Azam Jinnah: A Chronology.* Prepared by Riaz Ahmad. Karachi, Pakistan: Quaid-i-Azam Academy.

Nazar, Naheed. 1988. *Sang-i-Giran Hai Zindigi.* n.p.: Shahbaz Khan Danyal Khan.

Note on the Khaksar Movement. 1940. Reprint (Reproduction), Chicago, Illinois, USA: University of Chicago Photoduplication Department. Microfilm.

The Pakistan Times (Lahore, Pakistan).

Peerbhoy, Akbar A. [1943] 1986. *Jinnah Faces An Assassin.* Karachi, Pakistan: East and West Publishing Company.

Pirzada, Syed Sharifuddin, Editor. 1966. *Quaid-e-Azam Jinnah's Correspondence.* 2nd ed. (Revised). Karachi, Pakistan: Guild Publishing House.

Pirzada, Syed Sharifuddin, Editor. 1977. *Quaid-e-Azam Jinnah's Correspondence.* 3rd ed. (Revised and Enlarged). Karachi, Pakistan: EWP East and West Publishing Company.

Pirzada, Syed Sharifuddin, Editor. 1990. *Foundations of Pakistan: All-India Muslim League Documents: 1906-1947* (Volume 3). Karachi, Pakistan: Royal Book Company.

Pyarelal. 1958. *Mahatma Gandhi The Last Phase Vol II.* Ahmedabad, India: Jivandahyabhai Desai Navajivan Press.

Riddick, John. 1998. *Who Was Who in British India.* USA: Greenwood Publishers.

Saleemi, Safdar. 1967. *Khaksar-i-Azam Aur Khaksar Tehrik*. Lahore, Pakistan: Bab Al-Ishaat Khaksar Tehrik.

The Sind Observer (Karachi, Pakistan).

The Star (London, England).

The Star of India (Calcutta, India).

The Statesman (Calcutta, India).

Talbot, Ian, and Gurharpal Singh, Editors. 1999. *Region and Partition: Bengal, Punjab, and the Partition of the Subcontinent*. Oxford, U.K. and New York, USA: Oxford University Press.

The Telegraph (London, England).

The Times (London, England).

The Tribune (Lahore, Pakistan).

Weekly Report of the Director, Intelligence Bureau, Home Department, Government of India [Secret]. New Delhi/Simla, India: Home Department, Government of India.

The Westminster Gazette (England).

The Yorkshire Post (England).

Yousaf, Nasim. 2003. *Allama Mashriqi & Dr. Akhtar Hameed Khan: Two Legends of Pakistan*. New York, USA: Nasim Yousaf.

Zaidi, Z.H. n.d. *M.A. Jinnah: Ispahani Correspondence 1936-1948*. Karachi, Pakistan: Forward Publications Trust.

Zaidi, Z.H., Editor. 1993. *Quaid-i-Azam Mohammad Ali Jinnah Papers: Prelude to Pakistan, 20 February-2 June 1947* (First Series, Vol.1, Part 1). Lahore, Pakistan: Quaid-i-Azam Papers Project, National Archives of Pakistan, Islamabad.

Zaman, Sher. 1986. *Khaksar Tehrik Ki Jiddo Juhad Volume 1*. Rawalpindi, Pakistan: Khaksar Sher Zaman c/o Al-Tazkirah Publications.

Zaman, Sher. 1987. *Khaksar Tehrik Ki Jiddo Juhad Volume 2*. Rawalpindi, Pakistan: Khaksar Sher Zaman c/o Al-Tazkirah Publications.

Zaman, Sher. 1988. *Khaksar Tehrik Ki Jiddo Juhad Volume 3*. Rawalpindi, Pakistan: Khaksar Sher Zaman c/o Al-Tazkirah Publications.

Zaman, Sher. 1992. *Sir Syed, Jinnah, Mashriqi*. Rawalpindi, Pakistan: Khaksar Sher Zaman c/o Al-Tazkirah Publications.

Zamindar.

www.ingramcontent.com/pod-product-compliance
Lightning Source LLC
Chambersburg PA
CBHW031910020426

42338CB00031B/1707/J